A History Of The Upper Country Of South Carolina

From The Earliest Periods To The Close Of The War Of Independence (Volume I)

John Henry Logan

Alpha Editions

This Edition Published in 2021

ISBN: 9789354500732

Design and Setting By
Alpha Editions
www.alphaedis.com
Email – info@alphaedis.com

A HISTORY OF THE UPPER COUNTRY OF SOUTH CAROLINA,

FROM THE

EARLIEST PERIODS

TO THE

CLOSE OF THE WAR OF INDEPENDENCE.

BY

JOHN H. LOGAN, A. M.

VOL. I.

PUBLISHED BY
S. G. COURTENAY & CO., CHARLESTON,
P. B. GLASS, COLUMBIA.
1859.

WALKER, EVANS & CO., PRINTERS, CHARLESTON.

TO THE

PEOPLE OF UPPER CAROLINA,

AND THE

CITIZENS OF CHARLESTON,

INTIMATELY ASSOCIATED, AND CLOSELY UNITED BY TIES OF TRADE, AND OF COMMON STRUGGLES, AND SUFFERINGS, FROM THE EARLIEST PERIODS OF THEIR COTEMPORANEOUS HISTORY; AND NOW CONSTITUTING, AFTER THE LAPSE OF MORE THAN ONE HUNDRED YEARS, THE NORTH AND SOUTH POLES OF OUR POLITICAL MAGNET,

THIS WORK IS MOST RESPECTFULLY DEDICATED

BY

THE AUTHOR.

PREFACE.

A few words will be sufficient to introduce to an indulgent public my first effort of literary labor. Employed, as I have been, ever since leaving my Alma Mater, in the arduous business of instructing youth, I felt, with many others of like employment, the want of a popular, well-written School History of South Carolina; one whose perspicuity combined with that simplicity of style, and lively detail of personal and local history, so attractive to the young, would render it both useful and interesting to that important class of readers.

Having some leisure and inclination, without any boasted fitness for such an enterprise, I conceived the design of preparing a brief juvenile history, for the use of my own pupils, and of as many others as might be pleased to adopt it. A specimen of this work, accompanied by a beautiful map of Abbeville District, executed by Miss E. C. N., of my Senior Class, was exhibited at the State Agricultural Fair of 1857.

Unfortunately, however—myself being judge—for this conception of a school history, I had been, for several years previous, but with no very definite object, busy collecting, from various sources, original matter relating to the unpublished and traditionary history of the upper-country; and, unable to free myself from this fascinating crotchet, I was insensibly led by it to a stand-point, from which I was astonished to discover, stretching far back of any cultivated ground, a field rich in native historic lore yet unexplored, and wholly unknown beyond the circle of a privileged few.

The temptation to expatiate here, and cull all that is interesting, was too strong to be resisted; and the humble design of a juvenile book has swollen to the proportions of an imposing volume of history. My aims and views enlarged with my increased labors and widened field, and I came, at last, to write for the pleasure and information of the people. From them, if it is meet, must come my reward; and if I have written anything, or brought anything to light that will lead them to a better knowledge of the history of their fathers, and a juster appreciation of their noble institutions and State, the main object of my enterprise is accomplished.

It may be well to add that I wrote in the country, cut off, in great part, from the public and private libraries in which is deposited much information essential to the integrity of my work; and a large portion of its composition was performed in the short daily recesses from labor in the Academy.

GREENWOOD, S. C., Nov. 24th, 1859.

CONTENTS.

CHAPTER IX.—PAGE 204.

CHAPTER X.—PAGE 241.

CHAPTER XI.—PAGE 280.

CHAPTER XII.—PAGE 311.

CHAPTER I.

Early appearance of the Upper-Country—Uncultivated and unabused by the Indians—The Upper-Country defined—The origin of its peculiar features and soil—The richness and magnificence of its scenery—Primitive beauties of the territory of Fairfield—Opinion of Lord Cornwallis—Wild Buffaloes, &c.

At this day the upper-country of South Carolina presents a very different aspect from that of the same territory in the middle of the eighteenth century. It was then new and beautiful, and as remarkable for the luxuriant richness of its landscape as it is still for the striking features of its rolling hills and towering mountains; but under the iron tread of what is called a progressive civilization, its ancient glories of forest, and flora, and fertile soil have been well nigh wasted and ruined.

When in the possession of the Indian hunter, it is true that its natural, productive energies were left uncultivated and undirected, except so far as satisfied the simple wants of his savage nature. He built no palaces, reared no cities, set in motion no time-saving machinery, and whitened no sea with the floating canvas of a wide-spread commerce; but then, while he used, to the full extent of his capabilities, the talent confided to his care, he never abused it; that sin cannot be laid at the door of the poor Indian.

He never wantonly took the life even of the least useful of the animals of his forest. His landed patrimony was given him from the hands of God a magnificent country, and a magnificent country still, he yielded it up to the more vigorous race which supplanted him.

In mapping out, for our purpose, that portion of the State, which may be styled the upper-country, we shall be guided not so much by its geographical limits, as by its revolutionary and primitive relations. The territory embraced in the modern Districts of Abbeville, Anderson, Edgefield, Greenville, Pickens, Newberry, Laurens, Union, Spartanburg, Fairfield, Chester, Lancaster, York and Richland, *is the classic ground of the American Revolution*. It abounds in associations of the "evil time," richer in romance, and the stern trials of the patriot's heart, than even the boasted fields of the section that would arrogate to itself all that is worth recounting in the past and present history of the country. It is hallowed too by associations connected with events long prior to the Revolution; and these, in their proper place, it shall be our business and pleasure to develope first.

The natural characteristics of this region present just such features of climate, surface, soil, and vegetable growth, as would attract and fix upon its valleys and hills, the energetic race, which, we shall see, by-and-by, were the first to clear away its forests and appropriate its vast agricultural resources. A country, whose landscape was neither wholly rugged with mountains, nor monotonously tame with unbroken plains, but a scene of mingled elevated ranges, undulating hills, and flowery vales, formed a glorious analogue of the true Scotch-Irishman's heart and nature.

Rising abruptly from the sandy barrier that extends some sixty or a hundred miles into the interior, first in gentle undulations, then in higher, wave-like hills, bristling here and there with huge piles of granite, and last, in towering mountain heaps, whose blue tops stand like giant embattlements against the northern skies, it imparts, at a glance, the lesson taught by the geologist, that at a distant period in the past, some revolutionary convulsion of nature upturned the country, breaking its surface into a thousand hills and higher elevations, and driving the incumbent waters far to the south to occupy their present bed.

These subterranean forces, however, and the vast denudations which followed, were limited in their sway; the upheaved surface, like some agitated molten matter suddenly congealed, assumed a permanent form, and soon the tree and plant, after their kinds, whose indestructible germs lay locked up in its soil from the beginning, were developed into the shady woods and grassy plains, which rendered it a fit habitation for men and animals. When and how these, first found their way here, we shall leave to the speculative philosophers to determine, only reserving to ourself the right of deciding upon the truth or absurdity of their opinions.

It is sufficient to remark, that when our fathers

first penetrated this region, it was mostly covered with a wild, luxuriant vegetation, and possessed by a race of people totally different from themselves, in complexion, manners, customs, and religion. They were scarcely less struck, however, with its fertility and magnificent scenery, than with the remarkable race which inhabited it.

Ancient hunters and journalists spoke of these with rapturous enthusiasm. An old trader,* describing his impressions of the Blue Ridge in Carolina, says: "From the historical descriptions of the Alps, and a personal view of the Cherokee mountains, I conclude the Alps are much inferior to several of those mountains, both in height and rockiness; the last are also of a prodigeous extent, and frequently impassable by an enemy."

One of the earlier and most intelligent Governors of Carolina,† wrote a description of this section of the province, in connection with a larger territory, which we found still in manuscript in the office of Secretary of State: "The country lying between the Atlantic Ocean and the Mississippi River, is about a thousand miles in depth from east to west; it is intersected by a ridge of mountains running from north to south, called in Virginia the Blue Mountains or Alleghany, and in this province the Cherokee or Appalanthian Mountains. The rivers that flow from the east side of them have an easterly course, verging towards the south, and after running

* James Adair. † James Glen.

four hundred miles, fall into the sea, as those from the west side, after a much larger course westward, fall into the Mississippi. Some of the most sensible and credible of the Cherokee Indians, who have often traversed every part of the country, both in going to war and hunting, describe it to me as the most delightful, as well as the most fertile in the world; abounding in large, extensive plains and savannahs, swarming with deer and buffalo. I should be afraid to indulge myself with the liberty of copying, lest I should be thought to be drawing a picture or painting a landscape.

Numbers of rivulets water it; but it is the bed principally, of three great rivers. I have not rested satisfied with a verbal description of the country from the Indians, but have often made them trace the lines on the floor with chalk, and also on paper, and it is surprising how near they approach to our best maps.

It would not be difficult to demonstrate the benefits that must accrue to Great Britain by peopling and settling this country of which I am speaking; but all I plead for is, that we may, with the good will of the Indians, take, and keep, possession of it by means of forts."*

This last remark will be of great importance in the decision of an interesting question, discussed in a future chapter.

The beauty and fertility of this region, however,

* 5th Vol. of Indian Books, in Sec. of St. Off., Columbia.

were not confined to the mountains; the valleys and ridges that lay along the rivers and creeks of the eastern slope, to the utmost limits of the Cherokee country on the south, abounded in forests, fertile lands, prairies, and every species of American game. This was the favorite hunting-ground of the lower Cherokees, whose principal settlements were situated on the head waters of the Savannah.

Pearson, in his manuscript history of Fairfield, described the region of country embraced in the present Districts of Richland, Fairfield, Chester, and York, as peculiarly noted in primitive times, for the great abundance of its game. Farther back than any aboriginal history runneth—perhaps for centuries—it had been an uninhabited waste. When the English came, they found this beautiful peninsular a dividing, and common hunting-ground between the Cherokees and Catawbas. The tradition related by the same writer, to account for this singular fact, is exceedingly interesting. It will be given in its proper place.

In the cane brakes of the Saluda,* Long-cane, Ennoree, Broad River, Buffalo of York, and numerous other streams, and on the extensive prairie ridges, the early pioneers and hunters found large herds ot buffaloes and elks; while in the higher woodland country, deer abounded in vast numbers. Even here, though the blue tops of the mountains were only here and there dimly seen in the distance,

* Corrupted from Saluta.

the country exhibited many pleasant and romantic scenes.

The face of this region of romance, interspersed with forests, and prairies, and vast brakes of cane—the latter often stretching in unbroken lines of evergreen for hundreds of miles, from the alluvial country on the south, to the interior sources of the streams,* was not surpassed in picturesque beauty and grandeur, by the best portions of Texas of the present day; and its virgin soil was not then inferior to that of the same boasted State.

As late as 1775, the woodlands, carpeted with grass, and the wild pea-vine, growing as high as a horse's back, and wild flowers of every hue, were the constant admiration of the traveler and adventurous pioneer. The forests of those early times were far more imposing than any now remaining in this portion of the ancient Cherokee Nation. The trees were generally larger, and stood so wide apart that a deer or a buffalo could be easily seen at a long distance--there being nothing to obstruct the view but the rolling surface. On the elevated hill-tops the strolling hunter often took his stand, to sweep, at a single view, a large extent of country. The pea-vine and grasses occupied the place of the bushes and young forest growth that render the woods of the present time so gloomy and intricate.

The partizan soldiers of the Revolution, in Upper Carolina, frequently spoke of this striking feature of

---

* Adair's Hist. N. Am. Indians.

the country. It sometimes favored their enterprises, but as often proved the cause of premature detection and defeat.

Pearson's description of the primitive territory, now known as Fairfield, is quite a glowing picture; but, no doubt, in the main, truthful to nature. The natural scenery, composed of forests and rivers, rolling hills, undulating plains, and gushing springs, was grand as well as beautiful. It caught the eye of Lord Cornwallis, while encamped with his army at Winsboro', in the winter of 1780.

In that season of ice and snow, he pronounced it a paradise. Conversing, on one occasion, with Walter Roberson, he observed: "I can conceive of no finer region, taking into consideration its fertile soil, mild climate, its long-drawn beautiful valleys, and glorious highlands." The force of this remark will be somewhat heightened, when it is recollected that Cornwallis was, at that time, in no very favorable situation for being attracted by the beauties of nature. The indomitable Scotch-Irish Presbyterian hornets of Mecklenburg, and Upper Carolina, had allowed him little opportunity for the exercise of the poetic inspiration.

The same chronicler adds: "His lordship was right. Whoever remembers woodland Fairfield, has in his mind's eye, a vision of nature's best finish and kindest prodigality."*

The wild pea grew chiefly on the highlands, while

* Manuscript papers.

the cane flourished best in the valleys, and filled the lower grounds of all the streams.* Upper Carolina was then not inferior to any portion of the Great West, as a grazing country. On certain rich soils, however, the cane was frequently found by the earlier settlers, growing luxuriantly on the tops of the highest hills.

That fertile section of the Old Ninety-six District, which was afterwards known as the Flat-woods of Abbeville, presented to the view of the hunters, and pioneer settlers, the magnificent prospect of the hills and valleys of an extended tract of prairie country, waving under a rich growth of cane, from five to thirty feet in height. Patrick and William Calhoun who, with several others, built the first Scotch-Irish cabins ever erected in this section of the present district, often affirmed, that when they settled it, it was one vast brake of canes—not a tree or a bush appeared to break the view of the astonished beholder.†

This was, no doubt, the primitive condition of most, if not all, the lands of the ancient Long-canes, of Duncan's Creek, in the present territory of Laurens, and numerous other streams of the upper-country; not a few of them have treasured up in their names, lasting memorials of these facts in their primitive history. Besides its Long-cane, Abbeville has a Reedy Branch; Laurens its Reedy

* Both the pea-vine and maiden cane are still found in the up-country, but only in situations where they are shut in from hogs and cattle.

† Conversation of Col. John A. Calhoun and others.

Fork, and Reedy River; and Union, Spartanburg, Pickens, Lancaster, and Richland, their Cane Creeks.

When the first house was erected on the present site of Abbeville Village, it was designed to place it on the highest point of the hill; but afterwards, when the tall cane which covered the whole spot was cut away, an error of more than fifty yards was discovered. This house was built by Captain Andrew Hamilton, subsequent to the Revolution, and is still known as the Old Red House. One of the little shed-rooms of the same building, the same in which is still kept the village post-office, has become hallowed by a far more interesting association than that which connects it with the primitive scenery of the spot. It is the room which Mr. Calhoun used as his law-office, soon after commencing the practice of law in his native district. On the side-walk, immediately in front of this room, he was often seen standing, bareheaded, holding, in troublous times, with groups of his fellow-citizens, those inimitable conversations, for which he is still so fondly and gratefully remembered by hundreds, who were so fortunate as to be his auditors on such occasions. The Old Red House should be preserved as long as corroding time will suffer its perishable timbers to lie one upon another.*

The cane growth of the country soon became the standard by which the early settlers estimated the value of lands. If it grew no higher than five feet,

* It is built of logs.

or the height of a man's head, the soil was deemed ordinary; but a growth of twenty or thirty feet indicated the highest degree of fertility.* Hence, all the early settlements of the upper-country were planted on, or near, the rich hill-sides of the rivers and creeks. There was little danger to be apprehended then, from any billious diseases in such situations; even the old-fashion chill and fever were almost unknown, and the cabins, and premises of the pioneers, were far too recent to generate the miasm of the loathsome typhus.

Many wonderful accounts have been given of the prairies of the Great West. At the period when the hunters and cow-drivers first penetrated the upper-country, there were considerable portions of it, as before intimated, as destitute of trees, and as luxuriant in grass and flowers, as any prairie of modern times. The ordinary observer may discover that much of the forest of the present day is of comparatively recent growth; the greater number of the trees have sprung up in the memory of living men; few are so old as a hundred and sixty years, and only here and there, at immense intervals, towers a patriarchal pine or oak, whose germination dates back to the beginning of the sixteenth century.†

* Conversation of Joseph Duncan, of Duncan's Creek, one of the oldest residents of Laurens District.

† The concentric rings, easily counted in the trunk of a newly cut tree, indicate its age with mathematical precision. A pine was recently felled in the village of Greenwood, that began its growth in 1588.

It is well known that in the primitive history of the country, there were numerous prairies in the corresponding parts of Virginia and North Carolina. A judicious writer observes: "Emigration was encouraged and directed very much in the earliest periods, by the vast prairies, with pea-vine grass and cane brakes, which stretched across the States of Virginia and North Carolina. There are large forests now, in those two States, where, a hundred years ago, not a tree, and scarce a shrub, could be seen."*

It would be an interesting, as well as curious, subject of investigation, to inquire into the physical causes that have wrought so effectually in rearing noble forests of oak and pine on lands that were once flowered prairies. A reasonable solution of the question, would, no doubt, set at rest another, no less important: Why it is that lands once encumbered with heavy forests, have, on being cultivated a number of years, but not exhausted, and turned out, become as perfect prairies as any seen in Alabama or Texas. This is the present state of much of the land around old Ninety-six.

What remains of the oak forests of the Flatwoods, resembles, very much, the open woods of primitive times, and of many portions of the West, at the present day; and it is a fact not often observed in any Atlantic State, that so strongly is the soil impregnated with its own lime, that in a little while after the leaves have fallen from the trees in autumn,

* Foot's Sketches of North Carolina.

scarcely a shred of them can be seen upon the ground.*

These lands, it appears, were originally quite boggy, particularly in winter, and so full of ponds of water, inclosed in curious depressions of the surface, that many pioneers and land speculators, not well versed in the nature of these new soils, passed them by as inferior for agricultural purposes. Of one, especially, a wealthy speculator from Charleston, it is related, that having rode over, perhaps, the entire body of these lands, with the privilege of several fine selections, he rejected them all, and found himself better pleased with a section near the present site of Mt. Carmel.

A body of lands of the same formation, with those of the reedy flats of the Long-canes, and lying equally as well, but in their virgin state not quite so attractive to the emigrant and experienced farmer, were discovered extending several miles in a circuit around the future site of Ninety-six.

It does not appear from any records, or even from tradition, that this was, in old times, like the former, a prairie region. Its forest growth was quite similar to that of the country generally, while the luxuriant canes covered its whole surface, from the valleys to the tops of the highest hills. If it was ever, at any remote period, a prairie, it contrasted then no more singularly with the surrounding coun-

* Neither old leaves, nor ticks, nor stumps are ever seen in the Flat-woods.

try, than the larger portion of it does at this moment; for it is again, as before remarked, a natural prairie; and in spring and summer, scarcely less picturesque than when trod by the stealthy Cherokee, and roving herds of buffalo.

The fact is a curious one, and doubtless not yet accounted for, that since the oak and hickory have been cut from these lands, scarcely a solitary pine, and little of any other vegetable growth than a rich sward of grass, have sprung up to occupy their place. And this has not resulted from the sterility of exhaustion; for it is well known that if timber was convenient to enclose them, or a fence law in existence, the old Cambridge lands would, at once, command the highest market prices of the district.

We found among the records in Columbia, an old letter to Gov. Glen, from which may be learned several interesting particulars in regard to these lands, and many more of the upper-country, at the earliest period of its settlement. The following extract is sufficient for our present purpose: "The neighborhood begs leave humbly to propose to your Excellency, that one of the companies, at least, may be appointed to range these woods back of the settlements on the north side of the river;* for it is only there that the enemy can do us damage, there being no *livers* as yet at Ninety-Six, to receive any. The lands

* The writer refers here, to companies of rangers, just then organized for the protection of the traders and back-settlers, who were exposed to the incursions of the French, or northern Indians from the Ohio.

on and about Ninety-Six, are well known to be rich and good, but they are also known to be very thirsty, excepting what lies near the river Savannah. But those that lie to the north of us are of a kinder soil, generally, and far better watered with beautiful rivers and creeks, as far as the Catawba, and stand a fair chance to be sooner settled." This was written from Tugaloo, in the summer of 1751. We shall have occasion to refer to it in another place.

While upper Carolina thus abounded in attractions for the farmer and stock-raiser, it was no less inviting to the sportsman and hunter. Farther back than history or any tradition runneth, it had been the hunting-ground of the Cherokees.

In the swamps and low-grounds of the water-courses, the forest was often intricate and gloomy. The deep alluvial soil of those places nourished the largest trees and densest brakes. These afforded covert and food for wild animals of many kinds, and as numerous as those that lurk on the Trinity or Yellow-Stone; and with the natural pastures of the up-lands, rendered the country first the blest home of the Indian, and at a later period, the paradise of the Anglo-American hunter.

The buffalo, now to be met with only on the most distant plains of the great West, roamed in large herds through the open woods and prairies, and found both pasture and concealment in the cane-thickets of the rivers and creeks. At the earliest period of emigration into the upper-country, an old pioneer from Virginia often counted a hundred buffaloes grazing on a single acre of ground, in the present territory of Abbeville and Edgefield.*

When the first settlers of Duncan's Creek arrived from Pennsylvania, and began to erect their cabins on that fertile stream, they found its valleys and hills abounding in buffaloes. Their deep-worn trails, leading to favorite ranges and licks, marked the country in every direction, and long after the struggling settlement had become a flourishing community, and not a buffalo remained in those parts, these paths could still be traced along the creek and its tributaries.†

The old hunters killed great numbers of them, every year, solely for their skins and tongues; deer and wild turkeys were too abundant to make them an object of pursuit for the sake of their flesh. Attacked on all sides in a wooded country, and by hunters armed with the deadly rifle, the buffalo was quickly exterminated, or driven away into the deeper wilds of the west. They were the first, of all the original game of upper Carolina, except the timid elk, to disappear, and hence the little traditionary information now lingering among the people in relation to this remarkable animal.

In the old manuscript records of our collonial his-

* Henry Foster, father of the late Joseph Fox Foster, who died recently near Greenwood, at an advanced age. He settled first on the Saluda, in Edgefield, and afterwards on the place owned by his son at his death.

† Conversation of Joseph Duncan; asserted also by old Robert Long, one of the earliest settlers on the same creek, in evidence given in the trial of a case, many years ago, at Laurensville.

tory, reference is not unfrequently made to the wild animals of this region. The first mention, of any sort, that we discovered of the buffalo, is in the following note: "It is ordered by the Council for Indian Affairs, August, 1718, that the store-keeper in Charleston deliver Robert Blakeney, one buffalo skin from the public peltries, for his care in bringing down a periago* of skins and furs from Savannah Town."†

Bartram, in the narrative of his passage from this same ancient trading post, in 1773, by old Fort Charlotte to the Cherokee towns at the head of the Savannah, describes a spot, not far from the latter place, where he found large quantities of moss-covered bones, of both men and buffaloes, lying scattered indiscriminately over the ground.

The Cherokee Indians called the buffalo *yanasa* the very great bull, or the Bull of God; and this, says Adair, was the universal name among all the tribes of North America, for this animal—a presumptive proof of their common origin. The women fabricated from its thick, shaggy hair, a kind of cloth of great use among them for its warmth and durability. The gay young warriors often wore locks or rolls of this fur, drawn through their long slitted ears; and on great festive or military occasions, mounted upon their brows, already sufficiently hideous from paint,

* A periago was a kind of boat, used in the peltry trade; it is written in the Statutes of South Carolina, pettiauger. It was derived from the Spaniards.

† Savannah Town stood just below the present site of Hamburg. We will have much more to say of it.

a pair of buffalo horns, with the appendage of the tail, also, in its proper place.

The skins of the buffalo and the bear, formed the chief coverings for their beds; and like the white hunters, they destroyed great numbers of the former animal simply for their skins and tongues.* In the year 1760, a Mr. Graves, an old man, crossed the Wateree at Grave's Ford, and formed a settlement in the present territory of Fairfield. When his people had kindled their camp fires, soon after passing the river, he looked into the larder, and announced to the company that their meal and meat were both entirely exhausted; "but," said he, "as we crossed the river, I saw tracks in the paths, leading up from it into the woods, which must be those of the buffalo. Let the young men take their guns and waylay the trails, and they will, no doubt, soon take us a fresh supply of meat."

Reuben Harrison, who was one of the party, immediately formed a hunting band, and going out, as directed, was not long in killing three fat buffaloes, which they succeeded in bringing into the encampment. After cutting from their carcasses what they needed for their present necessities, the rest was divided into small pieces, and spread upon a log, to cool, during the night. The wolves, however, of the neighboring swamps, having got scent of it, surrounded the camp, with the most hideous howlings, and when day-light came, scarcely half of the game could

* Adair.

be found.* "But," adds our chronicler, "the loss was easily supplied."

The venerable Busby, who lived to the advanced age of one hundred and ten years, related, that he had often seen, at one time, three thousand buffaloes on the Long Meadows of Little River, in the same territory.†

In the time of the old hunters, or as late as when the early settlers were building their cabins on Buffalo Creek, on lands now embraced in York District, that stream was famous for its herds of the animal from which it derives its name. The valleys of this stream are exceedingly fertile, and their cane pastures afforded inexhaustible pasturage. The hunters, we are told, sought the buffalo here, more frequently than in any other of their haunts in that region. They not only found them in great numbers, but secured them as game with greater ease; for, after being shot, they seldom escaped by plunging into the water, as they often did on Broad River.‡

When closely pursued, and brought to bay, the buffalo was not surpassed in fierceness by any other animal of these wilds; and it is said by those who knew well his habits, that, heavy and awkward as he was, with his huge head, ponderous shoulders, and projecting hump, he was swifter than either the

* Pearson's MS.

† Pearson's MS. History of Fairfield.

‡ Conversation of the Hon. Wm. C. Black, of York District.

deer or elk. His great strength enabling him to plunge rapidly along over rolling hills as well as level plains.

Far back, in primitive times, the Cherokee Indians hunted the buffalo solely with the bow and spear, and on foot; and from its habit, so often witnessed at the present day, on the prairies of the West, of marching from one pasture to another, in a solid, compact body, the stealthy savages easily entered a herd, and singling out their victims, brought them down, at close quarters, with their flint-pointed arrows. At a later period, however, they were accustomed to hunt them on horseback, and armed with the rifle.

They occasionally resorted to the well-known method of driving them, when moving in large herds, over steep precipices. It was not often, however, they found them in a situation to allow of this advantage; and still less frequent were their necessities so great as to require this wholesale destruction of so noble an animal.

Adair, writing of the buffaloes in this region, about the commencement of the Revolution, tells us that they had then become scarce, as the thoughtless, wasteful Indians used to kill great numbers of them solely for their tongues and marrow-bones, leaving the rest of the carcass to the wild beasts.

The precise period when the last buffalo was seen in Upper Carolina, was, doubtless, never ascertained; they were abundant in Middle Tennessee, in 1775, and it was probably about that time that the last body of them disappeared from the country east of the Blue Ridge.

Long ago they ceased to graze on the rich valleys of Tennessee, and are now only to be found in the astonishing numbers of their primitive strength, on the most distant plains of the Great West; yet their range is still confined, it appears, to the region east of the Rocky Mountains. One of the officers of the United States Exploring Expedition on the Pacific, observes: "It will perhaps excite some surprise that I include the buffalo in the fawna of our Pacific States, as it is a common opinion that the buffalo is, and has always been, confined to the Atlantic slope of the Rocky Mountains. This is not true. The range of the buffalo does not now extend beyond the Rocky Mountains; but there are many Indian hunters, who have killed them in great numbers, to the west of the Mountains, on the head waters of Salmon River. Great numbers of their skulls were found on the prairie there."*

This monarch of the American forest and prairie, was formerly found throughout the entire Eastern portion of the United States, to the Atlantic Ocean, and as far south as Florida. To the south-west, it extended over the whole of the Mississippi Valley through Texas, and into Mexico.†

---

* United States Exploring Expedition.

† Ibid.

CHAPTER II.

The Deer of Primitive Times—Their great abundance—Associated with many animals of prey, whose screams and howls at Night made the Forests hideous—The Villages of Greenwood and Cokesbury—An Old Hunter—John Duncan, of Duncan's Creek—Ancient Buffalo and Deer Licks—The Meriwethers, Wardlaws, Moores, Browns, McAlasters, and Logans, of Little Wilson's Creek—Idle and Disorderly Persons begin, just after the Revolution, to wander over the country, to the great annoyance of the peaceable residents—Legislative enactments in regard to them—The Indian method of dressing a Deer-skin—The famous Bezoar stones of the Cherokees—Elks, &c.

Deer were so numerous, at this period, in the upper-country, that large herds of them were scarcely ever out of sight of the pioneer, even while standing in his cabin-door. They were more numerous than hares are at present, while panthers, wolves, bears, catamounts, and wild cats, prowled in incredible numbers in the swamps and thickets, making night hideous with their cries.

When reading the accounts given by travelers in Africa, of this fearful concomitant of the gloom and savageness of its woodland solitudes, few would realize the fact, that similar startling noises were the familiar serenades with which our emigrant fathers were nightly greeted in their cabins, in Upper Carolina. Lawson describes the cries and howlings of the wild animals at night, in the swamps of the Santee, even after that part of the province had been for some time in the possession of a European population, as terrific beyond measure.

On the beautiful ridge, the water shed between the Savannah and Saluda, and on which are situated, within eight miles of each other, the rural villages of Greenwood and Cokesbury, it was no uncommon occurrence in old times, to meet with herds of deer of sixty or seventy head. Deer Branch, that takes its rise in the former, just back of the residence of James Creswell, Esq., is a memorial of this fact, in its primitive history, not likely soon to perish. An old hunter is yet alive, though doubtless the very last survivor of his vigorous generation, who, in his youth, shot deer in great numbers, by means of blinds near their watering-places on the streams, that have their sources near those villages.*

It required of the hunter but a short walk, and ordinary skill with the rifle, to supply himself and family plentifully with venison and the flesh of the wild turkey. Old Anthony Park, who settled on lands now embraced in the District of Newberry, used to assert that a man could, at that time, stand in his own door, and kill more game than would be sufficient for the support of two families.†

When John Duncan built his house in a canebrake, on the creek, which bears his name, he opened

* Old Isaac Logan, now a resident of Greene County, Alabama.

† Pearson's MS.

a path, some fifteen paces long, through the cane to the stream, for the convenience of getting water. In after years he related to his children, that there was scarcely a minute in the day that he could not see some wild animal moving stealthily up or down the creek across that path."

Sitting, one evening at dusk, in his door, with his foot against the frame, a bear slily approached the the house, and threw him for a moment into a great fright, by springing suddenly over his leg into the cabin. Recovering himself, he seized his gun, and before the bold intruder could effect his escape, shot him dead upon the hearth.

After a while, however, as the English hunters became more numerous and aggressive, the deer grew wilder and scarcer; and they were now more frequently taken by being ambuscaded at their watering places and licks. These last were, many of them, famous spots, and well known to all the hunters for miles around. The indestructible marks of some of them still remain.

On a plantation,* a few miles south-east of the village of Greenwood, the traces of one are yet remarkable. When the buffalo and deer first frequented this spot, the lick was evidently on the edge of a small branch, under a sloping hill; in the course of years, however—perhaps of an age—they wore away, by the incessant application of their tongues, a large portion of the slope; and when the

* Near the residence of James Pert, Sen.

last of them visited it, the steep excavated sides of the hill had gradually extended some thirty or forty paces from the rivulet.

Around this lick the last of the Revolutionary hunters of Little Wilson's Creek had their deer blinds; here the Meriwethers, Wardlaws, Moors, Browns, Bakers, McAlasters and Logans often met at nightfall, to kill deer, and recount, with a social sympathy that only those old people felt and knew how to manifest, the news of the day and their last hunting adventure.

At a spot, about the same distance north-east from Greenwood, in a deep ravine, where the bases of several hills come together, there was, in the earliest periods, a celebrated lick, at which, it is probable that, far back in the traditionary history of the Indians, it was a place of resort for buffalo and deer, and perhaps for other animals now extinct.*

These licks abounded, however, in the upper country, from the Savannah to the Catawba. The early settlers and hunters easily discovered them, by following up the deep narrow paths that led to them from every direction.

Deer were so abundant in the woods around the site of old Ninety-six, even at the close of the eighteenth century, that the carcass of a buck brought no more than half a dollar in the streets of Cambridge. Now, not one of the species is to be found in all that region between the Savannah and Saluda.

---

* Near Chalk Level, on Dr. C. R. Mosely's plantation.

Of all the animals indigenous to this portion of the Cherokee country, the fallow deer was the most numerous and the most important; its flesh was the chief food of the Indians, and its skin one of the necessaries and luxuries of their domestic life. It was the material from which they constructed their mocassins, leggings and a hundred other things no less useful; while its strong, slender sinews served all the purposes of the most durable thread in their manufacture.

Next to success in war, the Indians honored the skill and good fortune of the warrior who took, in any season, the greatest number of deer. Success here was one of their great standards of worth; for, as in war, they regarded it as a special mark of divine favor, and of the moral purity of the hunter.

This was the taste of savages; but is it not more praiseworthy than that of a civilized Christian race, who make the ability to acquire wealth the chief standard of social excellence?

The Cherokee name for deer was *ahowwe*, and *awatahowwe*, a very common term among them, meant "the great deer-killer of God for the people." Says Adair: "since my time, this title was very honorable among them. Every town solemnly appointed one—him whom they saw that God had at sundry times blessed with better success than his brethren, in supplying them with a holy banquet, that they might eat and rejoice before the Divine Essence. But now it seems, by reason of their great intercourse with foreigners, they have left off that old social religious custom, and even their former noted hospitality."

They always sewed their moccasins with deers' sinews, though of a sharp, cutting quality, for they reckon them more fortunate than the wild hemp; but to eat such, they imagine would breed worms and other ailments, in proportion to the number they eat. And I have been assured by a gentleman of character, who is now an inhabitant of South Carolina, and well acquainted with the customs of the Northern Indians, that they also cut a piece out of the thigh of every deer they kill, and throw it away; and reckon it such a dangerous pollution to eat it, as to occasion sickness and other misfortunes, especially by spoiling their guns from shooting with proper force and direction.

It is also to be observed, that although they made constant use of the bears' oil, and even applied it to religious purposes, they had no such title as the *bear killer of God:* not regarding that animal so clean and sacred as the deer, and therefore not to be eaten in their religious feasts, in which they ate, sang and danced in the presence of Yohewah. Before dressing their fresh-killed venison, they always passed it through the smoke and flame of fire, as a sacrificial offering; and the first buck that fell before the hand of the hunter, either in his summer or winter chase, was often sacrificed entire, but most frequently merely the melt, or a piece of the fat, was so disposed of.

"In the woods, they cut a small piece out of the

lower part of the thighs of the deer they had killed, lengthways, and pretty deep. Among the great number of venison-hams they brought to the English trading-houses, not one was observed to be without this mark."

When in pursuit of deer, it was their habit to range over a large extent of country, often traveling more than thirty miles before they returned loaded to the camp.

Previous to their acquaintance with the English, in these enterprises, as in the chase of the buffalo, the bow-and-arrow was their chief weapon; and even after they had learned from the whites the use of the rifle, they never went on a hunt or a war expedition, without arming themselves as well with the bow and quiver.

Just before the Revolution, a large class of roving vagabonds, of whom we shall have more to say, spent their whole time sauntering alone through the woods, visiting their Indian mistresses, and shooting deer at all seasons, both the young and full grown, for the sake of their skins, to the great destruction of that useful animal, and detriment of the growing up-country settlements. The people, anxious at length, to preserve their deer, and to get rid of the vagrants, laid the matter before the Executive Council, and procured the enactment of a statute whose preamble well explains the grounds of the people's complaints.

"Whereas, many idle, loose, and disorderly persons, as well residents as non-residents in this province, have made, and do make, a constant practice of wandering up and down the same and of killing the deer merely for the sake of the skins, leaving the flesh to rot, whereby wolves, and other beasts of prey, are brought among the stocks of cattle, hogs and sheep, to the great annoyance and damage of the owners thereof; and whereas, the dangerous practice of hunting and killing of deer in the night-time, by carrying of lighted torches through the woods, is now become very common, by means whereof, several persons have been killed, and great numbers of all sorts of cattle are frequently destroyed, to the manifest injury of the owners of the same; for remedy thereof, and in order to prevent as much as may be, the like mischiefs in future, we humbly pray his most sacred Majesty that it may be enacted," &c.

Accordingly it was provided that no doe or fawn should be killed between the first day of January and the last of July, in any year ever after; nor any buck between the first day of September and the last Friday of October, and between the first day of March and the last of April. Two pounds of proclamation money, recoverable before any Justice of the Peace, was the penalty for the violation of this statute; and five pounds for the violation of the further provision; that no persons, whatever, (the Indians excepted,) should, in the night, hunt or kill deer, in any other place than their own grounds or enclosures.

It was finally enacted that no one should range the woods in search of game at a greater distance from his own residence than seven miles.* This Act was

* Statutes of South Carolina, Volume Fourth.

passed in August, 1769, the same year that by an order from the same authorities the first Court in the upper country was established at old Ninety-Six.

Two years after the Revolution, this interesting animal again became an object of legislative discussion and enactment. The people, it appears, were no longer annoyed by the offensive carcasses of deer slain around their plantations by the sauntering hunters; but a nuisance of greater magnitude had taken its place. Just as the manly tournament of the middle ages has degenerated into the effeminate, kid-glove exercise at arms of the present age, so the race of the old hero-hunters of Carolina had well nigh disappeared, and given place to a generation, not of hunters in the primitive sense of the term, but of night-walkers, whose chief skill in the art of taking deer, consisted in the ability to carry a pan, on which a bright lightwood torch blazed, to attract the eyes of their unsuspecting victims. This being effected, the magnanimous sportsman took deliberate aim, at his leisure, and as his musket, or great English shot-gun, carried a hand-full of buckshot, and the game was usually near at hand, he seldom missed his object. This method of killing deer was sufficiently objectionable, if only for the reason that it was greatly and wantonly destructive to them. But unfortunately for the peace and safety of these doughty pan-carriers, there were few of them who possessed the practical skill to distinguish, at night, between the eyes of a deer and those of a horse, or any other domestic animals; and many, it was strongly suspected at the time, were not very anxious to acquire a skill so discriminating. The indignation of the people was at last thoroughly aroused, and resulted in an enactment of the Legislature, October, 1785, the preamble of which reads as follows:

"Whereas, many idle and disorderly persons do make a practice of hunting with fire in the night-time, whereby great numbers of deer are unnecessarily destroyed, and the cattle and other stock of the good citizens of this State frequently injured; for remedy whereof, it was ordained, that any person who should thereafter hunt with fire, or kill any deer, or horse, or cattle, or stock of other kind, in the night-time, should pay the sum of twenty pounds sterling."*

This, we believe, was the last Act of the State Legislature in favor of the poor deer; but no statute passed there, or remonstrance from the better sort of people, availed to preserve them long after the country became more thickly settled, and the race of fire-hunters had once got a taste of their easy slaughter. Like the hapless red men, for whose subsistence a munificent Providence first provided it, the deer is now nearly extinct in the upper country. In the swamps of the Savannah, on the more northern tributaries of the Broad and Saluda rivers, near the foot of the mountains, and in the vast solitudes of the pine lands of Edgefield, a few may yet linger; but soon not a representative of the race will be found

*Statutes at Large, Volume 4, page 719.

east of the Blue Ridge, and another link be broken forever that connects the present with the stirring age of Carolina's romance.

Lawson declares that the Indians were frequently in the habit of eating the deer cooked entire with its stomach and intestines, and their contents. But their daintiest dish consisted of a pair of young fawns boiled as they lay in the water and womb of the mother.

The method which they used to dress the skins of the deer, and of other animals, so as to impart to them the exquisite softness and flexibility that rendered them so valuable in commerce, was exceedingly simple, and appears to be the same still in use in the upper-country for a similar purpose.

The skins were first soaked in water, and the hair curried off with an instrument made from a deer's shank bone or rib. This rude implement was displaced after a while by an English currying-knife of iron; the Indians used to say, however, that they could curry a skin with the bone, with more dispatch than with the sharp iron of the English.

After the removal of the hair, the skins were soaked for some time in a solution of deers' brains and water; the brains had been previously made into a cake and baked in the ashes. They remained in this mixture till all the water had been absorbed; they were then taken out and constantly rubbed or scraped with an oyster-shell or muscle, till perfectly dry; they were now sufficiently soft and pliant for all purposes when not exposed to water. To secure them from being hardened by moisture, it was necessary as at present, to tan them with bark. The Indians often used, in the first part of the process, the soft grains of their roasting-ears beaten to a pulp, instead of the deers' brains.

The same author observes that the famous bezoar stone, so much prized for its wonderful powers in medicine, was found chiefly in the deer that range near the mountains. The Indians valued it very highly; they were accustomed to reduce it to powder and carry it with them, in leathern pouches, on their expeditions. Lawson thus describes, in his journal, an interview which he had with a party of Indians, who were, no doubt, Cherokees, though he gives them a different name:

"This evening came down some Torteros—tall, likely men—having great plenty of buffaloes, elks, and bears, with other sort of deer amongst them, which strong food makes large, robust bodies. Inquiring of them if they never got any of the bezoar stone, and giving them a description how it was found, the Indians told me they had great plenty of it, and asked me what use I could make of it? I answered them that the white men used it in physic, and that I would buy some of them if they would get it against I came that way again. Thereupon one of them pulled out a leather pouch wherein was some of it in powder; he was a notable hunter, and affirmed to me that that powder blown into the eyes strengthened the sight and brain exceedingly—that being the most common use they made of it."*

* Lawson's Carolina, page 45.

It appears from this that the many strange stories related of the bezoars' never failing to extract the venom of the most poisonous reptiles, are unsustained by the experience and practice of the Indians. They were known to trust to other agents for the cure of the rattle-snake's bite, and that of other serpents nearly as deadly. The bezoar stone, it is now well ascertained, is nothing more than a calcareous formation in the deer and many other animals, like that which produces the painful disease of gravel in man.

Many wonderful stories are told of its curative powers. The bite of the most venemous serpent was harmless if a bezoar was at hand to absorb the poison from the wound; and here and there an old woman is still to be found in the upper-country whose child-like faith in all the virtues claimed for it is not surpassed by her belief in the creed or the gospel of St. John.

It is not, perhaps, generally known that the swift-footed, majestic elk was once an inhabitant of Upper Carolina. This animal "is a highly valued species of the deer, now only found in considerable herds in the wilds of the west, and north-west, to about the 50th degree of north latitude. The great forests were their favorite haunts, where were plenty of buds, and tender twigs; on those wide prairies, and plains, where man is seldom seen, but nature is bountiful in her supplies of verdant food."*

* Thatcher.

The elk is a large stately animal, and beautifully proportioned in all his parts. The towering antlers of the male are several feet in length, and have long been the admiration of the naturalist, as well as the hunter. His fleetness was incredible. When first aroused by the hunter, he disdained to fly at once, but bounded along a few paces only, as if trying his strength for flight. He stops to turn half round, and gaze again at his pursuer; then throwing back his branching horns upon his neck, and projecting his taper nose forward, he springs onward at a rate, which soon leaves the hunter far in the back ground.*

When wounded, and at bay, he was no less fierce, and dangerous than the buffalo or panther; the wary hunter knew better than to approach him, without great caution, under these circumstances. The name given him by the Indians was *hissooba;* they greatly prized his carcass, not so much for the sake of the flesh—for, like that of the buffalo, it was coarser, and not so sweet as venison—but for the horns and skin. The former, in their soft state, they esteemed excellent food; and when hard, and fully developed, they formed from them the best bows of which they were possessed. The latter they used in the manufacture of a great variety of domestic articles.

This exceedingly timid animal, was the first to disappear from the ancient hunting grounds of the upper-country, at the approach of the strange hunt-

* Thatcher.

ers and settlers, with their echoing axes, and louder pealing rifles. Its only genial home was the deep solitudes of uncultivated tracts. Scarcely a tradition lingers among the people to cast a gleam of light upon the early history of the elk in Upper Carolina. Its memorials passed away with the last generation of the Indians, and English hunters, who pursued it in its native wilds, ere it disappeared forever beyond the Alleghany range.

We are informed, however, in Pearson's manuscript, that the last of the species, which was seen in the famous neutral hunting-ground between the Broad and Catawba Rivers, already described, was killed near Winn's Bridge in the present District of Fairfield. He thus relates the incident: "For a short time after the settlers began to clear their lands, the elk was frequently met with; but the strange sounds which now began to invade his haunts, soon drove him off into the uninhabited wilderness. The last one that remained was shot near Winn's Bridge, by Robert Newton. One of the hams, and the magnificent antlers of the slain animal, were presented to Capt. John Pearson, who, like a true Englishman, ate the ham, and sent the antlers to a museum in England. At that period no such institution as a museum was known in the upper-country; neither did the people possess the taste or the inclination, to collect, and preserve its curiosities—their mission then, was to clear, to plant and to build."

"The elk was once perhaps more widely distributed over the North American Continent than any other quadruped; it existed throughout the entire territory lying between the northern provinces of Mexico and Hudson's Bay, and between the Atlantic and Pacific Oceans. Within the United States, east of the Mississippi, very few are left, except in the region bordering Lake Superior. On the western tributaries of the Mississippi it is still very common, and perhaps equally so in California and Oregon. West of the Rocky Mountains, it was formerly most abundant, in California, where it is still far from rare. In the rich pasture lands of the San Joaquin and Sacramento, the old residents tell us, it formerly was to be seen in immense droves, and with the antelope, the black tailed deer, the wild cattle and mustangs, covered those plains with herds rivalling those of the buffalo east of the mountains, or of the antelope in South Africa."

The favorite haunts of the elk in California, are the wide stretches of "tule" bordering the rivers and lakes I have mention. It is said that unlike most large quadrupeds, the elk can never be "bogged," and he traverses these marshy districts with a facility possessed by no other animal.

During the rutting season, when the bucks are rushing through the tule in search of the females, a common mode of hunting them is to mount a horse, and riding along the edge of the marshes to call the buck by an imitation of the cry of the doe. He comes plunging on his course, marked for a long distance by the trembling rushes, till, led on by the fatal signal, he bursts out of the cover with streaming sides, and, tossing his antlers, looks around to find the object of his search. This is the moment improved by the hunter to plant in his shaggy breast the fatal bullet.

The elk of the western coast, differs in nothing, so far as I could see from that of the Eastern States. Near Humboldt Bay, I am assured by intelligent men, that eight hundred, and even one thousand pounds, is not an unusual weight, and that individuals have been killed there, which are said to have weighed twelve hundred pounds. We saw the tracks of elks in the Cascade Mountains which were scarcely less in size than those of a bullock."*

Nothing gives us so vivid an idea of the vastness and fertility of the ancient natural pastures of this region, as these great herds of buffalo, deer, and elk, that in primitive times roamed over its hills and valleys. Our people are apt to forget, in view of their well-nigh exhausted and denuded soil, that at the period when this country bore to the inhabited and cultivated north-east the same relation that the unappropriated parts of Texas and Arkansas do at present to it, it was scarcely inferior to them in strength of soil or any natural production. And since its climate remains the same, and the stamina of its energies are not yet completely exhausted, a sure basis is afforded for the hope of its future resuscitation, and a progressive improvement, that shall ultimately as

* Explorations of Lieut. R. S. Williamson on the western slope of the Rocky Mountains.—Vol. vi. p. 66 of Explorations, Surveys, &c.

far surpass its present productiveness or the wildest luxuriance of its primitive vigor, as the genius of the civilized man surpasses that of the improvident, untutored savage.

Bears were so numerous, at this period, in the upper-country, wherever they could find the covert of rocks, hollow trees, and cane-brakes, that a hunter of ordinary skill could kill, in a single season, enough to make him some three thousand pounds of bacon.*

This animal, coarse as he was, was hardly less useful to the Indians than the deer or the buffalo. From his skin were formed their warmest and most substantial winter shoes, and their most comfortable clothing for the same season. The oil extracted from his fat, was one of the essentials of their domestic and religious life.

The Cherokee priests and prophets were inducted into office by the unction of bears' oil. "All the Indian Americans," says Adair, "especially the female sex, reckon their bears' oil or grease very valuable, and use it after the same manner as the Asiatics did their fine essences and sweet perfumes. The young warriors and women are uneasy unless their hair is always shining with it; which is probably the reason that none of their heads are bald."

It is related that they were sometimes reduced to great straits from the difficulty of procuring this oil, both for their domestic and sacred uses, after the bear began to be less abundant in the woods, or the hunt-

* Dr. Ramsay.

ers more indolent and less skillful than they had been previous to their intercourse with the whites.

The flesh of the bear was esteemed to be excellent food, and the traders and hunters from the English settlements soon learned to relish it as much as the Cherokees. "The industrious old traders have still a plenty of hogs, which they raise in folds, mostly on the weeds of the fields during the whole time the crops are in the ground; likewise some hundreds of fowls at once—plenty of venison—the dried flesh of bears and buffaloes—wild turkeys, ducks, geese, and pigeons, during the proper season of their being fat and plenty; for the former sort of fowls are lean in the summer, and the others are in these moderate climates only during the winter, for they return northward with the sun. The traders commonly make bacon of the bears in winter; but the Indians mostly flay off a thick tier of fat which lies over the flesh, and the latter they cut up into small pieces and thrust them on reeds or suckers of sweet tasted hickory or sassafras, which they barbacue over a slow fire. The fat they fry into clear, well-tasted oil, mixing plenty of sassafras and wild cinnamon with it over the fire, which keeps sweet from one winter to another, in large earthen jars covered in the ground. It is of a light digestion, and nutritive to hair. All who are acquainted with its qualities prefer it to any oil for any use whatever; smooth Florence is not to be compared in this respect with rough America.

"I have known gentlemen of the nicest taste, who, on the beginning of their first trip into the Indian country, were so greatly prejudiced against eating bears' flesh, that they vehemently protested they would as soon eat part of a barbecued rib of a wolf, or any other beast of prey, as a spare-rib of a young bear; but by the help of a good appetite, which their exercise and change of air procured, they ventured to taste a little; and presently they fed on it more plentifully than others, to make up the loss they had sustained by their former squeamishness and neglect. In the spring of the year, bear bacon is a favorite dish with the traders, along with herbs that the woods afford in plenty; especially with the young tops of poke. And this method they pursue year by year as a physical regimen in order to purge their blood.

Though most of the traders who go to the remote Indian countries, have tame stock, as already described, and are very expert at fire-arms, and ranging the woods a hunting; yet every servant that each of them fits out for the winter's hunt, brings home to his master a large heap of fat barbacued briskets, rumps, and tongues of buffalo and deer, as well as plenty of bears' ribs, which are piled on large racks; these are laid up and used, not for necessity, but for the sake of variety."*

The Indians regarded all animals that subsisted on flesh or disgusting food—as hogs, wolves, panthers, foxes, and cats, as unfit to be eaten—they were forbidden as polluted. The only animal which may be ranked among beasts of prey, that they exempted from this proscription, was the bear.

* Adair.

The male bear invariably made his den in the ground, under the upturned root of some fallen tree, or the cavity of some precipitous hill-side, to which he generally retired for winter quarters, at the first fall of snow. The female sought a safer retreat in the highest parts of hollow trees, and here bore her young, and nourished them till sufficiently large to take care of themselves.

"About Christmas the he and she bears always separate. The former usually snaps off a great many branches of trees, with which he makes the bottom of his wirter's bed, and carefully raises it to a proper height with the green tops of large canes; he choses such solitary thickets as are impenetrable by the sunbeams. The she bear takes an old, large, hollow tree, for her yeaning winter house, and chooses to have the door above, to protect her young ones from danger. When anything disturbs them, they gallop up a tree, champing their teeth and bristling their hair in a frightful manner; and when they are wounded, it is surprising from what a height they will pitch on the ground, with their weighty bodies, and how soon they get up and run off. When they take up their winter quarters, they continue the greater part of two months in almost an entire state of inactivity. During that time, their tracks reach no farther than to the next water, of which they seldom drink, as they frequently suck their paws in their lonely recess, and impoverish their bodies to nourish them.

While they are thus employed, they cannot contain themselves in silence, but are so well pleased with their repast, that they continue singing "*hum-um-um*; and as their pipes are none of the weakest, the Indians, by this means, often are led to them from a considerable distance, and they are then easily knocked on the head. But the hunters are forced to cut a hole near the root of the tree, wherein the she bear and her cubs are lodged, in order to drive them out by the force of fire and suffocating smoke; and as the tree is partly rotten, and the inside dry, it soon takes fire. In this case they become very fierce, and would fight any kind of an enemy; but commonly at the first shot they are either killed or mortally wounded. If the hunter, however, chance to miss his aim he speedily makes off to a sapling, which the bear, by overclasping, cannot climb; the crafty hunting dogs then act their part, by biting behind and gnawing its hams till it takes up a tree. I have been often assured, both by Indians and others who get their bread by hunting in the woods, that the she bear always endeavors to keep apart from the male during the helpless state of her young ones; otherwise he would endeavor to kill them; and that they had frequently seen the she bear kill the male on the spot, after a desperate engagement, in defence of her young ones." *

Lawson during his travels and residence in Carolina, became well acquainted with this animal, and, from his account of it, it was scarcely less useful to the Indians than the deer. Its flesh was not inferior

* Adair.

to the best pork, and that of the cubs, a dish to tempt the palate of the most fastidious epicure. The fat was as white as snow, and a melted quart of it taken upon the stomach would not rise in acidity. Fish, and other meats prepared in it, as the English use the fat of the hog, were peculiarly excellent.

When in its season, the berry of the black gum tree was the favorite diet of the bear; but then its flesh was good for nothing, on account of a nauseous taste imparted to it by this food; and the same effect was produced in those that ranged so low down on the rivers as to prey periodically on the shoals of herrings which ran up from the sea. They devoured great quantities of acorns, and while in search of these, they occasionally, in times of scarcity, seized upon and made prey of as many hogs as came in their way.

The corn-patches of the Indians were frequently invaded by them, and in a short time completely destroyed, if the voracious intruders were not quickly driven off; for they broke down and trampled under their feet more than they could eat. The bear was particularly fond of the sweet potato, and when once a patch of them was so unlucky as to receive a visit from him, it was usually swept clean of its contents. He was often detected in the act of fishing for herrings and other fish, by watching his opportunity on the bank of some stream, to dash them on shore by a sudden stroke of his paw. His cousin, the raccoon, it is often related, had a similar habit of catching crabs with the end of his tail.

The same chronicler informs us of a very curious fact in the history of the Carolina bear. No man, whether Christian or savage, was ever known to kill a she bear big with young. It was accounted for by supposing that as soon as the females had conceived, they retired to some impenetrable fastness, where they lay concealed, till past the season of pregnancy. Yet it appears unaccountable that in no instance they should have been discovered by the Indians, who time immemorial had hunted in every covert of the woods with the sagacity of dogs.

A few years before Lawson's arrival in Carolina, there were killed in two counties of Virginia, during a single winter, as many as five hundred bears, and among them all there were but two females, and neither of them pregnant. We leave the solution of this curious problem in natural history to the philosophy of the reader.

The English hunters pursued the bear as often for the sake of the rare sport his chase and capture afforded, as for his skin and flesh. They hunted him with dogs, well trained for the purpose, and when once fairly in pursuit of their game, they did not cease to press him till he was forced to take a tree, whence the unerring rifle soon brought him to the ground. Two or three shots were always reserved, however, by the hunters, to be used in case he should come down merely stunned by the balls already fired at him ; for, though not naturally ferocious, the bear when wounded becomes exceedingly fierce and dan gerous. The dogs sometimes brought him to bay on the ground, and in these close quarters the hunters used their pistols, which they always carried in their girdles. "If a dog," says the old chronicler, "is apt to fasten upon, and run into a bear, he is not good, for the best dog in Europe is nothing in their paws; but if ever they get him in their clutches they blow his skin from his flesh like a bladder, and often kill him; or if he recovers it he is never good for anything after."

As the hump of the buffalo was regarded as the most delicious portion of his body, so the paws of the bear were eaten with most avidity by the Indians and old hunters. The head was thrown away as good for nothing.

In preparing the oil to be used for anointing their hair and persons, and the bodies of their dead, the Indians mixed with it a root known to the whites as the "blood root," which they gathered near the mountains. When this could not be procured, they used paccoon root, or sanguinaria; either of which gave it a strong medicinal, and anteceptic power, as well as beautiful color. This unguent was regarded as a sovereign remedy for strains, aches and old pains.

The Indians endeavored always to take this animal in its winter's den, for it was then exceedingly fat; they used to say, that for a short time even, after it had emerged again in the spring, it was still found to be in good condition. The bear is now extinct in the upper-country, probably not one of the species can be found east of the Blue Ridge.*

The beaver, so deeply interesting for its wonderful sagacity, and for so long a time invaluable for its thick, strong fur, to the commerce of the world, and now only found in the remote regions of the west, was once abundant on all the creeks and rivulets of the upper-country. The waters of Fair-forest, Longcanes, Coronaka, and numerous other streams, were as famous for their beavers, as they were for their rich cane-brake bottoms.

A hunter has been known to take as many as twenty beavers in one season on the Fair-forest† of Union and Spartanburg, a large number, considering the value of their skins, and the difficulty of trapping this sagacious animal. It was exceedingly wary of any device of man to entangle it; and if way laid, and shot, unless killed dead on the spot, it most always managed to plunge into the water and dive into its burrow, before the hunter could secure it.

There is a history of the beaver, and of other animals that made their homes, in olden times, on the streams of the upper-conutry, far more truthful, and enduring than the records of the historian. Scarcely a neighborhood of its modern divisions, is without its "beaver" or "beaver dam" creek. And the

* In all the minute records, in the Secretary of State's office, Columbia, of the peltry trade between the Cherokees and Carolina, I found the skin of the bear not once mentioned; those of the deer and beaver seemed to be chiefly in demand.

† Dr. Ramsay's South Carolina.

creeks of the bear, the wolf, the wild-cat, buffalo, and panther are no less numerous. York District, in one of its finest tributaries of Broad River, has a lasting memorial of its ancient herds of buffaloes. In the same district, three "beaver dams," a wolf, and turkey creek, are similar mementoes of the animals whose names they bear. Abbeville has its "Deerbranch," its Turkey and Buffalo creeks. Greenville records the history of its beavers, wild-cats, and panthers, in a "beaver dam" and "wild-cat" creek, and the "panther's fork." The wild turkey has also its commemorative stream in Edgefield and Chester, and the beaver its constant memorial. Like Abbeville and York, Newberry cannot forget its buffaloes of primitive times, while its most south-eastern water course bears its tributary currents to the Saluda.

The upper-country is full of monuments like these—a rich, unobtrusive history of the past. "It might at first sight appear as if language apart, that is, from literature, and books, and where these did not exist, was the frailest, the most untrustworthy of all the vehicles of knowledge, and that most likely to betray its charge: yet is it in fact the great, often times, the only connecting link between the present and the remotest past, an ark riding above the water-floods that have swept away every other landmark and memorial of ages and generations."*

Adair remarks of the southern Indians, "They rank all amphibious animals in the class of those

* French on the Study of Words.

prohibited for food. Our old traders remember when they first began the custom of eating beavers; and to this day none eat of them except those who kill them; though the flesh is very wholesome, on account of the bark of trees they live upon."

A curious tradition, however, has been discovered that would seem to prove that religious scruples of a different kind from those that feared contact with polluted things, caused this reluctance of the Indians to pursue the beaver as an object of food. It is too interesting to be omitted in its proper place.

Notwithstanding the great abundance of this animal at the opening of the Indian trade, so rapid was its destruction with the improved methods of trapping and hunting introduced by the whites, that it soon became very scarce, and, it is probable, wholly extinct before the end of the eighteenth century. The last one seen on the Coronaka, is said to have been taken by an old hunter living near that stream, in the last year of that period.

Few, if any, traditions relating to it are now to be found among the descendants of the early settlers and hunters of the upper-country.

The Indians named the beaver *keenta;* and by combining that word with *ooka*, water, and *heenna*, a path, formed the very expressive appellative, *keentookheenna*, a beaver dam, or the beaver's path over the water.*

"The beaver once inhabited all portions of the

* Adair.

globe lying in the northern temperate zone; yet from England, continental Europe, China, and all the eastern portions of the United States, it has been entirely exterminated, and a war so universal and relentless, has been waged upon this defenseless animal; his great intelligence has been so generally opposed by the intelligence of man, that it has seemed certain, unless some kind Providence should interpose, it must soon be found only in a fossil state. Happily, that Providence did interpose, through a certain ingenious somebody, who first suggested the use of silk in place of fur for the covering of hats. The beavers are not yet exterminated from Western America; and now since they are not "worth the killing," in those inhospitable regions where there is no encouragement to American enterprise or cupidity, we may hope that they will always there retain existence in a home exclusively their own.

In the streams flowing from the Rocky, the Blue and Cascade Mountains—the old stamping ground of Bill Williams, and that host of Black-foot-hating,* death-defying "mountain men," whose adventures and escapes, half fiction, and half fact, cover so broad a page of modern story—the sagacious beavers are still numerous; but it was in the fastnesses of the Cascades, one hundred and fifty miles south of Columbia, in the clear, cold streams which, trickling down from the eternal snows, flow, now bright and sparkling, now deep and still, through mountain

* Blackfeet Indians.

meadows, green as emerald, and daisy-decked, in a region never before profaned by the foot of a white man, and unoccupied by savages, that we found the beaver in numbers, of which, when applied to beavers, I had no conception. The sides of these streams were literally lined with their habitations, though we never saw their houses, and seldom a dam made by them, but usually their burrows pierced the sides of the stream, a sufficiently large and long excavation being made to form warm, roomy and comfortable quarters. From the point where these burrows terminate in the water, trails lead off to thickets of pine or willow, where the beavers find their food. These thickets exhibit the most surprising proofs of the power and industry of these animals; whole groves of young pine trees cut down within a few inches of the ground and carried off bodily. So well was the work done that one could hardly resist the conviction that the woodman's axe had not there been plied vigorously and well. These trees, when felled, are cut into convenient lengths and carried to the burrows, there to be stripped of their bark, and then thrown into the stream. We often saw trees of considerable size cut down by the beavers; the largest which I noticed was a spruce pine twelve inches in diameter.

In California the beaver is quite common, though less so than in Oregon. On Cotton-wood Creek, near Fort Reading, they abound, and have cut the cotton-wood trees, which line the banks of the stream, of a diameter from fifteen to eighteen inches. To any one who has never seen the beaver in his native haunts the accounts of his mechanical skill and general intelligence, as exhibited in his dams, and "clearings," must seem almost fabulous; and when he has seen these with his own eyes, he cannot fail to feel that the profound respect entertained by the Indians and trappers for this sagacious animal is in a great degree deserved.

The value of beaver skins has so much depreciated that they were offered to some of our party, by the bale, at twenty-five cents each."*

* Lieut. R. S. Williamson, corps of Topographical Engineers, Explorations on the Pacific.

CHAPTER III.

The Panther—Wild Cat—Adventure of Sally Whitaker in the present territory of York—The last Panther seen on Long-Cane—Old John Ravelin and Capt. John Sanders—The Catamount—Adventure on Indian Creek—The Wolf—Adventure of Robert Long on Duncan's Creek—Old James Mosely near Grindal's Shoals, &c.

After the Indians, the most troublesome enemies with which the early settlers had to contend were the panther, wolf, and wild cat. They prowled around their houses at night, and so frequent were their onslaughts on the folds and poultry yards, that it was difficult for them to keep any domestic animals at all.

The panther, although by nature cowardly, and always ready to flee at the sight of a human being, yet when wounded or pressed by hunger, became exceedingly bold and ferocious. While hunting its prey it was not unfrequently known to leap fearlessly into the very midst of the pioneer's households. We were shown near the Ennoree, on a part of the very scene, where in after years the gallant Williams and Clark charged with fearful energy upon far different prey, the site of a ruined cabin, through the door of which a panther, one night, leaped over the shoulders of one Mrs. Ford.

This animal, when thoroughly aroused, was undoubtedly more formidable than any other in all this portion of the American Continent. The Indians called it the *cat of God*, and selected it as one of their great religious emblems. Their male children were made to sleep upon its skin, from infancy to manhood, that they might imbibe from it some portion of the cunning, strength, and prodigious spring of the animal to which it belonged. On the same principle their female offspring were reared on the soft skins of fawns and buffalo calves, that they might become gentle and obedient.

The panther has borne different names among the white settlers who took possession of his solitudes. He has been called the American lion, the tiger, and cougar; and his claims to be ranked with the king of beasts, or the great tiger of India, will hardly be disputed on the score of deficiency of size and strength, when it is related that individuals have been killed, in the woods of Carolina, measuring three feet in height, and eight feet from the tip of the nose to the root of the tail. Audubon fixes his average weight at one hundred and fifty pounds. His body was larger than the common sheep, and when seen in the forest appeared precisely of the same color with the Virginia deer."*

The usual cry of the panther when prowling in the woods, was exceeding melancholy, and so nearly resembling the distressed wail of an infant, as to

* The jaguar of South America is the nearest relative of the panther

be sometimes mistaken for that of a child lost in the forest, even by those accustomed to his habits.

It is related of a Miss Sally Whitaker, of whose heroism and romantic wanderings on the singular mountain, in York District, that still bears her name, we found some traditions, that on one occasion when strolling alone on the mountain, she caught, as she imagined, the sound of a child's cry in the distance; all her sympathies were instantly aroused, and quickening her pace in the direction whence it came, she found it grew rapidly more and more distinct, till, at last, it seemed to proceed from a covert near at hand; she pressed forward with increased eagerness, and drawing aside the intervening grass and bushes, discovered—not a child—but face to face with her, a large American lion. It is not related how she extricated herself from the dilemma; but the assertion may be ventured that the panther scampered off as fast as his legs could carry him, while Sally Whitaker neither fainted on the spot nor ran off in the opposite direction.

The Cherokees used to affirm that they had often come upon the panther, in the woods, lying at rest between two deer that he had just taken and killed. And they invidiously compared him, when thus situated, to the white man, who, they said, instead of being satisfied, like the Indian, with enough for his present necessities, and no more, was covetously eager, as the cougar, to pile around him far more property and substance than it was possible for him to consume upon himself.

It was about the year 1797 that old John Ravelin and Capt. John Sanders killed the last panther on Long-Cane Creek. The incident is related as follows by an old man yet living:* "When a small boy, I went up, on one occasion, from the vicinity of old Cambridge to visit an aunt, Mrs. Archy McCoy, who lived on the place now occupied by Mrs. John Kellar. Her house stood about eighty yards from the road, on the side opposite to the present buildings. Late the following night, I was awaked from a sound sleep by dismal screams, which seemed to come at regular intervals from the direction of Long-Cane Creek. Much frightened, for I had never before heard so strange a cry, I aroused my aunt, and asked her what it meant? After listening a moment, she told me to go to sleep again, that it was only the scream of the panther in the swamp. Very early next morning word was sent to John Ravelin and Capt. Sanders, that a panther had been heard in the swamp the previous night. These men were famous hunters at that period, and lived but a short distance from my aunt's."† Nothing pleased them better than the excitement of an ordinary hunt, but the prospect of a rare adventure with a panther kindled all the enthusiasm of their youth.

With their dogs and rifles they were soon on the ground, and almost as soon in hot pursuit of the game. It gave them a chase of several miles; but,

* J. Pert, Senr.

† Sanders lived at Westley Cromer's place. Ravelin lower down the creek.

at length was forced by the dogs to take a tree, from which it was brought to the ground by a few well directed shots, when the dogs rushing upon it, quickly finishing the work. This was probably the last panther that lingered in the swamps of Long-Cane. This creek, we learned from old men, was celebrated in early times both for its panthers and wild cats.

During the day, these animals were accustomed, like their kind, to keep themselves close in their dens of the cane-brakes, and under the rocks of the granite ridges; but at night, crept stealthily out in quest of food, and often rendered their neighborhood dismal with melancholy cries.

The chief food of the panther in primitive times, was the flesh of deer; to which, after the founding of the English settlements, he added the easier prey of the sluggish hog, and other domestic animals. Of all the beasts of Carolina, he was the most destructive to the interests of the pioneers, and most dreaded for his strength and fierceness when encountered in the woods. Like the cat, he was particularly clean and nice in his habits; whatever was left, after gorging himself from the victims of a night's hunt, he covered up carefully in the leaves, for another repast; but if, in the mean time, any other animal disturbed it, he would eat no more of it. In his moments of fondness, he purred precisely like the cat; but if taken when young, no care nor training could ever win him from his savage nature and habits. When first encountered in the forest by the hunter, he was exceedingly cowardly, the least dog could hurry him into a tree; the wary woodsman knew well, however, the importance of giving him a fatal shot at the first fire; for if he came to the ground only slightly wounded and enraged, the battle upon him was terrible. When wounded he is said to have hallooed like a man.

The flesh of this animal had a tempting appearance, and many, in old times, were in the habit of eating it with as much relish as that of the bear. The Indians made from his skin their best gloves, and shoes for their women.

Adair says, that no savages were equal to the Choctaws in killing bears, panthers, and wild cats, which resort in thick cane swamps, that are sometimes two or three miles wide, and a hundred in length, without any break on either side of the stream.

The American panther, though no longer found in this region, is still abundant from the 60th degree of north latitude to the extreme southern point of South America—being more widely distributed than any other species of his numerous family.

The wild cat was once exceedingly numerous and destructive, and when wounded no mean antagonist for the hunter. It is now well nigh extinct; an occasional straggler may sometimes still be chased into the deepest solitudes of the large river swamps, but not one in ten thousand of the present inhabitants of the upper-country, ever saw a native specimen of the race. In 1856, however, it was advertised by an amateur huntsman* on the Savannah, that he had just killed in a swamp of that stream, after a hard struggle, a large wild cat.

A larger, and once well known species of the wild cat, the active catamount, or cat of the mountain, has almost become a creature of fable; yet the first settlers on the streams of the upper-country often suffered severely by his fierceness and rapacity.

A few years ago, a man, while passing through a forest on Indian creek, of Newberry District, was startled by seeing a strange animal run into a tree not far from him; but he could give it no name; he had never before beheld such a creature. Others attracted by his calls soon came to the spot; and presently half the sober neighborhood had collected around the tree to witness the extraordinary sight. They, at length, dispatched it with their rifles and dogs, and having submitted the carcass to competent authority, it was pronounced a catamount, and was no doubt the last representative of its kind in all that region.

The wild cat might have been called the American leopard; for he was often quite spotted, though not so beautiful as that animal. Like all his kind, he was a beast of prey, and, next to the panther, the most blood-thirsty, fierce and destructive in the woods of Carolina. A great leaper, and little swift of foot, he took his prey by stealth and cunning. It was his

* J. W. Jones, Esq., published that year, in the Abbeville Banner, that he had killed a wild cat on the Savannah.

habit, as well as the panther's, to conceal himself in the thick brush of some overhanging tree or bush, and spring suddenly upon any animal passing in his reach, with which he could safely contend. The Indians declared it was no unusual sight, in their woods, to see a wild cat clinging to the back of a hapless deer, running at the top of its speed, upon which he had just sprung from his ambush; and though the frightened animal plunged madly through brakes and brambles, in its efforts to throw off its deadly foe, he would never relinquish his hold, but continue to suck the hot blood of his victim till it fell from sheer weakness and exhaustion; after which he devoured, at his leisure, as much of the carcass as he could gorge, and left the rest to other animals less nice than himself. The thick, warm fur of this animal was in great repute among the Indians.

Of all the wild animals, however, which the old settlers found in these woods, none proved more troublesome or destructive than the wolf. It was exceedingly numerous, abounding in the coverts of both the uplands and swamps. Stealthy, sagacious, swift of foot, and insatiably rapacious, only its utter extermination relieved the pioneer from its ravages. Rendered savage and desperate by famine, which was not unfrequently the case in the long cold winters of primitive times, the belated settler or traveler knew well the danger of encountering a pack of them when alone on the path. Many instances are still related of men passing alone through the forests, who, hearing the distant yelp of hungry wolves in hot pursuit of them, quickly divested themselves of every incumbrance, and ran for their lives to the nearest settlement.

Robert Long, one of the first settlers of Duncan's Creek, in the vicinity of the Old Church, was, one winter's night, returning home through the swamp, with several carpenter's tools upon his shoulder, when he heard behind him the familiar howl of a pack of wolves hunting in a body for their prey; apprehending his danger he quickly threw down his load, and setting off, did not cease to run till he found himself safe within the door of his house.

An old pioneer of the Pacolet, near Grindal's Shoals, James Mosely, who was famous as a hunter and woodsman, and at a later day as an intrepid whig scout, was late one evening returning from a hunt in which he had taken a small deer, that he carried on his shoulder. The wolves got a scent of the game, and were soon howling on the trail of the hunter. He heard them, and knew that an effort must be made to save both himself and his deer. Turning a little from the path he hastily sunk the carcass in a creek, and running some distance further, just had time to climb with his rifle into the branches of a post oak tree, as the pack came up in full cry. It was now too dark for him to use his rifle with effect, and he silently watched them as they circled, incessantly yelping and barking around him.

They bayed him in this manner all night. At the approach of day, however, their circle began to grow larger; and as soon as he could see through his sights he singled out the leader of the troop and shot him; the rest instantly ran off to their dens. Mosely was afterwards asked why he did not fire among them sooner? He replied that he was perfectly safe in the tree, but felt a sort of pride in waiting till daylight that he might pick off the leader and the largest of the gang.

The venerable tree connected with this story is still a living witness of the occurrence, and known to all the surrounding country as Mosely's Oak; no sacrilegious hand would dare approach it with an axe. It stands immediately on the road leading to Grindal's Shoals, and a short distance from the house of Garland Meng, Esq.

It appears that two distinct species of the wolf were anciently found in Carolina, as well as in Georgia and Florida, the black and the gray. The Indians greatly prized the skin of the former, either on account of its beautiful color, or for some superior quality of its fur.

The gray was the fiercer, and more hardy—better adapted to the long, cold winters of a primitive country. It is now found in great numbers in the high latitudes of Oregon and Washington territories; while the black species is still common in Florida.

The wolf delighted to make his den under large rocks, especially on the elevated sides of craggy precipices and hills, in which places natural cavities were most frequently found. There is scarcely a hollow granite rock in the upper country, or cavernous steep, that did not, when deep buried in its primitive woods, give shelter to some of these prowling pests.

No sooner did the colonists at the mouth of the Ashley and Cooper, begin to extend their settlements, and lay out farms a little way from Charleston towards the interior, than the panther, bear, and wild cat, with the voracious wolf at their head, made such terrible havoc in their poultry yards and folds, as to become a serious obstacle to the further growth and prosperity of the province. Hence among the first statutes of the Assembly, we find stringent laws for the destruction and extirpation of those animals. The first was enacted in March 1695, and is entitled an Act for destroying beasts of prey. The quaint expression, and ancient orthography of these old statutes, are no less historical than the facts to which they relate.

The first reads as follows:

"Be it enacted by his Excellency, William Earl of Craven, Pallatine, and the rest of the true and absolute Lords and Proprietors of the Province of Carolina, by and with the advice, and consent of the rest of the members of the General Assembly now met at Charlestowne for the south-west part of this Province. That every Indian bowman, capable to kill deere as aforesaid, of the several nations of Indians before named, shall sometime before the twenty-fifth day of November, one thousand six hundred and ninety-six, and soe yearly for ever, bring in to such person as shall be appoynted by the Governor for the tyme one woolfe's skinn, or one tiger's skinn, or one beare skinn, or two catt skinns. And if any Indian as aforesaid, shall not bring in to the receiver, one wolfes skinn, or one tigers skinn, or two catt skinns, the casique or cheife of every nation, together with assistance of his captains, and those men which have before delivered to the receiver as before appoynted, is hereby required, the Indian or Indians soe neglecting, to bring to Charlestowne some time before the twenty-fifth day of December one thousand eight hundred and ninety six, and soe yearly forever, and the same there upon his bare back, severely whipp in sight of the inhabitants of said towne, which *whipping shall be instead of that skinn, which otherwise the saide Indian ought to have given to the receiver.* And all and every of the several nations of Indians before named, which shall neglect or refuse to bring skinns as appoynted, or in lieu thereof to punish by whipping every severall neglecting Indian of their respective nations, shall be, and declared to be out of the protection of this Government, and shall not designedly receive any benefit thereby."

Surely nothing short of a pressing necessity could have urged the enactment of a law so stringent and unjust as this towards the Indians.

The next legislation on the same subject followed in 1700; and in this statute may be observed a marked improvement, not only in orthography, but also in justice and practical wisdom. Instead of compulsion under the penalty of the whipping-post, the Indian hunters are to receive a pecuniary reward for their useful services:

"And be it enacted that whatsoever white man shall destroy and kill, wolf, tyger, wild catt, or bear, shall have ten shillings for each, bringing the head thereof to the next justice as above exprest; and every Indian for killing every wolf, tyger or wild catt, shall have for each five shillings, to be paid by the justice, and be reimbursed by the receiver; and the heads of the said beasts are presently to be burnt or their ears cut off, in the presence of them that brings the same."*

Three years after, nearly the same statute was re-enacted; it differed from the last only in the fact, that but half the premium of ten shillings was now offered for the head of a wild cat. This animal had, perhaps, already become scarce in the vicinity of Charleston, or less aggressive in his habits.

But the settlements of Carolina were gradually extending towards the interior, and thence to the wild, unoccupied haunts of the upper-country; and in process of time, the homesteads and farms on the Saluda, Broad, Tyger, and Ennoree Rivers, and Fishing, Fair-Forest, and Long-Cane creeks, required the same fostering care of the Legislative authorities to protect them from the destructive encroachments of the same animals of prey.

We find among the statutes, therefore, acts similar to the above, frequently repeated, and continued in

* Statutes of South Carolina. Vol. 2d.

force for a limited period. The last that was probably enacted is before us, passed by the State Legislature in March 1786, and entitled an Act to encourage the destroying of beasts of prey:

"Whereas it is found necessary to give some encouragement to the destroying of beasts of prey, which, of late, have been very mischievous to some of the interior parts of the State; it is therefore ordained, that every person, who shall hereafter kill, in this State, any of the beasts of prey herein mentioned, shall have the following rewards: for a panther or tiger ten shillings; for a wolf ten shillings; for a wild cat five shillings. He shall carry the scalp and two ears of such beasts to any justice of the peace, and receive from him, on proof of the same, a certificate gratis."*

It is not a little surprising that notwithstanding these strong measures so long enforced, and the rapid increase of the population, who laid bare the country, and found exciting sport, as well as profit, in an incessant war upon these obnoxious animals, they continued for so many years to subsist in many parts of it. It was probably some time after the commencement of the nineteenth century, ere the last panther ceased to range the forest of the upper-country in search of his wonted prey. The wolf disappeared at a still later period; and the wild cat is not yet extinct.

The Indians were accustomed to take the wolf by means of the dead fall of logs and stones, baited

* Statutes of South Carolina. Vol. 4th, p. 726.

with a piece of deer or buffalo's flesh. The pioneers and hunters improving on this, introduced for his especial benefit a large sort of steel trap, which did such good execution in ridding the country of his presence, that the name, "wolf-trap," has ever since distinguished that instrument from all others of the kind, and is likely to remain an enduring memorial of those early times.

It appears, however, from the following incident, that the white men did not always follow the example of the Indians in baiting their traps with the flesh of wild beasts.

In the midst of that darkest period in the history of the upper-country, when, at the first hostile movement of the Revolution in the South, the Cherokees burst from their mountains in vengeful fury upon the defenceless Whigs. Col. Pickens, at the head of a trusty band, having chased a large party of them from the settlements, pressed them so closely in their retreat towards the Nation, as to force them to take refuge in an old deserted house in the neighborhood of Little River in the present territory of Abbeville. And when—it is to be hoped—he could not succeed in dislodging them by a less cruel means, he set fire to the building. The greater number of the wretches perished without an effort or a murmur in the flames, while a few were shot by the riflemen, as they rushed from the burning house in the vain hope of escape.*

Late the following night, Capt. Wm. Black was

* We will say more of this in its proper place.

riding by the spot on his way home from Miller's Block House on Little River, when his attention was arrested by the rattling of chains, a short distance from the path he was pursuing. Reining up to ascertain the source of a noise so singular in that place, he discovered a fellow of the neighborhood, whom he well knew, coolly in the act of baiting his wolf-trap with a piece of one of the dead Indians; the human carcasses had already attracted large numbers of that animal to the spot, and the unscrupulous trapper was making the best of his opportunity.

In both ancient and modern history, the wolf is famous as being the scavenger of battle fields; he tore the slain on the plains of Cannæ, and Pharsalia, and fatened on the dead and dying in the great retreat from Moscow.

It is the tradition in the vicinity of King's Mountain, that long after the great battle fought there, no spot in the upper-country was so much frequented for the purpose of hunting and trapping wolves.

The domesticated wolf was the dog of the Indian; and never were dog and master more alike. They, or a cross upon them, however, appear to have been very sagacious. Bartram, in his travels in Florida, observed in one place: "A remarkable occurrence here, was a troop of horses, under the care and control of a single black dog, which seemed to differ in no respect from the black wolf of Florida, except his being able to bark as a common dog. He was very industrious in keeping them together; and if any one strolled from the rest at too great a distance, the dog would spring up, head him, and bring him back to the company. The owner of these horse; is an Indian, who, out of humor and experiment trained his dog up from a puppy to this businesss he follows his master's horses only, keeping them in a separate company, where they range; and when he is hungry or wants to see his master, in the evening, he returns to town, but never stays at home at night."

The wolf made prey of the deer, and usually united in large droves to hunt them at night. It was nothing unusual, however, to see a single one run down a deer. In times when game was scarce with them, they became so lank and poor, as to be hardly able to run; and they then resorted to the miserable shift of filling their stomachs with swamp mud. But when in this condition, if they should chance to take any game, they instantly disgorged the mud, and devoured the prey. While hunting in troops in the dead hours of night, their noise was exceedingly annoying, and sometimes terrific.

A wounded buffalo or elk was the sure prey of this insatiable prowler; and the Indians and earliest English hunters frequently, in their wanderings, came upon packs of them when just in the act of pulling down the largest bull of some scattered herd, that had long retained sufficient strength in his last extremity to keep them at bay.

This animal was once extremely abundant on Hardlabor and Cuffytown Creeks. The last of the famous hunters of that region were the Hendersons—William and James. It is said that

Old Jimmy—the name by which the latter was better known—killed in their den, under a pile of rocks, near the present site of Scotch Cross, the last wolves probably that lingered in Abbeville District.

It would appear from the following incident, related by the same author, quoted above, in his History of Carolina, that the young wolves, the whole litter, as soon as they were strong enough, ventured to ramble alone through the woods:

"We had not proceeded far—in an excursion through Alabama—before our people roused a litter of young wolves, to which, giving chase, we soon caught one of them, it being entangled in high grass. One of the men caught it by the hind legs, and another beat out its brains with the but of his gun. This creature was about the size of a small cur dog, and quite black."

Bartram also remarks that the wolf was frequently met with, variegated with spots of white and black.

The fox is more familiar to the people than any of the native animals of the upper-country, whose history has been detailed in our previous pages. Yet there are some curious facts in his history that are not perhaps generally known. When the first settlers built their cabins in this region, the gray fox was the only variety that then inhabited the woods, and he was exceedingly abundant; his sprightly bark was one of the familiar sounds of the country, and it was as usual to see him stealing from covert to covert, as the hare at present. It was only as an occasional pilferer of the roost that he was noticed at all by the pioneers. His ears were then, and long after, unaccustomed to the bay of the hound, and the stirring echoes of the huntsman's horn. A people who had before them the work of erecting houses for their families, and clearing away the obstructions of a new forest-covered country, could spare no leisure to be devoted to the mere pleasures of the chase. His home was in the thick grass and brush of the woods, he was never seen in the open fields or prairies; and as the forest fell before the encroachments of the axeman and farmer, the gray fox like the whip-poor-will, receded towards the west, and soon became rare, if at all seen, in the best cultivated portions of the country. But, as our hunters well know, his place was not suffered to remain vacant; the same cause, the general denudation of the land, that drove away the gray, attracted from the east the smaller, but hardier, swifter and more intelligent red fox. The gray fox made his den deep in the forest, under the brush-wood and rocks; the red fox finds a retreat equally comfortable and far more safe in the deep intricate burrows which his ingenuity enables him to construct in the open sedge fields.

This sagacious pest of the farm, has become, of late years, so numerous in many parts of the upper-country as to make it impossible, without great care, to keep up a stock of hogs—a litter of young pigs is its favorite food. This is particularly the case at present around the mountain in Abbeville District. The female is exceedingly prolific; the hunters frequently take them when in a fair way of adding as many as nine at a single birth, to the numbers already teeming in the country.

But the den formed by this animal is the most curious part of its history; it is perhaps the most remarkable object, connected at this time, with all the natural history of the upper-country. When ready to perform this important work, it is usual for two or three of them to unite, and having selected a spot that pleases them—which is generally at the edge of an old field, and as convenient to water as possible—they set to work with all their force tunneling out the earth, and shaping their course as they go down at a considerable angle to the horizon. The dirt, as they push it out, is heaped up at the mouth of the hole, and becomes, after a while, quite a mound, sometimes several feet in height.

After they have delved in this manner, usually for more than thirty-five or forty feet, sometimes ninety or a hundred, they cease to tunnel, and begin the less laborious work of constructing their dormitories or sleeping-rooms. These they arrange with singular art, excavating them in receding galleries; so that, if we were to view the bottom of the burrow, even from the front, it would appear, at first sight, to be entirely empty.

The apartment destined for that one of the company whose lot it is to occupy the basement story, is elevated like a step some distance above the main floor, and on this his bed of leaves and straw is carefully prepared. At the same distance above this, and directly back of it, the second room is constructed, on which the second fox fixes his bed; and if there is still another in the company a third dormitory is excavated in the same manner, in relation to the second, and a similar bed made upon it.

It is obvious that several important advantages are gained by this ingenious arrangement. It affords them at all times, a dry, warm berth; it enables them, on any emergency requiring it, to run all out together with the greatest ease to themselves, through their long narrow tunnel; but chiefly, in case of sudden invasion from an enemy, their galleries serve as so many admirably constructed citadels, into which they can retreat in succession, with a powerful advantage, at the narrow entrance to each, over the boldest and most dangerous intruder.*

That security, when pressed by their enemies, is the principal aim, in planning their burrows after this fashion, is confirmed by the fact that they not unfrequently, after boring the first tunnel, and forming their bed-rooms, construct a second one from the back of the last dormitory an equal distance to the surface of the ground with the first; thus securing, in the last extremity, a safe retreat in, at least, one direction. In this case, the whole den extends through some sixty or a hundred feet. Where can the lover of nature find a more beautiful illustration of the intelligence and sagacity of brute animals?

* A den, similar to the one just described, was recently laid open on the bank of Long-Cane, by several hunters on that stream. It cost them a hard day's work.

The quadrupeds whose history we have endeavored to present, as intimately connected with that of primitive Upper-Carolina, are all that properly belong to her historical fauna. What remains worthy of notice still exist more or less abundantly in the country, such as the otter, raccoon, opossum, musk-rat, and squirrel. These animals, however, are every year diminishing, as the population grows denser, and the area of open, cultivated country is enlarged. The otter especially, has already become extinct in many streams where, in old times, he abounded. It may be observed, too, of another animal not before mentioned, the fœtid pole-cat, that it has now nearly, if not wholly disappeared from a large portion of the upper-country. The skin of this animal is exceedingly beautiful, and nothing prevented its extensive use, even for the most delicate fabrics, but its intolerable and indestructable odor.

The opossum has long enjoyed an enviable scientific notoriety; he is still, we believe, a sort of *pons assinorum*, of naturalists. Their patient investigations, however, have enabled them to arrive at a much more accurate knowledge of his nature and habits than had been attained in the time of an old author, who published a book in London, on Carolina, in 1741, in which he describes the opossum as "*a rat having a bag under its throat wherein it conveys its young when forced to fly.*" This animal ranges from the Hudson to the Rocky Mountains. The Cherokees gave it the name of *sesqua*; their names for the pole-cat and fox were *ookoonne* and *choochola*, or chicora.

CHAPTER IV.

Fish exceedingly abundant in the Upper-Country—Ancient shoals of Herrings—Old Legislative enactment for the protection of Shad Fisheries in Broad, Saluda, Ennoree, Tiger and Pacolet Rivers, and Stevens' Creek, of Edgefield—The Fish Sluice Law violently enforced—Incident at Lorick's Mill, on the Saluda—The Historian Adair and Indians harpooning Sturgeon in Savannah River, &c.

At the period to which our history relates, and even in later times, the rivers and smaller streams of the upper-country abounded in fish. The Catawba, Savannah, Saluda, and Broad, were not surpassed in this respect by the most prolific streams of the teeming south-west. Besides the numerous well-known varieties that live constantly in the fresh waters, vast numbers of shad came up every spring, and filled not only the rivers, and their larger tributaries, but the smaller creeks and rivulets; the waters of Bullock's and Stevens' Creek, of the Long-Cane, and Seneca, and Sandy Rivers, were famous with the early sportsmen and settlers for their shad fisheries. In the earliest periods, even shoals of herring were annually expected by the Indians to come a great way up into the fresh waters of the upper-country. Their time of running was in March and April.

Lawson says, that the savages took vast quantities of them at those seasons in crails and artificial ponds into which the fish were directed by means of hedges. It is not generally known, at least in the upper-country, that the shores of Carolina are the utmost southern limit of the migrations of those vast shoals of herring, which, for ages, have annually rolled from within the arctic circle to the warmer seas of the south, for the purpose of depositing their spawn. Why they so early discontinued their visits up the rivers and fresh water streamlets of the country, described by Lawson, we are unable to give any information. The herring is the most valuable fish yet discovered.*

Just previous to the Revolution, or immediately after, the gradual increase of population, and the consequent erection of dams and mills on the streams, so obstructed the ancient passages through which the shad were accustomed to run up to the numerous fisheries, famous from the time of the earliest settlers for their productiveness, and manly sport, that the communities, which were interested, complained loudly of the failure of their annual supplies of fish. This was particularly the case on the Broad, Saluda, Ennoree, Tiger, and Pacolet Rivers, and Stevens' Creek, in the present territory of Edgefield. The matter became a subject of Legislative investigation, and resulted, in March, 1784, in the following enactment, entitled an Act "to prevent the damming up of Broad, Saluda, Ennoree, Tiger, and Pacolet Rivers, and Stevens' Creek, or otherwise obstructing the fish from passing up the said rivers, and to oblige

* Encyclo. Amer.

such persons as had already dammed them, to remove the obstructions, so that the fish could pass up."

Such, however, was the value of good mills, and the necessity of stopping every passage at the river falls, in order to have them, that the "fish sluice statute" proved gradually, from the beginning, a dead letter. And the people, though greatly regretting the loss of their time-honored luxury and sport of spring fish and fishing, aware that the sacrifice must be made to greater interests that had sprung up in the rapid development of their section of the State, at length silently acquiesced, and nothing more was heard of fish sluices, or of shad catching, at the old fisheries, except at certain points on the Broad and Savannah Rivers.

The last two or three generations of the upper-country population have scarcely heard, from tradition, of those ancient migrations from the ocean, as far up even as the little streams and brooks that lie above the dashing shoals which stretch across the entire width of the State, in a magnificent series of foaming cataracts—an imperishable granite breakwater of God's building that separates the lands of oaks, and hickory, and luxuriant grain, from the sombre pines and alluvial sands of the middle and lower country.

It must not be supposed, however, that these important fishing privileges of the upper-country were yielded without a struggle. The innate selfishness of even enlightened men blinds them often to the legitimate results of the very progress which they themselves love, and are earnestly striving to promote.

In 1824, a company of twenty men, living near the Saluda, in the Districts of Abbeville and Laurens, assembled at the old Swansey's Ferry, with a boat in readiness to proceed down the river, according to a previous agreement, for the purpose of cutting through a dam that had effectually prevented the passage of shad to the long-established fishery at that point. At the head of the party were Dr. John ——, of Abbeville, and Captain Robert ——, of Laurens, and among them Nimrod Overby, Thomas Harris, Harrison Long, and —— Jolly.

Their point of destination was Lorick's Mill, some forty miles lower down, between the Districts of Newberry and Edgefield. The dam at this place had been built with public funds, under the auspices of Colonel A. Blanding, and in connection with his splendid folly of river and canal navigation of the Saluda.* A strong frame-work, supported by pens of rock, formed the material of the dam in which, with a semblance of respect to the statute, a small gap had been left, but not so deep as to afford, in the spirit of the Act, a sluice for the passage of fish.

The ardor of the party abated somewhat, on a close view of the work before them; they were not men, however, to be driven from a purpose once deliberately formed, and went resolutely to the task of throwing out the rip-rapped stone, and cutting away

* We shall speak of this fully in its proper place.

the timbers with their axes. Numerous spectators collected, in the meantime, on both banks of the river to witness the process of demolition; but no opposition was offered. Thus they toiled for three days, and in that time succeeded in opening a deeper passage not more than some six feet wide; but thinking this sufficient for their purpose, the party desisted, and returned home. A short time after the breach in the obnoxious dam was more effectually closed than before, and not a shad perhaps since that day has extended its migrations in the Saluda as far as Swansey's Ferry. This was doubtless the last attempt made in the up-country to enforce the fish sluice statute of 1784.

The gigantic rock fish—a delicacy for the table of a king—lurked especially in the deep waters of the Broad, while the sturgeon, trout, sucker, and perch, the fierce pike and voracious cat, were yet more numerous in that river, and the others that have been mentioned. Says an old writer: "Those Indians who are unacquainted with the use of barbed iron are very expert in striking large fish out of their canoes, with long, sharp-pointed green canes, which are well bearded, and hardened in the fire. In Savannah River, I have often accompanied them in killing sturgeons, with those green swamp harpoons, and which they did with much pleasure and ease; for when we discovered the fish, we soon thrust into their bodies one of the harpoons. As the fish would immediately strike deep, and rush away to the bottom very rapidly, their strength was soon exhausted by their violent struggles against the buoyant force of the green darts; as soon as the top-end of them appeared again on the surface of the water, we made up to them, renewed the attack, and in like manner continued it, till we secured our game."*

Fish was one of the staple articles of food with the Cherokees and other Indians in this region. When they were unable, by their simple methods, to take the usual supply of game from the woods, they seldom failed to procure, at all seasons, an abundance of fish in the rivers and creeks.

And it was chiefly for this reason that all their towns and settlements were situated on the banks of considerable streams. And these were then clear and beautiful—as limpid as transparent crystal; the clay and loosened soil, from a thousand wasting fields and plantations, had not yet imparted to them their modern turbidness. In such waters the simple spear and net served all the purposes of a complete fishing tackle.

No where in the up-country are the remains of a single Indian town found in a spot remote from a creek or river; and two historical facts may be safe-.y inferred for every such locality: it was once abundantly supplied with fish, and possessed a soil admirably adapted to the production of corn.

"There is a favorite method among them of fishing with hand nets. The nets are about three feet

* Adair.

deep, and of the same diameter at the opening, made of the wild hemp, and knotted after the usual manner of our nets. On each side of the mouth, they tie, very securely, a strong elastic green cane, to which the ends are fastened. Prepared with these, the warriors abreast jump in at the end of a long pond, swimming under water with their net stretched open with both hands, and the canes in a horizontal position. In this manner they will continue, either till their breath is expended by want of respiration, or till the net is so ponderous as to force them to empty it ashore or in a basket, fixed in a proper place for that purpose; by removing one hand the canes instantly spring together. I have been engaged half a day at a time, and half drowned with this diversion. When any of us was so unfortunate as to catch water-snakes in our sweep, and emptied them ashore, we had the ranting voice of the whole company whooping against us, till another party was so unlucky as to meet with the like misfortune. During this exercise the women are fishing ashore with coarse baskets, to catch the fish that escape our nets. At the end of our friendly diversion, we cheerfully return home, and in an innocent friendly manner eat together, studiously diverting each other on the incidents of the day, and make a cheerful night."

There was another primitive method of taking fish, so much like one still in vogue with the whites, that there is no doubt, it was originally borrowed from the Indians, who were accustomed to use it in the identical places in the streams of the upper-country, where our people use it at the present day.

It consisted in laying long, tapering baskets, precisely similar, it seems, to those now called "fish baskets," but much larger, and constructed chiefly of canes, in the middle of a shoal or slight waterfall, at a point where two sloping rows of stones, running, one from each bank, are made to meet. The fish following the natural swift current of the stream, would pass into the baskets, and, in those prolific times, soon fill them up. When a larger number than usual was wanted, as on the occasion of a village feast, the Indians used to expedite the process by what may be called a *drive of the fish*. They stretched a grape-vine across the stream, above the baskets, which they contrived to sink by hanging stones to it, that dragged the bottom; thus prepared, they sometimes swam a mile, plunging and whooping, and driving the fish before them into the baskets. In this way they frequently succeeded in taking incredible numbers, of which, according to Adair, they sometimes made a feast of love—every one in the village partaking of it in the most friendly manner—and afterwards they dance together, singing *halelujah*, and the rest of their usual praises to God for his bountiful gifts to the beloved people.

Another method not unfrequently practiced by the Cherokees in the art of taking fish, is somewhat curious, and illustrates not only their ingenuity, but that acute observation of the nature and properties of plants for which they have ever been celebrated.

It is thus described: "In a dry summer season, they gather horse-chestnuts, and different sorts of roots, which, having pounded pretty fine, and steeped awhile in a trough, they scatter over the surface of a middle-sized pond, and stir it about with poles, tlll the water is sufficiently impregnated with the intoxicating bitter. The fish are all soon drunk, and make to the surface of the water with their bellies uppermost. They are then gathered in baskets, and the largest barbacued—being carefully covered over at night to preserve them from the supposed putrifying influence of the moon. It seems that the fish caught in this manner, are not poisoned,* but only stupified; for they prove very wholesome food. By experiments, when they are speedily moved into good water, they revive in a few minutes."†

With these facts before us, it is no difficult task for the imagination to reanimate a thousand scenes in as many spots on the streams of the upper-country, that were the realities of the period, when it was yet the possession of its aboriginal people, and long before the restless foot of the white man had desecrated the soil. Those whose dispositions are sufficiently antiquarian to find delight in the study of the past—in deciphering through its associations with the present, a language and a history, too subtle for types

*The horse-chestnut is better known as the common "buck eye" of our woods—the Aesculus glabra of the botanists.

† Adair.

or even for the comprehension of less curious minds—may here enjoy a feast peculiarly their own. They may sit and muse by the Fairforest, the Tiger, the Ennoree, and the beautiful Savannah, and fancy they hear mingling, with the dashing roar or gentle murmur of their waters, the joyous shouts of the red men once more at their sports, or gladsome toil in the element they loved so well.

To complete this picture of luxuriant animal production, the usual varieties of wild foul were not wanting to the woods and waters. The rivers and their tributaries abounded with duck and wild geese; but not only did the former bird swarm in those streams, it was also found in great numbers in every woodland lake. In the vicinity of Greenwood, and Cokesbury, in the Flatwoods, and many other localities of the entire country, there were found in old times innumerable ponds or lakes, long since dried up, in which they collected in such quantities as to attract the attention of the early, and even more recent hunters. Possibly none may now live; but we are assured, that there were men, who shot duck on the elevated ridges of Greenwood and Cokesbury.

The noise, and denudations of civilized life, have affected this game, as they did the buffalo and elk, have driven it away forever from its ancient haunts. To see, at the present day, a flock of wild geese quietly feeding upon the ground or gamboling in the waters of the upper-country, would be an event surprising enough, while the peculiar whistle, and splashing roar of the great duck, gathering by thousands at night-fall in the creeks and woodland lakes, are heard no more.

The incredible numbers of wild turkeys that once existed in this region, is sufficiently attested both by tradition, and the fact that, although they are exceedingly shy, and the forests, their natural coverts, are well nigh cut away, they are still in many places quite numerous, and are likely to continue to subsist in the country as long as any portion of secluded woods is suffered to stand. Lawson declares, in his History of Carolina, published as early as 1718, that he had seen in the forest as many as five hundred wild turkeys in a single flock; indeed, they seemed to be seldom out of his sight, as he traversed the country from Charleston towards North Carolina. Bartram, the botonist and traveler, also mentions the astonishing numbers he encountered, of this bird, while traversing Carolina and East Florida. "Having rested very well during the night, I was awakened in the morning early, by the cheering converse of the wild turkey-cocks, saluting one another from the sun brightened tops of the lofty cypresses. They begin at early dawn, and continue till sun-rise, from March to the last of April. The high forests ring with the noise, like the crowing of the domestic cock, of these social sentinels; the watchword being caught and repeated from one to another, for hundreds of miles around; in so much that the whole country is, for an hour or more, in an universal shout. A little after sun-rise they quit the trees, and alighting on the earth, strut and dance around the coy female, while the deep forests seem to tremble with their shrill noise."*

In the methods of taking this splendid fowl, the Anglo-American hunters made no improvements on those practiced by the Indians in the earliest periods. No artificial contrivance, and no other human mouth, could surpass their imitations of the natural call of both the male and female. It was then, too, far less shy than after it had become frightened into a habitual wariness by the constant report of the pioneer's rifle. The Indians were also accustomed to entrap it in what are still known as "turkey pens," which they baited with maize.

The dried breast of the wild turkey, is said to have been frequently used, by the early settlers, as a substitute for bread.

The history of the partridge is similar to that of the bee and red fox, it rather followed than preceded the footsteps of the pioneers. When these western wilds were first penetrated by the whites, it was seldom, if ever seen; even in luxuriant Kentucky,† it was not till after the forest had been partially cleared away, and waving fields of golden grain had taken its place, that flocks of this, now familiar bird, began to gather around the cabins and farms of the settlers. The cry of "bob white," and the buz of the bee, became warning notes to the Indians of coming white men, and civilization.

* Bartram's Carolina, p. 81. † Hall's Sketches of the West.

CHAPTER V.

The Rattlesnake--Its powers of fascination--An object of veneration to all the tribes of the Continent—This curious fact probably connected in some way with their origin as a people—Cosmogony of the Cherokees or their notions of the world's creation--Great Rattlesnakes seen by Bernal Diaz in Mexico—Beautiful tradition of the Algonquins with whom the Cherokees were allied by blood--Curious account of the Horn-Snake, &c.

In the primitive history of Carolina, besides its quadrupeds and birds, there were a few reptiles, whose remarkable natural qualities, and singular association with the Indians and early white settlers, render them worthy here, of a notice of some length. The most important of these was the rattlesnake.

This interesting, but dangerous creature, occupies in the reptile kingdom the same position that the African lion does among beasts. He may be styled the king of snakes. Not that he was physically stronger than all others of his kind—for there were serpents that mastered him in strength and cunning, as there are quadrupeds which find no great difficulty in mastering the lion. But they resemble each other in the greatness of their absolute power, and in the generosity and nobility of their natures.

The vigor of the rattlesnake, however, did not consist so much in strength of muscles and hugeness of proportions—though the largest serpent in America—as in the wonderful fascination of his eye, and deadly energy of his venom, whenever hunger prompted the one, and the encroachments of an enemy elicited the other.

It was partly on account of these qualities, there can be no doubt, that the Indians regarded it with so much veneration, if not as an object of worship. The most striking feature, perhaps, in the Indian character, was the great respect which they entertained for the virtues of generosity, independence and courage; a brave, generous enemy never failed to win their sympathy and admiration.

Veneration for the rattlesnake was not peculiar to the Cherokees, or any other southern tribe; it was known to exist among all the natives of the Continent. Thatcher mentions it as an object of worship, even among the more northern tribes, under the name of *manito-kinibic.* From Central America to the Great Lakes, it enjoyed the religious regard and affection of the aborigines; they were accustomed to address it as their grandfather, and the king of serpents. On no account would they destroy it themselves, even when struck by its deadly fangs, while wandering in the woods, nor suffer a white man to do it, if it was in their power to prevent it.

But while this curious respect for the rattlesnake was not peculiar to any one tribe, neither was it conferred exclusively upon that serpent; all the snakes of the country enjoyed a share of it, though in a less degree. The Indians suffered them all to live unmolested. Some other cause, therefore, must be sought than the dangerous power and generosity of the rattlesnake, to account for these singular facts. It becomes an interesting subject of inquiry. Philosophers have written much to account for the origin of the aborigines; but we do not recollect to have seen this serpent-worship used among their speculations as an argument in favor of their having come from the East. It is, certainly, in some way connected with the story of the temptation and fall in the garden by the waters of the Euphrates.

It is impossible to read the curious cosmogony of the Cherokees, or their notion of the world's creation, without being forcibly reminded of the Scriptural account of the origin of evil and death. They believed that a number of beings were engaged in the work of creation. The sun was created first. The intention of the creators was that men should live always; but the sun, when he passed over, told them that there was not land enough, and that people had better die. At length the daughter of the sun, who was with them, was bitten by a serpent and died. The sun, on his return, inquired for her, and was told that she was dead. He then consented that human beings might live always; and told them to take a box, and go where the spirit of his daughter had fled, and bring it back to her body, charging them at the same time, that when they had obtained her spirit, they should not look into the box, until they had returned with it to the place where her body had been left. Impelled however by curiosity, they disobeyed the sun's injunctions, and opened the box, upon which the spirit escaped, and the fate of all men was decided—they were doomed to die.*

The Cherokees,† as their name imports, were worshippers of fire, and they extended their adoration to the serpent, because they believed it to be the fire's messenger.

Bernal Diaz, in his account of the march of Cortez to the city of Mexico, says: "We to-day arrived at a place called Terraguco, which we named the town of the serpents, on account of the enormous figures of those reptiles, which we found in their temples, and which they worship as gods." Living rattlesnakes were kept in the great temple of Mexico as sacred objects. "Moreover," he adds, "in that accursed house, they kept vipers and venemous snakes, which had something at their tails that sounded like morris-bells, and these are the worst of vipers. They are kept in cradles, and barrels, and in earthen vessels, upon feathers; and there they layed their eggs and nursed up their snakelings; and they were fed with the bodies of the sacrificed,‡ and with dogs' flesh.§

The Natchezs on the Mississippi, had the figure of a rattlesnake, carved from wood, placed upon the altar of their temple, and paid it peculiar honors. The Linni Lenape held it in great respect, and like-

* Archæological Researches. † Chera means fire.

‡ This is no more wonderful than many things stated by Mr. Prescott of the ancient Mexicans, on the same authorities.

§ Squire's Archæ. Researches.

wise the Hurons. We are told of a Menominee Indian who carried a rattlesnake constantly with him, and called it his great father. Sculptures of this serpent have been repeatedly taken from the mounds of the West.

There is a tradition of this remarkable reptile, once current among all the Algonquin stock of the aborigines, that is too interesting to be omitted in this connection. It is known as the Algonquin tradition of the evil serpent. Manabozho, the famous teacher of the Algonquins, was always regarded as an enemy to a great serpent; and he is represented as in constant conflict with his antagonist.

"One day, returning to his lodge, from a long journey, Manabozho missed from it his young cousin, who resided with him; he called his name aloud but received no answer. He looked around on the sand for the tracks of his feet, and he there for the first time discovered the trail of Meshekinibic, the great rattlesnake. He then knew that his cousin had been seized by his terrible enemy. He armed himself and followed on his track; he crossed the great river, and passed mountains and valleys to the shores of the deep and gloomy lake, now called Manitou Lake, or the Lake of Devils. The trail of Meshekinibic led to the edge of the water.

At the bottom of this lake was the dwelling of the serpent, and it was filled with spirits, his attendants and companions. Their forms were monstrous and terrible, but most of them, like their master, bore the semblance of serpents. In the centre of this horrible assembly, was Meshekinibic himself, coiling his volumes around the hapless cousin of Manabozho. His head was red, as with blood, and his eyes were fierce, and glowed like coals of fire. His body was all over armed with hard and glistening scales of every shade and color.

Manabozho looked down upon the writhing spirits of evil, and vowed a deep revenge. He directed the clouds to disappear from the heavens, the winds to be still, and the air to become stagnant over the lake of the Manitous, and bade the sun to shine upon it with his fierceness; for thus he sought to drive his enemy forth, to seek the cool shadows of the trees that grew upon its banks, so that he might be able to take vengeance upon him.

Meantime Manabozho seized his bow and arrows and placed himself near the spot, where he deemed the serpent wonld come to enjoy the shade. He then changed himself into the broken stump of a withered tree, so that they might not discover him.

The winds became still, the air stagnant, and the sun shone hot upon the lake of the evil spirits. By-and-by the waters became troubled, and bubbles rose to the surface; for the rays of the sun penetrated to the horrible brood within its depths. The commotion increased, and a serpent lifted its head high above the centre of the lake, and gazed around the shores. Directly another came to the surface, and they listened for the footsteps of Manabozho; but they heard him no where on the face of the earth, and said one to another, "Manabozho sleeps." And then they plunged again beneath the waters, which seemed to hiss as they closed over them.

It was not long before the lake became more troubled than before; it boiled from its very depths, and the hot waves dashed wildly against the rocks on its shores. The commotion increased, and soon the great rattlesnake emerged slowly to the surface, and moved towards the shore. His blood-red crest glowed with a deeper hue, and the reflection from his glancing scales was like the blinding glitter of a sleet-covered forest in the morning sun of winter. He was followed by all the evil spirits, and so great was their number that they covered the shores of the lake with their foul-trailing carcasses.

They saw the stump into which Manabozho had changed himself, and suspecting it might be one of his disguises, for they knew his cunning, one of them approached, and wound his tail around it, and made an effort to drag it down. But Manabozho stood firm, though he could hardly refrain from crying aloud; for the tail of the monster tickled his sides.

The great serpent wound his tail among the trees of the forest, and the rest also sought the shade, while one was left to listen for the steps of Manabozho.

When they all slept, Manabozho silently drew an arrow from his quiver, and placing it in his bow, aimed it where he saw the heart beat against the sides of the great serpent. He let it fly, and with a howl that shook the mountains, and startled the wild beasts in their caves, the monster awoke, and followed by his frightened companions uttering mingled sounds of rage and terror, plunged again into the lake. Here they vented their fury upon the helpless cousin of Manabozho, whose body they tore into a thousand pieces; his mangled lungs rose to the surface, and covered it with whiteness. And this is the origin of the foam on the water.

When the serpent knew that he was mortally wounded, both he and the evil spirits around him were rendered ten-fold more terrible by their great wrath, and they rose to overwhelm Manabozho. The waters of the lake swelled upwards from their dark depths, and with a sound like many thunders, it rolled madly on his track, bearing the rocks and trees before it with resistless fury. High on the crest of the foremost wave, black as midnight, rode the writhing form of the wounded Meshekinibic, and red eyes glared around, and the hot breath of the monstrous brood hissed fiercely above the retreating Manabozho. Then thought Manabozho of his Indian children, and he ran by their villages, and in a voice of alarm, bade them flee to the mountains, for the great serpent was deluging the earth in expiring wrath, sparing no living thing. The Indians caught up their children, and wildly sought safety where he bade them. But Manabozho continued his flight along the base of the western hills, and finally took refuge on a high mountain beyond Lake Superior far towards the north. There he found many men and animals that had fled from the flood, that already covered the villages, and plains, and even the highest hills. Still the waters continued to rise, and soon all the mountains were overwhelmed, save that on which stood Manabozho. Then he gathered together timbers and made a raft, upon which the men, and women, and the animals, that were with him, all placed themselves. No sooner had they done so than the rising floods closed over the mountain, and they floated alone on the surface of the waters. And thus they floated for many days; and some died, and the rest became sorrowful and reproached Manabozho, that he did not disperse the waters, and renew the earth, that they might live.

But though he knew that his great enemy was by this time dead, yet could not Manabozho renew the world, unless he had some earth in his hand wherewith to begin the work. And this he explained to them that were with him, and said, that were it ever so little, even a few grains of earth, then could he disperse the waters and renew the world. Then the beaver volunteered to go to the bottom of the deep, and get some earth, and they all applauded his design. He plunged in; they waited long, and when he returned he was dead; they opened his hands but there was no earth in them. Then said the otter, 'will I seek the earth,' and the bold swimmer dived from the raft. The otter was gone still longer than the beaver, and when he returned to the surface, he too was dead, and there was no earth in his claws. 'Who shall find the earth,' exclaimed all on the raft, 'now that the beaver and otter are dead?' And they desponded more than before, crying, 'who shall find the earth?'

'That will I,' said the muskrat, and he quickly disappeared between the logs of the raft. The muskrat was gone very long, much longer than the otter, and it was thought he would never return, when he suddenly rose near by; but he was too weak to speak, and swam slowly towards the raft. He had hardly got upon it, when he too died from his great exertion. They opened his little hands, and there closely clasped between the fingers they found a few grains of fresh earth.

These Manabozho carefully collected and dried them in the sun, and then he rubbed them into fine powder in his palms, and rising up blew them abroad upon the waters. No sooner was this done than the flood began to subside, and soon the trees on the mountains were seen, and then the mountains and hills emerged from the deep, and the plains and the valleys came into view, and the waters disappeared from the land, leaving no trace but a thick sediment which was the dust that Manabozho had blown abroad from the raft.

Then it was found that Meshekinibic was dead, and that the evil Manitous, his companions, had returned to the depths of the lake of spirits, from which, for fear of Manabozho, they never more dared to come forth. And in gratitude to the beaver, the otter and muskrat, these animals were ever after held sacred by the Indians, and they became their brethren, and they never killed nor molested them, until the medicine of the stranger made them forget their relations, and turned their hearts to ingratitude."*

In this beautiful tradition, worthy of the deep, poetic feeling of the red men, it requires no great knowledge of the Bible to discover many of the most striking points, though confused and jumbled, in the pathetic story of man's redemption, and the ancient account of the universal deluge.

The history of the aborigines furnishes no stronger presumptive proof than this of their Asiatic origin, and the error into which those intensely scientific philosophers have probably fallen, who teach that Noah's flood did not extend to the New World, and that the Indians bear no blood relationship to the first parents of the Anglo-Saxon and other races of men. The latter inference is necessarily included as a corollary in the first; for if the Indian originated in America, then the deluge could not have been universal; unless it can be shown with certainty that this Manabozho represents a real American Noah, and the mountain spoken of far beyond Lake Superior towards the North, an American Ararat; which would be a vastly more difficult feat than to prove the absolute historical truthfulness of the whole story of Manabozho and the serpent.

Arguments drawn from manners, customs, arts, and even language, in order to establish an identity

---

* American Review.

of origin between two people, long widely separated, are far less reliable than those derived from striking analogies plainly traceable in their ancient traditions, and cosmogonies.

This fable of Manabozho and the serpent, or something near akin to it, possibly entered into the religious belief of tribes much farther south than those living around Rainy Lake. Adair asserts that the Southern Indians never ate of the otter and musk-rat; and the Cherokees were closely related, through the Powhattans, to the Algonquin race.*

"Our old traders remember when they first began the custom of eating beavers; and to this day, none eat of them except those who kill them, though the flesh is very wholesome on account of the bark of trees they live upon. It must be acknowledged, they are all degenerating apace."

But, whatever may have been the source of this singular veneration with which the aborigines regarded the rattlesnake, it was exceedingly favorable to its growth and increase in every part of the country. The old traders and hunters met with them in alarming numbers, and of proportions sufficiently large to excite the awe and respect of the least devout of the natives; for though they had many endearing names for them, and refused to kill them, they knew well what a respectful distance was, when they chanced to come upon one in the woods, drawn up in his defiant coil, and sounding his notes of alarm.

* Pickett's History of Alabama.

The following description of one of their famous haunts in the Cherokee Nation, must be given in the quaint style of the old trader who relates it:

"Between the heads of the northern branch of the lower Cherokee* River, and the heads of that of Tuckasehchee, winding around in a long course by the late Fort Loudon, and afterwards into the Mississippi, there is, both in its nature and circumstances, a great phenomenon. Between two high mountains,† nearly covered with old mossy rocks, lofty cedars and pines, in the valleys of which the beams of the sun reflects a powerful heat, there are, as the Indians affirm, some bright old inhabitants, or rattlesnakes, of a more enormous size than is mentioned in history. They are so large and unwieldy that they take a circle about as wide as their length to crawl round in their shortest orbit; but bountiful nature compensates the heavy motion of their bodies; for, as they say, no living creature moves within reach of their sight, but they can draw it to them; which is agreeable to what we observe through the whole system of animated beings. Nature endues them with proper capacities to sustain life; as they cannot support themselves by their speed, or cunning,

* The Little Tennessee.

† If our author has reference here to the two head branches of the Little Tennessee, the locality which he would describe, lies somewhere among the mountains of the present Macon County in North Carolina, a few miles south-east of the village of Franklin. Fort Loudon stood on the same river in the territory of Tennessee, in the fork between it and the Tellico.

to spring from an ambuscade, it is needful they should have the bewitching craft of their eyes, and forked tongues.

The descriptions the Indians give of their color is as various as what we are told of the camelion; they seem to the spectator to change their color by every different position he may view them in, which proceeds from the piercing rays of light that blaze from their foreheads, so as to dazzle the eyes; for in each of their heads there is a large carbuncle, which not only repels, but they affirm, sullies the meridian beams of the sun.

They reckon it so dangerous to disturb these creatures that no temptation can induce them to betray their secret recess to the profane. An old trader of Cheeowhee told me that for the reward of two pieces of stroud cloth he engaged a couple of young warriors to show him the place of their resort; but the head men would not, by any means, allow it on account of a tradition, by which they fancy the killing of them would expose them to the danger of being bit by the other species of the serpentine tribe."*

Due allowance must be made in this singular narrative, for the superstition of the Indians; but there can be little doubt, from what has just been stated, that even more than one such horrible abode of those venemous reptiles existed at that period, in the gloomy recesses of the Blue Ridge, and granite hills of the upper-country. Many such dens have been

* Adair.

brought to light by the advancing settlements in the far west.

Notwithstanding their religious regard for the rattlesnake, and their perfect knowledge of the fatal influence of his venom, it does not appear that the Indians feared to approach, and even to handle him, when armed with their famous antidotes. "I once saw," says Adair, "the high-priest of the Chickasaws chew some snake-root, blow it on his hands, and then take up a rattlesnake without damage soon afterwards he laid it down in a hollow tree with great care, lest I should have killed it. Once on their trading war path, a little above the country of the Creeks, as I was returning to camp from hunting, I found in a large cane swamp, a fellow-traveler, an old Indian trader, inebriated and naked except his Indian breeches, and moccasins; in that habit he sat holding a great rattlesnake round the neck, with his left hand besmeared with the juice of proper roots; and with the other applying the roots to the teeth of the reptile, in order to repel the poison before he drew them out; and having effected this, he laid it down tenderly at a little distance from him. I then killed it, to his great mortification, as he was afraid it would occasion misfortunes to himself and me. And he did indeed perish, not long after, by the hands of the Choctaws, under French influence, on the Chickasaw path."

There once lived in Tomassee—a town situated a few miles above the site of old Fort Prince George—a great "divine man," a famous rain-prophet of the lower Cherokees, who, we are told, possessed a carbuncle nearly as large as a hen's egg, which he was reported to have found near where a great rattlesnake lay dead. It sparkled with such surprising lustre as to illuminate his dark winter house; like strong flashes of continued lightning its brightness appeared, to the great terror of the weak, who were afraid of being struck with sudden death, if they should approach the place where it had been deposited.

On the death of this prophet, according to the Indian custom, he was buried and the dreadful carbuncle with him, under the town-house of Tomassee, which stood on the extreme western side of the town. The remains of Tomassee can, no doubt, be traced; and it may be possible that this splendid relic of an age of romance, and of the curious serpent-worship of the aborigines, can yet be found, if diligently sought. It lies in the precise spot where it was interred with the beloved prophet, unless some rapacious white man discovered the secret of its history.

This is stated on the authority of Adair, who thus concludes his account of it. * * * "They who will run the risk of searching, may luckily find it; but if any of the rattle snake family detect them in disturbing the bones of their beloved relation, they would resent it as the basest act of hostility."

Lawson, in his surveying expeditions through the woods of Carolina, often met with the rattle snake; he gives a few curious particulars of its history. He frequently stumbled over them, but was never once bitten. On one occasion, when out in the forest, he witnessed its remarkable powers of fascination in the case of a squirrel, which ran directly into the open jaws of one of them. When dead, and even when alive, we will see farther on, the Indians made great use of it in medicine. The cast-off skin was a remedy in some diseases; the rattles were reduced to powder, and given to lying-in women, to expedite their labor. The gall, made into pills with clay, was regarded as so great a remedy in fevers and small-pox, as to be regarded as one of the precious secrets of nature. This nostrum was borrowed at an early day from the Indians by the people of Connecticut, and it soon became famous under the imposing name of the *trochisci Connecticotiani*. It was deemed important that the rattle snakes should be taken in the spring, when a little meal or chalk mixed with their gall, and rolled into pills, formed the celebrated *trochisci*. Connecticut has been prolific of nostrums and notions ever since. The troches were anodyne.

The ancient surveyor must himself relate the instance in which the whole reptile, alive, was applied in a notable case. A certain planter had been long suffering under a lingering disease, which none of the regular physicians in his reach were able to remove, though with great patience he had tried them, one after the other, at the expense of all that he was worth. At last, almost in despair, he threw himself upon the skill of an Indian, well known in his neighborhood by the name of Jack.

"After the bargain was concluded, the Indian went into the woods, and brought in both herbs and roots, of which he made a decoction, and gave it to the man to drink, and bade him go to bed, saying it should not be long before he came again, which the patient performed, as he had ordered; and the portion he had administered made him sweat after the most violent manner that could be, whereby he smelled very offensively. But in the evening, towards night, Jack came with a great rattle snake in his hand, alive, which frightened the people almost out of their senses. And he told his patient that he must take that to bed with him; at which the man was in a great consternation, and told the Indian he was resolved to let no snake come into his bed, for he might as well die of the distemper he had, as be killed by the bite of that serpent; to which the Indian replied, he could not bite him now, for he had taken out his poison-teeth, and showed him that they were gone. At last, with much persuasion, he admitted the snake's company, which the Indian put about his middle, and ordered nobody to take him away upon any account; which was strictly observed, although the snake girded him as hard, for a great while, as if he had been drawn in by a belt, which one pulled at with all his strength. At last, the snake's twitches grew weaker and weaker, till, by degrees, he felt him not; and, opening the bed, he was found dead, and the man thought himself better. The Indian came in the morning, and finding the snake dead, told the man that his distemper was dead along with that snake, which proved so, as he said; for the man speedily recovered his health, and became perfectly well."*

Bartram, as late as 1775, frequently encountered the rattlesnake in his adventurous travels through Florida and the Carolinas. In one place he relates: "An occurrence happened this day, by which I had an opportunity of observing the extraordinary veneration or dread the Indians have for the rattlesnake. I was busy in my room in the council-house, drawing some curious flowers, when, on a sudden, my attention was taken off by a tumult without, at the Indian camp. I stepped to the door, where I met my friend, the old interpreter, who informed me that there was a very large rattlesnake in the Indian camp, which had taken possession of it, having driven the men, women and children out; and he heard them saying they would send for Puc-puggy, (that was the name they had given me, signifying the flower-hunter,) to kill him or take him out of the camp. I answered that I would have nothing to do with him, apprehending some disagreeable consequences. My old friend turned about, to carry my answer to the Indians, when I heard them approaching, calling for Puc-puggy. Starting up, to escape from their sight by a back-door, a party consisting of three young fellows, richly dressed and ornamented,

* Lawson's Carolina, page 219.

stepped in, and with noble simplicity and complaisance, requested me to accompany them to their encampment. I desired them to excuse me. They entreated, however, that I should go, for none of them had the courage to expel the rattlesnake from their camp; and, understanding that it was my pleasure to collect all their animals and other natural productions, that I was welcome to him, if I would come and take him away. I at length consented, and went with them to the encampment, where I beheld the Indians greatly disturbed indeed; the men with sticks and tomahawks, and the women and children collected together in affright and trepidation, while the dreaded serpent leisurely traversed the camp, visiting the fire-places, from one to another, picking up fragments of their provisions, and licking their platters. The men gathered round me, exciting me to remove him. Arming myself with a light wood knot, I approached the reptile, which instantly collected himself in a vast coil; upon which, I cast the knot at him, and luckily taking him on his head, dispatched him instantly. I took out my knife, and cut the head from his body, then, turning to the Indians, they complimented me with every demonstration of satisfaction for my heroism and friendship for them. I carried off the head of the serpent, bleeding in my hand, as a trophy of victory, and, taking out the mortal fangs, deposited them carefully among my collections."*

* Bartram, page 258.

The amiable traveler's adventure with this serpent, however, was not yet over; he had scarcely returned to his drawing, before he was, a second time, aroused by a tumult among the Indians. They had been deliberating on the death of the rattlesnake, and had come to the conclusion that his spirit must be appeased by inflicting upon Puc-puggy their customary punishment—he must be *dry-scratched* with the teeth of rattlesnakes; and they now approached with their instruments ready for the execution. Having surrounded him in his room, without the least intimation of their design, they attempted to lay hold of him. They now informed him that he was too heroic and violent, and that it would be good for him to lose some of his blood, to make him milder and tamer; and had therefore come to *scratch* him. Alarmed for the safety of his skin—for he knew well what they meant by a *dry-scratch*—he instinctively sprang to his feet, and stood on the defensive. At this point, when he seemed really in danger of the fate of having his skin lacerated by a process of the most exquisite and diabolical torture, a young warrior interposed in his behalf, when instantly the whole troop changed their countenaces, caught him by the hands, and proclaimed him a brave warrior, and a sincere friend to the Indians. They then returned to their camp, having, by this farcical demonstration, appeased the manes of the dead snake, and satisfied the superstitious prejudices of their people.

The instrument for dry-scratching was a curious

specimen of savage ingenuity. It was made in the following manner: A piece of split cane having been first flattened and smoothed at one extremity, a number of rattlesnakes' fangs were then inserted, with their points all turned towards the handle, and fastened securely, so that, when finished, it resembled very much a miniature brush or comb. The head men of every town or camp, it appears, were furnished with one or more of these implements, with which, for certain offences against the decorum or religion of the Nation, they were in the habit of inflicting the severest tortures upon the offenders. It will be seen in other places, that they not only scratched their children and young people with this horrible instrument, but even their most noted head men and warriors.

Lawson found it also in great use among them as a scarificator for drawing blood in disease, which they did in a very expeditious manner with their mouths, after the skin had been punctured with the snakes' teeth. There were two degrees of this torture when used as a punishment. If the culprit was deemed worthy of its severest application, he was instantly stripped, and the sharp penetrating fangs applied to the dry unyielding surface. This was termed *dry-scratching*. The milder form of it permitted the skin to be first softened and mollified with warm water.

In the first settlement of Carolina and Georgia, it is said that rattlesnakes were not unfrequently met with, seven, eight, and even ten feet in length, and from eighteen inches to more than two feet in circumference. Some time before the period of the Revolution, however, these monsters of a primitive age, and pampered gods of the simple red men, had disappeared forever from their ancient lurking places. A race of men had invaded them who knew and honored the true Manabozho, and, for his sake, cherished undying enmity towards all the venemous serpent tribes.

Bartram again relates, that on one occasion, in Georgia, having wandered a little distance from the spot where he had pitched his camp, his steps were suddenly arrested by a huge rattlesnake that lay in easy reach of him, already coiled for the fatal stroke. He affirms, that the volume of this reptile, as he lay in that position, formed a spiral mound half as high as his knees. His generous forbearance in withholding his blow when the botanist was fairly in his power, made so great an impression upon him, that he and his companions voted him his life and a quiet retreat.

Some years after this, when, in company with his father at Old Fort Picolata, on the St. John's River, attending a congress between the authorities of Florida and the Creek Indians, they employed their leisure hours in making botanical collections in the woods around the fort. "The morning the treaty commenced," he writes, "we had been rambling in a swamp about a quarter of a mile from the camp, I being a head a few paces, when my father suddenly bid me observe the rattlesnake just at my feet. I stopped, and saw the monster formed in a high spiral coil, not half his length from me. Another step forward and I must have stumbled over him. The fright I was thrown into at once excited resentment; at that time I was insensible to gratitude or mercy. I instantly cut off a little sapling and soon dispatched him.

This serpent was about six feet in length and as thick as an ordinary man's leg. Having fastened a vine to his neck, I dragged him after me, his scaly body sounding over the ground; and entering the camp with him in triumph, was soon surrounded by the amazed multitude, both Indians and my countrymen. The adventure reaching the ears of the commander, he sent an officer to request that, if the snake had not bit himself, he might have him served up for his dinner. I readily delivered his body to the cooks, and being that day invited to dine at the governor's table, saw the snake served up in several dishes, Governor Grant being very fond of the flesh of the rattlesnake. I tasted of it, but could swallow none of it down."

This Governor Grant of Florida, was the same officer who, as Colonel Grant, in the spring of 1761, had carried fire and sword among the Cherokees. It is highly probable that he found leisure and opportunity, while on that expedition, to rid some of those gloomy lurking places in the Cherokee mountains of their ancient reptile denizens of the jeweled heads, in the same easy, cheerful manner in which he disposed of the snake killed by Bartram.

It would appear, from an item which we find in a schedule of government charges, published with the statutes of South Carolina, that as late even as 1764, the rattlesnake was still sufficiently numerous and mischievous, to elicit from the legislative authorities so decided a notice as a handsome appropriation to secure, as far as possible, an abatement of the nuisance. In that year, a negro fellow, named Sampson, who claimed to have discovered an antidote for its venom, was voted an *annuity* of one hundred and four pounds sterling for his valuable service to the province.

There is no record of Sampson's famous recipe; it was, doubtless, nothing more than one of the potent native herbs that had been used by the Indians, for the same purpose, time immemorial.

During all his forty years' residence among them, Adair asserts, that he never knew one to die from the bite of the rattlesnake or any other venemous reptile, although frequently struck by the most dangerous species. When going into the woods, or upon an expedition, every Indian provided himself a pouch of the best snake-root, such as the seneca or fern snake-root, or the wild horehound, wild plantain, St. Andrew's cross, or some other of a variety of plants equally efficacious and well known in the forests of Carolina.

It will not be out of place to describe and name more particularly the most important of these primitive antidotes indigenous in our woods, and once so powerful in the hands of the savages who first discovered them. The seneca snake-root—*senega polygala*—is abundant throughout all Upper Carolina. It is said to have derived its name from the fancied resemblance between its root and the rattle of the serpent, with whose history it is so intimately associated. It is more probable, however, that its English name originated from its well-known use among the Indians. They may have possibly been led first by that resemblance to apply it as a remedy for the bite of the rattlesnake. It grows in an erect, smooth stem, with alternate lance-like leaves. The flowers are white, closely clustered on the top of a spike or stem growing up from the root, and in bloom most of the summer. Given in moderate doses, the seneca is a warming stimulant, imparting a general glow to the system, and exciting profuse perspiration. In larger doses it proves both emetic and cathartic.

The Virginia snake-root—*aristolochia serpentaria*—is a perennial plant, and, like the seneca, abounds in the upper-country on dry ridges and uplands. It is easily distinguished from the latter—its leaves, stem and root are all totally different from those of the seneca. The stem is hairy and zigzag, like that of the wire-grass; the leaves heart-shaped and oblong; the white flowers expand themselves, not on a single spike, but on several little stems or peduncles rising from the root, and sometimes under the surface of the ground. It grows from eight to ten inches in height, and blooms through the summer. The root, however, is its greatest peculiarity, being exceedingly fibrous; it appears like a collection of a great number of orange-colored strings, all branching out from the same point.

Like the seneca, however, it is powerfully stimulant and sweat-producing, with the additional claim of being both a tonic and preventive of putrifaction. Mr. Eberle, in his Therapeutics, remarks of these plants, that they have been discovered to be utterly useless as antidotes to the poison of venemous serpents. A moment's reflection, however, will reveal the reason of this, and vindicate both the credibility of their history and the good sense of the Indians, who asked for no other remedy when struck by the fangs of the deadly rattlesnake. The truth is, there is not now, nor never was, any sure remedy for the bite of that dangerous serpent, unless it was immediately at hand, to be applied the moment the venom was injected into the blood. The Indians knew this better than any learned writer on modern materia-medica, and seldom ventured into the woods without a safe supply of such remedies, as their experience and observation had taught them to be perfectly reliable when seasonably used.

In later times, however, after the god-rattlesnake of the supplanted red men, began to bruise the heels of the English, and Anglo-Americans, in the greater number of instances, it was under circumstances when no remedy could be applied at all, before the poison had become completely incorporated with the blood, and then these ancient, famous plants being prescribed, and necessarily failing, were set down as utterly valueless. Besides, the manner in which it was directed to apply them—beaten into cataplasms, or infused in water or spirits, was enough, even though ready at hand, to insure the death of the patient, by the loss of precious time. The Indians knew nothing of this; the instant one of them felt himself struck by a serpent, he sat down, took the root from his pouch, chewed it as rapidly as possible, so as to swallow in time the necessary quantity of juice, and then taking it from his mouth applied it to the wound. In this way he had already set up in his system a powerful antagonism to the venom of the serpent, while the man of the pharmacopæia would have been beating up his poultice or preparing his infusion. The Indians fought the venom of the rattlesnake as Napoleon I. fought the Austrians; the learned faculty, as the Archduke of Austria fought Napoleon. The analogy would be complete, if the former had had the weakness to lay his defeat upon the want of strength in the metal of his arms.

After swallowing his medicine, "for a short space of time," says one who often witnessed its operation, "there is a terrible conflict through all the body of the Indian by the jarring qualities of the burning poison, and the strong antidote; but the poison is soon repelled through the same channel it entered, and the patient is cured."

There were other antidotes, not less trustworthy with the American savage, and scarcely less famous than the snake-roots. The wild horehound, the rattlesnake's master, or the rattlesnake's plantain, frequently formed the only store of his indispensable medicine pouch. These plants are quite common on all the dry soils of the upper-country. On the high ridge between the Savannah and Saluda Rivers, particularly in the vicinity of the villages of Greenwood and Cokesbury, few native plants are more abundant.

The wild horehound is a *eupatorium*, and belongs to the same natural family with the well-known *bone-set*; it grows, however, on highlands, while the *bone-set* is chiefly found in wet marshy places. It attains a height of two or three feet; the stem is hairy, the leaves triangular in shape, coarsely notched on their edges, and so arranged in pairs, as to cross one another at right angles. During the months of July and September, its white flowers are full blown, and may be readily recognized by their resemblance to those of the bone-set, clustered in a dense, flat corymb at the top of the stem.

The rattlesnake's master—*liatris squarrosa*—abounds on dry soils and shady woods. It can be easily distinguished by its green grass-like leaves and purple flowers, arranged on their spike, like those of the hyacinth. They are in bloom through September and October.

The rattlesnake's plantain—*goodyera pubescens*—found in the same situations, belongs to the tuberous root family. It grows from six to ten inches in height, having a stem quite hairy towards the top, with egg-shaped leaves, and a spike of white flowers.

Besides the virtues of these plants, as reliable antidotes for the poison of serpents, when applied in time, they are invaluable as remedies in a variety of diseases; for which the seneca and serpentaria, at least, have been greatly extolled in the regular practice.

Dr. Bartholomew Parr, in his huge folio Dictionary of Medicine, published in 1819, makes mention of a specific remedy for the bite of the rattlesnake, that had been discovered by a negro, which may possibly be the same for which South Carolina so generously paid the annuity recorded in the Statutes. It is doubtless worthy of a resurrection from its ponderous tomb; for it consists wholly in the united strength of two of the most potent of the antidotes whose powers and natural history have just been detailed.

"Take of the roots of plantain and horehound—in summer the whole herb—a sufficient quantity; bruise them and squeeze out the juice, and give immediately a large spoonful. If the patient is swelled pour it down his throat. If it does not relieve in one hour, give a second dose, which never fails. The roots, when dry, should be bruised in water."

Besides the rattlesnake, there was one other, in the early periods, sometimes seen and felt in the woods of the upper-country, that is worthy of a brief notice. Around the history of the *horned serpent*, there hangs an obscurity, which, perhaps, no research will ever fully clear away. Some, indeed, have wholly denied that such a reptile was found on the Continent. Others admit its primitive existence and describe it as a curious and harmless creature. There are others, again, who, while they regard it as having once belonged to the catalogue of our native serpents, describe it as possessed of a venom, whose fatal energy no antidote was ever known to master.

Bartram met with a reptile which he calls the horn-snake in his travels in Carolina, and speaks of it as follows:

"The pine or bull-snake is very large and inoffensive, with respect to mankind, but devours squirrels, birds, rabbits and every other creature it can take as food. They are the largest snake yet known in North America, except the rattlesnake, and perhaps exceed him in length; they are pied black and white. They utter a terrible loud, hissing noise, sounding very hollow, and like distant thunder, when irritated, or at the time of incubation, when the males contend with one another for the desired female. These serpents are also called *horn-snakes*, from their tail terminating with a hard, horny spur, which they vibrate very quick when disturbed, but they never attempt to strike with it. They have dens in the earth, whither they retreat precipitately when apprehensive of danger."*

Lawson, who traversed the same region about seventy years earlier than the botonist, describes another under the name of the horn-snake serpent, of a totally different character. "Of the horn-snakes," he says, "I never saw but two, that I remember.

* Bartram, p. 272.

They are like the rattlesnake in color, but rather lighter. They hiss exactly like a goose, when anything approaches them. They strike at their enemy with their tail, and kill whatsoever they wound with it, which is armed at the end with a horny substance like a cock's spur. This is their weapon. I have heard it credibly reported, by those who said they were eye witnesses, that a small locust-tree, about the thickness of a man's arm, being struck by one of these snakes at ten o'clock in the morning, then verdant and flourishing, at four in the afternoon was dead, and the leaves red and withered. Doubtless, be it how it will, they are very venomous. I think, the Indians do not pretend to cure their wound."

This singular statement of the old surveyor, in relation to the locust-tree, could scarcely have ever come to the knowledge of the good, but plain people living on Coronaka and Wilson's Creeks; yet there is still extant in that region, a tradition, in which it is related, that many years ago, a man in the lower part of the district or in Edgefield, being closely pursued by a horn-snake, took refuge behind a tree, when the enraged serpent, rolling swiftly after him, like a trundled hoop, plunged its horny sting deep into its trunk, where it was made fast, and so diffused its venom into the circulating sap, as to destroy completely, in a few hours, the vitality of the tree.

Bartram, with all his acuteness and enthusiasm as a naturalist, has certainly confounded the names of two distinct native serpents of Carolina. The bull-snake, as he describes it, was well known in the upper-country at the period of his visit, and long after; but the old people had seen, and talked much of the horn-snake as well, whose sting they dreaded as the visitation of death. Hewit informs us, that the horn-snake was found in Carolina, and owed its name, not to a horny excrescence growing upon its head, as some have supposed, but to the horn-like sting at the extremity of its tail, with which it defended itself, striking it with great force into every aggressor. It was also deemed exceedingly venemous; and the Indians, when stung by it, did not resort to their usual antidotes, but instantly cut out the wounded part, as the only safe preventive of the deadly poison's being infused through the system.* Mills, in his Statistics, enumerates, among the indigenous reptiles of Carolina, both the horn and bull-snake. The former must, however, have been exceedingly rare; for, at a comparatively early period, it had already become a creature of curious tradition. Lawson, it has been observed, saw but two of them as early as 1718, notwithstanding no white man of his day enjoyed better opportunities for making such discoveries in Carolina. Among the innumerable facts that may be gathered from natural history illustrative of God's goodness, there are few more deserving of notice than this rareness of a reptile so fierce,

* Carroll's His. Col. p. 82.

and deadly as the horn-snake must unquestionably have been. Had it been as abundant, as the other venemous species, the Indians even, though furnished with their potent antidotes, could hardly have inhabited the country. The imagination is taxed to conceive of an object more repulsive or truly terrible. It possessed scarcely a single redeeming feature; there was nothing of the admirable craft of the eye—nothing of the beautiful changing colors or characteristic magnanimity of the rattlesnake—but with dull eye, insensate skin, and vengeful spite, ready to dart its dreadful sting into every approaching intruder, it lay a horrible compound of all the hated qualities of its race—the incarnation of death.

On an afternoon, nearly forty years ago, a party of gentlemen were riding from Abbeville Village towards the Calhoun settlement, and when approaching the place now known as the Cabins, they passed a dwelling near the wayside, just at the moment when a little girl, whom they had seen to cross the road some distance before them, gave a piercing shriek, and ran back into the house in an agony of pain and fright. Perceiving that something serious had occurred, they hastily alighted to ascertain the matter; and entering the room, found the child stretched upon a bed, and already a *corpse.* She had lived long enough, however, to whisper to her mother that a snake had struck her, while she was in the act of gathering fire-wood on the road-side. The party instantly sought the spot, and there discovered a large specimen of the horn-snake which they dispatched. The skin of this serpent was stuffed, and preserved by an intelligent gentleman* of the neighborhood; and it was long an object of great curiosity at his residence, and afterwards at Old Cambridge, where it was last seen.†

* Captain Thomas Parker.

† Conversation of James Taggart, Esq., and others.

CHAPTER VI.

Conjectures in relation to vast mineral wealth in Upper-Carolina—Old French and Spanish miners—The gold mania of that treasure-seeking age—The restless energy born of the love of money more efficient for good than money—Treasures not essential either to the support or the progress of truth, &c.

The wild animals of the upper-country, particularly those that supplied the Indians and hunters with food, and the valuable peltries, which, it will be presently seen, became the much-desired commodities of a lucrative traffic, chiefly attracted the attention of the first white men who penetrated these north-western wilds. They were not, however, the only objects of pursuit; the supposed vast mineral wealth of the same region had, from a very early period, excited the romantic speculations of adventurers from all the leading colonizing nations of Europe. The beetling crags, towering mountain knobs, and quartz-bearing hills of the upper-country, were peculiarly alluring to the gold-loving rapacity of the French and Spaniards.

The treasure-seeking mania of this active age was remarkable; but only because turned for a time into an extraordinary channel. The previous and succeeding periods, with the one in which the present generations are pushing their fortunes, are to be regarded as not a whit less, but perhaps more calmly sordid. It has often been a subject of serious regret that so small a portion of the acquired treasures of the world are devoted to the cause of truth; yet many striking facts attending the gold mania of this era, as well as that we have witnessed in our own, clearly indicate that there is much less of efficacy for good in gold itself, than in the unceasing, restless activity and energy engendered by the depraved love of it.

Those who express such regret either forget, or do not perceive, that money is not only the representative of the values created by the sweat and self-sacrifice of the enslaved toiling million, but equally, in a moral sense, of the depravity of the race. Wherever wealth inordinately accumulates, there very soon are developed the most hideous forms of human iniquity and misery. "Where the carcass is, there the eagles gather together," and that carcass is the laboring poor of Free-soil society.

Even in the South, where the institution of African slavery fosters the purest and healthiest social organization the world has ever seen, men of wealth may be almost daily met, stiff and stark with the self-complacency that proclaims to others, "stand aside, I am holier than thou." Yet so little is there of essential potency in money to promote and sustain the true dignity of man, that it cannot be regarded as an element even in the moral progress of humanity. The glory and stay of the country is its real Christianity, whose maintenance actually costs it thousands less than its dogs and annual supply of tobacco and strong drink. Indeed, the Church would continue to live with vigorous efficiency, though every cent were emptied from its coffers.

The Great Teacher, who needed not that any should tell him what was in man, when organizing his visible church on earth, evidently avoided the self-sufficient power of money. Two only of its representatives were intimately associated with his humiliation: one of them sold him for thirty pieces of silver, and the other, frightened in the last moment to his duty by the awful manifestations of nature at the crucifixion of his master, assumed his true character, and begging the body, put upon it the equivocal honor of laying it in his own sumptuous tomb. The worst deformity of modern society is not poverty and its evils, but the inordinate love and accumulation of barren money, the superciliousness of the purse-proud, and the heartless selfishness of a large and growing class, which mistake worldly prosperity for the distinguishing favors of Heaven.

Like the numerous useful discoveries however that resulted incidentally from the lonely studies of the crazy alchymists of the middle ages, the gold fever of this period achieved the exploration of large and valuable tracts of country, that must have otherwise lain a much longer time utterly unknown to civilized men. It is quite probable that even before the commencement of the eighteenth century many adventurers landed in Charleston and St. Augustine, who, after a brief rest, and the necessary inquiries, set off with gun and knapsack in search of the hidden treasures, which rumor had declared only awaited the enterprise of the skillful explorer among the granite hills and wild mountain ridges of the upper-country.

Indeed, the famous territory of Cofachiqui, so often mentioned, and so minutely described by the chroniclers of the celebrated gold-hunting expedition undertaken by Ferdinand De Soto, in 1538, through the dreary wilderness, afterwards embraced in the States of Florida, Georgia, Alabama and Mississippi, had its centre on the western limits of the present territory of Upper Carolina. Its capital and chief town stood upon the tongue of land between the Broad River of Georgia, and the Savannah, just opposite the modern District of Abbeville.

"Early in March, 1540, De Soto broke up his winter quarters, and set out for the north-east, in search of the Province of Cofachiqui, which was supposed, from Indian accounts, to be the rich country for which he was in search. He had been informed by the guides and other Indians, that it lay a long distance off, towards the north-east, and that it abounded in gold, silver and pearls. From Anhayca they passed northward, probably crossing the Flint River, and pursuing their marsh in the valley on the west side, for nearly twenty days, until they reached the southern part of the Cherokee country, called Achalaque; then they directed their route to the northeast, crossing, in the course of the next twenty days' march, two large rivers, in all probability, the Ocmulgee and Oconee Rivers, in the vicinity of Macon and Milledgeville, in Georgia.

At length, after an entire march and sojourn of more than two months, the Spanish army arrived in the Province of Cofachiqui, about the middle of May. This province was situated on, or near, the head waters of the Savannah River, and the chief town, probably, in the peninsula, at the juncture of the Broad and Savannah Rivers. They found the country ruled by a beautiful Indian queen, or female Cacique, who entertained the Spanish governor and his army with great ceremony." *

The generous hospitality of Xualla—for that was the name of the Indian queen—was, however, ill requited by the avaricious strangers. They soon discovered that there were numerous mounds or tombs in the vicinity of the town, filled with rich treasures, that had been deposited with the bodies of distinguished chiefs. These sacred relics were plundered for the jewels which they contained; they were the only riches found, and, although many and valuable, were to be obtained in large quantities only by plundering the vaults of the dead.

The old chroniclers severely test the faith of the reader, in respect to these treasures. The Portuguese narrator, the most reliable historian of DeSoto's expedition, informs us that the amiable queen, tired of the presence of the ungrateful Spaniards, offered

* Monette's History of Valley of the Mississippi.

them, if they would be gone, two hundred horse-loads of pearls. They took, however, from the mounds, or temples, only fourteen bushels, which were sent to Havana, as a specimen of the natural wealth of the country. Garcellasso, another historian and eye-witness, affirms that in the country surrounding the capital of Xualla, the Spaniards calculated that a thousand bushels of pearls could have been gathered.

These gems, though very pretty, were, doubtless, not of the most valuable kind; but the fact that they were found in such incredible quantities, and the product of the muscle, once so common on all the streams of the upper-country, is sufficiently astonishing. None, we believe, have ever been discovered in the same region since the time of De Soto's expedition; and even the muscles themselves are now seldom met with.

Were the Indians in possession of a secret process, by which these gems were engendered in the shells of the muscle, that was never revealed either to Spaniards or English? But where are the muscles, which, in 1540, were found in such vast numbers around the Indian settlements on the Savannah and in the country north-west of it? A living muscle is now seldom seen on the Corenaka, yet, in our boyhood, we remember to have seen them there in considerable quantities; and the minute fragments of their shells mingled everywhere with the sand and pebbles, indicate a great abundance of them in primitive times.

The Spaniards found, also, in the capital of the Indian queen, hatchets formed from an alloy of gold and copper. These objects greatly excited their cupidity, and encouraged them in the belief that they had at last discovered in Cofachiqui, a country abounding in the precious deposits they had so long sought. And so they indeed had, but it was neither their good fortune nor their desert, to find out the precise spot where they could be obtained. In less than fifteen miles south-east of the town, on the opposite side of the Savannah, lay one of the most extraordinary gold deposits in the world.

It is true that the Cherokees knew nothing of excavations on the present site of the Dorn Mine, or on any of its rich branching veins; but they were well acquainted with the locality, which is shown by the numerous relics of their handy-work scattered around it; and there can be little doubt that the massy nuggets of its out-cropping gold supplied them abundantly with the finer metal of the alloy that so attracted the eyes of the Spaniards. It is well known to mineralogists that the out-croppings of most gold and copper regions, are far richer than their deep, but more permanently productive veins. And, it is no less known to a few who have inquired into the traditions of the aborigines, that the gold and copper found in their possession, in the form of solid masses and curious trinkets, by the first white men who visited the country, were obtained from those sources.

But by what method did they succeed in smelting

these metals? It was one of the most remarkable devices of savage ingenuity; in practical efficiency, the famous blow-pipe of Dr. Hare was scarcely superior.

Having first hollowed out a flat stone in the form of a basin, they filled it with charcoal, and upon this laid the nuggets of metal. A number of Indians now seated themselves in a circle around the basin, (and this circle was larger or smaller in proportion to the size and number of the nuggets to be melted,) each one having in his hand a long reed pierced through its entire length, and armed at one end with a clay tube or pipe. Everything being ready, fire was applied to the charcoal, and the whole mass instantly blown into a powerful heat through the reeds, the clay-extremities of which were inserted in the basin, while the Indians blew through them upon the charcoal with all their might, and with protracted expiration.

No ordinary lump of either gold or copper could long maintain its solidity in such a crucible. With this process the Indians could easily produce any variety of ornament from those metals, using them either alone or in alloy. This method was known to have been in use among the Indians who lived upon the gold-producing lands of North Carolina, and the same process must have been known to the Cherokees.

It is quite probable that had the Spaniards conducted themselves properly while in the capital of Cofachiqui, Xualla would have revealed to them the precise spot whence the gold of the wonderful hatchets was obtained—the renowned mineral treasury of Cofachiqui. But such was the deep disgust and resentment with which the whole native population were inspired by their rudeness and inhumanity, that they would have preferred to die rather than impart information so agreeable to their hated visitors.

Every effort was used therefore to induce them to leave the province; and none succeeded so well, as the declarations of the queen, whom De Soto had made his captive, and of her attendants, that the gold deposits for which the Spaniards were searching lay some distance off towards the north-west, among the mountains. He had learned this too on the banks of the Flint River, and now set off across the territory of Georgia in search of the yellow stone quarries of Dahlonega."*

Some time after leaving Cofachiqui, two of his followers volunteering their services, were sent by De Soto to explore the country in search of the mines whence the gold was obtained he saw in the hatchets on the Savannah. After several weeks of toilsome wanderings among rolling hills and mountains of stupendous rocks, they returned to him at one of his camps in the territory of Alabama, having made no discovery of any mineral, and bringing back with them nothing more valuable than a buffalo's skin, which they conjectured to have been taken from an

* Dahlonega in Cherokee means the place of the *yellow stone*.

animal of huge size, and that partook of the nature of the ox and the sheep.*

There is much confusion even in Monette, in regard to the Province of Cofachiqui and the country of the Cherokees. He speaks of the Spaniards, when marching up Flint River, as having reached, just as they turned towards the north-east in search of Cofachiqui, the southern boundary of the Cherokees, whose country was called Achalaque. Yet after De Soto has left the Savannah, and is marching north-westwardly towards the present site of Rome, in Georgia, the same historian adds: "Through this means—the captivity of Xualla—the Spaniards procured a safe march through the territory of Cofachiqui to the country of the Cherokees, called the Province of Chalaque.

The truth is, from the moment he reached the southern boundary of the Cherokees on the Flint, till he met the beautiful Queen of Cofachiqui on the banks of the Savannah, he had been marching over Cherokee territory.

Xualla's capital, at the mouth of Broad River, was no more the centre of Cofachiqui than it was of the country of the Lower Cherokees.

The old map published by Adair with his History of the North American Indians, represents the southern boundary of the Cherokees as running directly eastward from the Flint to the Savannah, considerably south of the mouth of Broad River. At a later

* Pickett.

period, however, this line appears to have been obliterated, and Broad River came to be the dividing line between the lands of the Cherokees and Creeks. It is so laid down by Mouzon and Cook. This brought those warlike savages in close proximity with the early settlers of Ninety-Six District, on the Savannah; and it was for their protection that Fort Charlotte was built, and garrisoned a few years before the breaking out of the Revolution. The father of Robert Long, who settled on Duncan's Creek, in 1769, often assured his family, if we mistake not, that not long after his arrival in Ninety-Six District, he had taken from the government, and executed the contract of building Fort Charlotte.*

We have in another place traced in this and other portions of the upper-country, the scattered remains of the towns and villages of a numerous people that once lived upon its fertile valleys and streams. It is highly probable that those settlements were the provincial towns of Cofachiqui—the richest and most flourishing district of the Lower Cherokees—that they were yet standing and prosperous, at the period of De Soto's visit, the events, whatever they were, having subsequently transpired, which reduced them to ruin and decay.

The ancient mounds and terraces that distinguished the site of Xualla's capital, are seen at this day, though much wasted, at the mouth of Broad River. Many have been the speculations in regard

* Conversation of Miss Susan Long.

to them, by the farmers of their vicinity, both in Elbert County and Abbeville District.

The spot was visited by Bartram in 1776, and the following description given of it in his rare book of travels in Carolina: "After conferring with gentlemen in Augusta, conversant in Indian affairs, concerning my future travels in those distant, unexplored regions, and obtaining letters to their agents in the Indian territories, I set off, proceeding for Fort James, Dartmouth, at the confluence of Broad River with Savannah—the road leading me near the banks of the river for the distance of near thirty miles. Towards evening I crossed Broad River at a good ford, just above its confluence with the Savannah, and arrived at Fort James, which is a four-square stockade, with salient bastions at each angle, mounted with a block-house, where are some swivel guns, one story higher than the curtains, which are pierced with loop-holes, breast-high, and defended by small-arms.

"The fortification encloses about an acre of ground, where is the governor's or commandant's house—a good building, which is flanked on each side by buildings for the officers and barracks of the garrison, consisting of fifty rangers, including officers; each having a good horse, well-equipped, a rifle, two dragoon-pistols and a hanger, besides a powder-horn, shot-pouch, and tomahawk.

"The fort stands on an eminence in the fork between the Savannah and Broad Rivers, about one mile above Fort Charlotte, which is situated near the banks of the Savannah, on the Carolina side. Fort James is situated nearly at an equal distance from the banks of the two rivers, and from the extreme point of land that separates them. The point or peninsula between the two rivers, for the distance of two miles back from the fort, is laid out for a town, by the name of Dartmouth, in honor of the Earl of Dartmouth, who, by his interest and influence in the British councils, obtained from the king a grant and powers in favor of the Indian Trading Company of Georgia, to treat with the Creeks for the cession of a quantity of land sufficient to discharge their debts to the traders; for the security and defence of which territory this fortress was established.

"I made a little excursion up the Savannah River, four or five miles above the fort, with the surgeon of the garrison, who was so polite as to attend me and to show me some remarkable Indian monuments, which are worthy of every traveler's notice. These wonderful labors of the ancients stand in a level plain, very near the banks of the river, now twenty or thirty yards from it.

"They consist of conical mounds of earth and four square terraces. The great mound is in the form of a cone, about forty or fifty feet high, and the circumference of its base two or three hundred yards, entirely composed of the loamy rich earth of the low grounds. The top or apex is flat; a spiral path or track leading from the ground up to the top is still visible, where now grows a large, beautiful red cedar. There appear four niches excavated out of the side of this hill, at different heights from the base, fronting the four cardinal points; these niches are entered from the winding path, and seem to have been meant for resting places or look-outs. The surrounding level grounds are cleared, and planted with Indian corn at present; and I think the proprietor of these lands, who accompanied us to this place, said that the mound itself yielded above one hundred bushels in one season; the lands hereabouts are exceedingly fertile and productive.

"It is altogether unknown to us, what could have induced the Indians to raise such a heap of earth in this place, the ground for a great space around being subject to inundations, at least once a year, from which circumstance we may conclude they had no town or settled habitations here. Some imagine these tumuli were constructed for look-out towers. It is reasonable to suppose, however, that they were intended to serve some important purpose in those days, as they were public works, and would have required the united labors and attention of a whole nation, circumstanced as they were, to have constructed one of them almost in an age.

"There are several less ones round about the great one, with some very large tetragon terraces on each side, near one hundred yards in length, and their surfaces, four, six, eight and ten feet above the ground on which they stand.

"We may, however, hazard a conjecture, that as there is a narrow space or ridge in these low lands, immediately bordering on the river's bank, which is eight or ten feet higher than the adjoining low grounds that lie betwixt the stream, and the heights of the adjacent mainland, which, when the river overflows its banks, are many feet under water, when at the same time this ridge on the river bank is above water and dry, and, at such inundations, appears as an island in the river these people might have had a town on this ridge, and this mount raised for a retreat and refuge in case of inundations, which are unforeseen, and surprise them very suddenly every spring and autumn."

Such, more than eighty years ago, were the ruins of the great capital of Cofachiqui. From the period of De Soto's expedition to the time of Bartram's visit, nearly two hundred and fifty years had passed away; and when two centuries more shall have imprinted their wasting footprints upon the same spot, its unsculptured, unlettered tumuli will still tell the passing stranger their simple story of the departed red men.

De Soto, not long after leaving Cofachiqui, found a magnificent though melancholy grave in the bosom of the Mississippi; but no treasure of the beautiful yellow stone either from the mines of Dahlonega or the more lightly covered deposits of Abbeville.

We are informed by Adair that shortly after the settlement of Augusta a company of desperate adventurers, of what nation we are not told, were found working with success a silver mine, which they had opened in one of the solitudes of the Blue Ridge, probably not far from, if not on the very spot, where a similar vein is now being wrought by a Charleston company in Cheohee Old Fields, at the head of Little River, in Pickens District. This place is rich in Indian remains. A few years ago an adventurous miner threw out, from the depth of some fifteen feet below the surface, a curious cup of exquisite form and color, which is still preserved by a lady residing in Clarksville, Georgia.

They found the ore at the depth of some thirty feet, and so rich did it prove, that they were soon enabled to combine with their mining operations the then lucrative business of coining large quantities of counterfeit money which was conveyed to Augusta in wagons. A heavy load of it was, on one occasion, detected by the public officers passing over the usual route that had been destined for the purchase of negroes in that town.

This mine, like many others in the same region, has been utterly lost to the cupidity of succeeding generations, unless it be really true that Kughtmann has struck upon the identical vein in Cheohee Old Fields. It is well to remember, however, that even at this early period, a villainous class of arrant counterfeiters found, in the shady recesses of the mountains, and in the lawless society of the border, a retreat sufficiently favorable to their nefarious occupation; and they were not men whose wits were so dull as not to perceive that the popular belief in the existence of gold and silver in this region gave them license to prosecute it with the utmost boldness and energy. They spared no pains, therefore, to extend and deepen this belief; and hence the great number of legendary stories still to be met with in the upper-country, of ancient gold and silver mines, that were once well known and worked with wonderous profit, but now lost.

There can be no doubt, however, that at this period, the old English traders among the Cherokees were confident in the opinion that their hills and mountains were as rich in the precious metals as any portion of Mexico or South America. One affirms, that so thoroughly were the rocks and soil impregnated with them and other valuable metallic substances, that the mountains glistened in view of the passing traveler; and even the blades of grass were bright with their subtle exhalations. "On the tops of those mountains I have seen tufts of grass deeply tinctured with mineral exhalations. If skillful alchymists made experiments on these mountains, they could soon satisfy themselves as to the value of their contents, and probably would find their account in it."*

Lawson declares that the Indians, time immemorial, were acquainted with valuable mines of gold and silver in Upper Carolina; but that nothing could ever induce them to discover their locality to Europeans. Their reason for concealing them was, that they knew the English and Spaniards greatly coveted the precious metals, and if their mines were once known to them, they would come up and settle near their

* Adair, p. 236.

mountains, and bereave them of their hunting-grounds.*

Another chronicler, no less ancient and quaint, tells us of a quicksilver mine, situated somewhere in the same region of Carolina. He is exceedingly vague as to its locality, but describes minutely the method used by the Indians for extracting the metal from the ore. They used it in preparing the colors with which they painted their bodies in time of war and great festivals.

The ore was broken into small pieces, and placed in earthen pots, from which a strong heat sublimed the quicksilver—that is, drove it off in the form of vapor. The pots had long necks, and these being inserted in others full of water, and half-buried in the ground; the vapor was received by the water, and condensed into the fluid metal.

Arranged in rows close to one another, three or four men could attend to a thousand retorts, all heating at once†.

The traditions of the olden time, and some curious facts that have come to light in more recent periods do not appear to confine the deposits of silver, at least, to the mountainous portions of the upper-country. Many years ago, there were picked up on the bank of Bush River, in Newberry District, several ancient Indian ornaments, consisting of pieces of black marble, rudely set in silver. Dr. Flannagan, who then lived on the Ennoree, and into whose pos-

---

* Page 205.

† Cox's Carolina.

session these interesting relics came, conjectured that both the silver and the marble were originally procured in that portion of the Cherokee Nation that lay beyond the mountains. As late as 1815, he had ascertained that the Indians, who still resided there, were secretly working a very rich silver mine near a town named Shainrack, which they carefully concealed from the whites. By artful persuasions, he was on the eve of making its discovery, through an Indian, who had already consented to lead him to the spot, when his hopes were disappointed by the interference of a mixed-blood, a prominent character among them, by the name of Johnson.*

Would it not be just as plausible, however, to conjecture that the silver contained in those old mementoes of Indian vanity, was originally found near the spot where they were picked up—at least, nearer to Bush River—than the country over the hills?

A tradition of an ancient silver mine that was once known and worked on Coronaka Creek in the present District of Abbeville, still lingers among the people, who live around the old Rock Church. This tradition is scarcely known to the rising generation, but is cherished with deep interest by a few venerable men whose years link them with the age that conversed with the emigrant fathers.

We shall relate it just as we received it from the lips of one of them when a boy. Many years ago, when the whole up-country was yet covered with its

* Mills's Statistics.

primitive forest, and scarcely known even to English adventurers, a party of enterprising Spaniards penetrated, in their search for gold and silver, into the territory now embraced in this district; and on a spot somewhere near the present site of the Old Rock Church, observing signs of one of the precious metals, applied their pick-axes, and brought to light a promising vein of silver ore. Fixing themselves permanently, they, in a short time, laid open a mine, whose wealth surpassed belief.

Such was their avidity, however, says the tradition, to acquire treasures, that they wholly neglected to procure for themselves the necessary means of subsistence—finding it more convenient to obtain them by force from the neighboring Indians, whose corn patches lay on the fertile valleys of the Coronaka. This, the generous Cherokees endured for a time; but on its being frequently repeated, they became exasperated, and attacking the Spaniards in their excavation, massacred the whole party, except two, who escaped and fled towards North Carolina. The Indians then threw the entire mass of the accursed metal they had raised and melted, back into the mine, and so completely restored the spot to its primitive aspect, that no vigilance or skill of civilized men has since availed to recover the lost treasure. The precious secret, doubtless, passed away forever with the red men.

These Spaniards may possibly have been a party of straggling deserters from De Soto's camp on the Savannah. In process of time, however, the Cherokee war of 1760 broke out, and brought up from Charleston into the back-woods an army, composed of soldiers and volunteers drawn from many different sources. On their return from the campaign in the Nation, they formed an encampment, and rested several days at a ford of Little Wilson's Creek, on a piece of ground afterwards embraced in a plantation owned by Rev. Joel Townsend, a short distance south of the Pointing Rock and the Old Rock Church. The ancient Keowee trail, it will be more fully shown, passed between and near both of these conspicuous spots.

The surrounding settlers were soon familiar in the camp; indeed, some of them had served as volunteers in the recent foray against the Cherokees, where, among other things, they learned, from certain old soldiers, this curious story of a silver mine of untold value having been discovered and lost, in the manner described, not far from the very place on which they were encamped.

They were moreover informed, that the Pointing Rock, which stood close on the side of the old Keowee trail, had been noted by the escaped Spaniards as a land-mark by which their treasure might be once more found. *It lay just two miles east of that rock.**

Such is the tradition of the lost mine of the Spaniards. It is now well nigh forgotten; but in a former age the influence which it exerted upon the sons

* Conversations with my father and with Joseph Fox Foster, who recently died near the Rock Church, at an advanced age.

of the old men of the Coronaka settlement, who had served in Grant's army, and who can scarcely be charged with being inordinately sentimental or romantic, was near akin to that exercised by their belief in the final perseverance of the saints.

Early in the present century, a company was formed of several of the most practical men of the neighborhood for the purpose of making a thorough search for the old Spanish mine. Among them, were old Dr. Zachary Meriwether, Colonel John Logan, Captain John Irwin, and Wm. Buchanan—all of them Revolutionary soldiers, except Dr. Meriwether. They began by carefully taking from the Pointing Rock the traditionary bearing which led them to quite a promising-looking spot on a hill-side, a short distance above the east bank of Coronaka, and a little way south of the site of old Captain *Slunge*. John Calhoun's Revolutionary tub-mill, afterwards Logan's. Here, with brilliant expectations, the company broke ground, and sunk a shaft some sixty or seventy feet in depth.

Often, in the hunting rambles of our boyhood, while yet ignorant of the traditions of the old settlement, we wandered to the brink of this strange excavation deep in the shadows of primitive woods, and there mused, with far more imagination than philosophy, on its probable cause. The land belonged at the time the shaft was sunk, to Buchanan; and such was his faith in the ancient tradition, that even at this day it may be seen in the conveyance by which it passed from his to other hands, that one or more acres were reserved, in the midst of which the excavation had been made.*

The work went bravely on, with a few interruptions, for several weeks; the adventurous miners examining closely every bucket-load of earth and stones as it came up, expecting each successive one to disclose, at last, the identical silver that had been smelted perhaps more than a century before by the less fortunate Spaniards.

The precise spot on which this delving was going forward had been ascertained by Captain Irwin, who professed, as well as most of his neighbors, unwavering faith in his ability to discover veins or deposits of the precious metals beneath the earth's surface. He had in his possession a forked divining-rod, still preserved by his descendants, which was never known, in his hands, to fail to detect the hiding-place of any noble metal, if it lay near enough the surface to be within its influence.

On one occasion, soon after the Revolution, having been called down on the Saluda, to search with his rod for the spot in which a well-known Tory had concealed, it was reported, a considerable sum of gold; he discovered with little difficulty that it lay near the root of a tree, which leaned several feet over the water of the river; for, on looking more closely, after repeated trials of the rod, had fixed indubitably upon that spot, there, sure enough, an old powder-horn was found hanging from one of the

* It is at present the property of Thomas Stuart.

upper limbs, just over the very point where, in the opinion of all concerned, the stupid fellow had consigned his money to the faithless waters. After this feat, the old soldier's brass rod was as potent over men's minds as it was over hidden treasures.

Our grandfather was the first, at length, to suspect the virtues of the magic rod; though his faith continued as firm as ever in the teachings of the old tradition; but keeping his doubts to himself, he resolved to give it a private test that would infallibly settle the question in his own mind.

Happening one day at the excavation, when a rock was thrown out, whose almost spherical shape and metalic appearance drew the attention of all present, he placed it on the pummel of his saddle and carried it home with him, and throwing it down in the yard, concealed under it four silver dollars, so as to put the fairness of the test beyond doubt, and then sent for Capt. Irwin to come with his rod, as he suspected the existence of silver near his house. The enthusiastic old man was soon at the spot; but after a thorough search, he pronounced confidently the opinion, that the place was utterly destitute of any deposit of the precious metals.

Nothing, of course, was said about the ruse of the hidden coins; but the operations at the shaft ceased soon after, never more to be resumed. It was not long, however, before another considerable excavation was made in the same bootless search, near the head of the branch that runs into Coronaka through the lands and close to the house owned at present by

Franklin Crawford. It was on the plantation, if we mistake not, of the venerable Benjamin Puliam, so well remembered, though long dead, for his unbounded hospitality and native goodness of heart. He lived and died on this place, afterwards embraced in the lands of the late Capt. T. B. Byrd.

The chief laborer employed in sinking the shaft on the Coronaka was old Nick, the faithful and well known negro, who died in the possession of our father at an advanced age in 1850. He had belonged, when a boy, to Capt. John Calhoun, and passed with that intrepid partizan soldier through many of the troublous scenes enacted on the Saluda and Coronaka during the Revolution. To the last day of his life nothing gave him so much pleasure as to recount the incidents to which he had been an eye witness at that trying period; especially the rough handlings the Tories received at the hands of his old master.

With uncommon intelligence for a slave, he combined the admirable humility so characteristic of the negroes of his times; and even, in his old age, would have gloried in shouldering his musket against Tory or *Abolitionist*, in defence of his master and his master's family. We are not ashamed to confess that many happy moments of our boyhood were spent in listening to his graphic stories of the olden time. On one occasion, he was captured at his master's house, during his absence, by a band of plundering Tories, who carried him into North Carolina, and concealed him, with several other negroes taken in the same manner, in the hollow of a huge sycamore that stood under a hill in a thick swamp. "We like to have starved to death in this place," he related; "a man came only once or twice a day to the top of the hill, and rolled down a few ash cakes, which broke into a hundred fragments before reaching its foot, and the strongest among us fared best in the fierce struggle that followed for the scattered crumbs." His master succeeded, after some time, in tracing him to the neighborhood in which he was concealed, and making a foray into it with several of his Whig comrades, overtook and recovered him from the Tory when in the act of conveying him farther away. His joy, on seeing his master once more, he used to relate, was too full for utterance; seizing his hand as he rode up, he leaped behind him on his horse, and together they dashed on in pursuit of the retreating marauders. We shall have more to say of Captain Calhoun in another place.

The old Spanish mine is yet undiscovered. It may be, however, that when all is forgotten—when the tradition itself has faded from the memory of men, and the last witness of its influence upon the minds and imaginations of our grandfathers is no more—some fortunate farmer, while enlarging with enlightened judgment the operations of his agricultural improvements, deepening his furrows, and lengthening his ditches, will one day, unexpectedly lay open the lost mine and treasures of the Spaniards.

An old chronicler adds: "Metals or minerals, I know not of any, yet it is supposed and generally believed, that the Apalatean Mountains, which lie far within the land, yield ore both of gold and silver; that the Spaniards, in their running searches of this country, saw it, but had not time to open them, or at least for the present were unwilling to make any farther discovery, till their mines of Peru and Mexico were exhausted, or as others assert, that they were politically fearful that, if the riches of the country should be exposed, it would be an allure to encourage a foreign invader. Poverty preserving riches often times the cause that property is lost, usurped, and invaded; but whether it be this or that reason, time will discover." *

There are reasons for believing that the knowledge of valuable mineral deposits in the upper-country was not confined to the Indians or Spanish adventurers. An old Mrs. Moss, who died a few years ago, in the north-west corner of York District, at an advanced age, frequently affirmed that her husband, during the Revolution, had obtained from a mine on Dolittle Creek, all the lead from which he cast the balls used in his rifle at that troublous period.

The whole family of that name—and there were not a few of them—were famous hunters. Since that time we are not aware that a particle of lead in any form has been found on the same stream, though it runs through a country rich in mineral productions.

* Gent's Carolina, Carroll's Hist. Col.

CHAPTER VII.

The primitive Hunter, Cow-Driver and Indian Trader of Upper Carolina—Patrick and William Calhoun—The Business of Stock-raising—Cow-pens—The thorough-bred Horses of Colonial times—The Statute of 1700 relating to Horses—The Wild Horses of Carolina—Old Jesse Gladden, &c.

We have now presented most that is important in the natural history of Upper-Carolina. A country thus abounding in magnificent woods and prairies, and so rich in its production of animal life, must have offered, as similar regions of the west at the present day, rare attractions to the hunter and stock-raiser; and if all other information on the subject had been wholly lost, it would not be difficult to conjecture what sort of men first ventured to penetrate its unexplored wilds.

There were three remarkable classes of men who preceded, by several years, the regular settlers of north-western Carolina; these were the hunters, cow-drivers and Indian traders. The hunter, though no pioneer—for he appropriated no lands, leveled no forest, and cultivated but little soil—yet served by his adventurous life many valuable purposes; he conciliated the jealous savages, impressed them, as Indians were easily impressed, by his romantic courage and unrivaled skill in the use of the rifle, with sentiments of respect for the character and prowess of white men; and in his wanderings over vast tracts of wild territory, having a keen eye, as well for the virtues of the soil and beauties of the country, as for the immediate objects of his pursuit, brought back to the border settlements glowing accounts of Elysian spots he had seen in the wilderness, and thus opened the way to the most eligible sections for succeeding groups of advancing settlers.

Patrick and William Calhoun, the pioneers of western Abbeville, were induced to visit the Long-Canes, by such descriptions of the fertility and loveliness of the country there, which they had obtained from a band of hunters at the Waxhaws.

No man now living east of the great western plains, may claim to be the modern representative of the ancient hunter of Upper-Carolina. He was the peculiar product of his age, and passed away forever with the deer and buffalo, as they disappeared before the aggressive axe of the pioneers. He was the Kitt Carson of primitive times; and, like Kitt Carson, was an extraordinary man. Poor, but scorning the arts and trammels of civilized society, with no companion but his dog, he passed his solitary life in the depths of the forest, undisturbed by the world's busy industry, and far out of reach of the dishonest strategy of its respectable thrift. And when the line of advancing settlements approached his haunt, and the sound of the settlers' axe began to mingle with the sharp echoes of his rifle, seizing the simple moveables of his log shanty, he removed a corresponding distance into the yet unappropriated wilderness.

A life like this, indolent and aimless as it may seem, illured no ordinary men. His powers were just of that kind, which in all ages, have elicited the warmest admiration of mankind. Nothing daunted him;

and to lion-like courage, strength and endurance, he added the activity of the catamount and the vigilance of the hawk—his eye was never at rest. Even when he was on a temporary visit to the settlements, or in Charleston procuring a fresh supply of ammunition its ceaseless activity—scrutinizing every nook, and sweeping every view—betrayed his habits and wild haunts.

Not far from the log-hut of the hunter stood that of the *cow-driver*, a character likewise worthy of note, but inferior to the hunter, in the attributes of a chivalrous manhood, in just the proportion of his greater sordidness.

Besides his association with the Indians, and their gloomy wilds, there was little romance about him; yet his life was one of self-reliance, hardship, and active vigilance; and in it were trained, for eminent usefulness, many of the backwoods soldiers of the Revolution. General Andrew Williamson, of White Hall, had been a cow-driver in his youth on the cane pastures of the Hard-Labor.

The business of stock-raising, at this period, on the frontiers, was scarcely less profitable than it is at present in similar regions of the west; and numbers of enterprising men engaged in it, either personally or through their agents. Having selected a tract, where cane and pea-vine grass grew most luxuriantly, they erected in the midst of it temporary cabins, and spacious pens. These were used as enclosures, in which to collect the cattle at proper seasons, for the purpose of counting and branding them; and from many such places in the upper-country, vast numbers of beeves were annually driven to the distant markets of Charleston, Philadelphia, and even to New York.

In 1740, Nightingale, the maternal grandfather of the late Judge William Johnston, established a *ranch* or *cow-pen*, six miles from the present site of Winnsboro', at a spot afterwards owned on Little Cedar Creek by the lamented General Strother. A man by the name of Howell, from the Congaree, soon after, formed a similar establishment, at a place near Winn's Bridge, on Little River. Several years after the Revolution, General Andrew Pickens was engaged in the business of stock-raising near his new residence in old Pendleton, and drove beeves to the market in New York.

At an earlier day, a *cow-pen* was quite an important institution. It was usually officered with a superintendent, and a corps of sub-agents—all active men, experienced woodsmen, and unfailing shots at long or short sight with the rifle. For these a hamlet of cabins were erected, besides the large enclosures for the stock; all of which, with a considerable plat of cleared land in the vicinity for the cultivation of corn, made quite an opening in the woods; and when all were at home, and the cattle in the pens, a very noisy, civilized scene, in the midst of the savage wilderness.

These rude establishments became afterwards, wherever they were formed, the great centres of settlements founded by the cultivators of the soil, who followed just behind the cow-drivers in their enterprising search for unappropriated, productive lands. They never failed to afford them abundant provisions, some society, and a sure protection from the Indians and not less terrible white marauders, who now began to infest the border.*

The professional cow-drivers, however, did not monopolize the business; few of the old settlers neglected the raising of stock in a country so admirably adapted to it, and generally came well provided for the purpose. They brought with them, from Pennsylvania, Virginia, and North Carolina, many animals of superior blood, and from this race sprang the famous chargers of the Revolutionary partizans, so often celebrated in the thrilling stories of that period. At no day since have there been so many thorough-bred riding-horses in Upper-Carolina—horses whose mettle and prowess admirably adapted them to the heroic service of the spirited men who bestrode them. May it not be fairly regarded as by no means one of the least significant signs of the present degeneracy, that the splendid, thorough-bred saddle-horses of the olden time have long ago ceased from the land, and men and women are both alike content to loll lazily in cushioned buggies and sumptuous carriages?

The generous emulation of that day, was, who could appear on the finest and most spirited horse: now the base struggle is, who can drive out with the largest amount of glitter and glare upon his carriage and harness. If giants were not in those days, men there were, at least, who, like Alexander with Bucephalus, prided themselves in being able to mount and

* Pearson's MS. History of Fairfield.

subdue steeds, whose mettle was worthy of kings and warriors.

Yet it would appear from an old statute, enacted in 1700, but repealed seven years after, that not all the horses brought at that early period into the province from Virginia, and other eastern colonies, were of the most desirable either for their blood or breeding. Its preamble runs as follows: "Whereas great numbers of horses have of late been brought from Virginia and other northern plantations into this Colony, and daily more may be expected, which hath, and will prove disadvantageous and detrimental to the inhabitants hereof; for the prevention of which, and for the better encouragement of more serviceable horses to be bred amongst us, be it enacted," &c.*

This statute, no doubt, acted as efficiently in Virginia and Pennsylvania as in Carolina "for the encouragement of more serviceable horses to be bred," and greatly contributed to that improvement of their breeds, by importations from Europe, which a half century after, enabled the Scotch-Irish emigrants from these colonies to bring with them into Upper-Carolina a superior race of that noble animal. Many fine horses were also brought directly from abroad into Carolina, that likewise proved an important source of spirit and energy to the stock of the revolutionary period in every part of the province.

While on the subject of the horse, it will not be

* Statutes of South Carolina.

uninteresting to many to say something of the wild breed of Carolina and Southern America. Pearson, in his unpublished History of Fairfield, labors through several pages, and with considerable plausibility, to prove that the horse was a native of the Continent, and well known to the Indians long before the first visits of the Europeans. Some of his statements are at least novel.

At the period, he affirms, of the settlement of Carolina by Sayle and his followers, in 1670, immense droves of wild horses were found subsisting upon the natural pastures of the country. The colonists soon learned to take them in snares, and great numbers of them, it is related by old settlers, were caught in this way. Old Jessy Gladden, long since dead, pointing on one occasion to a valley on his estate near the Wateree Creek, observed: "In my boyhood I often saw large herds of wild horses rushing along that valley in a wild stampede; and so great were their numbers that the ground on which our cabin stood shook under their tread."

The opinion that this noble quadruped is not a native of America, seems to have originated chiefly from a few casual remarks, found in the chronicles of the first discoverers and explorers. It is a striking incident related, and often repeated, of the cavaliers of Cortez, in his invasion of Mexico, that they were taken by the simple natives, when first seen approaching on horseback, to be so many monsters composed partly of the body of the horse, and partly of that of a man. From this it was hastily concluded that they had never before seen the horse, while there is clearly an equal probability that their astonishment did not arise from the sight of the horses, but the novel complexion, strange costume, and extraordinary pageantry of the stern cavaliers who rode upon them; and so great was the impression made upon their imaginations, that it was easy for them to fancy a natural connection between the Spaniards and their steeds.

But neither the pageantry nor the wonderful race of men thus presented to the view of the Mexicans, was requisite to produce such an effect upon their unsophisticated minds. It is well known that the buffalo was originally found roaming over the whole extent of the Southern Atlantic and Gulf States; but no Indian or Mexican had ever used them for purposes of draught or burden.* Suppose, therefore, that instead of horses, the Spaniards had approached the City of Mexico mounted upon the backs of domesticated buffaloes, would the astonishment of the natives have been less or their imaginations less active?

An incident is related in the primitive history of Carolina, which precisely illustrates the point in view. When the Catawba Indians first heard of the arrival of Sayle on the coast, they instantly—so the tradition runs—dispatched a war party to reconnoitre the movements and appearance of the strangers.

* The Mexicans never used brute animals for draught or burden. A hundred men of burden bore a present from Montezuma to Cortez. —American History, vol. 11, p. 35.

Proceeding to the banks of the Ashley, the party concealed themselves in a glade in full view of the sea, and there, for the first time, beheld the ships of the white men, as they rode at anchor. "*What great birds!*" they exclaimed to one another, and very soon they saw the English themselves hurrying to and fro, with strange notions and yet stranger dress, both in the vessels and on land. But an object now appeared that astonished them almost as much as the ships—a man leading out a horse with a bell on his neck, which he proceeded to tether to grass on the glade not far from their hiding place.

On their return to the Nation, this circumstance of the horse was related as a subject of peculiar interest, yet the country, at that period, abounded in wild horses; they must have seen hundreds of them on the path, as they passed to and from the coast; but a horse with a bell on, and tethered to grass, was a sight sufficient to excite the wonder of any savage on the Continent.

In this plausible manner, the amiable chronicler of Fairfield ventures to lay claim to the American nativity of the horse. The argument, however, is more ingenious than historically truthful. It cannot be denied that the Spaniards introduced into the country the original stock, from which the wild breed of the prairie, both of that period and of the present, are descended.* After much observation

*For the privilege of using the interesting historical papers left by Mr. Pearson, of Fairfield, we are indebted to the kindness of Major W. S. Lyles, of that district.

among the Southern Indians, Bartram informs us that the horse was not originally found in their possession. Of the wild horses of the Seminoles, which he met with in East Florida, he thus writes:—"They are the most beautiful and sprightly species of that noble creature, perhaps, anywhere to be seen, but are of a small breed, and as delicately formed as the American roe-buck. The horse in the Creek tongue, is *echoclucco*, the great deer. The Seminole horses are said to have descended from the Andalusian breed, brought here by the Spaniards, when they first established the colony of East Florida. From the forehead to their nose is a little arched or aquiline, and so are the fine Choctaw horses among the upper Creeks, which are said to have been brought thither from New Mexico across the Mississippi, by those nations of Indians who emigrated from the West, beyond the river. These horses are everywhere like the Seminole breed, only larger, and perhaps not so lively and capricious. It is a matter of conjecture, whether or not the different soil and situation of the country may have contributed, in some measure, in forming the difference in size and other qualities between them. I have observed the horses, and other animals in the high, hilly country of Carolina, are of a much larger and stronger make than those which are bred in the flat country next the sea-coast. A buck-skin of the Cherokees, will weigh twice as much as those bred in the low, flat country of Carolina."

Lawson, though he gives us quite a curious and

minute journal of an excursion which he made early in the beginning of the eighteenth century, from Charleston, through portions of the middle and upper-country, appears to have seen no wild horses, unless he includes them in the general term cattle. He speaks of "passing several large savannahs, wherein are curious ranges for cattle."* In a description which follows, however, of a grand town-dance that he witnessed among the Waxhaws, in the present territory of Lancaster, he speaks of the women leading off in the joyous circle, having hawks' bells about their necks, and great bells for *horses* fastened to their legs.

On the luxuriant cane pastures of the Tugaloo and Keowee Rivers, and, doubtless, at quite an early period, on the richer savannahs of the Long-Cane and Saluda, as well as beyond the mountains, the Cherokees kept immense droves of horses that roamed as wild and free as the deer of the same region. These horses are said to have been of very superior quality; the Cherokees were famous jockeys, and exceedingly shrewd in their judgment of those animals.

In the famine, however, that followed in the Nation, the ruinous onslaught, made in 1761, upon their towns by Col. Grant, of rattle snake memory, the discomfited Cherokees were reduced to the hard necessity of shooting and eating most of their horses. At the conclusion of the war, however, they soon

* Lawson's Carolina, p. 211.

replenished their herds from the English settlements with a breed as excellent as that they had lost.*

The white traders who settled among the Cherokees, encouraged by the many natural advantages offered by a country abounding in grasses, turned their attention to the raising of horses; and some of them laid claim to stocks of a hundred and fifty head, running at large upon the common pastures. They are described as being of good size, well made, hard-hoofed, handsome, strong, and fit for the saddle or draft. The old chronicler adds, however, "a person runs too great a risk to buy any to take them out of the country, because every spring season most of them make for their native range."

The Andalusian or Spanish horse, from which sprung the wild horse of America, was itself derived from the Barbary stock, the nearest approach, perhaps, in existence, to the pure Arabian bloed, descended direct from Mohammed's celebrated mare, whose spotless genealogy is carefully preserved among the archives of Mecca. The horse of Andalusia is still much prized; it is small, but beautifully formed. Its head is, however, rather large in proportion to the body, the mane thick, the ears long, the eyes animated, the breast full, the legs finely shaped, the pastern large, and the hoof high."† This is closely descriptive of the perfect horse, as drawn by an old writer, Camerarius; "he should have the breast broad, the hips round and the mane long, the coun-

* Adair. † Encyclo. Amer.

tenance fierce like a lion, a nose like a sheep, the legs, head and skin of a deer, the throat and neck of a wolf, and the ear and tail of a fox."

The excellence and beauty of many of the wild horses found at the present day on the plains of the far West, is a striking proof of the indestructible vigor and purity of original noble blood.

Lieut. R. S. Williamson, in the field notes of his explorations on the great Pacific slope, makes the following observation of the Klamath Lake Indians: "They own many horses, some of which were valuable animals. No offer would tempt them to sell any of the latter, although they were eager to dispose of a few miserable hacks, too worthless to purchase. The idea which prevails in Oregon, that all Indian horses are of inferior breed, doubtless arises from the fact that such only are brought to the settlements for sale. Near Klamath marsh, we saw a few animals of a pie-bald color, whose graceful forms and clear, piercing eyes, showed very superior blood. It may be that their genealogy extends back to the Barbary steeds, introduced by the Spaniards into Mexico, and supposed to be the progenitors of the wild horses of the prairies."*

It is a question not unworthy of consideration, how it came to pass, that a people who must undoubtedly have sprung from some stock of eastern origin, were yet found to be destitute of the horse, and to-

* Explorations and Surveys from the Mississippi to the Pacific, made and published under the direction of the U. S. Secretary of War, Vol. vi. p. 70.

tally ignorant, even, of the use of any beasts of burden. The horse has been the useful friend, almost the companion, of men in the Old World, from a period up to which no history runneth. It is not known, certainly, where he originated. He is mentioned in the Pentateuch, and is the subject of description in one of the most magnificent passages of Job. Why, then, did he not accompany the ancient and first pilgrims to the New World? It may be urged for the Indians, in relation to animals of burden, that, finding themselves in the midst of a country abounding in game, and a genial soil, they quickly fell into a manner of life whose simplicity required no assistance from such animals. A curious fact of a philological character, mentioned incidentally by Adair, would appear to give force to the supposition. In the dialect of one of the southern tribes the name of a horse-rope, *hissoobistarakshe*, "is derived from *tarakshe*, 'to tie,' and *hissooba*, an elk or horse that carries a burden; which suggests that they formerly saw elks carry burdens, though not, perhaps, in the northern provinces."

The primitive Mexicans were, however, quite advanced in civilization, which they must have derived either from their progenitors, or from some partially enlightened colony; for no savage people can elevate themselves. They practiced gardening and agriculture, built great public edifices, lived in cities of no mean splendor, and, in practical astronomy, surpassed even the enlightenment of the best days of Greece; yet they knew nothing of the horse or the ox, and, though surrounded by multitudes of buffaloes, they had never learned the simple art of turning their strength and docility to the useful purposes of draught.

To our mind, a stronger presumptive argument for the western, local origin of the aborigines, may be derived from this singular historical fact, than all the chronological and ethnological deductions of the sciolists. We shall make of it, however, a better use. Is it not curiously, at least, suggestive of the manner in which the primitive race came from the Old World to America? If they found a pathway by land, crossing from Northern Asia, where the Aleutian Islands and the peninsula of Alaska yet in great part lie, or from the southern portion of the same continent, by Malacca, which, it is equally probable was, at some time in the history of the world, connected by an unbroken isthmus, along the fifteenth degree of south latitude, with the western shore of South America, would they not, unquestionably have brought the horse with them? He would have been exceedingly useful to them in so long a journey.

But two suppositions, therefore, remain, in regard to the means by which they effected their great migratory passage to the West. They were either a small party—a single pair it may have been—blown away in a frail bark of primitive times, from the eastern shore of Asia and cast upon the western coast of America, as it happened to a company of unfortunate Japanese, in 1836, near the coast of

California, or, they voluntarily achieved the passage of Bhering's Strait, in large numbers, and under such circumstances as precluded the transportation of the horse and every other animal of burden.

This is not presented as a demonstrative argument on the subject; it is, however, not a whit less conclusive than the bulk of the speculations on the same difficult problem by men of philosophy and genius.

Zimmerman believed they effected their migration by the way of South-eastern Asia; Mr. Jefferson argued that the aborigines knew no relationship to the races of the Old World, having originated on the soil; while another, of less celebrity, urged the claims of North-eastern Asia.

Dr. Livingston makes the same curious remark of the tribes visited by him in Africa—that neither the ox nor the horse were originally known to the aborigines of that continent. The horse and ox are, however, not the only animals of burden for which the New World is indebted to the European colonists.

It is generally believed that the present effort of the United States Government to introduce the camel into the South, and to naturalize it upon the great prairies, is the first attempt of the kind that was ever made. There is decided and venerable testimony to the contrary. Shortly after the Spaniards had supplied America with horses, that active people, then the most enterprising in Europe, imported from Africa a number of camels to be used for purposes of transportation on the plains of Mexico; and some of them were doubtless used on the very prairies to which the more recent enterprise has consigned a second importation of the same noble animal. The old chronicler to whom we are indebted for this information,* remarks that the strange climate seemed to suit them well, and they promised to thrive and answer all the purposes for which they had been introduced. The experiment must, however, in some way have proved a total failure; the camels became extinct early enough to escape the notice of living generations, and we know of no other writer who has recorded the fact that such an attempt was ever made by any other than our own government.

There was a sandy plain on the bank of the Enoree, quite famous in old times, at which the settlers on that stream, and from Duncan's Creek, were accustomed to assemble for the purpose of breaking their young horses to the saddle. John Duncan, the first settler of Laurens, drove with him from Pennsylvania to that region of country a fine stud of horses. It was not then necessary, however, to strip the corn of its blades and ship hay from the meadows of the North in order to sustain them; they kept rolling fat throughout the year on the natural grasses that abounded in the woods and valleys.†

The small or maiden cane was especially valuable

---

*Cox's Carolina: published for Olive Payne, in Pope's Head Alley, Corn Hill. 1741 South Carolina College Library.

†Conversation of Joseph Duncan, grandson of the pioneer, and now in his 86th year.

for this purpose—it was exceedingly rich in nutritive qualities. "When slender it never grows higher than from four to seven feet: it shoots up in one summer, but produces no seeds until the following year. It is an evergreen, and is perhaps the most nourishing food for cattle upon earth. No other milk or butter has such flavor and richness as that which is produced from cows which feed upon cane. Horses that feed upon it work nearly as well as if they were fed upon corn, provided care be taken to give them, once in three or four days, a handful of salt.*

During the Revolution, this with the other grasses of the soil, was the chief food of the cavalry of both Whig and Tory in the campaigns of the upper-country.

In the deed of conveyance by which certain territory was ceded to the Province of Carolina, preparatory to the building of old Fort Prince George, the grass pastures lying between the Keowee and the Long-Canes, are, among other lands, particularly mentioned.†

* Narrative of Capt. Imlay in his descriptions of Kentucky previous to 1793.

† State Records.

CHAPTER VIII.

The Indian Trader—Old Anthony Park—Daugherty the first trader among the Cherokees—Peltries and Packhorses—First legislative Act in relation to the trade—The character of the traders—The Governor of Carolina interested in the traffic—Alexander Cameron—The first Board of Commissioners, &c.

The Indian trader of the Cherokee Nation was a far more interesting character than either the hunter or cow-driver. Devoted as he was to the arts and wrangle of gain, he nevertheless possessed not only a fearless intrepidity, but a high order of intelligence; and in more than one instance education and extraordinary learning. "He advanced without ceremony into the heart of Indian settlements;" and for the sake of pushing his lucrative business, was content to live, in many instances, a long life-time, deprived of the comforts and amenities of civilized society.

Speculative men have drawn comparisons between savage and civilized life, highly colored in favor of the former. Their theories have been acted upon ever since the discovery of America by individuals, who, turning their backs upon the society in which they were reared, have voluntarily chosen a residence among the Indians. Of this description there were several, who, at an early day, had settled among the Indians, at a great distance from the white people. Anthony Park—of whom we have already spoken—one of the first settlers of the back-country, and who lived to a very advanced age in Newberry District, traveled, in 1758, a few hundred miles among the Indians to the west of the Alleghany Mountains. He found several white men, chiefly Scotch or Irish, who said that they had lived among the Indians as traders twenty years, a few from forty to fifty, and one sixty years. One of these said that he had upwards of seventy children and grandchildren in the Nation. If these accounts be correct, the oldest of these traders must have taken up his abode among the savages four hundred miles to the west of Charleston before the close of the seventeenth century, when the white population of Carolina scarcely extended twenty miles from the sea coast.*

In 1690, several years before the English settlers on the Ashley knew that such a people as the Cherokees existed, one Daugherty, a trader from Virginia, ventured to take up his residence among them for the purposes of traffic.† And from this time, numerous adventurers in search of trade and fortune, began to frequent all the towns, and great war-paths of the Nation. The business proved, for a considerable time, exceedingly profitable; vast quantities of peltry were purchased from the Indians, and being conveyed on pack-horses, sometimes by water, to the markets of Charleston, and other ports, were readily

* Dr. Ramsay, vol. I.

† Ramsey's Anls. of Tennessee.

disposed of to merchants, who entered largely into the traffic.

This system of exchange was exceedingly advantageous to the English adventurer; for a few trinkets, looking-glasses, pieces of colored cloth, hatchets, and guns of small value, he could procure, on the Savannah and Catawba, peltries which, in Charleston, would command many times their original cost. And unequal as it appears, it would have conferred real benefits upon the Indians, as well, if it had been possible thus to introduce among them many articles of which, in their savage state, they stood in real need, without introducing, at the same time, evils that first corrupted and afterwards ruined them.

The trade during this period, and until 1716, was conducted solely under the auspices of individual enterprise. But now partly for the sake of its enormous profits, and partly with the design of having better control of the Indians, in view of the public safety, the Provincial Government assumed the direction of all its affairs, and conducted them, ever after, as a great public monopoly. And, like all public monopolies, it was not long before it began to exhibit a lack of the energy and life that had previously made it the most lucrative business in America.

So true it is that commerce even with savages, as all other institutions growing out of the natural wants and activity of human society, has its laws, that may not be violated with impunity. Even-handed justice would have required, however, that the evil results which followed should fall exclusively upon the offenders; it will be seen that they fell heaviest upon the poor Indians.

As early as 1707, the exciting abuses of the trade, the rapid profits of which, had allured into the Indian nations many irresponsible men of the most despicable character, induced the passage of an Act by the Assembly, by which a Board of Commissioners was instituted to manage and direct everything relating to the traffic with the Indians; and all traders were compelled, under heavy penalties, to take out a license as their authority in the nation.

The same Act embodies all the principles, and most of the regulations, by which the trade was henceforth to be conducted, and contains, besides, no little incidental history, in relation to the Indians and the times:

"Whereas, the greater number of those persons that trade among the Indians in amity with this government, do generally lead loose, vicious lives, to the scandal of the Christian religion, and do likewise oppress the people among whom they live, by their unjust and illegal actions, which, if not prevented, may in time tend to the destruction of this province; therefore, be it enacted, that after the first day of October next, every trader that shall live and deal with any Indians, except the Itawans, Sewees, Santees, Stonoes, Kiawas, Kussoes, Edistoes, and St. Helenas, for the purpose of trading in furs, skins, slaves, or any other commodity, shall first have a license under the hand and seal of the Commissioners hereafter to be named; for which he shall pay the public receiver the full sum of eight pounds current money. The license shall continue in force one year and no longer, and he shall give a surety of one hundred pounds currency. One of the conditions to which he was bound under this surety was, never to sell or give to the Indians, under any pretence whatever, any rum or other spirituous liquors. We shall have ample reason to observe with what conscientious strictness this obligation was discharged. No ammunition was to be disposed of to hostile Indians, under the penalty of being declared guilty of felony, and deprived of the benefit of clergy.

The Commissioners were to frame general instructions, to be given to every trader applying for a license, and likewise particular instructions and orders, according to the diversity of time, place, and other circumstances. To these instructions the traders were to give implicit obedience, under the penalty of forfeiting their license. They were forbidden, under heavy penalties, to seize the person of any free Indian, and sell him as a slave; they were not to extort from the Indians any skins or other goods by means of threats and abuse. Previous to this, it appears, that the Governors of the Province had been greatly benefited, and perhaps too much influenced by the numerous valuable presents made them by the various Indians in alliance with the authorities in Charleston. It is now provided that the public receiver, pay to the present Governor the sum of one hundred pounds annually, in lieu of all

Indian presents whatsoever; and the same provision shall effect his successors forever.

The Act fixes the equivalent for these Indian presents at one hundred pounds; it was in reality, however, twice as large. In the manuscript Records of Columbia, there has been ferreted out an old correspondence between Gov. Nath. Johnson and the Assembly, "in which two hundred pounds were offered as an equivalent for his Indian perquisites, and refused. In 1716 the annual compensation was two hundred pounds."*

By the same statute was also appointed the first General Indian Agent, whose duty it was to reside during the entire year—excepting two months, allowed him for business in Charleston—among the Indians, for the purpose of inquiring into and redressing their grievances, and deciding all disputes between them and the traders. He was also to act as a magistrate and justice of the peace, with power to decide cases involving sums of one hundred and fifty dollars—there being the right of appeal to the commissioners.

Many will recollect that Alexander Cameron, the deputy superintendent of the celebrated John Steuart, was a leading magistrate, at his residence of Lochaber, in the present territory of Abbeville, at the commencement of the Revolution. John Steuart was one of the last general superintendents of Southern Indians in alliance with Great Britain, as Thomas

*Prof. Wm. J. Rivers.

Nairne—appointed under the Act whose provisions we are considering—was the first agent. Of both Steuart and Cameron we shall have much to say in another place.

The bond of the agent, or superintendent, was fixed at two hundred pounds, and his salary at two hundred and fifty—equivalent to about twelve hundred and fifty dollars. There is a curious item in this old statute, assigning a special duty to the agent, which savors of the ancient belief that something wonderful and enriching was yet to be disclosed in the deep solitudes of the north-western wild: "It is also ordered, that if the agent, or his lawful successors, can procure any person residing among the Indians, or who may hereafter go amongst them, to undertake to make any new discovery, or settle any new trade, such person shall be rewarded by the House of Commons for such discovery as they shall think fit."

It was finally enacted that nine commissioners should be appointed, to direct, as before related, the whole business of the trade. The first Board was composed of the following gentlemen: Ralph Izard, James Cochran, Robert Fenwick, Col. George Logan, Lewis Pasquereau, Richard Beresford, John Ash, John A. Motte, and Major John Fenwick.*

Such were the first public enactments, and provisions, for the management of the Indian trade. All else, however, was free and untrammelled; the

---

* Statutes of South Carolina, Vol. II.

traders went and came, as they pleased; trafficked, as yet, in any part of the Nation; bought their own goods, and bartered them on terms sufficiently remunerative to the Indians for peltries and slaves, which they disposed of in Charleston with equal freedom. And the laudable designs of the government, with no mean pecuniary advantages, would still, in great part, have been secured, if the commissioners had continued to adhere rigidly to the spirit of these provisions.

One of the principal grievances which they sought to remove was the employment, in the Indian country, of men of vicious practices, who brought disgrace upon the English name, and endangered, by their crimes, the safety of the province; yet, it was not long before the temptations of the license fee, or a want of foresight, induced them to proceed in such a manner as to increase, rather than diminish, the evil. Bad men were now licensed to do violence to the poor Indian, and to the principles of justice and humanity; and so great a number of traders of all characters found authority to drive their fortunes in the traffic, that a far worse state of things was soon experienced than ever before.

The adventurous, wild life of the trader, as well as the prospect of enormous profits, held out peculiar attractions to men who, anxious to acquire wealth, cared nothing for the means by which they attained their end. The Cherokee towns, as well as those of the Creeks and Chickasaws, lay far beyond the border; and though frequently visited by their watchful agent, were yet well fitted for the residence and operations of the lawless.

A large portion of the commissioners' time, at each meeting of the Board, was consumed in hearing and considering abuses in the Nation, and on the trading paths. Their records abound with the minute particulars of these perplexing irregularities.

At one of their meetings, in 1710, Richard Edghill, P—— G———, and Captain Musgrove, were cited to answer for the alleged crime of having reduced to slavery several free Indians. G——— had seized an Indian fellow named Ventusa, and his wife; Musgrove, Masoony; and Edghill, Diego. They were required by the Board to prove these Indians lawful subjects of slavery. Musgrove, it appears, was exceedingly oppressive and troublesome to the Indians. They brought another complaint against him, to the effect, that in the spring of the same year, he had gone to one of their towns and ordered all the people to turn out and hoe his corn, under penalty of a severe flogging for every one that refused.

Capt. Musgrove is also mentioned as commandant of a caravan of twenty-three pack-horses, which was sent from Carolina to the factory among the Creeks, in the winter of 1817; and he is, without doubt, the same successful, though unscrupulous trader whose history has been given, in good part, by the historians of Georgia, under the name of John Musgrove.

Oglethorpe, on his first ascent of the Savannah

River, found him established, with his famous half-breed wife, Mary, on the same bluff where now stands the chief city of Georgia. "This Indian, Mary, was born in the year 1700, at the town of Coweta, upon the Chattahooche, in Alabama. Her Indian name was Consaponaheso, and, by maternal descent, she was one of the Queens of the Muscogee Nation, and the Indians conceded to her the title of Princess. When ten years of age, her father took her to Ponpon, in South Carolina, where she was baptized, educated, and instructed in the principles of Christianity. Afterwards, she fled back to her forest home, laid aside the civilization of the English, and assumed the ease and freedom of the happy Muscogee. In 1716, Col. John Musgrove was dispatched to the Chattahooche, by the government of Carolina, to form a treaty of alliance with the Creeks, with whom that colony had been at war. It was there stipulated that the Creeks were to remain the free occupants of all the lands east, as far as the Savannah River. The son of the British negotiator, John Musgrove, had accompanied his father to Coweta, and falling in love with the Princess Mary, made her his wife. After remaining in the Nation several years, and after the birth of their only child, they removed to South Carolina. There residing several years, in much happiness, they afterwards established themselves upon Yamacraw Bluff, at the head of an extensive trading house, where Oglethorpe found them. By his alliance with this remarkable woman, who was well versed in the Indian and English languages, Musgrove obtained considerable influence over the natives, and became exceedingly wealthy. Mary was afterwards the warm friend of Oglethorpe, and several times saved the early colonists of Georgia from savage butchery.*

On the death of Musgrove, she married Captain Jacob Mathews; and, becoming the second time a widow, was finally married to Thomas Bosomworth, a clergyman of the Church of England, and of notorious memory. We will not inflict upon our readers the voluminous details of her subsequent history; it fills, with that of her ambitious husband, a large and inglorious part of the early annals of Georgia and Carolina. After her death, the disconsolate Bosomworth married her chambermaid.† They lie buried on St. Catharine's Island.

One Joss Crosley, a trader, having become jealous of his Indian mistress, laid hold of a suspected Indian and abused him in a most barbarous manner; and when Cocket, another trader, and who acted as interpreter on this occasion before the Board, interfered to save the fellow's life, Crosley turned upon him, and beat him till the blood issued from his mouth.

P—— G——— took an Indian girl, against her will, to be his mistress, and when she objected to his

* Pickett's History of Alabama.

† Whoever is fond of investigating the truth of history under difficulties, can be amply gratified in the numerous closely-written manuscript pages devoted to the Bosomworths in the Journals of the Secretary of State's Office, Columbia.

violence, he cruelly beat her. He also conceived a jealousy, even, of the girl's own brother, because he had accepted from her a trifling present of a few beads, and beat him as he had done the sister. These things, it is recorded, greatly grieved the Indians. On another occasion, he made a girl drunk with rum, and locking her in his room, threatened to take the life of her mother if she did not go off, and leave her daughter with him.

It was often the case, when the licenses of many of the traders expired—which they did at the end of one year—that they continued to traffic, nevertheless, without renewing them according to law. In 1710, the following traders had their bonds put in suit for this offence: Capt. John Jones, Matthew Smallwood, Anthony Probat, James Lucas, Abram Pierce, Joseph Crosley, Roger Hoskins, Alex. Clark, William Smith, Theophilus Hastings, William Scarlett, and John Jones. A few of these delinquents were sufficiently refractory to tear to pieces, in the presence of the agent, the warrants that had been sent up for their arrest. James Lucas reported to the Board that Capt. Musgrove had unjustly detained two of his Indian slaves; and one Capt. Fitch brought the complaint that the Appalechian Indians had killed his *ram*, for which he had seized two of their guns. A Captain Peterson was also notorious for his abuses among the Indians. From a letter addressed by the Board to their agent in the Pocotalligo towns, we made the following extract: "We will do all we can to assist you in abating these abuses, particularly the settling of the white men upon the Indian lands. We are but a bare Board, and your complaints being of so high and grievous a nature, as we with you believe, tend to the utter ruin and desolation of the government, if not timely prevented; we thought fit to send you this in answer, and that we would have you proceed with vigor in the defence of the province."

This same agent, one Wright, came down soon after from the Yamassee towns and reported to the Board the bonds of several traders who desired licenses; among them were, Even Lewis, James Patterson, William Ford, Thomas Simonds, Alex. Mackey, Nicholas Deas, Thomas Seabrook, and Capt. John Cochran. He presented on the same occasion several of the Yamassee chiefs, who had come down to make some inquiries in relation to certain abuses of the traders. They were introduced with two interpreters, Bray and Cocket, and the conference began by the Indians representing to the Board, that an agent had been sent up to their towns to redress their grievances, and to acquaint them that their *rum debts* should be forgiven them. They added, that they had come down, to learn, themselves, from the Commissioners, if this was true. The president assured them that such was the fact, and more: not only were their rum debts not to be exacted of them, but they should not be required to pay the debts contracted with the traders by the relations of any of them, for whom they had not engaged to stand.

The traders were in the habit of selling goods

without scruple to the most worthless of the Indians, with the expectation of persuading or of compelling, if necessary, their more active and thrifty relatives to discharge the debt. The president of the Board finally remarked to the chiefs, that it was impossible to prevent unprincipled traders from carrying up rum to their country. They further complained of several white men, who were encroaching upon their hunting grounds; these were Thomas Jones, John Whitehead, Joseph Bryan, Robert Steel, John Palmer, and Barnaby Bull. The Board promised that they should be removed.

The following year Capt. John Cochran was charged with having sold a free Indian as a slave; and one Cornelius McCarty, with the seizure of the wife and child of a warrior, who was absent on a war expedition against the enemy. The Board decided that the woman and child should be sent for and brought back from New York, where McCarty had sold them as slaves.

This forcible reduction of free Indians to slavery, became, at this time, so great an evil, that the Board ordered, as something of a preventive of the nuisance, that no trader should purchase an Indian as a slave, until he had been, at least, three days in the town of the warrior who captured him. None were subject to slavery but those taken fairly in war; and so profitable was the traffic, even under this general restriction, that the traders in their scrambles for the newly captured prisoners, in the possession of friendly bands of Indians returning from war, that they hastened to meet them even in the woods, and at distant points on the war-paths—every one struggling to acquire for himself the largest profits from the last spoils of the war.

The oppressive abuses, necessarily growing out of such irregularities as these, called loudly for the interference of the public authorities.

The first introduction of the Cherokee Indians to the people of Carolina, took place in Charleston in 1793, on an occasion similar to that which we have just seen brought down the Yamassees, to complain to the Governor and Council, that the Savannahs and Congarees had attacked their extreme eastern settlements—now the territory of Chester and Fairfield—captured their people and sold them as slaves to certain merchants of Charleston.*

In 1711, Stephen Beadon was summoned before the Board, and asked what he knew of one John Frazer's beating the King of Tomatly? He answered, the common report was, that Frazer was apt to beat and abuse the Indians; he had forcibly made a slave of one of the people of Cohassee, and had sold an Indian boy into slavery, which he had been ordered to hold, until it could be ascertained whether or not he was a slave.

It was in the summer of the same year, that circumstances arising from some of these abuses, occasioned the first notice in the State records of the Waxhaw Indians, and the warlike Catawbas. The

* Pickett's History of Alabama.

superintendent, John Wright, was ordered by the Board to proceed with all expedition to Savannah Town—(of this more in another place)—and thence send messengers to the Waxhaws, Esaws, and Catabas, inviting their head men to meet him and the chiefs of Savannah Town at the house of one Benjamin Clea, where he was to inquire strictly into all the complaints recently made to the government by those nations.

Notwithstanding this display of confidence on the part of the Board towards this agent, he was not long after charged with having forcibly taken possession of Ahela, a relative of the King of Tugaloo, whom he sold into slavery, though she was declared to be a free woman of the Cherokees. He was likewise instrumental, it was asserted, in driving the Alabama Indians away from the Carolina trade to that of Mobile, by seizing several slaves belonging to a man of that nation, and giving them up to one Gower, to whom the Indian owed nothing.

The first mention made of the Cherokees in the old State records, occurs in 1713, in the following entry: Two Cherokee women it was asserted before the Board, were held in slavery by one Peter St. Julian, a farmer, who lived in the country on the road leading from Charleston to the Congarees. He was ordered to appear before the Board and answer the charge.

At this period, therefore, it is obvious, that many of the traders engaged in the commerce with the Indians, were much more intent on dealing in slaves or Indian captives, than on legitimate barter of goods and peltries. And the greater portion of the testimony afforded by the ancient records of the trade, in relation to its abuses and irregularities, are found principally connected with the wrongs and oppressions of the authorized commerce in Indian slaves. It came to be a custom with a few of the most hardened to keep a body of slaves around them in the Nation, whom they sent out to war with the other Indians, in order to add yet more largely and expeditiously to their profits arising from the sale of captive enemies.

In 1711, the Board, fully aware of this inhuman practice of some of its licensed traders, issued the following order to them all: "You shall permit none of your slaves to go to war on any account whatever." Yet not long after this, the complaint, in one instance, at least, was brought down, that a trader had sent out a body of his slaves to war against the enemy.

We shall present, from the same source,* but one more example on this head; and it is one which for cool, diabolical atrocity, was surely never surpassed, even in the gloomy traditions of Guinea and Dahomey. There lived at this time near the present Silver Bluff, in Barnwell District, a small detached tribe of Indians, known as the Euchees.†

* Records of Indian Affairs, in the Secretary of State's office, Columbia.

† Their lands extended from Brier Creek south, to the site of a town afterwards built by the Georgians and named Ebenezer.

The name of their town was Chestowee. Two men connected with the Indian trade, Alex. Long and Eleazer Wiggon, had frequent dealings with these people as well as with the more numerous Cherokees, and their chief object, it appears, were the gains arising from the sale of captive Indians. Be that as it may, it happened, on a certain occasion, that Long, and an Indian from Chestowee, had some difficulty in their trafficking, and came to blows and a struggle, in which the Euchee tore away from Long's head a portion of his hair. Long, not less vindictive than the savages around him, from that moment vowed vengeance against the whole Euchee race. But his desire to be avenged, though deep and lasting, was not without a method and calculation that looked to the main profits of his trade.

He resolved upon the destruction of Chestowee, and the capture, from its ruins, of as many slaves as he could get for his portion, among the several accomplices necessary for the accomplishment of such a scheme. His plan was soon arranged, and no trader in the Nation, it appeared, was better acquainted with the men best fitted to assist him in the work. Eleazer Wiggon, a kindred spirit, was let into the secret, and was to share in the expenses and profits of the venture. Crossing the mountains, he paid a seeming business visit to some of his acquaintances among the Over-Hill Cherokees, and was soon in close conference with three or four of their head men—with the leading warrior of Euchasee, and a Capt. Flint, and Cæsar, and some three others. Everything was settled to his satisfaction; it was agreed that these Indians should pass stealthily beyond the mountains, and make a clandestine attack upon the unsuspecting and defenceless Euchees. The pretext was, that the Euchees, some time before, had murdered some of their people. Long, in order to make sure of his game, exhibited to his accomplices a forged order from the Governor, ordering the destruction of the Euchee town, for the alleged offence against the Cherokees. He was to supply the powder and ball necessary for the enterprise, and the spoil was to be equally divided among them. It was afterwards confessed, that the reason they did not invite the lower Cherokees to join them was, that there would have been too many to claim shares in the anticipated spoil. Cæsar and his companions set out, and having crossed into the lower settlements, passed silently through, and came at night fall, like hungry panthers, in striking distance of Chestowee. They then halted, and having coolly painted and decorated themselves for the diabolical work, rushed, with a whoop upon the town, and soon wrapped it in flames. The frightened Euchees, completely surprised, made, it appears, little resistance, but suspecting the object of their enemies, hastened to collect their wives and children in the war-house of the town, and preferring to see them dead rather than the slaves of their persecutors, cut the throats of them all with their own hands.

Long afterwards testified before the Board, that he and Wiggon had received, as their portion of the

16

spoil, but one woman and five children, which they had claimed in lieu of a debt due them by the unfortunate Euchees. It is only necessary to add, that others swore, on the same occasion, that both Long and Wiggon, had been heard to declare that if they could bring about the destruction of Chestowee, there would be a "*fine parcel of slaves in the market.*"

After a patient hearing of the case—for it was brought, at once, before the Board—it was resolved that Long and Wiggon were guilty, their licenses were taken from them, their bonds put in suit, and a request made the Governor that he would proceed with the utmost rigor against them in the Court of Sessions.

These practices were a disgrace to the people and the times, and impartial truth requires this account of them at our hands. It cannot be shown, however, and no recreant Southerner or God-forsaken agitator of another section needs assume it as true, that South Carolina for one moment winked at these abuses, in order to enhance the profits of a lucrative traffic.

Full and special instructions, on this head, were repeatedly, and from the first public recognition of the trade, enjoined upon all connected with it. "You are," said the Board to its agents, "to acquaint all persons trading among the Indians with the duty incumbent upon them by this Act, which you are hereby ordered to publish and read to them, and to give them such other instructions as you shall think good for the safety of the province and the trade.

"You are to use your utmost endeavors to regulate the *lives of the traders*, so that they give no offence to the Indians, and bring no scandal against the Christian religion; keep them, at least, within the bounds of morality, and to this end rebuke all actions that tend to the contrary. If any one so rebuked, persist in his course, let us know him."

In the statute of 1707, already mentioned, a special clause was provided for this abuse, "That if any person trading among the Indians, shall, by his own confession or verdict of a jury in any Court of Session or gaol delivery, be convicted of selling any free Indian for a slave, at any time after the ratification of this Act, shall, for every such offence, forfeit the sum of sixty pounds current money of this province; and for want of such payment shall receive such corporal punishment as the Judges of the General Sessions shall think fit, not extending to life or limb, and upon conviction of such offender the Indian slave so sold is hereby declared free."

"It shall be your constant aim to promote peace and good-will among all nations of Indians with whom we trade, and to engage as many others as possible, to embrace our friendship and amity."

This last clause, so far even from a *legitimate* provision for the trade in captives, was the severest blow that could have been given its prosperity; for it will be recollected, that none but the prisoners of tribes at war with Carolina, and her Indian allies, were subject to slavery. In the proportion therefore, that she extend her amity and trade to the surrounding nations, in the same measure was the field lessened for the operations of the Indian slave trade.

But one of the expressed designs of the Assembly, in assuming some authority in the direction of the lucrative commerce with the Indians, was to secure the safety of the province by the abatement of its abuses.

The question, however, may be asked, should a Christian people have tolerated such a practice under any form, with or without its abuse?

The circumstances by which the colony was then surrounded, clearly vindicate its humanity as well as its discretion, in the measures enacted for the enslavement of even the poor Indians. As late as 1703, the entire population of Carolina, did not exceed four thousand souls; out of these, there could scarcely have been mustered eight hundred fighting men; yet they were surrounded on every side, except that of the sea, by countless hordes of warlike savages, whose prowess in arms they had already too many reasons to know was formidable; while still more bitter and impressive had been their experience of the remorseless cruelty with which they disposed of their unfortunate captives—a calm, untortured death at the stake even, being far too tame and unexciting to gratify the devilish spirit of revenge, which it was both their nature and glory to indulge.

It was impossible that the colonists could have dealt with such enemies by the ordinary rules of humanity and policy. When captured, as they often were, in the conflicts which took place on the border, or far beyond it, between hostile tribes and friendly nations in alliance with the English, it was absolutely necessary to destroy them there—to shoot them in cold blood in the streets of Charleston, imprison them for life, or ship them to the West Indies as slaves.

A healthful sensibility will hasten to choose the last alternative as the one most honorable, as well as prudential, for an intelligent Christian people; and this was just the course adopted by our forefathers. The famous traffic in African slaves had already begun under the auspicies of the motherland, and her slave ships were opportunely at hand, provided with every necessary appliance for securing similar cargoes on the coasts of Carolina, whence they conveyed them to the West Indies or to the more northern colonies.

This traffic began under the wise administration of Gov. West, and was continued just so long as the safety of the colony required that its numerous Indian captives should be so disposed of, or massacred in the province.

It would appear, however, from the following letter, written by a Catawba trader, one Matthew Toole, to the Board, that this plea for its continuance was protracted through many years. "The Catawbas held a council yesterday in the king's house, and have resolved to go with the English against the French. They want me and my people to go with them, and we are willing to do so, even without pay, on one condition—that we be allowed to keep, as our own property, whatever plunder in the way of *Indian slaves* we may be able to capture." This transpired as late as 1754, in the midst of Braddock's war, and there are frequent intimations in the records, as we approach this period, that Indian captives were used as slaves, and not merely styled such from long previous, but now obsolete usage. Their regular delivery in Charleston, however, and exportation from the province, had, doubtless, ceased long before this period. Few of them were suffered to remain in Charleston after being once disposed of in the market, and the owners of those few, it appears, were to treat them as wards or apprentices. Col. Barnwell, it is recorded, took an Indian boy, and stipulated with the authorities to have him taught letters and a useful trade.

He purchased him for the term of nineteen years, paying down ten pounds, and entering into bonds in the penal sum of five hundred pounds to the Commissioners and their successors, for setting free the said boy at the expiration of that time, and that he shall not export him; and shall, further, educate him in a Christian-like manner, and cause him to be taught some useful trade.*

Those who are at all acquainted with the Indian character, know that the mere fact of their being almost constantly at war among themselves, formed no just ground for the conclusion that either the

* Journal of Indian Affairs.

English, or any other civilized people in contact with them, instigated their hostilities. War was their passion—the necessary excitement to their otherwise indolent natures. Adair says, of the Cherokees, that it was impossible for them to live without war.

The traffic in Indian slaves began about four years after the first settlement of Charleston. The English colonists had already made considerable openings in the forest around their town, and were planting and embellishing farms, and rearing on them in great abundance the domestic animals and fowls, so necessary to the comfort, as well as beauty of an Englishman's home, when the Stono Indians, whose hunting grounds joined the plantations on the west, not caring, or not being able, in their frequent hunting rambles on the border, to discriminate very readily between the tame geese, turkeys and stock of the planters, and the wild birds and animals belonging to the wilderness, freely made game of them to the great injury of the English.

The latter vigorously resented these encroachments, and killed several of the savages while in the act of depredating upon their property. An Indian war was the consequence, in which many of the whites suffered death in return, with the usual barbarities of the red man's vengeance. A strong military force was called for. Those of tho colonists who were not immediately interested in defending the farms, or in retaliating upon the Indians for the loss of relatives, manifested great reluctance to obey the summons. Indeed the treasury was low, and men are not apt to turn out in the public defence without pay.

Gov. West, in this emergency, resorted to the plan of fixing a price upon every savage that should be taken and brought alive into Charleston.

Numerous adventurers now volunteered their services, and the war, after a protracted struggle, was brought to a close by the overthrow of the refractory Stonoes, and the lucrative transportation of many of them to the West Indies. The plan worked well. It was applied to succeeding Indian wars—even to those waged between hostile tribes and the red allies of the English. Hundreds of dangerous savages were thus disposed of in the most humane manner possible under the circumstances, and with a pecuniary reward to the struggling farmers, of which they stood in much need; for their lands, tilled as yet by no efficient laborers, had returned them little else than their bread. A new impulse was imparted to every branch of business, and prepared the way, in a great measure, for the speedy reciprocal introduction into the colony of savages of a darker hue from Africa, whose magic touch converted the before almost valueless plantations into mines of wealth.

And so long as this traffic was regularly and honestly conducted, neither humanity nor good policy had, perhaps, anything to regret. It was not purer, however, than other wordly interests, whose profits are sufficient to excite the rapacity of bad men, and abuses followed apace. We have already shown with what care and assiduity the authorities of Carolina labored to remove these, and to load her with the odium of their existence, is as illogical as it is historically unjust. As well may the whole body of bank officials in the country be charged with robbery, since several of their number proved disgracefully untrustworthy in the last financial panic.

As well may the whole population of the free-soil States of the Union, be charged with the horrors of the middle passage, because so many of their own citizens and seamen are the chief agents in promoting the present contraband slave trade; or the entire people of New England with evils, which surpass, according to a truthful eye-witness, all the calamities of the slave traffic itself, inflicted upon the natives of Western Africa, by the annual importation of her *rum.**

As in the case of the African slave trade, evidently ordered, despite the whining fanaticism of both North and South, in the righteous providence of God, for a blessing upon the negro race, infinitely nobler in its magnitude and preciousness than any ever granted from the same source to the perishing red man; the

* This is asserted by the Rev. Leighton Wilson, missionary to Africa, in his recent interesting work on the tribes of Western Africa. It is very probable that the saintly people of New England are not aware of the fact, that while Southern slave-holders are oppressing the poor negroes with the stupendous wrong of making them work in their cotton and rice fields, *they* are *murdering* them by wholesale, at long shot, with mean rum, in Africa; for, Mr. Wilson being a Southerner, his book has doubtless never reached the luminous regions around Massachusetts Bay.

duty of the colonists was to guide, with a firm hand, the passing course of events which they were appointed to direct, mitigating, as far as possible, the necessary abuses as they arose, and committing the gracious results to the wisdom of Him who first designed them.

Seventeen years after the Stono war, so considerable and lucrative had the peltry trade become, that it was decreed by the Assembly, that an impost duty laid upon its commodities, should supply a revenue to be used in all such emergencies as had inaugurated the traffic in Indian captives. Their preamble strongly sets forth the straitened and exposed condition of the colony. "In the former several invasions of this province, the want of a public treasure hath occasioned such delays in the preparations, and in providing such necessary provisions, men, arms, boats and ammunition, as might easily—by God's blessing—have repelled and utterly defeated the enemy, which, for want thereof, have inflicted and done great depredations on the persons of theire Majesties' subjects and estates in this colony. And since the several persons who employ themselves in trading with the Indians, by reason of the distance, the most convenient place for that trading lyes from the settled part of this colony, cannot possibly, upon like occasions, if any such happens, (which God forbid,) personally give their assistance in defence of this colony; it is, therefore, enacted, that a duty be laid on all skins and furs exported from any part of this province; for every deer skin not stamped or tanned, three pence; for every pound avoirdupois of beaver, seven pence half-penny; for every otter skin, three pence; for every fox or calf skin, one penny; for every boare* skin, six pence; and for every raccoone skin, one half-penny, and soe proportionably for a greater or less quantity to be disposed of, as is hereafter provided." †

In 1695, it was again enacted, for the same purpose, that every skin shipped from Charleston should pay a duty of one penny each. A little later, a specific sum was raised from this impost to discharge the debt incurred by the first expedition against St. Augustine. Indeed, during these early calamitous years of the colony's history, and until the introduction of an efficient complement of laborers by the welcome providence of the African slave trade, her only source of regular revenue was the active peltry traffic with the Indians. As late even as 1686, a fund of three hundred pounds was raised, by assessment on all the people, to defray the expenses of the public defence against the hostile incursions of the Spaniard: for he had "several tymes made incursion into his Majestie's colony, robbing and burning several of the inhabitants' houses, pillaging their stores, and murthering and carrying away divers of his Majestie's subjects."

It cannot be denied, that the government of South Carolina instituted and sustained for years the traffic

* This must be a misprint for bear.

† Statutes of South Carolina, Vol. ii.

in Indian captives and slaves—just as she chooses now to maintain the traffic in negroes—yet has neither the increased enlightenment, nor the enlarged humanity of her people, tended in the least to convince them that in so doing they have been guilty of any great moral wrong. Indeed, thanks to the abuse and opposition of their enemies, the fierce discussions and patient investigations into which they have been driven in defence of their rights and safety involved in this momentous question, have led them almost insensibly, but surely, to an elevated stand-point, from which they decry, at one view, the tottering, crazy systems of social reform that fanatics would foist upon them, and the truthfulness, the unspeakable superiority of their own well-tried institutions.

The full time has come when our people are to light their torches of wisdom from purer fires than those that burn on the altars of Northern fanaticism. The slave trade is no more incompatible with the genius of Christianity, than are the evils incident to poverty and disease in the ordinary providence of God. While the dispositions of mankind remain as they are, certainly no greater calamity could befall the race than that men should become universally prosperous and healthful. In a like sense, has the slave trade been indirectly productive of incalculable moral good; to millions of benighted Africans, and to millions more of native bondmen, it has been as a rock in the heated desert, as a house of refuge from the storm and tempest.

The inexorable logic brought to bear upon this question by numerous able writers of the South is telling silently, but widely, upon the popular mind. The chief obstacle in the way of a complete apprehension of this view of the question appears to be the laudable scruples of many who are yet unable to reconcile the practical details of the traffic in slaves with the right precepts of morality and religion.

Do they not, who thus hesitate, overlook the important fact, that in the arrangements of divine Providence, however distasteful to men, or incongruous with their notions of morality, there are many things that must be left without a word to the decrees of the all-wise Governor of the world. Gamaliel was a good philosopher as well as learned teacher, and his famous argument in relation to a far nobler institution than any that has since attracted the attention of mankind, is not out of place here. If this thing be of God, it will prosper, and the world be vastly the better for it. If it is not, it will speedily come to naught.

It is unnecessary to relate, how that for more than four hundred years, the African slave trade has continued to subsist with various fortunes, but steadfast energy; how the efforts that have been put forth by the great powers of the earth to suppress it, have resulted chiefly in augmenting in a tenfold degree the enormities of its abuses, and how at this moment, the unscrupulous monarchies of Europe, bitterly repentant of their egregious blunder of emancipation, but not of their hatred to the cotton-producing

States of America, have already set about restoring it to more than its pristine vigor, under the fraudulent device of the "apprentice system."

The practical relations of the traffic to the principles and sentiments of a Christian civilization, may be familiarly illustrated. The manufacture of brandy, notwithstanding its lamentable abuse by many, yet supplies the world with one of the necessaries of its domestic and mechanical uses. That was a day of fanaticism and crude notions, which declared the manufacture, and all use of alcoholic liquors unnecessary, and a foul blot upon the piety of the people. Who now, will, so far, risk his reputation, as to persist openly in such an opinion? Yet it is not inconsistent to say, that the *Christian* may not become a professed manufacturer or vender of strong drink, any more than he should become a fanatical shrieker against all who do make such employments their daily business. The abuse of them, is the only legitimate object of his reprobation and attack.

A Christian citizen of South Carolina may not engage in the Southern, domestic trade in negroes; but will he take the ground that *nobody* should do it, because inconsistent with his character and profession? If he does, then, as a consistent, as well as conscientious man, it becomes him to speak out boldly, and assert before the world the injustice and atrocity of all Southern slavery. Let the question be reviewed as it may, there is no neutral ground to stand upon in a fair discussion of it. It is either right in the sight of God, and frought with blessings for both master and slave, or it is not, and deserves the opprobrium and condemnation of every good man. If the first view be the true one, then in no sense, can negro trading be condemned any more, at least, than the manufacture and legitimate vending of alcoholic liquors can be.

Again, war is sometimes a necessary evil, and will continue to be so, as long as sin and pride find a resting-place in the human heart, despite all the unspeakably sublime and foolish morality of the Elihu Burrett school. The manufacture and sale of bowie-knives and Colt's revolvers, becomes, therefore, one of the necessities of national progress and defence, and even, under some circumstances, of individual safety;* and while the intelligent Christian may not resort, for a livelihood, to the manufacture and dissemination of those deadly weapons, he cannot cry down those who do, nor refuse, when duty and patriotism prompt the act, to buy and use them in his own and country's defence with all the strength with which God has endowed him. The opposite sentiment is the prevailing morality of that section, where, for *a consideration*, all the bowie-knives and revolvers used in the country are manufactured.

These illustrations afford, as we conceive, a strong popular argument in favor of slavery as it exists in the South; for there are specific benefits inherent in the institution, and the foreign slave trade, *properly*

---

*The habit, however of carrying deadly weapons should stigmatize every one guilty of it, as a coward and unfit for the society of the decent and virtuous.

conducted, which surpass all the ordinary claims in favor of the uses of alcoholic liquors, and weapons of defence. The following remarks on this important subject from the able and judicious pen of Bishop Elliott, formerly of the South Carolina College, should be read and studied deeply by the people of the upper-country; for the time is already upon them, when manfully, they must contend, as they have never yet contended, for the rights and institutions with which a munificent God has entrusted them; and a soldier fights all the better, for having a clear view, and an immovable appreciation of the faith that is within him:

"It is well for Christians and philanthropists to consider whether, by their interference with this institution, they may not be checking and impeding a work which is manifestly providential. For nearly a hundred years the English and American churches have been striving to civilize and Christianize Western Africa, and with what result? Around Sierra Leone, and in the neighborhood of Cape Palmas, a few natives have been made Christians, and some nations have been partially civilized; but what a small number in comparison with the thousands, nay, I may say millions, who have learned the way to heaven, and, who have been made to know their Saviour, through the means of African slavery! At this very moment there are from three to four millions of Africans educating for earth and for heaven in the so vilified Southern States—educating a thousand ways of which the world knows nothing—educating in our nurseries, in our chambers, in our parlors, in our workshops, in our fields as well as in our churches; learning the very best lessons for a semi-barbarous people—lessons of self control, of obedience, of perseverance, of adaption of means to ends; learning, above all, where their weakness lies, and how they may acquire strength for the battle of life.

"These considerations satisfy me with their condition, and assure me that it is the best relation they can, for the present, be made to occupy. As a race, they are steadily improving. So far from the institution degrading the negro, and keeping him in degradation, it has elevated him in the scale of being much above his nature and race, and it is continuing to do so. Place an imported African—of whom a few still remain—side by side with one of the third or fourth generation, and the difference is so marked that they look almost like distinct races—not only in mind and knowledge, but in physical structure.

"That monkey face, the result of an excessively obtuse facial angle, has become, without any admixture of blood, almost as human as that we are accustomed to see in the white race; and it has a facial angle, as distinctly a right angle as that which belongs to the Caucasian family. The thick lips have become thin; the dull eye is beaming with cunning, if not with intelligence; the understanding is acute and ingenious. Their knowledge, when they have been instructed by missionaries or by owners, is respectable. A man has been made out of a barbarian—an intelligent and useful laborer out of an ignorant savage—a Christian and a child of God out of a heathen: and this is called degrading the African race, by holding them in slavery! Such language is only of a piece with miserably false sentimentalism which is pervading the world: such sentimentalism as thinks it cruel that a child should be disciplined or a criminal punished—which looks so tenderly upon the means as quite to overlook the great *end those means may be working out.* God's ways are not discordant with this way of slavery. He who sees everything in its true aspect—with whom a thousand years is as one day—in whose sight the light affliction of this life, which is but for a moment, is far outweighed by the glory which is to follow, cares very little for the present means through which his will is working. What is it that a man should be a slave, if through that means he may become a Christian? What is it that one, or even ten generations should be slaves, if by that arrangement a race be training for future glory and self-dependence? What are the sufferings—putting them at the worst—which the inhumanity and self-interest, and the restraints of law, can inflict for a few generations, when compared with the blessings which may thus be wrought out for countless nations inhabiting a continent? What is to be the course and what the end of this relation, God only knows. My feeling just now is, that I would *de-*

fend it against all interference, just as I should defend my children from any one who would tempt them to an improper independence; just as I should defend any relation of life which man was attempting to break or to violate, ere the purpose of God in it had been worked out."

CHAPTER IX.

The sites of ancient Cherokee towns abounding in Upper-Carolina—The original limits of the Nation defined—The divisions of Ayrate and Otarre, Upper and Lower Cherokee—Statistics of the Nation, extracted from an original paper copied in London—Catalogue of towns with the names of a few of their chiefs—Seneca, Tugaloo, Keowee, Mudlick, Coronaka and Johnson's Creeks, &c.

Thus far we have taken a general view of the ancient Indian trade, especially so far as it related to the traffic in slaves; we are, however, more particularly interested in that portion of it which belongs to the history of the Cherokees. These were the aboriginal possessors of the upper-country, and the remains of their once populous towns, and the sites of their rude homes, are still to be seen on our valleys and verdant hills. Here the brave Cherokees were intimately associated with the English during all the gloomy years of their colonial history, sometimes as friends and allies, at others as treacherous, dangerous enemies.

The manners, customs and traditions of this once noble people—the curious antiquities that lie scattered over every part of the upper-country, illustrative of their warlike and domestic life—the details and thrilling incidents of the wars waged by them upon the frontier settlements of Carolina, Georgia and Virginia—their romantic conflicts on the border with our Scotch-Irish forefathers—the midnight alarms and horrid butcheries of helpless women and children, and the terrible scenes of their more dreadful tortures in captivity and at the stake, have not yet received due notice at the hands of any chronicler.

We resume, however, for the present, further details of the ancient commercial relations that so long bound together the old English adventurers and Carolinians of Charleston, and the great Nation of the Cherokees. It is important, however, to define, first, as accurately as can now be done, the ancient limits of the Nation, and to trace the names and sites of its then flourishing settlements.

The first white men who penetrated the wilderness of north-western Carolina and northern Georgia, found it in the possession of the Cherokees; and no history relates when their settlements here were formed. Mr. Pickett, in his History of Alabama, informs us—but on what authority it is not stated—that a powerful branch of the tribe at one time occupied lands much farther south than those now embraced in the upper-country. "About the same period," he says—1623—"a large branch of the Cherokees came from the territory of South Carolina, near Charleston, and formed towns upon the main Tennessee, extending as far as the Muscle Shoals."*

---

* Page 154, Vol. i.

The Over-hill settlements, on the Tellico and Little Tennessee, were established, according to the same author, in 1623, by a branch of the Cherokees, who had been driven from the Appomattox by the first settlers of Virginia. Adair thus minutely describes the boundaries of the Nation, as it existed at the period of his sojourn among the southern Indians. "The country lies in about thirty-four degrees of north latitude, at the distance of three hundred computed miles to the north-west of Charleston, one hundred and forty miles west south-west from the Catawba Nation, and almost two hundred miles to the north of the Creek country. The Cherokees are settled nearly in an east and west course, about one hundred and forty miles in length, from the lower towns, where Fort Prince George stands. to the late unfortunate Fort London. They make two divisions of their country, which they term *Ayrate* and *Otarre*, the one signifying 'low,' and the other 'mountainous.' The former division is on the head branches of the beautiful Savannah, and the latter on those of the easternmost river of the great Mississippi."*

The earliest account that has been preserved of the Cherokees, from which it is possible to glean any reliable information in regard to their numbers, and the extent of their settlements, is found in a very interesting paper, taken from the records in London, for Mr. Bancroft, a copy of which was presented by him to Prof. Rivers. This document, prepared origi-

* Page 226—History of North American Indians.

nally by the highest official authority in Carolina, contains a minute statistical report of the strength and locality, in relation to Charleston, of many Indian tribes, in and around the province. It has never before, if we mistake not, been published.*

Just before the Revolution of 1719, the proprietors had made the request of Gov. Robert Johnson, to furnish them with a full statement of the strength of the colony, and of the aboriginal tribes around the English settlement. We select chiefly that portion of the governor's report which relates to the Cherokees. He says: "By the within accounts of the number of Indians subject to the government of South Carolina, in the year 1715, your lordships will find upwards of eight and twenty thousand souls, of which there were nine thousand men who traded with Carolina, besides several small tribes, such as the Congarees, Santees, Seawees, Pedees, Waxhaws, and some Corsaboys; so that by war, pestilence and civil conflicts among themselves, the Cherokees may be computed as reduced to about ten thousand souls, and the Northern Indians to two thousand five hundred.

The Cherokee upper settlements contain 19 towns, 900 men, 480 women, 980 boys, 400 girls; middle settlements, 30 towns, 2,500 men, 900 women, 2,000 boys, 950 girls; lower settlements, 11 towns, 600 men, 480 women, 620 boys, 400 girls—total, 11,210.

It would be a very difficult task to extract from

* Professor Rivers, with his usual kindness and liberality, allowed us the free use we have here made of this valuable record.

the records in Columbia, a complete list of the towns embraced, at any period, in the two divisions of the Cherokee Nation, so confused is the orthography of the names there given, and so indefinite the information relating to their respective situations. In 1751, the following entry was made in one of the Indian books, from the report of a trader:

*Keowee.**—29 warriors, 3 chiefs, viz., Skiagusta, or the Old Warrior; Oruste, the Catawba king, and the Chote king.

Estatowee.—9 warriors, 1 chief, Clugoitosh, the Good Warrior.

Tucksoie.—7 warriors, 2 chiefs, Osquosoftoi and the Raven.

Jommantoo.—1 warrior, 1 chief, Schollokoskie.

Chewohee.—7 warriors, 1 chief, Skiagusta.

Oussazlay.—4 warriors, 1 chief, Johnny.

Kowee.—1 warrior, 1 chief, Jaccutee.

Oustate.—4 warriors, 1 chief, the Yellow Bird.

Stocowee.—3 warriors, 1 chief, Tacitee.

Noquossee.—4 warriors, 0 chief.

Jacasechoo.—5 warriors, 1 chief, Chuchachoo.

Inforshee.—12 warriors, 3 chiefs, the Beaver, his son Skiacow, and Tacitee, the Notched Warrior.

Little Tellico.—7 warriors, 2 chiefs, Sananulohoo and Onaloee.

Tommotly.—7 warriors, 0 chief.

Jollohee.—1 chief, the Prince.

Great Tellico.—16 warriors, 2 chiefs, the Blind Warrior and Cæsar.

* Written Kewhohee.

This is obviously an imperfect statement of the strength of the Nation, at this period. The list presents, however, a few names nowhere else found. Some four years afterwards, in new-modeling the trade, the whole Cherokee country was subdivided into what were called hunting districts, from the record of which we are enabled to extract the following more complete catalogue of towns:

FIRST DISTRICT.

Over Hills.—Great Tellico, Chatuge; Tennessee, Chote and Toqua; Sittiquo and Tallasse.

Valley Towns.—Enforsee, Conastee and Little Telliquo; Cotocanahut, Uayowee, Tomatly, and Chewohee.

Middle Towns.—Joree, Watoge, Nuckasee.

Keowee.—Keowee, Tricentee, Echoee, Torsee; Cowee, Tarsalla, Coweeshee, and Elejoy.

Out Towns.—Tucarechee, Kittowa, Conontoroy; Steecoy, Oustanole, and Tuckasegee.

Lower Towns.—Tomassee, Oustestee; Cheowie, Estatoie, Tosawa; Keowee, Oustenalle.

In the spring of 1776, the Cherokee Nation was visited by Bartram, who supplies, in his interesting journal, several additional names of towns then existing, or just deserted.

Over-hills on the Tennessee and its branches.—Nucassee, Ticoleasa, Conisca, Nowe, Noewe, Clennuse, Ocunnolufte, Chewe, Quanuse, Tellowe, Hiwassee, Chewase, Nuanha, Chelowe, Sette, Joco, Tahasse, Tamahle, Tuskege, Nilaque, Niowe.

Lower towns east of the mountains.—Seneca.

On the Keowee.—Keowee, Kulsage or Sugaw-Town.

On the Tugaloo.—Tugoola, Estotowe.

On Flint River.—Qualatche, Chote.

On other rivers.—Great Estotowe, Allagae, Jore, Nacooche.

Mouzon's map, in Carroll's Collection, adds to the lower Cherokees the following names of towns that were standing as late as 1771, and which we have seen nowhere else recorded.

On the Tugaloo and its branches.—Tururaw, Old Estatohe, Noyowee, Tetohe, Chagee, Tussee, Chicherohe, Echay, Takwashuaw.

On the Keowee.—New Keowee, Quacoretchie.

On the Seneca.—Aconnee.

Adair observes, that several of their best towns on the southern branch of the Savannah are now forsaken and destroyed: as Ishtatohe, Echia, Tugaloo, and others, and they are brought into a narrower compass. At the conclusion of the war of 1760, the traders calculated the number of their warriors to consist of about two thousand three hundred, which is a great diminution in so short a space of time. The Cherokee towns were generally built wide of each other, owing to the scarcity of good situations on the rivers and creeks; it being rare to find in that mountainous region a tract of four hundred level acres.

In the rich valleys, however, of the Keowee,* Seneca and Tugaloo, they were numerous and exceedingly populous; not yet have the leveling operations of Anglo-American progress completely effaced here the deep traces of aboriginal art and life; but when all else have been obliterated, when no wigwam's site or tumbling sacrificial pillar shall remain, the beautiful names of the Seneca, Tugaloo, Keowee and Isundiga,† will continue to proclaim a history of the once blest Cherokee, in accents as soft as the murmur of their waters, and as enduring as their granite falls.

The towns situated on the head waters of the Savannah were not the only Cherokee settlements in that portion of their beautiful Ayrate embraced in the present territory of Upper Carolina. Straggling villages and solitary wigwams were discovered to

---

*Isundiga was the Cherokee name for the ancient Keowee and Savannah. The present name of Savannah was derived from the Shawano or Savannah Indians; a warlike tribe that once lived on its western bank, near the present site of Augusta. Some time after the settlement of Carolina they removed beyond the Ohio. Adair declares they were driven away by the foolish measures of the English. We shall have much more to say of them.

† The name Isundiga, we believe, is now nowhere known in the territory of Pickens District. It should be revived and preserved in the name of some new village or educational institution.

have once stood on all the rivers and creeks whose waters abounded in fish, from the Congarees to the mountains. Several of these were, no doubt, standing as late even as the period when the Scotch-Irish began their settlements in Laureus, Newberry, and other districts.

Eight miles from Dorn's Gold Mine, in a valley of the Long-Cane, on lands belonging to Benjamin McKittrick, is an ancient Indian mound, nearly one hundred yards in length by thirty in breadth. It appears to have been once a lofty as well as capacious terrace, on which might have conveniently stood several other buildings besides the usual great town-house.

This mound was evidently constructed of earth, brought with vast labor from some other spot than the one on which it was reared; and notwithstanding the wastes of time, and the yet more ruinous washings of centuries of floods in the creek, it still rises some three or four feet above the general level of the valley.

When John Duncan arrived upon Duncan's Creek, quite a flourishing Indian village stood upon a hill in the plantation now owned by Major Wm. Young, of that neighborhood in Laurens. The site is still conspicuous for its monumental heaps and other aboriginal remains.*

On the west bank of the Saluda, about a half-mile

* Conversation of Joseph Duncan.

below the old Swansey's Ferry, in Abbeville, is a broad level area excavated from the hill-side, on which stood, in the recollection of the early settlers, an Indian town. A fertile promontory juts from the east into the Coronaka, at the point of its juncture with Black Rock Creek.* On this spot the Cherokees, in primitive times, had a teeming settlement. The ground has been in cultivation time out of mind; yet to this day the instruments of their husbandry and savage arts continue to be turned up from the soil. The spring which supplied them with water still issues from the foot of the hill. The creeks afforded inexhaustible quantities of game and fish. Long after the Cherokees had retired forever from the territory of Carolina, these streams were famous for their fisheries. It is said, too, that the Coronaka,† like the Saluda, was remarkable, in the early periods, for its production of corn. During the Revolution, if tradition is to be credited, many a seasonable supply was gathered from its fertile valleys.

On the west bank of Johnson's Creek, in sight of the Wards road, on the plantation now occupied by Mrs. John Black, is another spot where also abound

* Now Rocky Creek.

† There is no clue to the meaning of the Indian name, Coronaka. We are scarcely better informed of its correct orthography. In Drayton's Memoirs, it is written Cornacre; in Tarleton's Campaigns, Coronacre; in the old district land-plats, Coronaceo, and sometimes Coronaco; in the Indian books, Corenacay, and as often Coronaca. In other records it is written Coronaka; and this method we have adopted.

the unmistakable relics of an ancient Indian town or settlement. They lie scattered over a cultivated field, and among them are the fragments of a rude pottery, which display some taste of design.

In a plantation on Cane Creek, of Pickens District, well known as the Moultrie Tract—having been originally granted by the State to that distinguished officer of the Revolution, but now the property of Major Robert Maxwell—is a famous spot still called Black-bird's Hill, on which, in the memory of living men, a flourishing Cherokee town once stood. Black-bird, the last of its chiefs, and a man of mark among his people, bequeathed his name to the place, after it had borne, perhaps for centuries, the more euphonious Indian name of Cananaska. Like all the grounds in this region on which were found old Indian settlements or their remains, the soil of Black-bird's Hill and its vicinity is remarkably fertile.

In a field on Mudlick Creek, a part of a plantation belonging to Colonel John D. Williams, of Laurens, are five mounds still rising several feet above the level of the valley. These occupy the site of an ancient Cherokee burying-ground, and mark a spot near by on which once stood a flourishing town. They have never been opened; but a sufficient excavation would scarcely fail to disclose their usual contents of human bones, fragments of vases, pipes, and implements of war.

Deep in a forest, on lands attached to the old Colcock Place, now the property of Dr. H. W. Leland,

and in sight nearly of the star-redoubt at Ninety-Six, is a large mound, in which were deposited the bones of generations, perhaps, of the inhabitants of an Indian town, that evidently once existed in a waste field of the same plantation, lying a short distance north of the mound. The usual relics of a once populous Cherokee community are abundant everywhere in its vicinity, as they are also on the hills and valleys of the opposite bank of Ninety-six Creek, in lands owned at present by Captain James Creswell and others.

The Indians were no agriculturists, but they possessed an instinctive appreciation of fertile soil; and hence, for ages, doubtless, before the rich, cane-covered lands of old Ninety-Six greeted the covetous eyes of English speculators and pioneers, they had given sustenance to teeming settlements of the native red men.

There is an interesting mound on the Tiger in Union District, just opposite the battle field of Blackstocks. It stands, if we mistake not, on lands belonging to Dr. Winnsmith, of Spartanburg: it has never been excavated. These curious burial places of the aboriginese are the more interesting from the fact that they were reared, most of them, long anterior to the landing of any white man in America, and are the only notable monuments that now remain in the upper-country, of its native races.

Adair informs us that, till the Cherokees fell under the influence of the English, they were accustomed to deposit, in the same grave with the dead, all the implements and trinkets of which they had been possessed before death. They soon learned, however, from the traders, to preserve these things for the use of surviving relatives and friends. The contents of a mound must therefore often fix the time of its construction, either nearly coeval with the coming of the English, or at a period indefinitely anterior to that event.

Besides these earthern tumuli, found usually in the fertile valleys of the streams, and near the ancient habitations of the Indians, they frequently raised monumental piles of loose stones on the tops of their mountains, hills, and near famous passes. These were in honor of departed chiefs, and other great men. Sometimes the stones were collected and piled on the very spot where a distinguished warrior had fallen in battle; and though rough and unlettered, these rude monuments have mocked, in their durability, thousands of structures of marble and brass, whose exquisite forms were carved and fashioned by the hand of genius and civilization. Many of them are standing at this day, nearly as entire as when the last stone was placed upon their conical summits, at a period in the fabulous past, up to which no history runneth. But whether standing erect or scattered promiscuously around their original sites, they are equally monumental, and never fail to teach the curious passer-by the simple story they contain of aboriginal history.

An old chronicler* observes: "To perpetuate the

* Adair.

memory of any remarkable warriors killed in the woods, I must here remark that every Indian traveler, as he passes that way, throws a stone on the place, according as he likes or dislikes the occasion or manner of the death of the deceased. In the woods we often see innumerable heaps of small stones in those places, where, according to tradition, some of their distinguished people were either killed or buried, and their bones suffered to remain till they could be gathered for regular sepulture at home. On these piles they added Pelion to Ossa, still increasing each heap, as a lasting monument and honor to them, and an incentive to great actions."

Several of these Indian cairns were standing a few years ago, on the romantic top of Gilkey's Knob near Limestone Springs. They were built of white quartz rocks, and looked, in the deep shade of the huge chestnut oaks that surrounded them, like so many motionless spectres on a visit from the blest abodes of the ancient warriors in whose memory they were reared.

We found on the summit of Whitaker Mountain, in the north-west corner of York District, a group of interesting *cairns*. This knob is itself worthy of a visit, for the sake of its noble views. On one side is seen, dotting a vast area, the farm-houses and cultivated fields of North Carolina, fenced in the back ground by the magnificent sierra of the Blue Ridge, encircling nearly one quarter of the horizon. On the east towers near by, in solitary grandeur, the sharp pinnacle of the King's Mountain, supported on the right by its spur of lesser knobs, and among them the humble, but far more interesting summit, on which Ferguson made his last stand against the enemies of his king. Far away on the west, rising from the banks of Broad River, are the wooded hills and plantations of Spartanburg and Union, while the fertile valleys of that noble stream are traced by the deeper green, and denser shade of their forest growth, stretching many miles to the south. The greatest warrior of a more refined race than the Cherokees, might well be proud of a grave and a mausoleum on such a spot.

There are too distinct piles on this mountain: one on each extremity of the oblong top, extending more than a mile from the north-east to the south-west. They are remarkable for their peculiar arrangement. Each monument consisted of a group of cones several feet in height, and placed in an exact circle, some ten or fifteen feet in diameter; a low wall connected them all, presenting the figure of a miniature fortification thickly set with towers. The stones have, long ago, tumbled from their places, or were pulled down by some one curious to discover any treasure they might conceal, and now the whole fabric exhibits a striking resemblance to Ptolemy's ancient diagram of the epicycular motions of the moon.

A great variety of interesting relics of these aboriginal people are found throughout the Valley of Broad River; such as mounds, and the familiar stone implements of their warlike and domestic arts.

But among them some are occasionally brought to view, so curiously and perfectly wrought, as to force the conclusion that they came from the hands of a people far more civilized and ingenious than the race of mound-builders supplanted by our forefathers. We saw in York District a stone, the exquisite carving of which attracted more attention than the singularity of its shape, or the impenetrable mystery of its use.

It had been wrought from the hardest material—one of the yellow quartz pebbles found abundantly in the shoals of the river. Having first trimmed it to an exact cylinder, four or five inches in diameter, and an inch in thickness, the skillful artist then neatly rounded the sharp edges, and, on each of the flat sides, described as perfect a circle as could be constructed by the most improved mathematical instruments. These being described, with some other implement he managed to excavate them to the depth of a quarter of an inch or more into the solid quartz, leaving the edges of the circumference at bottom and top perfectly sharp and smooth. No modern lapidary, with all the tools and appliances of his difficult art, could have given it a better finish.

The traders inform us that the Cherokees—the most skillful artists of all the native tribes—wrought very slowly while carving in wood and stone. It was a month's work for a warrior to fashion one of his ornamented pipes; and they speak of seeing no such fabrication as the above among them, in all their conversations and reports.

In a letter recently received by the author from Dr. Ramsey, of Tennessee, the accomplished writer of the Annals of his State, and whose collection of Indian antiquities, is perhaps unsurpassed in the Union,* he observes of this remarkable stone, that it is, without doubt, a relic of the ancient mound-builders, whose mysterious history has so long puzzled the brains of philosophers.

The use they made of it can scarcely be conjectured; from its elaborate finish, however, it would appear to have belonged to some part of their ceremonial worship. This opinion is corroborated by the fact that a few others, besides the one seen in York District, have been discovered in places widely separated: yet they are all precisely alike, carved with the same exactness, and from the same material—the yellow rolled quartz of the river's bed. If they had been designed for one of their games of amusement, or for some mechanical use, they would scarcely have been wrought with so much elaborate care. One of these stones is preserved in the valuable museum recently presented by Dr. E. R. Calhoun of Greenwood, to the Laurensville Female Academy. It was originally contributed by Dr. Ramsey, of Tennessee. There is another in the extensive private museum of the late Dr. John Barret, of Abbeville: and a third one is in the possession of a gentleman of his vicinity, who procured it while acting as engineer among the ancient sites of the Over-hill Cherokees.

* See Archeological Researches by Squire.

One of the most singular remains of the primitive inhabitants of the upper-country, was discovered a few years ago in the thickest settled part of the village of Greenwood. The objects themselves are not worthy of particular notice; but the situation in which they are found may well excite surprise, and give rise to interesting conjecture. They consist of a number of aboriginal graves, scattered at random over an area of some one or two hundred yards square. One of the mounds lies a few paces in the rear of the Presbyterian Chapel, and is still shaded by the woods. The rest were found south-eastward of this point on the opposite side of the main street.

The question has been often asked by a few, who are interested in such inquiries, when, and under what circumstances were these ancient interments made? Was this retired, densely-wooded spot, used as a burying ground, in early times, by the Cherokees, who had their settlements on the Coronaka and other contiguous streams? Or is it a primitive battle-field on which their warriors met in deadly conflict the more southern tribes, or the warlike Muscogees, in one of their hostile incursions from beyond the Savannah.

With the view of investigating the subject, a few years ago, several gentlemen opened one of the graves, near the house occupied at present by Capt. Wm. H. Griffin. It was found to contain, besides distinct fragments of human bones, the implements that have been described as peculiar to the earliest known sepulture of the Cherokees. A very curious pipe, taken from this grave, was deposited, together with the bones, among the collections of the Laurensville College Museum.

These mounds, unlike the tumuli, already described as forming the common burying place of a village, contain, each of them, the remains of a single body. But like the flint rock cairns, their construction was evidently designed with great simplicity and skill, to secure an imperishable durability. The bones of the dead, with the articles to be interred with them, were first placed upon the surface of the ground; they were then covered, to the depth of several inches, with a mixture of charcoal and ashes—the charcoal being most abundant—and the burial completed by a layer of clay brought from some other place, and piled compactly on till a mound was formed several feet in height.

This simple fabric obviously possessed a property similar to that which constitutes the strength of the arch; the storms of centuries only served to beat more firmly together the mass of clay, and indestructible carbon; so that at this day, though embosomed in primitive woods, and covered with the fallen leaves of an age of autumns, it is still perceptible, and not to be mistaken for any natural formation.

The stratum of clay passed through in the excavation, was a foot and a half in thickness, and, with the ashes and charcoal, formed the only protection to the contents of the mound. It would appear therefore, that only the bones had been originally gathered up and deposited in these graves; for otherwise the beasts of prey that then abounded in these wilds, would scarcely have waited for the departure of those who performed the rites of burial, to tear them open and devour their contents. This was a mode of interment usual with most of the native tribes. It must also be inferred that the mounds were raised about the same time; and the question presents itself, why were so many formed at this spot? No Cherokee town or wigwam stood near it. The Indians never planted their settlements on dry ridges; and much less were their cemeteries found in solitary places. Neither, at the period when these graves were constructed, was there any frequented path passing near the spot. The great Keowee trail, of which we shall speak more fully hereafter, that lead by Old Ninety-Six to Charleston, ran some three miles to the east of this point.

We conclude, therefore, that these mounds mark the scene of an ancient battle; a conflict most probably between strolling war-parties of Cherokees and Creeks.* These powerful nations were constantly waging war upon each other; and abundant evidence will appear in future pages of the fact, that the warriors of the latter frequently crossed the Savannah to cut off the Cherokees, and lay waste their settlements in this portion of their territory.

The signs of aboriginal settlements are no less abundant on the Savannah and Congaree Rivers than

---

* The Muscogees and Creeks were the same people.

on the Broad. The last great floods in those streams washed up from their valleys, and exposed to view a variety of exceedingly curious and interesting remains; some of them belonging to the more modern Cherokees, and others evidently to the ancient mound builders.*

These facts prove incontestably, that, at an early period, though much later than the age of the mysterious race which was supplanted or succeeded by the Cherokees, the whole territory of the upper-country, from the southern border of Richland to the foot of the Blue Ridge, was alive with the flourishing settlements of that great nation. But about the time of the English settlement on the Ashley, they had all well nigh disappeared; their towns were found clustered on the head waters of the Savannah, and in the valleys beyond the mountains, leaving behind them a vast and fertile territory, yielded once more to the sway of wild beasts, and filled with the crumbling remains of their former habitations and rude barbarism. What vicissitudes of fortune, or hostile invasion, produced this wide-spread depopulation and ruin, we leave for those to determine who are better versed in the lore of aboriginal history and tradition.

It was before remarked, that Bartram, the natural-

* Several of the most important of the relics from the Congaree are preserved in the museum of the Presbyterian Theological Seminary at Columbia; and for an interesting description of these and other objects brought to light by the floods in the same locality, see a paper contributed by Dr. George Howe to Schoolcraft's great work on Indian antiquities.

ist and traveler, made an excursion through the Cherokee Nation, in 1776. His notes and observations of this journey are valuable and interesting; they form the only account which we have from so reliable a source, of the condition of the Cherokees at that momentous period. He was in the midst of their towns, pushing his investigations with the boldness and artless simplicity of the true philosopher, only a few weeks before the famous battle of Fort Moultrie, and the nearly simultaneous onslaught made by the deluded warriors upon the frontier settlements of the old Ninety-six District.

On the 15th of May, he set out from Lochaber, the residence of Mr. Deputy Cameron, in the present territory of Abbeville, and arrived late in the evening, after passing through an uninhabited wilderness, at the town of Seneca. He found this to be a very respectable settlement, situated on the east bank of the Keowee River, though the greater number of Indian habitations were on the opposite shore, where likewise stood the council-house, in a level plain, between the river and the range of beautiful hills, which seemed to bend over it and its green meadows. The house of the chief, and those of the traders, with a few Indian dwellings, were seated on the ascent of the heights, on the eastern bank, from which they enjoyed a magnificent view.

Seneca was a new town, had been re-built since the Cherokee war of 1760, when Gen. Middleton and his Carolina auxiliaries broke up the lower and middle settlements. The number of inhabitants was now estimated to be above five hundred, with one hundred warriors. Leaving Seneca the next day, he rode sixteen miles through a noble forest, covering excellent lands, to old Fort Prince George.

Keowee was a most charming situation; but its scenery could not drive from the mind of the traveler painful thoughts of his lonely, exposed situation—by himself in a wild Indian country, a thousand miles from his native land, and a vast distance from any settlements of white people. It was true, there were a few of his own color, but they were strangers; and though hospitable, their manners and customs of living were so different from his, as to afford him but little comfort. A long journey yet lay before him; the savages were vindictive from ill-treatment lately received by the frontier Virginians; blood had been spilt, and the injury not yet wiped away by treaty; the Cherokees naturally jealous of white people traveling about their country, especially if they should be seen peeping among rocks or digging up the earth.

The Vale of Keowee is seven or eight miles in length; it extended that distance from the little town of Kulsage, situated a mile above Keowee, southward, to a narrow pass between the approaching hills. After being detained three days at Keowee, waiting for an Indian guide, who was out hunting, he set out alone across the hills, passed the river at a good ford, just below the fort, which he found to be exactly one hundred yards wide, and riding two miles through delightful plains covered with strawberries, struck the rocky ridge of the rising hills.

Having gained a considerable elevation, a magnificent view burst upon him; the town and valley of Keowee appeared again, with the meandering river speeding through the bright green plains. Four miles farther, he came into another valley, watered by a beautiful river that crossed the path. On the left, he observed, at the base of a grassy ridge, the remains of a town once occupied by the ancients, and by the modern Cherokees, as amply appeared from the great number of mounds, terraces, pillars, and old peach and plum trees in view on the spot.

He passed, the same day, through the Oconee Valley, enriched with hills, and at the base of the Oconee Mountain, came upon the ruins of the town of the same name. Thence climbing to an elevated peak of the mountain, he beheld on all sides of him, a scene inexpressively magnificient and comprehensive. Beyond this mountain, he entered a valley surrounded with an amphitheatre of hills, on whose turf-covered bases he found the ruins of another ancient Indian town.

Early in the forenoon of the next day, after passing over a plain red with fields of ripe strawberries, he came upon a ridge of lofty hills, among which were the remains of the famous town of Sticoe.

Here was also a vast Indian mound and terrace, on which had stood the council-house; an embankment encircled it, and orchards of peach and plum, many of the trees still quite flourishing, were growing around.

He entered next the fertile Valley of Cowe, extending some sixty miles in length, and watered by the head branch of the Tenase. Strawberries were so abundant in the meadows through which his path led, as to dye the hoofs and ankles of his horse. The swelling hills that bounded this valley were a striking feature in its scenery. He observes of them, and of those in the vicinity of all the fertile vales of this region, that they appear to have been the constant situations of the towns and settlements of the ancient mound-builders, and of the more recent Cherokees. He soon after crossed the head branch of the Tenase, and not quite a mile beyond, came to the spot, where, as we shall see more fully in another place, General Middleton, at the head of the Carolinians, met the flower of the Nation, in a decisive and bloody battle. He found the field covered with the conical stone-heaps, in memory of the great number of warriors who fell here. These stood under the forest, on a spur of small hills that projected into the River Valley. The following night he spent in the cabin of a trader, who had married a Cherokee woman, and settled in the midst of the valley, some fifteen miles from its head, on the sources of the Little Tennessee. He was here most hospitably entertained with cream and strawberries, coffee, *bucanned* venison, hot corn-cakes, and butter and cheese. The fruit was brought in by a company of Indian girls, who belonged to a village among the hills, not far off.

Next morning, he set out again for Cowe, situated fifteen miles lower down the valley, and after riding four miles over lands of incredible fertility, he reached the town of Echoe, populous, and consisting of many good houses. Three miles farther, he came to Nucasse, and three more brought him to Whatoga. This was a large town, and riding through it, the road led him winding about through the little plantations of young corn, beans, and other vegetables, up to the great council-house, which was a very large dome or rotunda situated on the top of an ancient mound. The road here terminated, and he had a fine view of the scene, which consisted of innumerable miniature plantations, green and flourishing, with their mingled crops of maize and vegetables, and divided from one another by narrow borders of grass. These marked the bounds of their respective possessions, and every man's house stood in the midst of his lot.

He was now at a loss where to proceed, when he was discovered by the chief of the town, who led him across a grassy ravine, through which ran a beautiful rivulet, to his house on the top of a hill. He describes this chief of Whatoga as a very fine specimen of the physical man. He was about sixty years of age; but still upright, tall and perfectly formed; his countenance cheerful and lofty, and at the same time characteristic of the Indian—the brow being ferocious, and the eye active, fiery and piercing as the eagle's.

After being seated in the house of the chieftan, he was entertained by the women with their usual dishes of boiled venison and corn-cakes, to which was added on this occasion the famous Indian dish of boiled hominy, served with cool milk. Even his horse was furnished with a good bait of corn, which was an extraordinary favor; for the Indians regarded their maize, as given by God, to be used only as the food of man.

Tobacco and pipes were next introduced; the chief filled one of them, whose stem, about four feet long, was sheathed in a beautiful speckled snake skin, and adorned with feathers, and strings of wampum, and having lighted it, smoked a few whiffs, puffing the smoke first towards the sun, then towards the four cardinal points, and lastly over the breast of his guest, after which he handed it to him, as ready for his use. In the conversation that ensued, the Indian inquired if he had come from Charleston, and if he knew John Stewart?

He was greatly pleased with Bartram's answers and manner, and assured him of both friendship and protection in his country.* Setting out from Whatoga, he was accompanied several miles by the friendly chief, towards Cowe, where he arrived at noon, having passed over much exceedingly rich soil. The vale of Cowe exhibited one of the most charming natural landscapes, perhaps, in the world; ridges of hills rising, grand and sublime, one above and beyond another; some boldly projecting into the

* It would appear from this hospitable reception of the botanist by the valley towns, that at this critical juncture, as were the Over-hills, in the beginning of the War of 1760, they were less disposed than any other portion of the Nation to break peace with the English or Carolinians.

verdant plain, their bases bathed with the silver flood of the Tenasse; while others, far distant, veiled in blue mists, mounted aloft with yet greater majesty, and ovelooked vast regions.

In Cowe, he was entertained at the house of Mr. Galahan, an Irishman and a trader, who had been many years among the Indians, and was greatly esteemed by them, for his humanity and probity—a character to which few white men in the same employment could lay claim. He had often been protected by the Cherokees, when all others around him were broken up, their property seized, and themselves either driven from the Nation, or killed in the fury of the exasperated savages.

The next day he went with a trader a few miles out upon the summits of the surrounding hills, to view some remarkable scenes; and having reached the highest point, enjoyed a magnificent prospect of the enchanting Vale of Keowee, not less fertile or beautiful, perhaps, than the famous fields of Pharsalia or the Valley of Tempe; the town itself, the elevated peak of the Jore mountains, a distant prospect of the Jore village in a beautiful lawn, many thousand feet above the position on which he stood; and numerous other towns and settlements on the sides of the mountains, at various distances and elevations.

Descending again towards the town, he came suddenly upon a scene that appears to have interested him even more than the landscape he had just been so rapturously admiring; a company of Cherokee girls sporting in all the freedom of their wild nature in a shady vale of the hills. Some were gathering the fruit of the strawberry; others, having already filled their baskets, lay reclining under the shade, or bathed their limbs in a brook, while a few more gay, were wantonly chasing their companions over the lawn. This was a sight, he declares, too enticing for younger men than himself to behold. He arrived safely, however, soon afterwards, at Cowe.

This town consisted of one hundred houses, built near and on both sides of the Little Tennessee. The Cherokees constructed their dwellings on a plan different from that of the Creeks; they formed an oblong square building of one story, with notched logs, stripped of their bark, and plastered the walls both inside and out with clay, mixed with grass; the whole was roofed with the bark of the chestnut or with oaken boards, and partitioned transversely into three apartments, which opened into each other by inside doors. Their manner of conducting this work was curiously similar to that of the ancient builders of Solomon's Temple; each log and piece of timber was carefully notched and prepared in the woods, and then brought on their shoulders and laid in its proper place upon the building, till the entire fabric was completed.

The council-house at Cowe was a large rotunda, of sufficient capacity to hold conveniently several hundred people. It stood on the summit of an ancient mound of earth that had been thrown up some twenty feet in height; and the building itself being quite thirty more, its pinnacle reaches an elevation of nearly sixty feet above the surface of the earth. This was the usual form, and the artificial mound the common site of the council-houses of all th towns. The Cherokees themselves knew nothing of the origin or first design of those mounds. Their forefathers found them in their present situations when they came from the West and took possession of the country, and the race they supplanted gave no more satisfactory account of them. They were probably used by their builders as sacrificial altars in the public manifestations of their superstitious belief.

The council-house was an imposing fabric, and was thus constructed. They first fixed in the ground a circle of posts about six feet high, equally distant from one another, and notched at the top, for the reception of wall plates. Inside of this was planted another circle of very strong posts, more than twice as high as the first, and likewise notched for a range of beams or plates. Within this again a third circle was ranged of yet larger, stronger and loftier pillars, but fewer in number, and at a greater distance apart. Lastly, in the centre rose the great pillar which formed the pinnacle of the building, at whose top were fastened the upper extremities of the rafters, rising in a sharp pyramid from the last range of plates. Laths, nailed across, secured the rafters and supported the roof, which was usually of bark. The walls were also formed in the same manner. A single large door gave access to the interior, and supplied all the light from without. The Indians harangued and deliberated in their town meetings by the light of their never-absent council-fires. Next to the wall settees were ranged in several circles, one above another, for the accommodation of the people, who assembled in the town-house almost every night in the year, to enjoy some festival or their favorite dances and songs. The settees were covered with mats, curiously woven, of thin splints of the ash or oak.

From Cowe, he penetrated some distance into the country of the Over-hills, but was deterred from proceeding farther in that direction by the dangerous ill-humor of the Indians in this section of the Nation, arising from recent conflicts between them and the frontier settlers of Virginia. Most of the traders had retired from the Over-hill towns. He returned to Cowe, after having turned the summit of the Jore Mountains; and, setting out next day for the low-country, arrived, after two days' travel, again at Keowee.

Renewing his explorations here, he observed in the environs of the town, on the bases of the rocky hills, ascending from the low grounds, a great number of exceedingly curious remains and antiquities. They appear to have been designed by the ancient mound-builders either for tombs or sacrificial altars, and were constructed in the following manner: Three flat stones being set on edge together, were covered by a fourth at top, forming a box-like enclosure, open at one end, and some five feet in length, two in height, and three in width. They were, however, of different dimensions. A trader who accompanied him regarded them as ancient ovens. The Indians themselves could give no other account of them than that their fathers found them in the places where they then stood.

There is scarcely, in all Upper Carolina, a lovelier spot than this ancient valley of the Keowee—more truthfully written Kewohee—or more interesting for its historical associations. True, its cheerful, animated scenes of aboriginal life are no more; not a trace, save a large conical mound near the river's brink, and a few broken relics scattered upon the cultivated soil, and here and there an ancient shade-tree remain to tell the passing stranger that two great Cherokee towns and an English fortress once occupied the spot.

The surpassingly fertile lands of the valley were not its only attractions to a people keenly alive both to agricultural advantages and the romantic combinations of Nature's loveliest forms. The first feature that strikes the traveler approaching it, at the present day, along the remains of the old Keowee trail, is the same that must have first attracted the gaze of the traders and English warriors, who frequented the spot in primitive times—its magnificent mountain scenery.

Just after reaching the head of the ravine in Gab Mountain—itself a historic spot, of which we shall speak in another place—the beautiful valley bursts suddenly upon the view in a grand vista of lofty hills or knobs, ranged on each side of the river, and terminating far away in the dim distance in the picturesque sierra of the Blue Ridge. These mountains are near enough to disclose to the eye their abrupt precipices and naked rocks, and are yet so far removed as to give the imagination full scope to revel among their misty summits, and the deeper gloom of their mysterious gorges.

That portion of the valley in which Keowee town and Fort Prince George stood, appears to the eye, a semi-circular area some four hundred yards in breadth from the river towards the east, and twice that distance from north to south. The Keowee, which runs almost perfectly straight through the valley, forms the base of the semi-circle, while the ranging hills stud the line of its circumference on the east. These hills are yet covered, in great part, with woods, and on their sides are still found the fragments of the ancient Indian works mentioned by Adair, now utterly demolished and scattered. Nearly opposite the point at which the Keowee trail entered the valley, passing close to the present site of Steel's house, was situated the ancient ford, just at the head of a beautiful shoal, that connected Kulsarge, or Sugar-Town, with Keowee. A short distance above this ford, on the west side, the hills suddenly recede from the river, forming another valley of considerable extent, sufficient for the site of Sugar-Town, and a little lower down, at an earlier period, for that of Old Keowee. It was on the demolition or desertion of this town, that New Keowee was built on the eastern bank, opposite to Kulsarge. The oldest Cherokee Indian now living east of the Mississippi, and who spent most of his life near the head branches of the Savannah, or in the Valley of Cowe, informed us, that when Kewhohee was first founded, it was called by that name, but on the erection of a town-house it was changed to Tacite—the meaning of which in English is Sugar-Town. The old man's memory was, doubtless, at fault in this; he probably referred to the town already mentioned by that name, on the western side of the river, and which is often spoken of in the Indian books, not as Tacite but Sugaw, of which Sugar-Town is evidently an English corruption. Sugaw may possibly have been first called Kewhohee, and the name afterwards transferred to the more recent New Kewhohee, when the former received the name of Sugaw. Bartram gives the name of Kulsarge to the town corresponding with Sugaw.

The same venerable Indian, Oosqualooyaie, or the Otter, whom we found living with some fifteen hundred Cherokees on the Tuckasege—a branch of the Tennessee in western North Carolina—informed us further, that Kewhohee, or Keowee, means, in their language, the river of *mulberries;* just as the same race, far back in immemorial time, named their beautiful Ennoree, the river of *muscadines.* The Ennoree is now a turbid stream, discolored by the dissolving clay of a wasting soil; but whatever there is of poetry or beauty in the name Kewhohee,* the stream that bears it merits it all, and more; for we venture nothing in the declaration, that the Kewhohee is the most beautiful river in Carolina. Its waters are still as pure and transparent as when they bathed the limbs of the first boisterous group of Cherokee youths, who lived upon its fertile banks; and when viewed in relation to its numerous dashing shoals, picturesque valleys, and magnificent mountain scenery, it is certainly not surpassed by any stream of equal size and length in the South. There are scenes of beauty on the banks of the Kewhohee and Seneca which are yet destined to awaken in song and architectural combinations the most elaborate manifestations of genius and cultivated taste.

A few miles above Kewhohee, near the juncture of the Toxawaw and Estatoe, is the ancient site of Toxawaw, and on the latter stream, those of Quacoretchie and Estatoe. The latter stood wholly on the west bank of the stream, while the former occupied, in part, both its right and left shores.

Some twenty miles from the juncture of the Seneca with the Tugaloo, near the mouth of Chauga, and in the vicinity of the present site of Bachelor's Retreat, there once stood a cluster of Cherokee towns. On the east side of the Tugaloo, close to one another, were the towns of Old Estatoe, Noyo-

* The Otter is our authority for writing this name, Kewhohee, as well as the various spelling of Keowee and Kewhohee, found in the Indian books.

wee, Tugaloo, Toogoola and Takwashaw. On the west, those of Tehoe, Chagee, Tussee, and two others, a few miles lower down the Tugaloo, whose names are lost, if they are not identical with those mentioned by Adair as having been destroyed by the warlike Muscogees. They have been referred to in another place.

The town of Seneca, which took its name from an immigrant tribe, or the migratory remnant of a tribe, from the province of New York, stood sixteen miles south of Kewhohee, not far from the juncture of the present Little River with the Kewhohee, on the west side of the river. Previous to the coming of the Senecas, it is said that the entire eastern branch of the Savannah was known only as the Keowee. In the old map of Monzon, however, neither the name Kewhohee nor Keowee, appears as belonging to any stream in this region. It gives the name of Keshwee to the present Keowee, from its source to its juncture with the Seneca; and at this point began the ancient Cherokee appellative for the more modern Savannah, which it then bore throughout its entire course to the ocean—the Isundiga.

It would appear from this that the restless Sawannos, like the Senecas, had the address, at a comparatively recent period, to displace from one of the finest rivers of the South, the beautiful name it had, doubtless, borne for immemorial ages, and impress upon its fleeting waters their own forever.

From Keowee he proceeded to Seneca, in which town he again met Alexander Cameron, holding a talk with the lower chiefs on the important question at that time agitating the entire Nation. The Indians were undetermined what course to pursue, and a general council was appointed to assemble as soon as possible in one of the Over-Hill towns. It was from this talk that they rushed, tomahawk in hand, July 1st, 1776, upon the defenceless settlements of the old Ninety-Six District.

CHAPTER X.

First Packs of Goods sent up by the Board to the Cherokee Towns—Col. James Moore and Charite Hayge, the Great Conjurer of Tugaloo—They agree upon a Commercial Treaty—A Trading Post and Fort to be erected at the Congarees—John Sharp and Sam. Muckleroy—Incursions of the Yamassees from Florida, &c.

No direct mention is made in the State records of a traffic with the Cherokees, previous to the assumption of the management of the peltry trade by the public authorities of the province in 1716. In that year it is stated that goods had been sent up by order of the Assembly for their use. This was done in compliance with a sort of commercial treaty, formed at this period, with the Cherokees through the diplomacy, on the one side, of Col. James Moore, and of Charite Hayge, a distinguished conjurer and friend of the English, on the other. It was stipulated that there should be a regular exchange of goods and peltries between Charleston and the Nation. The goods were to be transported from the former place by water or by pack-horse trains as far as Savannah Town,* where the Indians had promised to bring

* Savannah Town or Fort Moore. It stood a short distance below the present site of Hamburg.

their peltries and furs, and thence convey the goods back to their settlements.

It was also agreed that a trading house and fort should be built the approaching fall, at a place known as the Congarees, the Conjurer promising to repair thither, at that time, with eighty warriors—one half of whom were to assist in cutting logs for the fort, and the other to carry the goods, expected to be brought up by the English that far, the remainder of the distance to the Cherokee towns.

According to the present value of the pound sterling in our currency, ten thousand dollars' worth of goods were sent up to Savannah Town as soon after the conclusion of this treaty as pack-horses could be procured to convey them; and it is perhaps worth relating, that a pair of white horses, kept by Robert Daniel, the then presiding Governor, for his carriage, were among those that formed the first great pack-train that went up from Charleston, under provincial authority, to a Cherokee trading post. They had strayed away from their stalls in town, and having been taken up in the country by those who were out in search on the common range for horses to be used in the pack-train, were pressed into that service, the Governor being indemnified from the public funds.

The first chief agent who is mentioned as having been placed by the commissioners over the factory at Savannah Town, was Capt. Theopholus Hastings, assisted by John Sharp and Sam Muckleroy. Hastings appears to have been a competent and reliable officer, enjoying the full confidence of the Board. At a later period, in some important emergency relating to the Chickasaws, he was sent to reside among that people. Previous to this change, however, he had presided for some time over the Cherokee trade at the town of Tugaloo.

Major Wm. Blackeney succeeded him at Savannah Town with the assistance of Capt. Charlesworth Glover.

The colony was suffering greatly at this juncture from the terrible effects of the general Indian war, that had broken out the year before. It continued to be harrassed by vengeful attacks of the Yamassees, who, though driven into Florida from their ancient seats in Carolina, frequently came up in stealthy scalping parties, and fell upon the defenceless families living on the outskirts of the settlements. Pressed by these dangers, the public authorities had erected on the frontiers two small forts, and besides their garrisons, kept in the same region of country a body of mounted rangers. Capt. James Moore, it appears, commanded these, and was discharging the duties of that position when he negotiated the treaty of commerce and amity with Charite Hayge.

Of the forts thus built, one was placed in Apalachia, the present territory of Georgia, and the other at Savannah Town, about a mile below the modern town of Hamburg in Edgefield, destined to become a great centre of trade with the Cherokees, who were now at peace with the English. It received the name of Fort Moore, in honor of James Moore, the father of the Colonel of Rangers, who, a short time before, had been governor of the province; and in the latter part of his term had led a triumphant foray against the Apalachian Indians. Col. James Moore, the son, became, afterwards, no less distinguished than his father, by finishing the work begun by Col. Barnwell against the Tuscaroras and other Indians of North Carolina, whom he completely subdued.

Though Fort Moore, and the one beyond the Savannah, were built in 1716, that at the Congarees, contrary to the agreement with Charite Hayge, was not erected till two years later. The reason assigned by the Board for deferring the work was, that the trading house and garrison at Savannah Town were sufficent for the trade until the Cherokees had concluded the war they were at that time waging with a branch of the Muscogees.

Hewit remarks of this fort that with the others it was erected for the special purpose of defence and against the same dangers. If the records must be credited, however, it would appear that the Cherokees themselves requested that it should be built in view of their increasing traffic with the English; and it was in compliance with that request, and the enlarged demands of the trade, that in the summer of 1718 a body of men was sent up from Charleston to be employed in its construction.

In August of that year, Capt. Charles Russell, who, at the recommendation of the Board, had been appointed by the governor the first commandant of the fort, was ordered to proceed to the country, and there enlist the men who were to constitute its garrison as soon as it should be completed. Among those who were thus enlisted for this service, were Ralph Dayton, John Evans, and Edward Darlsley, the first soldiers who ever did duty in the old fort at the Congarees.

We have before us an extract from the instructions given by the Board to one Dauge, an assistant agent among the Cherokees, in relation to the public work at Congarees:

"You are to proceed at once to the Cherokee Nation, and, on your arrival, inform the Conjurer and other head-men that, in a month or six weeks, we shall have a settlement at the Congarees, to which place they may resort, and procure whatever goods they may need; that we would have built the fort earlier than this, if some of our people had not run away with the boat which had been prepared to carry up the men and implements necessary for its construction. Inform the Conjurer also, that we expect him to hasten down in order to meet at the Congarees with a supply of provisions, the train of pack horses, which is now on its way with the men and tools to be employed on the fort, and with a quantity of ammunition for the Cherokees."

In the fall of the previous year, 1717, the Board had said to a trader just setting off for the Nation: "Acquaint Charite Hayge that our new Governor Johnson has arrived, and we will speedily fix a garrison and factory at the Congarees, whence the

Cherokees may be supplied with arms and ammunition.*

Samuel Kinsman was the head carpenter, who executed the work, and was paid nine pounds per month for his services. As this fortress was designed simply as a safeguard for the goods and other property belonging to the trade, accumulated here, it was of no more formidable construction than a common stockade inclosure.

The name was derived from the Congaree Indians, in whose settlement it had been built. It stood on or near the site occupied, in after-years, by old Fort St. John's, a short distance above the mouth of Congaree Creek, near the present City of Columbia. Here was once the great centre of trade for the Catawbas, and Middle and Lower Cherokees. The Over-hills traded chiefly at Savannah Town.

Lawson visited this spot in his explorations in Carolina, long before it became of any importance to the English, and while yet in the possession of its native population. His description of the surrounding country will be readily recognized as a truthful picture by all who have once seen its modern aspect. "The next morning Santee Jack told us we should reach the Indian (Congarees) settlement betimes that day. About noon we passed by several fair savannas, very rich and dry, seeing great copses of many acres that bore nothing but bushes about the bigness of box trees, which, in their season, afford great

*State Journals in Secretary of State Office.

quantities of small black-berries, very pleasant fruit, and much like to our blue huckleberries that grow on heaths in England. Hard-by the savannas we found the town, where we halted. There was not above one man left with the women, the rest being gone a hunting, for a feast. The women were very busily engaged in gaming. The names or grounds of it I could not learn, though I looked on above two hours. They kept count with a heap of Indian grains.

"When the play was ended the king's wife invited us into her cabin. The Indian kings always entertain travelers, either English or Indian, taking it as a great affront if they pass by their cabins. The town consists of not above a dozen houses—they having other straggling plantations up and down the country, and are seated upon a small branch of Santee River. Their place hath curious, dry marshes, and savannas adjoining to it, and would prove an exceeding fine range for cattle and hogs, if the English were seated thereon.

"These Indians are a small people, having lost much of their former numbers by intestine broils; but most by the small-pox. We found here good store of chinkapin-nuts, which they gather in winter, great quantities of, drying them, and keeping them in great baskets. Likewise hickerie-nuts, which they beat betwixt too great stones, then sift to thicken their venison broth therewith; the small shells precipitating to the bottom of the pot whilst the kernels, in form of flour, mixes with the liquor.

"The Congarees are kind and affable to the English; the queen being very kind—giving us what varieties her cabin afforded—loblolly made with Indian corn and dryed peaches. These Congarees have abundance of storks and cranes in their savannas. They take them before they can fly, and breed them as tame as dung-hill fowls. They had a tame crane at one of their cabins that was scarce less than six foot in height, his head being round with a shining crimson hue, which they all have.

"These are a very comely sort of Indians, there being a strange difference in the proportion and beauty of these heathen. The women here being as handsome as most I have met withal, being several five-fingered brunettos amongst them. These lasses stick not upon hand long, for they marry when very young, as at twelve or fourteen years of age.

"We saw at the king's cabin the strangest spectacle of antiquity I ever knew—it being an old Indian squaw, that, had I been to have guessed her age by her aspect, old Parr's head, the Welch Methusalem, was a face in swadling clouts to hers. Her skin hung in reaves like a bag of tripe; by a fair computation, one might have justly thought it would have contained three such carcasses as hers then was. From what I could gather she was considerably above one hundred years old, yet she smoked tobacco, and eat her victuals, to all appearances, as heartily as one of eighteen. At night we were laid in the king's cabin, where the queen and the old squaw pigged in with us.

"In the morning we rose before day, having hired a guide the over night to conduct us on our way. The queen got us a good breakfast before we left her; she had a young child which was much afflicted with the colic, for which she infused a root in water, held in a gourd; this she took in her mouth, and spurted it into the mouth of the infant, which gave it ease. After we had eaten, we set out for the Wateree Indians."

Savannah Town received its name in the same manner as the Congarees, from the Sawannos or Savannah Indians, who once lived on the banks of the Savannah, and who, Adair tells us, were driven thence by the mismanagement of Carolina officials. It is certain, that, in the days of Gov. Glen, as we shall presently see, they became exceedingly troublesome to the northern settlements of the colony, from their new seats on the Ohio.

The ancient site of Fort Moore can now be scarcely traced, even by the most diligent antiquary. An old writer, who probably visited the spot at the commencement of the present century, thus describes it: "A little below Hamburg, Edgefield District, is the bluff on which formerly stood Fort Moore, so celebrated in the early history of this State. The site is precipitous, perhaps ninety or a hundred feet high. In the early settlement of the province, a frontier garrison was kept at this place, to protect its inhabitants against the Muscogee, or Creek Nation, and other Indians.

On one occasion, previous to the emigration of the

Savannahs, but after the erection of the fort, there was exhibited here, by a famous Muscogee warrior, a feat of cool, daring intrepidity, the relation of which will serve to impress upon the memories of our youthful readers, the history of this once interesting spot. This warrior had been taken prisoner by the Savannah Indians, and having been bastinadoed in the usual manner, he was condemned to be burnt. They bound him to a stake, where he underwent a great deal of torture without showing the least concern; his countenance and behavior were, as if he suffered nothing from the glowing hot irons applied by his enraged enemies to his naked body. He told them, in a manly voice, that he was a very noted warrior, and had acquired most of his martial honors at the expense of their people; and that now, in the act of dying, he was anxious to show them that he was still as much their superior as when he led against them his gallant war parties. That although he had fallen into their hands, by forfeiting the protection of the Divine Power through some impurity or other, when carrying the holy ark of war against his devoted enemies, yet he still had virtue enough remaining to enable him to punish himself more exquisitely than all their despicable ignorant crowd could possibly do, if they would but give him liberty by untying him, and hand him one of the red-hot gun barrels from the fire.

The proposal and manner of address appeared so exceedingly bold and unusual, that his request was granted. Whereupon, seizing suddenly one end of the red barrel, and brandishing it from side to side, he forced his way through the armed and astonished multitude, leaped down a prodigiously steep and high bank, into a branch of the river, dived through it, ran over a small island, and crossed the other branch, amidst a shower of bullets from the commanding ground, where Fort Moore, or New Windsor garrison, stood. And though numbers of his indignant enemies were in close pursuit of him, he took shelter in a bramble swamp, and in that naked, mangled condition, reached his own country without further injury.*

At this period, Savannah Town and the Congarees often presented scenes more boisterous and busy than many a commercial town of the present, with far more pretension in situation and trade. On their outskirts are encamped numerous caravans of pack-trains, with their roistering drivers, who are mostly mischievous boys. The smoke from a hundred camp-fires curl above the thick tops of the trees, and the woods resound with the neighing of horses, and the barking and howling of hungry Indian dogs. A large supply of goods has arrived from Charleston, and every pack-saddle came down from the Nation loaded with skins and furs, and these being now displayed to the best advantage, the work of barter begins.

In the open air and in the trading-house are congregated a motley assembly of pack-horsemen, tra-

---

* Mills' Statistics.

ders, hunters, squaws, children, soldiers, and stately Indian warriors—some silent and grave, seemingly uninterested in the scene; but the greater number loudly huxtering, and obstinately contending over their respective commodities in trade, in many barbarous tongues.

The hunters from distant wilds want a supply of powder and ball, each squaw fancies some bright-colored fabric for a new petticoat or dress, while the warriors and old men eagerly demand guns, ammunition and blankets.

The clamor begins, however, presently to subside, and at length the last bargain has been struck, and the goods and peltries have alike changed hands. The packs are once more made up: the goods for the Indian towns, and the skins for the market on the seaboard, and everything is again ready for the trail. The boys crack their whips, and with shouts and halloos that make the forests ring, the trains enter the narrow paths, and are soon far on their way, leaving the garrisons and agents of the posts to the dull monotony of the wilderness till their next visit.

The duties of the agents at these posts were simply, yet highly responsible. They were to take charge of all goods, wares and merchandise, sent up by the Board, and barter the same to the Indians in amity with the English, receiving in exchange skins, furs, leather, slaves, and whatever else of a marketable value they might offer.

No hostile Indians were to be supplied with arms and ammunition, and none connected with the trade were to be credited, even with the value of a single skin. This excellent rule was, however, never properly enforced; it soon fell into disuse, and many evil consequences, both to the whites and Indians, was the result. The principle of the cash system is sound and just for all parties, and should be observ-ed under every condition in which commerce offers her commodities to the necessities and wants of mankind.

The Board caused to be prepared in Charleston a special brand, with which the skins and slaves of the Cherokee traffic were all to be marked at the trading posts; a similar one had also been sent up to be used in the Catawba trade. The brand of the former was $^{C}_{H}$ cut in iron, which impression was to be burned into the skin of the slave by a heat sufficient for the purpose. This practice, it must be related, however, to the credit of the Board, was discontinued as far as slaves were concerned before the end of 1716. Instead of the brand of iron, the Board enjoined the use of gunpowder and oil, which was pricked into the skin of the slave, in the same manner as the Indians frequently tattooed themselves.

As late, however, as the summer of that year, we find it recorded, that one John Ballantine, a merchant of Charleston, was paid, by order of the Board, a pound and ten shillings for three iron brand marks, to be sent up for the use of the factors in marking the public skins and *slaves.*

To what part of the body these brands were applied we are not precisely informed. The Spaniards, who enjoy the honor of having first used this instrument in America, branded their Indian slaves upon the back of the shoulder, where the mark would be conspicuous, and not easily obliterated by the slave himself.

The following record was made February 1717: the public store-keeper, in Charleston, in the employment of the Board, informs them that he had bought six slaves from neighboring Indians. It is ordered that the slaves be sold next day at auction, with the condition that they be exported within a month. Further on it is again stated, that these captives had been accordingly sold, and singly, except a woman who had been put up with her child. Five others were sold in the same month in like manner, and brought one hundred and twenty-two pounds and five shillings the entire gang.

The traders and agents were prohibited from purchasing any male slave older than fourteen years; in a short time, this restriction was extended to thirty years, so much had the business of the traffic increased. No agent was allowed to trade on his own account, not even to receive a present from the Indians, except in behalf of the public.

The following were the rates of barter agreed upon by Col. Moore and the Conjurer: A gun was to be equal in value to thirty-five skins; one yard of strouds cloth to eight skins; a white duffil blanket to sixteen skins; a hatchet to three; a narrow hoe to three; a broad hoe to five; thirty bullets to one;

a pair of scissors to one; a knife and string of beads to one each; twelve flints to one; a laced broad-cloth coat to thirty; an axe to five; a pistol to twenty; a sword to ten; a shirt to five; a piece of steel to one; a calico petticoat to fourteen; and a red girdle to two.

The first adventure, in trade, made by the Board with the Cherokees was in March of 1716, and by the following November, so greatly had the traffic enlarged that Hastings requested of them to be allowed the services of five assistants instead of two. A laced hat brought readily, at Savannah Town, eight buck-skins; a calico petticoat twelve; and so great was the demand for salt, gunpowder, tea-kettles and looking-glasses, that the Commissioners fixed no price upon them, leaving the traders to exact as muc. as the savages were willing to pay for such things.

It was, no doubt, the abuse of this privilege that led the Indians at this time to complain to the Board of the high rates of barter agreed upon by Colonel Moore and the Conjurer.

Of the five assistants granted at the request of Hastings, one was placed at the town of Terrequa, one at Quanassee, one at Chote, one at Tugaloo, and one at a town towards the north.

The following articles, among others, were soon after sent up by the Board to Hastings, to be used at the branch of his agency situated in the town of Tugaloo: a lot of *brands*, *bolts*, *locks* and *shackles*. The traffic in rum was so exceedingly profitable that the Board found it impossible to restrain it within proper bounds; but hoping, at least, to mitigate its terrible effects upon the misguided Indians, it was permitted the unscrupulous white men who engaged in it, to make a legal admixture of one-third water and two of rum. The Indians, who were not wanting in penetration, nor in *taste*, when strong drink was in question, soon sent up the complaint, that their rum was so nearly water as to be unfit for use. The traders had taken advantage of the amiable concession of the Board, and reversed the standard mixture to *two-thirds water* and *one of rum*.

Moved by these complaints, and the deplorable inroads made by intemperance upon the Indian population, Governor Daniel, in a council of all the kings and head-men of the tribes in amity with Carolina, stipulated, at the request of the chiefs themselves, that no more rum should be carried up to their country; and further decreed a heavy penalty for the violation of this article of the treaty at that time solemnly ratified.*

He had just as well have treated, however, for the cessation of the daily motion of the earth; neither the traders nor the Indians observed it a moment longer than the delay necessarily incurred in conveying up a fresh supply of strong drink. The young men of the several tribes soon after took occasion to declare, in a body, their utter disgust at this article of the treaty, and threatened death to every head-man concerned in making it, if it was not set

* Lawson's Carolina, page 203.

aside, so that they might buy rum freely when they went to the houses of the English.

Lawson tells us, that the Indians themselves engaged in the business of bringing up and selling rum to their people; as much, at least, as remained over and above what they appropriated to their own use on the trail between Charleston and their Nation; for the same narrator adds: "Sometimes they cannot forbear breaking their cargo, but sit down in the woods and drink it all up, and then halloo and shout like so many Bedlamites. I accidentally once met with one of these drunken crews, and was amazed to see a parcel of drunken savages so far from any Englishman's house; but the Indians I had in company informed me, that they were *merchants*, and had drunk all their stock, as is very common for them to do.

"But when they happen to carry it safe—which is seldom, without drinking some part of it and filling it up with water—and come to an Indian town; those that buy rum of them have so many *mouthfuls* for a buck-skin—they never using any other measure—and, for this purpose, the buyer always makes choice of his man, which is one that has the greatest mouth, whom he brings to the market with a bowl to put the liquor in. The seller looks narrowly to the man's mouth that measures it, and if he happens to swallow any down, either through wilfulness or otherwise, the merchant, or some of his party, does not scruple to knock the fellow down, exclaiming against him for false measure. Thereupon the buyer finds another mouth-piece, so that this trading is very agreeable to the spectators, to see such a deal of quarreling and controversy as often happens about it, and is very diverting."

The rates of barter agreed upon could not, in the nature of the case, be long permanent; wild animals, after a while, grew scarcer and more difficult to entrap; the hunting range became much more extensive, and the business of pursuing them to their haunts a toilsome labor. The Indians soon began, therefore, to complain to the authorities that, with the greatest efforts and the most assiduous industry, they were unable to procure skins and furs in sufficient quantities to purchase for themselves, at the existing rates, the necessaries of life.

As may be now well conjectured, however, the greatest obstacle to the prosperity of the peltry trade, at this period, was not so much the scarcity of game, nor the increasing toil of taking it, as the rapid and marked degeneracy of the Indians themselves in native energy and manliness. The abuse of strong drink, to which they appear to have had an irresistible constitutional tendency, and which, we have seen, their agents and traders, with few exceptions, encouraged without stint, made sad havoc of their primitive strength and vigor. And no sooner did they see that the chief management of their trade had passed into the hands of the public authorities from those of the old traders, who used to traffic with them on their own account, and under circumstances altogether favorable to the independence and integrity of the Indian character, than they shrewdly conjectured, at a glance, the true cause of the change—not so much the importance of the peltry traffic as their own importance—a numerous warlike people on the mountain border of a growing civilized community, and from that moment like, all protegés and parasites of public patronage, relaxed their ancient manliness, and in all exigencies ceased to look so much to their own strength as to that of their great father in England and his white children of Carolina.

The visits of their head-men to Charleston became more and more frequent; their palavers or talks with the governors longer, and more insolent, and their demands for presents unceasing and annoying. So urgent indeed, oftentimes were their real wants, that notwithstanding the chief difficulty lay in their own indolence, they become objects, rather of our commisseration than contempt.

In order to maintain the trade at all, now that the Indians had been taught to look to it for the supply of all their wants, it was absolutely necessary for the Board, having already, under frequent complaints, greatly lowered the rates of traffic, to fix a point below which they must not go; and even to withhold goods, if the Indians were not prepared to comply with it. Better, by far, for them, however, both morally and physically, if they had never seen a white man—had never been made acquainted with the subtle arts of his civilized intercourse and commerce, nor learned to admire the bright colors of his fabrics and painted baubles; but have retained their old beloved manners and simplicity, though decked only in the skins of wild beasts, and armed with no other weapons than the rude club and bow and arrow. They were then a happier, and in every sense, a nobler people. Moral integrity and love of the first Great Cause, even among heathens, have their virtue and earthly rewards.

This state of things had a tendency, not only to subvert the Indian character, but to depreciate, as well that of the traders. The men of probity and tone, who once figured in these exciting scenes, were now well-nigh banished the nation; with here and there an honorable exception; the traders became as despicable as the barbarians among whom they lived—many of them were mere vagabonds, wandering from place to place in the country, subsisting as chance favored them—the objects of contempt even to the savages themselves. Many of this class had been attracted to the Nation by the easy opportunities it afforded them to furnish valuable peltries to other marts than Charleston, thus evading the prescribed duties, despite the authority of the Board, and securing to themselves the profitable immunity of under-selling the public agents of Carolina.

The colony of Virginia was most prolific of these intruders, and gave the Governor and Board of Indian Trade in Carolina much annoyance. They first remonstrate through their agents with the offending traders: "Say to the intruders from Virginia," it was often charged them when setting out from Charleston for the Nation, "that they have no right to traffic, either with the Cherokees or Catawbas, without a license from us; and that their peltries must be brought down to Charleston to be disposed of; or, if they choose to send them to other markets, they must be required to come themselves to Charleston, and pay on them the regular duties."

These independent traders, however, from Virginia, and not a few from Carolina herself, knew that while individual enterprise was forbidden, if they preferred to smuggle, the game was in their own hands, and hence paid little regard to such remonstrances. In 1718, Elieazer Wiggon, of Euchee memory, who was then trading with the Catawbas, represented to the Board, that that nation was greatly dissatisfied with the Charleston traffic: goods were ill-supplied them by the authorities there, and the few that came they were taxed to transport over the trail from the Congarees, where their warriors were frequently cut off by the lurking enemy. On the contrary, the Virginia traders, they assured him, brought them large quantities of goods on their own pack-horses, with their own drivers, giving the Indians no trouble whatever, which they sold at prices considerably lower than those that had been fixed by the Board in Charleston.

These complaints of the Indians were, therefore, wholly excusable, and the dangers to the public monopoly pressing. In a letter to Captain Hutton, of Tugaloo, the Commissioners remark: "As to what you say concerning the Virginian traders, we are sensible of the great mischief they do us, in more than one respect, by interfering with our Indian trade, and still hope that the Assembly will consider their case, and contrive some means of circumventing them."*

During many years, the Indians themselves, under the familiar name of "*burdeners*," carried on their backs all the goods and peltries that made up the staple of their trade with the English, except the cargo of an occasional pettiauger,† that risked the precarious water-route from Charleston to Savannah Town. These voyages were quite frequent in the early years of the trade; for though exceedingly dangerous, always detrimental to both peltries and goods, from long exposure to dampness and salt water, and much more protracted than a pack-horse carriage by the direct trading path; yet, in the fierce predatory wars that then so frequently subsisted between the Cherokees and Muscogees, the main current of the Savannah was a much safer place for rich cargoes of peltries and goods, than the woods and thickets where lurked stealthy bands of hostile Indians, watching for an opportunity to take both the goods and scalps of the carriers.

Now, towards the close of 1718, when all the Southern Indians had learned, in great part, the importance and justice of respecting one another's trade with the whites, partly from its growing lucrative-

* Journals in Secretary of State's Office.

† Spanish name for a kind of boat.

ness, but more from the ever-increasing wants and necessities engendered by all legitimate commerce, and peculiarly operative among a people just emerging from the simplicity and negative comforts of the savage state, we find in the Cherokee traffic that the hazardous pettiauger, and the oppressive custom of carriage on the path, by Indian burdeners, were abandoned for the safer and far more expeditious conveyance on the backs of pack-horses.

The country abounded in wild horses, and the sides of the trading path in luxuriant pastures of cane and grass. "Tell the Cherokees," writes the Board, to their agent at Tugaloo, "we shall hereafter endeavor to ease them of the labor and trouble of carrying burdens. Pack-horses are now being collected to take their places on the trail." In the summer of 1717, Captain Hastings had written from the same town, to General James Moore, the following missive: "I send by these fellows four hundred and seventy-three beaver-skins—fifteen packs and twenty-three skins over—thirty to the pack. Give each man for the carriage, one fourth yard of stroud-cloth, and to those you load back, a pair of *half-thicks* each, or cotton stockings."

A few months previous, the Conjurer, Charite Hayge, had, with the assistance of ninety-one burdeners, conveyed from Charleston to Tugaloo one thousand four hundred and thirty-seven pounds sterling worth of goods, for which service they each received *two yards* of duffil-cloth.

The Board likewise ordered, at this time, a good

pasture ground to be prepared at the town of Tugaloo, for the use of the horses, and provisions to be collected at the same place for their pack-horsemen.

The urgent complaints of the Indians, when used as burdeners in the trade, were truly well-founded. Their hardships were not alone confined to the toil of conveying on their heads or backs, often in the sultry heats of summer, heavy bales of skins and goods, more than three hundred miles, but while thus encumbered, they not unfrequently fell an easy prey to treacherous enemies, who ambushed their trails.

In the fall of 1717, a party of burdeners on their way from Keowee to Charleston, headed by a chief of that town, and conveyed by an assistant trader named John Sharp, was attacked on the path near Saluda Old Town by a party of roving Cowetas. Several of the burdeners were killed in the flight that necessarily ensued, and among them a son of the chief. Seven hundred and seventy skins were the booty of the assailants. The record adds—"And John Sharp was standing in front of the Keowee party when the Cowetas fell upon them."*

Bartram met an aged Indian in one of their towns of the Mississippi Valley, who could remember when his tribe used no implements but those of native manufacture; and he informed the naturalist that he was the first man who brought the white people's goods into his town, which he did on his back from

* Commissioners' Journal.

Charleston, five hundred miles on foot, for they had no horses then amongst them.

Notwithstanding the remonstrances of the Board, and the interested opposition of the Carolina traders, the intruders from Virginia continued, year after year, to disturb the traffic and lessen its profits. Yet among them there were several who conducted a regular and honorable commerce with the Indians, under licenses from the Board in Carolina. These were, Nath. Evans, Richard Smith, George Smith, David Crawly, John Evans, Richard Jones, Thomas Edwards, Henry Tally and Wm. Dettipoole.*

These ancient traders penetrated to the towns of the Over-hills by a famous war path that had been known to the Cherokees, and the more northern tribes, time immemorial. Passing down the North Fork of the Holston, into the modern territory of Tennessee, it crossed that stream near the present site of Rogersville, thence diverging to the south-west till it reached the French Broad, it pursued the northern bank of this river to within a short distance of its mouth, crossed into the valleys lying between it and the Little Tennessee, and thence across the latter stream, at the mouth of the Tellico and the Hiwassee, as far westward as the present town of Chattanooga.† In the valleys of the Little Tennessee and the Tellico, it branched in every direction among the villages and settlements of the Over-hills.

* Commissioners' Journal.

† Dr. Ramsay's History of Tennessee.

It is melancholy to relate, on authorities that can not well be doubted, that one of the most serious evils, both to the Indians and the whites, with which the trade had to contend at this period, was the settling on the border of ignorant, dissolute clergymen, who came, pretending to be missionaries of the Cross. Adair does not hesitate to affirm that this, with the general license system, lay at the bottom of all the misrule and abuses that prevailed. The Indian country was infested, the morals of the natives corrupted, and their civilization and improvement put far out of reach of common means.

But these scandalous sins of commission in high places, were not all the offence—would to God they had been! From the beginning of the colonial settlement a deep wrong had been done the wild children of the forest, in withholding from them not goods, not powder, and lead, and guns from Charleston, but the truth of the Gospel, whose whole tendency would have been to remove their savage ferocity, to elevate them as a people, and render them both more profitable and less dangerous as neighbors. Yet at this interesting period of their history was offered the golden opportunity—the only opportunity that could ever be presented for the hopeful operation of Christian influences upon their savage minds and passions, ere the canker of corruption had eaten too deep. It was a season fraught with great results, either of good or evil to the poor Cherokees, and it passed quickly away.

This neglect alone, under ordinary circumstances, was sufficiently inviting to the rebukes of Heaven;

but, in this particular case, fearfully so; and the reasons are not few or obscure, for believing that its special visitations were, in more than one instance, experienced in consequence.

It was in God's sight, and the sight of all good men, a significant and important article in the charter granted by Charles Second to the lords-proprietors, which declared to the world, that one of their chief motives in undertaking the great enterprise of settling Carolina, was a profound Christian sympathy for the poor native heathen, who inhabited its wilds, and an active zeal to propagate among them the truths of the Gospel; yet it is the testimony of history that just this much of their charter, and no more, was sheer pretence and hypocrisy. During the whole period in which they governed the province, not one effort was made, in the exercise of their own power, to disseminate the truths of Christianity, either among the destitute colonists, whom their self-interest had allured from Christian homes in Europe, or among the benighted Indians of the surrounding wilderness.

"Until the Society for the Propagation of the Gospel in foreign parts, sent out a missionary to South Carolina in 1701, that State had been entirely without a minister; and Oldmixon informs us, that the only instruction which the Indians received prior to that time, was from a French dancing-master, who settled in Craven county, and taught the natives to dance and play upon the flute.*

* Note in Carroll's Collections.

Samuel Thomas was the missionary sent to the South. He began his labors among the Yamassees, and is spoken of as a worthy, earnest man; but he did not long survive the heat and malaria of his new field of toil. It will not be irrelevant to add here a paragraph which appeared a few months ago in the Register of Winnsboro': "Died at his plantation, in Fairfield District, January 1, 1859, John Peyere Thomas, M.D., aged sixty-two years. Dr. Thomas was born December 23, 1796, in St. Stephen's Parish, South Carolina. He was a lineal descendant of Mr. Samuel Thomas, who, in the year 1702, was appointed by the Society for the Propagation of the Gospel in Foreign Parts, their first missionary to South Carolina; and who, after having laid by his industry and devotion, a good foundation for his successors to carry on the work he had begun, died much lamented for his sound doctrine and exemplary life. Dr. Thomas graduated in the South Carolina College in the class of 1816. He afterwards graduated in Medicine in the City of New York, having been a pupil of Valentine Mott, with whom he maintained a long friendship and correspondence."

The society soon sent out other missionaries, both for the town and country, but we hear nothing of their labors among the Cherokees and Catawbas, either in their villages or on the border. At this time the fierce controversy between the Dissenters and Episcopalians, which had so long distracted the colony, was still raging: the latter had, however, for a moment triumphed—had become, not only the dominant party of the province, but the established church, in the same manner as the Episcopacy was the established church in the mother-country.

The Dissenters were accustomed to say, however—and it does not appear that they were moved altogether by prejudice or ill-will—that the clergy sent over by the society, were far too intent upon making proselytes to the Episcopal party, both among whites and Indians, to be of any great service to the manners or souls of either.

A few years later occurred the dreadful massacre of Pocatalligo, in the famous Indian war of 1715. Cotton Mather, who then edited the Magnolia in the colony of Massachusetts, wrote in a number of that now invaluable record of colonial times, that such was the vengeance of Heaven upon a spirit among men, which sought more to gain adherents to a creed than converts to Christ.

These time-serving, ambitious efforts, were even plied among the savages in their distant wilds. An old trader tells us, in his own off-hand, original style, of an incident, in point, which took place near the border. He is sketching the character of a Cherokee *beauty*, then well-known to the traders and to many in Charleston. We will have occasion to refer, ourself, to her again. "The conversion of this *rara avis* was in the following extraordinary manner: There was a gentleman who married her according to the custom of the Cherokees, but observing that marriages were commonly of short duration in that wanton female government, he flattered himself that he could better secure her affection by having her confirmed, and baptized by a priest of the church, and taught the duties of the conjugal relation by virtue of a new Christian name and marriage. As she was no stranger in the English settlements, he soon persuaded her to go with him to the Congarees to have the ceremony performed, and to get a supply of fine things besides. The priest was one of those sons of wisdom the church sent us in her maternal benevolence, both to keep and draw us from dangerous errors, and, grasping at the opportunity of making a valuable convert, he changed her from a wild savage to a believing Christian in a trice.

He asked her a few articles of her creed, which were soon answered by the bridegroom, as interpreter, after asking her a trifling question, relating to other subjects than the matter before them. When the priest proposed to her a religious question, the bridegroom, by reason of her low ideas and peculiar dialect, was obliged to mention some of the virtues, and say he recommended to her a very strict chastity in the married state. "Very well," said she, "that's a good speech, and fit for every woman alike, unless she is very old." The interpreter, after a short pause, replied, that he was urging her to use a proper care in domestic life. "You evil spirit," said she, "when was I wasteful or careless at home?" He replied, "never." "Well, then," said she, "tell him his speech is troublesome and light. But, where are those fine things you promised me?" He bid her be patient a little, and she should have plenty of everything she liked best; at this she smiled. Now the religious man was fully confirmed in the hope of her conversion; however, he asked her if she understood and believed the doctrine of the Trinity? The bridegroom swore heartily, that if he brought out all the other articles of his old book, she both knew and believed them, for she was a sensible young woman.

The bridegroom had a very difficult part to act, both to please the humor of his Venus, and to satisfy the inquisitive temper of our religious son of Apollo; he behaved pretty well, however, till he was desired to ask her belief of the uni-trinity, and tri-unity of the Deity, which the clergyman endeavored to explain; upon this he assured the priest that the Indians did not mind what religion the women were of, or whether they had any; and that the bride would take it very kindly if he shortened his discourse, as nothing can disturb the Indian women so much as long lectures.

The *Dark-lantern* (which was the name of the bride) became very uneasy, both by the delay of time, and the various passions she read in the bridegroom's face and speech, and she asked him sharply the meaning of such a long discourse? He instantly cried out that the whole affair was spoiled unless it was brought to a speedy conclusion; but the clergyman insisted on her belief of that article, before he could proceed any farther. But, by way of comfort, he assured him, it should be the very last question he would propose, till he put the holy water on her face, and read over the marriage ceremony. The bridegroom, revived at this good news, immediately sent the bowl around with a cheerful countenance, which the bride observing, she asked him the reason of his sudden joyful looks. The answer he gave her caused her to smile; whereupon the priest imagining her cheerful looks, proceeded from her swallowing his doctrine, immediately called for a bowl of water to initiate his new convert. As the bridegroom could not mediate here, he persuaded her to let the beloved man put some beloved water on her face, and it would be a sure pledge of a lasting friendship between her and the English, and entitle her to everything she liked best. She at last consented, with this promise, and had the constancy, though so ignorant a noviciate in our sacred mysteries, to go through our catechism and the long marriage ceremony. Her name was soon entered in capital letters to grace the first title-page of the priest's church-book of converts, which he often showed to his English sheep, and, with much satisfaction, would inform them, how, through his instrumentality, an Indian Dark-lantern had been changed into a lamp of Christian light. Afterwards, however, to his great grief, he was obliged, on account of her adulteries, to erace her name, and enter it anew on one of the crowded pages of his female delinquents. The same author adds: "I must here beg leave to be indulged in a few observations on our own American missionaries. Many evils are produced by sending out ignorant, and wicked persons as clergymen. Of the few I know, two of them dare not venture on repeating but a few collects in the common-prayer. The very rudiments of learning, not to say of religion, are wanting in several of our missionary evangelists. The best apology I have heard in their behalf is that of an English nobleman, who asked a certain bishop why he conferred holy orders on such an arrant set of blockheads? He replied, because it was better to have the ground plowed by asses than leave it a waste, full of thistles. It seems very surprising that those who are invested with a power of conferring ecclesiastical orders, should be so careless in propagating the holy Gospel, and assiduous to profane holy things, in appointing and ordaining illiterate, irreligious persons to the service. What is it but saying, go teach the American fools? My blessing is enough. Cherish confidence, and depend upon it they will not have the boldness to laugh at you. Leave the remote and poor settlements to the care of divine Providence, who is diffusive of his rich gifts. The harvest is great elsewhere. Only endeavor to episcopize the northern colonies; it is enough—there they are numerous, and able to pay Peter's pence, as well as our old Jewish and new parliamentary tithes; and in time, your labors will be crowned with success.

"What can we think at this distance, when we see the number of blind guides our spiritual fathers at home have sent us, to lead us clear of the wages of error, but that they think of us with indifference, and are studiously bent on their own temporal interest, instead of our spiritual welfare. There are thousands of the Americans, who, I believe, have not heard six sermons in the space of above thirty years; and in fact they have more knowledge than the teachers who are sent to them, and too much religion to associate with them.

"And even the blinder sort of the laity, not finding truth sufficiently supported by their blind guides, grew proud of their own imaginary knowledge, and some thereby proudly commenced teachers, by which means they rend the church asunder; and, instead of peace and love, they plant envy, contempt, hatred and revilings."*

In the several manuscript volumes relating to Indian affairs, preserved in the Secretary of State's office, we remember to have noticed but two or three instances in which the mental or moral interest of the Indians is at all mentioned or referred to. One has already been related, of the little Indian boy, who was apprenticed to Col. John Barnwell, on the condition that he should be taught English and the principles of Christianity. In a conference, to be hereafter described, that was held between the Governor of Virginia and a self-appointed delegation from the Over-hill Cherokees,—the former, among other promises, assured the Indians that he would take their children and have them educated in the college just then established in that colony. This was William and Mary's, recently burned to the ground with its more precious treasure of old and rare books.

* Adair.

In one of Gov. Glen's Indian talks in Charleston he expressed the desire that an opportunity might some day be offered of having all the Indians instructed in the truths of Christianity. These fair promises or good wishes were the nearest approximation ever made, by either Church or State, to a full conscientious discharge of its obligations to take care of the religious and moral welfare of the savages on the border. Yet at the period when they first became acquainted with them, particularly the Cherokees and Catawbas, there was doubtless no nobler or more susceptible people to be found on the American Continent.

If, at that time, the same religious sympathy had been manifested in their behalf, and the same practical schemes set in operation for their instruction and moral improvement, that have since been so effectual in their new home beyond the Mississippi, combined with free schools and the institution of slavery, in elevating them from a condition of deep degeneracy to their present superior position in the scale of civilization, who can estimate the good that must have accrued to them as a nation, by their happy alliance with the conscientious English colonists? And how much of the suffering, how many of the horrors and dark scenes of torture, of ruin and of blood, would have been prevented on the border, and long years of the reign of savage vengeance and rapine?

While on this subject, we must be allowed to anticipate for one moment: There is a curious and very valuable old manuscript journal of a Rev. Hugh McAden, which was snatched, as it were, from the flames kindled by Lord Cornwallis in North Carolina, with the libraries and papers of Presbyterian ministers, that sheds considerable light on the religious condition of the upper-country in its early periods.

The reverend journalist, having traversed a large portion of the settled backwoods of North Carolina, crossed the Catawba, and penetrated some distance into the almost primitive wilds of the more southern colony. It was in the fall of 1755: "On Monday, 20th of October, took my journey for Broad River—sixty miles to the southward—in company with two young men, who came this far to conduct me thither—a place where never any of our missionaries had been." Here, unfortunately, just at the point of the expedition most interesting to us, several leaves are missing from the journal. Twelve days, however, after leaving Broad River, still moving towards the south, the narrator resumes: "Monday, 2d of November—preached to a number of those poor baptized infidels, many of whom, I was informed, had never heard a sermon in all their lives before, and yet several of them had families."

He here inserts an anecdote of an old man who, he was told, had said to Governor Glen, when on a visit in the upper-country, for the purpose of forming a treaty with the Cherokees, that he had never seen a shirt, been in a fair, heard a sermon, or seen a minister in all his life. Upon which the Governor promised to send him up a minister, that he might hear one sermon before he died. The minister came and preached; *and this was all the preaching that had been heard in the upper part of South Carolina before McAden's visit.**

We shall have occasion to recur to this journal when we come to treat of the early settlers and settlements in Upper Carolina.

At the head of the society that had been formed in England for the propagation of the Gospel among the heathens of the New World was the celebrated Robert Boyle, equally as well known in the highest walks of science as in many benevolent enterprises for doing good to men. His measures were afterwards warmly seconded by the excellent Queen Mary, of Orange, and Dr. Compton, Bishop of London; and if their plans had been forwarded in America, in the English settlements and on the frontiers among Indians and traders, by agents as conscientious and pious as themselves, great results must have followed.

Dr. Tennison, Archbishop of Canterbury, was, however, the immediate founder of the society to which we have referred as having been chartered for the propagation of the Gospel in foreign parts. The people of England, we are told, welcomed the enterprise with their usual ardor, and made the society many munificent benefactions; so that in a short time it was enabled to send out and support

* Foot's Sketches of North Carolina.

numerous missionaries in the plantations. A contemporary of this period thus describes the religious and moral destitution of that portion of their field which was embraced in Carolina: "About this time the number of inhabitants in the colony amounted to between five and six thousand, besides Indians and negroes. In Charleston they had one minister of the Church of England, and another of the Church of Scotland; but in the country there was no such thing as public worship, nor schools for the education of children; and the people living thus scattered through a forest were likely in time to sink by degrees into the same state of ignorance and barbarism with the natural inhabitants of the wilderness."* This was at the beginning of the eighteenth century.

It is not to our purpose to detail what the society did for Carolina; it is enough to know it did nothing for the Cherokees and whites of the upper-country. The old journal of McAden anticipates more than half a century of the time before us, and he is sufficiently explicit on that point. His statement, too, in regard to the startling destitution among the settlers on the border is singularly corroborated by an Act of that period, which we find in the Statutes of South Carolina:† "And whereas, the inhabitants of the Congarees and the Waterees have *never had any minister of the Gospel to preach and perform divine service among them*,—be it therefore enacted by the

* Hewit. † Vol. iv., p. 20.

authority aforesaid, that the public treasurer of this province, for the time being, shall pay to such minister of the Gospel of the Established Church as shall statedly preach and perform divine service at Saxe-Gotha, or such other centrical place in the Congarees as the Commissioners hereinafter named shall direct, and six times a year, at least, at the most populous places within forty miles of the same, the sum of seven hundred pounds, current money, per annum." The same *favor* was likewise extended to the settlers in the old Fredericksburg township, at the Pine Tree, now Camden, and all surrounding settlements within forty miles. This statute was ratified in the council chamber, January 27th, 1756.

If this was the first religious instruction that had been supplied the people of the Congarees and Pine Tree, we may well agree with McAden and others, who assert, that up to this late period the Indians and traders, and scattered pioneers of the upper-country, were still utterly destitute of any stated religious services.

And now, at last, the provincial establishment had awakened, too late, to a sense of duty and to aggressive enterprise. Already were the pious, church-loving Scotch-Irishry beginning to pour by steady streams into the long-neglected, unoccupied wilderness of north-western Carolina. The Lyleses had built their cabins and were leveling the forest on Broad River in the present territory of Fairfield. The Gowdies were at Ninety-Six, and the Calhouns, on their way to the rich cane-pastures of the flat-woods; but we must not anticipate.

CHAPTER XI.

Unprincipled white men the originators of most of the disturbances that afflicted the trade—No class more safe in the Nation than horse-thieves and pilferers—The declaration, in regard to these abuses, of Anthony Dean, a Trader singularly learned and sagacious—The Traders become too numerous—They compete with one another as pedlers and skulking hucksters of trifles and intoxicating liquors—the office of Agent either discontinued or of no practical efficiency—Blakeney, Chicken, Hastings and Charlesworth Glover—Punch-houses are set up on the border—The Indians become more and more idle and depraved—The profits of the trade fall off, &c.

It must be confessed, that unprincipled white men were ever concerned with or at the bottom of most of the difficulties that continued to disturb the Nation. And no wonder, when every horse-thief could find means to screen himself from justice, and instigate the Indians to persecute and harass the traders. This state of things could not have existed, if the trade, after being properly regulated, had been judiciously and firmly directed; if suitable officers had been placed and maintained in the Cherokee towns, to superintend its interest, and see that justice was done to all parties. It is a matter of surprise to us at this day, that a government so remarkable for the energy and excellence of its laws, and for its large sympathies for the distressed of mankind, did not take this decaying branch of traffic in hand, to correct its abuses and relieve the sufferings of hundreds connected with it. The more especially since it would have formed a powerful barrier between the outer English settlements and a nation of wild people whose friendship was ever too fickle to be implicitly trusted; and it might have been brought to approximate, at least, its former lucrativeness.

This neglect, it must be supposed, originated in the want of truthful representations to the governor and members of the Assembly; otherwise the numerous complaints, that constantly came down, would have been heard, the grievances redressed, and those engaged in the trade could not have been forgotten. The country would have been free from some of the burden of taxation, the merchants have received their dues, the poor trader subsistence, and the Indians satisfaction and peace. Such is the substance of a communication written by Anthony Dean—himself a trader among the Cherokees and a man of singular learning—to the Governor and Commissioners.*

"Formerly, each trader had a license for two towns or villages; but according to the present unwise plan, two, and even three, Arab-like pedlers skulk about in a single town. Several of them, also, frequently emigrate into the woods with spirituous liquors and cheating trifles, after the Indian hunting camps in the winter season, to the great in-

* Indian Books, Columbia.

jury or the regular trader, who supplies them with all the conveniences of hunting: for, as they will sell even the shirts from their backs for intoxicating liquors, they must be supplied anew in the fall of the year by him, when they are in no condition to remunerate him for his goods. At my first setting out among them, a number of traders, who lived contiguous to one another, joined, through our various nations, in different companies, and were generally men of worth: of course, they would have a living price for their goods, which they carried on horse-back to the remote Indian countries, at very great expenses. These set an honest copy for the imitation of the natives: for, as they had much at stake, their own interest and that of the government coincided. As the trade was, in this wise manner, kept up to its just standard, the savages were industrious and frugal; but, having lowered it, through a mistaken notion of re-gaining their affections, we made ourselves too cheap to them, and they despised us for it. The trade should be raised again, to a reasonable fixed price; thus we shall keep them employed, and ourselves secure. Were we to lower the trade, even fifty per cent. below the prime cost of goods, they would become only the more discontented, by thinking we had been cheating them all the years past. A mean, submissive temper can never manage our Indian affairs. The qualities of a kind friend, sensible speaker, and active, brisk warrior, must constitute the character of a superintendent. Great care must be taken not to give the Indians offence, or a mean opinion of the people our superintendents represent."*

It was, at first, the practice of the government, in accordance with the statute, to have responsible agents to reside in the nation, in order to watch over the interest of the trade, and to regulate the manners of both Indians and traders; but this salutary custom had, it appears, already fallen into disuse. After Hastings, Blakeney, Charlesworth, Glover and Chicken, we scarcely hear the name of agent or superintendent mentioned in connection with the Nation or Indian affairs, till the time of the celebrated John Stuart, and his hardly less famous deputy, Alexander Cameron, of Lochaber, in the present territory of Abbeville District.

At the same time that the office of the Indian agent was thus practically abolished, it ceased, likewise, to be that a few worthy men, alone, were licensed to live and trade among the Indians, whose influence and ability would have compensated, in great part, for the loss of the accredited overseer. The license system was thrown open to every one who presented himself, with the legal fees, and the Nation was quickly overrun with a troop of vicious hucksters, whose depravity was only equalled by their utter worthlessness. Men of honesty and mercantile pride were deterred from embarking in the trade with such competitors.

Hence, the large and increasing traffic in rum with

* Adair.

the Indians; the establishment of punch-houses on the border; the idleness and debauchery of the savages; the rapid falling off of the profits of the trade, and the consequent ruin of the regular traders; the dissatisfaction, complaints and violence of the Indians, and their threatened defection to the French. A deputation of the Creeks complained to the Board in Charleston, that their people were unable to obtain a needed supply of goods, because their traders expended such quantities of those they brought to the Nation in clothing and decorating the persons of their Indian mistresses.

In the prime of the trade, before the complete deterioration of the Indian character, the life of the trader, to one whose courage and love of wild adventure adapted him to such scenes, was intensely fascinating. The Indians, upright, manly and industrious, were no mean or disagreeable companions; and their esteem and affection for the honest, bold trafficker knew no bounds. They watched for his welfare, and were ever ready to defend him with their lives against any assailant. In the frequent turmoils and dangers incident to a savage community, many of the traders owed their lives to this friendly disposition of their Indian allies. Adair, in several places, speaks of the great risk that any man would have run in attempting to assault or to arrest a trader of this description when surrounded by the Indians of his town.

In the latter periods, however, when both Indians and white men had sadly degenerated from their former hardy virtue, the endangered trader was much oftener indebted for his safety to the devotion and cunning of his corrupt Indian mistress. Many romantic instances of this kind could be related. There is one connected, by tradition, with the history of Old Ninety-six, which we will relate in its proper place.

Despite, however, the ardent attachments which the traders often had the address to inspire in the breasts of the savages, they were constantly beset with dangers, and many good and true men among them lost their lives. The records in the Secretary of State's office, relating to Indian affairs, and the old chroniclers of the times, abound in such incidents. Yet we may venture the assertion that the half has never been told; many are the dark deeds of atrocity and blood, perpetrated in the gloomy woods and recesses of the Cherokee nation alone, whose history no living soul shall know till that day come, when all such spots shall be required to yield up their dead, and their long-kept secrets as well.

Having fixed upon a village or town suited to his purpose, the trader went to work, with the assistance of the Indians, and soon built for himself and his handsome Indian wife, a dwelling house; nor was it a structure by any means uncomfortable or unsightly. It was usually put up in the regular Cherokee or pioneer style of notched logs, with a roof of boards; but, unlike most houses of the early immigrants, it was neatly plastered, both inside and out, with white porcelain clay. This was in the true

Cherokee manner, and greatly added to its comfort and appearance. Its inner conveniences and furniture were not altogether rude or barbarous. The trader's pack-horse trains, direct from Charleston, enabled him to gratify the vanity of his copper-colored bride with chairs and neat bedsteads, instead of the skins of buffaloes and bears, on which she had been brought up. The utensils of the house-keeping department, except a few heir-looms of savage life, were precisely similar to those of any immigrant's cabin on the border. If we were to mention a single article that seemed to be of prime domestic use, it would be the iron tea-kettle: the manuscript records frequently make mention of kettles, sent up by the merchants of Charleston to the Cherokee towns. In 1716, Elisha Prioleau was paid by the Board nine pounds seven shillings and six-pence, for a lot of seven kettles sent up to the Nation.

After the completion of his dwelling-house, the trader next built, hard by it, a store-room, for the reception of his goods and peltries, and for general business purposes. This was called his trading house. The erection of a poultry house, a corn crib, and sweating oven for the use of his wife and half-breed *responsibilities*, with which his cabin was soon well filled, completed his private improvements. The sweating oven was always fixed just in front of the dwelling, and was in great requisition.

If the town, in which he is settling, happens to be at war with any neighboring tribe, his whole establishment is placed so as to be surrounded by the houses of the Indians, in order to afford it the greater security in case of an attack from the enemy. But usually, as was the custom of the Indians, he built at a considerable distance from any other dwelling, for purposes of domestic convenience, in the rearing of useful animals and garden vegetables. Adair says, "that the Indian children of his time were as destructive to the pigs and poultry running at large about the villages as the wild-cats and foxes of the woods; and, for these mischievous offences, their fond, degenerate mothers, only called them 'mad-caps,' instead of *dry-scratching* them, as in former and better times."

The "*dry-scratch*" was a famous mode of punishment among all the savages of North America, and except, perhaps, the Turkish bastinado, no infliction upon the naked skin can be conceived more horrible. If any Anglo-American mother is amused with this, let her ask herself the question, whether there is not in the present day, and in her own household, a leniency towards her wayward offspring, which is filling our schools and colleges with unmanageable, lawless youth, just as the corrupt remissness of the ancient Cherokee mother, reared in her Nation a generation of truce-breakers and moral vipers, who, in due time, fell in savage fury upon the defenceless families of our immigrant fathers.

We learn from Lawson the reasons assigned by the traders for their intimate association with the Indian women. "The English traders are seldom without an Indian female for his temporary wife, alleging these reasons as sufficient to allow of such a familiarity. First, they being remote from any white people, that it preserves their friendship with the heathens, they esteeming children begotten by white men much above those by native husbands; the Indian mistress ever securing her white friend provisions whilst he stays amongst them. And, lastly, this correspondence makes them learn the Indian tongue much the sooner, they being of the Frenchman's opinion, how that an English wife teaches her husband more English in one day than a school-master in a week. But one great misfortune, which oftentimes attends those who converse with these savage women, is that their childen by them, are seldom educated otherwise than in a state of infidelity; for it is a certain rule and custom amongst all the savages of America, that I was ever acquainted withal, to let the children always fall to the woman's lot. When man and wife separate, all the children go along with the mother. And, therefore, on this score, it ever seems impossible for the Christians to get their children, which they have by these Indian women, away from them, whereby they might bring them up in the knowledge of Christian principles. Nevertheless, we often find that Englishmen and other Europeans, that have been accustomed to the conversation of these savage women and their way of living, have been so allured with that careless sort of life, as to be constant to their Indian wives, so long as they lived, without ever desiring to return again amongst the English, although they had very fair opportunities of advantages in their country, of which sort I have known several."

The education of their mongrel offspring in the precepts of Christianity, did not, it is quite probable, give many of the traders any great solicitude; but, it cannot be doubted, that they often found excellent wives in their beautiful savage consorts, and spent with them cheerful and contented lives. And it must not be taken for granted, that because the bold adventurer, thus associated himself with the barbarians, that he was, therefore, cut off from any of the necessaries of life, or even from many of its luxuries. Under the care of his thrifty wife, his crib was usually well stored with corn; the yard swarmed with poultry, and the common pastures with his swine, horses and cattle. Cherokee women of intelligence made the best housekeepers on the continent; in their habits and persons, they were as cleanly as purity itself, and yet knew from childhood what it was to labor with their own hands, and provide every domestic comfort. Lawson observes: "The floors of their cabins are never paved nor swept, so that they always have a loose earth on them, yet I never felt any ill or unsavory smell in them; should we live in our houses as they do, we should be poisoned with our own nastiness, which confirms these Indians to be, as they really are, some of the sweetest people in the world. They are of a very hale constitution; their breaths are as sweet as the air they breathe in, and their women

25

seem to be of that tender composition, which better fits them for the blandishments of love than the rough drudgery of labor." Bartram and other old chroniclers, speak in the same strong terms of the charms of the young Cherokee women.

In their proper seasons, the woods of the Nation abounded in many varieties of nuts, and delicious fruits. Milk and butter were plenty, and no great expense supplied them with sugar and other groceries from Charleston, with which materials the females were as expert in making savory pies, tarts, puddings, and cakes of different sorts, as the boasted housewives of the English settlements.

An old trader relates: "Till of late years the honest traders lived among the Indians in the greatest plenty. They abounded with hogs, which made very firm streaked bacon, and much preferable to that in English settlements, chiefly owing to the acorns, and hickory-nuts they feed on. But the Indians are now grown too proud and lazy by having goods too cheap and plenty, that very few raise any. There are, at least, five times the number of trading houses in all the western Indian nations, since general licenses, through the wisdom of our civil rulers, were first granted, than was formerly, while experience directed South Carolina to pursue and enforce proper measures. Such a number of lewd, idle white savages, are very hurtful to the honest part of the traders, by heightening the value of vegetables, especially in time of light crops, to an exorbitant price; for, by inebriating the Indians with their poisonous liquors, they purchase the necessaries of life, at four or five hundred per cent. cheaper than the orderly traders; which is a great check to the few who love their country, and observe the strict laws of trade.

"The industrious old traders, have still, however, a plenty of hogs, which they raise in folds, mostly on the weeds of the fields, during the whole time the crops are in the ground; likewise some hundreds of fowls at once, and plenty of venison."*

In another place the same narrator adds: "I am writing this by the side of an Indian female, as great a princess as ever lived among the ancient Peruvians or Mexicans, and she bids me be sure not to mark the paper wrong, as do most of the traders, otherwise it will spoil the making of good bread or hommony, and of course beget the ill will of our white women."

The every-day life of the trader in the Nation, was one of primitive and most delightful freedom and simplicity. No hollow-hearted etiquette, no grinding social customs, trammeled or annoyed him; he dressed as best suited him, and conformed to nothing except as his own taste or inclination prompted him. No mode of living could more nearly approximate than his the complete ideal of social liberty.

Yet there were privileges, which the dignity and self-respect, even of savages denied him. He could

* Adair.

not with impunity, pry into the sacred, religious rites of the Indians, nor abuse the sanctity of their marriage relations. Indeed he was made constantly to feel that the preservation of his character for sobriety, truthfulness, and fair-dealing, was as essential to his popularity, and pecuniary interest in the Nation, as in the civilized community he had left. A dishonest, drunken trader, was ever an object of contempt to the Indians, and his life worth but little, when the solitude of the forest or a drunken brawl, offered an opportunity to cut him off.

It is true that the Cherokees, unlike every other native tribe of the continent, were found to have no formal law against adultery; but it had not always been so; and though Adair uses the following language, it would appear that this heinous crime was not altogether free from danger of punishment, in his time, in the Nation: "They have been a considerable while under petticoat-government, and allow their women full liberty to plant their brows with horns, as oft as they please, without fear of punishment." Yet, he, immediately after, admits that he had known a case among this people, in which one of the guilty parties was arraigned, and proceeds to describe minutely the penalty awarded by the judges —an infliction too horrible to relate.

The ordinary punishment was severe enough. "They commonly begin with the adulterer, because of the two he is most capable of making his escape. They generally attack him at night, by a surprise, lest he should make a desperate resistance, and blood be shed to cry for blood. They fall on, eager and merciless, whooping their revengeful noise, and thrashing their captive with long-knoted flails; some over his head and face; others on his shoulders and back. His belly, sides, legs and arms are gashed all over, and at last, he happily seems to be insensible of pain; then they cut off his ears."

The same author adds: "The traders' ears are often in danger among the Indians by the sharpness of this law, and their practice of admitting the testimony of foolish children as legal evidence; but generally, either the tender-hearted females or their friends, give them timely notice of their danger. Then they fall to the rum-keg, and as soon as they see the pursuers approaching they stand to arms in a threatening parade. Formerly the traders, like so many British tars, kept them in proper awe, and consequently prevented them from attempting any mischief. But since the patenteed *daublers* set foot in their land, they have gradually become worse every year, murdering valuable, innocent British subjects at pleasure; and when they go down to Charleston, they receive presents as a tribute of fear, for which these Indians upbraid and threaten us. The Muscogees lately clipt off the ears of two white men for supposed adultery.

For the first offence, the ears of the adulterer were cut off close to the head; if he repeated the crime, his nose and upper lip were sacrificed; and for the third offence, he was sometimes put to death.

Bartram gives rather an amusing account of an affair of this kind, which he witnessed, while traveling through the Creek Nation, in 1777: "On my arrival at the town of Mucclasse, I was not a little surprised at a tragical revolution in the family of my friend the trader*—his stores shut up, and guarded by a party of Indians. In a few minutes, however, the whole affair was related to me. It appeared that this son of Adonis had been detected in an amorous intrigue with the wife of a young chief, the day after his arrival. The chief was out on a hunt, but came in next day; and upon information of the affair—the fact being confirmed—he, with his friends and kindred, resolved to exact legal satisfaction, which, in this case, is cutting off both ears of the delinquent close to the head. This being determined upon, he took the most secret and effectual method to effect his purpose. About a dozen young Indian fellows, conducted by the injured husband, having provided and armed themselves with knotty cudgels of green hickory, which they concealed under their mantles, in the dusk of the evening, paid a pretended friendly visit to the trader at his own house, when the husband, feigning a private matter of business, took him aside in the yard, then whistling through his fingers, he was instantly surrounded, knocked down, and stripped to his skin, and beaten with their knotty bludgeons. He had the cunning, however, to feign

* A Mr. Tap——y, with whose caravan he had just arrived from Mobile.

himself speechless before they had really killed him, which he supposed was their intention; and when he lay as if dead, the executioner drew out his knife with the intention of taking off his ears. This respite gave him time to reflect, when instantly springing up, he ran off, leaped the fence, and had the good fortune to get into a dark swamp, where he miraculously eluded the pursuit of his enemies, and finally made a safe retreat to the house of his father-in-law, the chief of the town, throwing himself under his protection, who gave him his word that he would do him all the favor that lay in his power. This account I had from his own mouth; for, hearing of my return, he sent a trusty messenger, by whom I found access to him. He farther informed me that there had been a council of the chiefs of the town convened to deliberate on the affair, and their final determination was that he must lose his ears or forfeit all his goods, which amounted to upwards of one thousand pounds sterling; and even that forfeiture would not save his ears unless Mr. George Gulphin interposed in his behalf; and after all, the injured Indian declares he will have his life. He entreated me with tears to make what speed I could to Silver Bluff, and represent his dangerous situation to Mr. Gulphin, and solicit that gentleman's speedy interference—which I assured him I would undertake."*

Of the success of our author's friendly mission to

* Bartram, p. 416.

Silver Bluff, and of the fate of the unfortunate trader, or his ears, we are left wholly to conjecture. It is quite probable, however. that long before the potent influence of Col. Gulphin could reach his case, his life, perhaps, had paid the penalty of his crime, and of the violated code of the Muscogee.

Those coy Indian beauties, while they were generally faithful to their English husbands, and made them industrious, thrifty wives, were nevertheless, not always the simple, unsophisticated creatures that many may be disposed to regard them from their wild breeding in the woods. The true feminine characteristics are observable in every form of society, and only await the proper opportunities and culture to be developed, either in the loveliness of an angel or the hateful depravity of Jezebel.

The same author quoted last, in the interesting narrative he gives of his explorations in East Florida, several years previous to the Revolution, tells the following story of a young trader from North Carolina, whom he met on the St. John's: "On our arrival at Spaulding's upper trading house, we found it occupied by a white trader, who had for a companion a very handsome young Seminole woman. Her father, who was a prince, by the name of the White Captain, was an old chief of the Seminoles, and, with part of his family, was encamped in an orange grove, near the stores, having lately come in from a hunt.

This white trader, soon after our arrival, delivered up the store-houses to my companion, and joining his father-in-law's camp, soon after went away into the forest on a hunting tour, and to trade with the flying camps of Seminoles. He is unhappy in his connection with his beautiful savage. It is but a few years since he came here, I think, from North Carolina, a stout, well-bred genteel man, active, and of a heroic, amiable disposition; and by his industry, honesty, and engaging manners, had gained the affections of the Indians, and soon made a little fortune by trafficking with the Seminoles; when, unfortunately, meeting with this potent charmer, they were married in the Indian fashion. He loves her sincerely, as she possesses every perfection in her person to render a man happy. Her features are beautiful, and manners engaging; innocence, modesty and love appear to a stranger in every action and movement; and these powerful graces she has so artfully played upon her beguiled and vanquished lover and unhappy slave, as already to have drained him of all his possessions, which she dishonestly distributes among her savage relations. He is now poor, emaciated, and half-distracted, often threatening to shoot her, and afterwards himself; yet, he cannot summon resolution enough even to leave her; but now endeavors to drown and forget his sorrows in deep draughts of brandy.

"This is a striking instance," he adds "of the power of beauty in a savage, and her art in improving it to her private ends." Does it not illustrate, as well, the fascinations of an artful beauty of many a civilized community? "It is, however, but doing justice to the virtue of the Seminoles, and of the American aborigines, to observe that the character of this woman is condemned and detested by her own people, of both sexes. If her husband were to turn her away she could not marry again, and would be regarded as a harlot."

The Cherokee towns were now swarming with the half-breed offspring from this opportune amalgamation of the vigorous, unadulterated English stock with the more beautiful and robust of the Indian females: and while the native blood was fast deteriorating from the fearful licentiousness of the women, and other causes already enumerated, this generation grew up into a race whose physical and intellectual energies have been active and prominent in developing the civilization of the modern Cherokees. The same remark is applicable to the other leading nations of the South, and the names of McGillivray, Ross, Ridge, and Adair, belong to the history of their maternal ancestry.

Alexander McGillivray, the celebrated Chief of the Creeks, was the son of a Scotchman named Lachlan McGillivray, by Sehoy Marchand, a princess of the wind, and whose father was a Captain Marchand, commandant of the old French Fort Toulouse. Lachlan ran away from wealthy parents, living in Dunmaglass, Scotland, when a boy of sixteen, and landed in Charleston in 1735. Pickett thus describes him: "He then had no property, except a shilling in his pocket, a suit of clothes upon his back, a red head, a stout frame, an honest heart, a fearless disposition, and cheerful spirits, which seldom became depressed."

The English were at this time conducting a lucrative commerce with the Chickasaws and a portion of the Creeks; Lachlan, while strolling over the town came upon the busy quarters of the traders in the western suburbs, and beheld with astonishment hundreds of pack-horses, pack-saddles, and curious looking men in half-savage garbs, together with huge piles of packed merchandize, ready for conveyance to the Indian country. He became a pack-horse driver on the spot. Ten years after he married Sehoy, at the Hickory-nut Ground, near old Fort Toulous, and became very rich. Alexander, their first child, studied Latin and Greek, in Charleston, and while yet a young man, succeeded, in right of his mother, to the Chieftaincy of the Creek Nation.

The regular experienced English trader was a man of no ordinary traits of character, he was always remarkable for enterprise, shrewdness, courage, and an astonishing fertility of expedients. Difficulties and dangers that appalled most men only served to stimulate his energy and sharpen his wit. He encountered many risks, as well as hardships, both on the lonely trading path and in the Indian country, while in the exciting pursuit of his favorite calling. And such were the charms of the wild adventures or the prospects it held out of speedily enriching all who engaged in it, that there were not wanting men at the head of the peltry trains, and in remote trading posts, whose learning and abilities might have raised them to places of distinction amid the rivalries of civilized society. In another place we shall have occasion to speak particularly of these.

Most of the traders from motives of expediency—a few no doubt from choice—adopted the dress and many of the habits of the savages. Indeed, we are told, that after a year or two's residence in the Nation, those who loved their wild life so well as to desire to obliterate the last remains of their Christian bringing-up, effected so great a change in their appearance and complexion by the strange dress they had assumed, by exposure, and the constant use of bear's oil on the skin, as to be almost undistinguishable from the native Indians.

It was a curious custom of the Cherokees that as soon as a trader had proved himself acceptible and popular in the Nation, some warrior would select him as a fast friend and confidant; and having exchanged his clothes for his, would thus exhibit to each other, and to all around them, a constant pledge of their mutual regard and affection. And this was no unmeaning parade, at least, on the part of the Indian; it bound his heart as firmly, as does the eating of bread with an enemy, the hand of the wandering Arab. In not a few instances it secured the lives of these bold adventurers when perhaps no other human instrumentality could have effected it.

We know of no custom like this among any other people, except the ancient Jews—could the Indians of America have derived it from them? "Then Jonathan and David made a covenant, because he loved him as his own soul. And Jonathan stripped himself of the robe that was upon him, and gave it to David, and his garments, even to his sword, and to his bow, and to his girdle."*

It was not often that a trader ventured upon the path, or in any part of the Nation, without being well armed. The frontiers were seldom free from the marauding cut-throats of their own color and race, and often swarmed with hostile Indians at war with the Cherokees and Catawbas. He was, moreover, too well versed in the subtleties of Indian character, not to know that even the friendly Cherokees were always the more respectful and trustworthy for being kept in awe of his prowess. They had a supreme contempt for any man, who either would not or could not stand up in his own defence.

On retiring to his bed at night, he took the invariable precaution to hang his arms—a gun, tomahawk, knife and pistols—on the wall just above his head, in quick reach of his hand. He knew not at what moment he might need them; vigilance being the watchword of his life. At this very period, or only a few years previous, a fearful massacre of a large number of traders had been perpetrated by the enraged Creeks, at Apalachucla—one of their ancient towns on the Chattahoochee. Nearly all the traders at that juncture, in the Nation, were cut off at a single blow.

They had repaired to Apalachucla from their dif-

* 1st Sam. ch. 18.

ferent towns, in hopes of finding refuge, on being apprized, by their temporary wives, that the Indians designed to attack them; and were all assembled in one house, under a promise from the chiefs, that they should be protected. But while the former were deliberating in council on the means of doing it, the Indians, in great numbers, surrounded the house, and set it on fire. All of them, to the number of eighteen or twenty, miserably perished in the flames. Bartram remarks of this tragedy: "I was shown by a trader the ruins of the house in which they were burned."

Adair and other narrators abound in thrilling incidents, illustrative of the perils that beset the traders in the Indian country. About the year 1750, there lived at the Congarees an experienced and much-respected Catawba trader, of the name of H. G.—Herman Geiger. We found in the manuscripts of the Secretary of State's Office, the name of Herman Geiger, as one of the first settlers and Indian traders at the Congarees. There can be little doubt that those initials, in Adair's history, refer to him.

On one occasion he had been employed, it seems, by the provincial authorities in Charleston, to go, in company with a member of the Board of Indian Trade, to the Cherokee Nation, in search of the precious metals, which were supposed to exist in inexhaustible abundance in that mountainous region. Having set out, and reached in safety one of the middle towns, they there discovered several of their friendly *settlement* Indians in the hands of a party of hostile Canadian savages, who had captured them near Charleston, and were carrying them prisoners to their towns in the north.

The *settlement* Indians were a class of the natives who, preferring the habits and customs of the whites, had settled in and around their plantations in the low country, and looked to them for protection, which they appear very much to have needed; for they were objects of contempt and hatred to all other Indians, and were little able to defend themselves when attacked by their enemies. In more than one place in the manuscript journals, they are called the *parch-corn Indians*—a name of derision which they had received, either from the lower class of whites, or the Indians of the Nation. They appear to have been very useful, and were evidently favorites on the plantations.

Geiger's pity, as well as patriotism, was aroused at the sight of these poor fellows in the hands of their merciless enemies; he knew full well the doom that awaited them at the end of their long journey, and resolved to rescue them at every hazard. At this period the old friendship of the Cherokees for the English had greatly waned; they were on terms of close amity with the Canadians and the bloodthirsty Savannahs of the Ohio, and, as before intimated, the captives were objects of their special aversion.

The assistance of the traders of the town was necessary, and through the mediation of one of them, the leading Cherokees at length consented to remain neutral in the affair.

Geiger now put himself at the head of several of the traders, among whom was Colonel Fox, and going to the camp of the Canadians, who were dancing, whooping, and cursing the English at a wild rate, seized and bore off the prisoners, despite the loud threats of the savages; and having placed them in a house, the bold Englishmen stood around it upon their arms, till an opportunity offered to supply them with provisions and send them safely home.

All was well so far; and little did Geiger think, that this act of kindness to the friendly Indians would one day cost him his life. But so it was. The following summer, having set out for the Catawba Nation, in company with a half-breed, the favorite son of T. B., a famous old trader, they were intercepted and captured by several of the very party of Canadians from whom Geiger had delivered the domestic Indians. The savages, fearful of the Catawbas, hastened with their captives beyond the mountains, but ventured to encamp several days a short distance from the Cherokees, apparently for no other purpose than to receive the congratulations of those already hostile Indians, who freely visited their camp and exulted with them in their good fortune.

The authorities of the province very soon hearing of Geiger's capture, dispatched an express to the towns of Keowee, Sugaw and Seneca, requesting the lower Cherokees to rescue the prisoners if they passed in reach of their part of the Nation; adding the inducement of a considerable reward. But so far from doing this; they threatened the lives of several of the traders who were preparing to attack the Canadians, in order to save their comrades; and they were thus suffered to escape.

The savages now resumed their flight, and bearing to the north-west, in order to avoid all possible danger from the intrepid Catawbas, they crossed the present territory of Tennessee and Kentucky, gradually turning due northward again towards their towns on the Ohio or in Canada. Geiger, worn-down at length by the fatigues of their rapid marches and the excessive heat of the weather, entreated them to put him to death and end his misery; but regarding this as only indicative of his warlike spirit, they conceived a respect for him, and having prepared a sort of litter, bore him with great care, in this manner, until they reached a point where the party were to divide on two different routes, each division taking a prisoner.

Geiger resolved to go no farther; his sufferings may have been great, but he, no doubt, anticipated the more dreadful tortures and death that awaited him in the enemy's country. Having bid his companion a last farewell, and seen him out of sight and hearing, he turned to the savages and told them to do their worst, for farther with them he would not go. Whereupon, enraged at his obstinacy, they buried their tomahawks in his head, and left him dead on the spot.

The old chronicler, who gives us these particulars, adds: "The half-breed afterwards got safe home, and told us of the death of our much-lamented friend, who died, as he lived, always despising life when it was to be preserved only in a state of slavery. And though he was lost to his family and the country by a manly performance of the duties of his office, in which he engaged by the pressing entreaties of the Governor,* yet his widow was treated ungenerously and basely, as was Capt. J. P.,† at the Congarees."

The winter months, with a portion of the spring, constituted the chief hunting-season in which the Indians collected their peltries. The traders frequently accompanied them, encamping with them in the woods to the end of the hunt; their packs were usually made up by the first of May, at which time they set out with the trains for Charleston or Augusta; leaving their wives and the Indian fellows to begin the operation of planting the crop of corn, beans, and other vegetables, for the year.

It has already been related, that the chief agents in the Nation, under the Commissioners, were Hastings, Glover and Blakeney. They were all, at different times, stationed at Savannah Town. Hastings served a short time besides at Tugaloo. Over and above their regular salaries, these agents were allowed twenty pounds yearly, to furnish their tables in the Nation, and defray expenses, when called on public business to Charleston. Hastings appears to

* Governor James Glen, against whose policy and acts Adair is often exceedingly severe.

† Who was Capt. J. P., of the Congarees?

have been a more conscientious public man than is usually met with in similar positions at the present day.

On one occasion, when expecting to pay a visit to Charleston, he sent down an humble petition from Tugaloo to the Board, begging, that he might be allowed to bring with him, on his own account, a lot of the beautiful baskets manufactured by the Cherokees, to be distributed as presents among his friends in town. The Commissioners had the littleness to deny the request; but the lasting record of it in their journals testifies as well to the petitioner's honesty and kindness of heart. John Chester and William Hatton were assistant factors in the Nation in 1717; the one at Keowee, and the other at Tugaloo.

There was a character of the name of Edward Maxwell, who is mentioned in several places of the records of this period for the performance of extraordinary express service between Charleston and the border. This appears to have been his business. He resided at Savannah Town. In one place it is ordered by the Board, that Edward Brailsford, Cashier of Indian Trade, pay to Edward Maxwell, or order, the sum of ten pounds, for an extraordinary express he had just rode from Savannah Town to Charleston; and for others that he had rode between the same points before this date.

In 1717, he brought down from Charlesworth Glover, Agent and Commandant at Fort Moore, to the Board, a letter giving an account of Colonel

Mackey's having been attacked by hostile Indians, three days' journey from Tugaloo towards Charleston, with the loss of a soldier, named Wilson, and an Indian killed, and several horses that fell into the hands of the enemy; and that no goods had yet been taken on the trading path. This adventure occurred on the old Keowee trail, and during the prevalence of a fierce war between the Creeks and Cherokees. We shall recur to it again, as affording a most remarkable confirmation of a well-known tradition, that accounts for the origin of the name of Wilson's Creek in Abbeville District.

Colonel Mackay was at this time the leader of a company of rangers, who scoured the country in the vicinity of the Cherokee border. "Tell the Indians," said the Commissioners at this period, to a trader just setting out for the Nation, "that we have a *ranging army* on our frontier or outer settlements." Henry Webb, and Benjamin Edwards, are also mentioned as traders, at this time, among the Cherokees. In 1717, John Sharp was assistant factor at Quanasse; Hill, at Cowee; Dange, at Terrequa and Tennassee. Charite Hayge, who has already been mentioned as an influential conjurer of Tugaloo, was greatly esteemed by the public authorities. In 1718, it was ordered by the Board, "that a keg of rum be provided, and sent up by the pack-train, now starting to the Nation, as a present to Charite Hayge, of Tugaloo, from the Commissioners, in remembrance of friendship." At the same time, John Coleman was appointed to be chief of the pack-horsemen, employed in the Cherokee trade; and John Milligan, Joseph Ponder, John O'Brian, John Poor, and John Carroll, to accompany and serve under him.

The present of a keg of rum from the Board, was the surest evidence of their regard for a head-man; for no gift could have been more acceptable, and it implied, at the same time, a confidence, on their part, that the chief would use it with discretion. In October of the same year, the Commissioners sent up a special messenger to inform Charite Hayge that they would soon erect, according to promise, the trading-house and fort at the Congarees. It has been before intimated, that the first attempt to establish this post proved a failure; the same messenger now acquaints the Conjurer with the reason. In the month of January previous, the Board purchased, from one Thomas Wilkinson, a periago boat, for the purpose of sending up men, provisions and utensils, to build the fort. On the 28th, Captain James Howe was ordered to take twelve men, and a carpenter named Sam Stanwood, and proceed up the river, in the periago, to the Congarees. Stanwood was to direct the work. The order was never, however, carried out by Howe. The very night, perhaps, before he was to embark, a party of marauding white men stole the Commissioners' boat, and succeeded in making off with it to safe quarters. This affair delayed the work till the following year, and placed it in the hands of a different party of men.

In June 1716, a great council was held at Tugaloo, presided over by the Conjuror, at which Hastings was present. The proceedings were sent, soon after, to Charleston, attested by the mark of the former. This was, in all probability, a treaty relating to the trade; for the important statute, already presented, by which it passed under the control of the government, was enacted by the Assembly, the last day of the same month.

CHAPTER XII.

The Pack-horsemen employed in the Trade—The Great Chickasaw Trading-path—Hostile Incursions of the Creeks into the Territory of the Cherokees and Catawbas—Description of a Caravan of Pack-horses—Old Fort Charlotte—George Whitfield, nephew of the celebrated Rev. George Whitfield—John Lewis Gervais—The Wedding at White Hall—Andrew Williamson—The Chickasaw Path between Charleston and Savannah Town—Peter St. Julian—The Old Savannah Trail connecting the Cherokee Towns with Savannah Town and Augusta—The Founding of Augusta. 1736—Bartram visits it in 1776—His Description of the ruins of Fort Moore, &c.

Next to the trader, the most interesting characters employed in the traffic with the Indian Nation, were the pack-horsemen. These frequently consisted, in part, of boys, under the direction of an experienced *voyageur*; and their life was one of exposure, hardships, and, not unfrequently, of thrilling adventure. In peace, and in war, and every vicissitude of weather, they were found upon the path. When menaced, however, by lurking enemies, it was usual for several caravans to unite for mutual protection; yet they were not unfrequently attacked, the drivers and traders murdered or routed, and their horses and goods seized by the marauders. Many instances of this kind could be related.

The great Chickasaw trading-path was particularly infested by hostile Creeks and Choctaws. The former were accustomed, when at war with the Cherokees and Catawbas—and they were not often on friendly terms with those nations, till the time of Governor Glen—to extend their predatory incursions beyond the Savannah, and lay in ambuscades on that portion of the old Keowee trail that traversed the territory now embraced in the Districts of Edgefield and Abbeville.

An illustration, from life, of the daily movements and stages of one of these caravans, will not be uninteresting. It occurs, however, at a period somewhat later than the one whose history we are now relating. Early in the spring of 1776, Bartram having completed his tour among the Lower and Overhill Cherokees, returned to Dartmouth, at the mouth of Broad River of Georgia, and there learned that a company of adventurers for the West were quite forward with their preparations for setting out. He determined to join them.

"Our place of rendezvous," he says, "was Fort Charlotte, on the opposite side of the Savannah, and about a mile from Fort James." Old Fort Charlotte stood close on the east bank of the Savannah, in the present District of Abbeville. The waste of time, and still more ruinous floods from the river, have not yet completely demolished the once powerful stone-walls and bastions of this venerable relic of the past. We shall have occasion to speak of it, yet again, in a more interesting connection.

"On the 22d of June, we set out from Fort Charlotte, in company with Mr. George Whitfield, who was chief of our caravan. We traveled about twenty miles, and lodged at the farm of Mons. St. Pierre, a French gentleman, who received and entertained us with great politeness and hospitality. Next morning, after breakfast, we set off again, continuing nine or ten miles farther down the river, where we stopped at a plantation, the property of one of our companions, where we were joined by the rest of the company. After dining here, we set off again, and proceeding six miles down the river, we crossed over into Georgia, taking a road which led us into the great trading path from Augusta to the Creek Nation. Early in the evening we arrived at the Flat Rock, where we lodged. This is a common rendezvous for the traders and Indians, and lies near the bank of one of the head branches of the Ogechee.

"This evening, two companies of Indian traders from Augusta arrived and encamped near us; and as they were bound for the Nation, we concluded to unite with them; it was a favorable opportunity, in case of necessity. Next morning, we set forward together.

"I thought worthy of note, a singular method the traders made use of to reduce the wild young horses to their hard duty. When one persisted in refusing to receive his load—if threats, the whip, and other abuse prove insufficient—after being haltered, a pack-horseman catches the tip of one of his ears between his teeth, and sharply pinches it, when instantly the furious creature trembling, stands perfectly still till he is loaded.

"Our caravan now consisted of about twenty men and sixty horses; we made a formidable appearance, having now little to apprehend from predatory bands or outlaws.

"At evening we came to camp on the banks of a beautiful creek, a branch of Great Ogechee, called Rocky Comfort, where we found excellent accommodations, there being pleasant, grassy spots to spread our beds upon, surrounded with extensive cane-meadows, affording the best of food for our horses.

"First of July, we encamped on the banks of the Oconee; it is here about two hundred and fifty yards over, and we crossed it next day by fording, and traveled twenty miles. The following day's journey, of twenty miles, carried us across the Ocmulge by a ford of three or four hundred yards over. At this point the Ocmulge is just forty miles distant from the Oconee. In the evening we encamped on the banks of Stony Creek—six miles beyond the river. The travel of the next day carried us over the Great and Little Tobosochte Creeks, to an encampment on Sweet Water, a beautiful brook. Afternoon of the following day, we crossed Flint River, through a ford of about two hundred and fifty yards.

"We had not gone far beyond the Flint, before the heat and burning flies began to torment our horses to such a degree, as to excite compassion even in the hearts of pack-horsemen. We traveled almost from sunrise to his setting, amidst a flying host of these persecuting spirits, that formed a vast cloud around our caravan, so thick as to obscure every distant object. The head, neck, and shoulders of the leading horses were continually in a gore of blood.

"The next day, being still oppressed and harassed by the stinging flies and heats, we halted at noon, being unable longer to support ourselves under such grievances. Two days after, we arrived at the Chatahooche,* opposite the Uchee Town, where, after unloading our horses, the Indians came across to us in large canoes, in which, with their assistance, we ferried over the merchandize, and afterwards swam over the horses."

We have thus conducted a caravan from Old Fort Charlotte, along the great trading path of the Creeks and Chichasaws, leading to Augusta and Charleston, from the towns of the former. The minute topography of the botanist will enable the reader, by reference to any good map of the country, to trace the entire route. Previous to 1736—the year in which Augusta was founded—Savannah Town, or Fort Moore, as we have already seen, was the great terminus on our western border, of this famous trail. From that point it ran to Charleston, first by the head of the Salkehatchie, through or near the present site of Barnwell Village, thence to the Ponds, in the north-west corner of Colleton District, from which it passed towards Conwayborough, and to the Ashley.

George Whitfield, who is mentioned as chief of the caravan, which Bartram accompanied to the

* Bartram writes it Chata-Uche.

Creek Nation, was a nephew of the celebrated Rev. George Whitfield, and father of the late Tyler Whitfield, of Anderson. He was also the grandfather of Drs. Charles and Thomas Wilson, of the Rev. John Wilson and Mrs. Amelia Simmons—all formerly of Abbeville District, but the first two now of Georgia, and the latter of Mississippi—and of Susan Winter Wilson, first wife of Dr. John Logan, of Greenwood.

Five years previous to this adventure he was married at White Hall, the then residence of Gen. Andrew Williamson, of Revolutionary memory, to Miss Frances Tyler of Virginia, sister to Mrs. Williamson, and Mrs. Leroy Hammond, of Snow Hill. John Lewis Gervais, a well-known German land speculator, and Justice of the Peace, who lived on the plantation at present owned by John Foster, near White Hall, officiated on the occasion—a minister not often being convenient at that early day for such a purpose.

A few days after the wedding, Gervais wrote as follows to his friend, Colonel Henry Laurens, of Charleston: "I had the honor, last week, at Mr. Williamson's, to marry Mr. George Whitfield, nephew of the late Rev. Mr. Whitfield, to Miss Frances Tyler, sister of Mrs. Williamson—a charming bride, who would have made a figure in Charleston, as well for her appearance as elegance of dress. A Justice less grave than myself might have been tempted to give, now and then, a sly look."*

* Charleston Courier of recent date.

This letter was dated from Herrenhausen—the name of the correspondent's residence—2d of October, 1771. The Rev. George Whitfield had died the month previous to the wedding at White Hall. At the time of Bartram's visit to Fort Charlotte, George Whitfield owned the old Fort Charlotte plantation, now the property of Col. Wm. Tatom, and was probably the commandant of that post. The year before it had been visited by the Rev. Wm. Tennent, as a Commissioner with Wm. Henry Drayton from the Provincial Congress, who, after examining its works and means of defence, wrote as follows in his journal: "I called for Captain Whitfield and consulted with him on the propriety of cutting down his corn around the fort."* The Tories and Loyalists were then gathering all their strength in Upper-Carolina preparatory for the great struggle, and an attack from them was expected every day upon the fort.

Several stages of a caravan, which was sent up to Savannah Town by the Board, in 1717, we found thus specified in the journals: They were to proceed from Charleston, first to one Peter St. Julien's, thence to Washmasaw, after which they were to pass to the Ponds, and at Edisto Garrison, where they would arrive after leaving the Ponds, they were to await Lieut. James Howe, who would conduct them to Fort Moore.

Peter St. Julien, it appears from other passages of the journals, lived at a point where the trails met

---

* Drayton's Memoirs.

coming respectively from the Congarees and Savannah Town to Charleston. It was a great camping place, and the Board frequently deposited corn there for the use of the public caravans. Lieut. Howe held the post of Lieutenant in the fort, and had been ordered, doubtless, on this occasion, to march with a guard to meet the approaching caravan and protect it over part of the path that was peculiarly exposed.

This much of the old Creek and Chickasaws trail formed the larger part of the first path of commercial communication that was ever opened up between Charleston and the Cherokees. Soon after the erection of a factory at Savannah Town, under the protection of Fort Moore, the Indians themselves cut a trail from their towns down the east bank of the Savannah to that place, of sufficient width and straightness for the conveyance of peltries and goods on the backs of "burdeners." As the traffic increased it gradually enlarged, and by the time the trading houses and fortress were erected at Augusta, in 1736, under the auspices of Oglethorpe, it had become a thoroughfare for caravans of pack-horses.

Savannah Town was now deserted, and Augusta became a great centre of trade. Caravans by the trail, and pettiaugers by the water route, were constantly in motion, bearing their loads of merchandize from Charleston to Augusta. She was soon a busy mart, and a large town full of houses and people—the first example on the continent of the astonishing growth of a western village into a populous town. The valuable trade of the three great Indian nations united its streams in her streets; and perhaps at no time since have they exhibited more stirring or business-like scenes.

An old writer thus describes Augusta at this period: "The trustees ordered the town of Augusta to be laid off in 1735, and garrisoned in 1736. Several ware-houses were built, and furnished with goods suitable to the Indian trade—boats were built by the inhabitants calculated to carry about ten thousand weight of peltry: making four or five voyages annually to Charleston. Augusta became a general resort for the Indian traders in the spring, where they purchased annually about two thousand pack-horse loads of peltry; and including townsmen, pack-horsemen and slaves, it was calculated that six hundred white persons were engaged in this trade. A path was opened to Savannah, which was passable on horseback."*

Bartram visited Augusta in the spring of 1776; but was too intent on his favorite study of flowers and animals, to make a single observation of its social, commercial or architectural advancement at that period. He did better for the site of Savannah Town, and old Fort Moore; and his notes, though brief in relation to it, show that a rapid decay had fallen upon everything there, after the founding of Augusta.

"In early times, the Carolinians had a fort, and kept a good garrison here, as a frontier and Indian

---

* McCall's History of Georgia, p. 59.

trading post, but Augusta superseding it, this place was dismantled; and since that time, which probably cannot exceed thirty years,* the river hath so much encroached upon the Carolina shore, that its bed now lies where the site of the fort then was; indeed, some told me that the opposite Georgia shore, where there is now a fine house and corn field, occupies the place."†

At length, after many fair promises to the Indians, the Commissioners, in 1718, erected at the Congarees, a fort and store-house. It was then that pack-horse trains from Charleston, first began to pass by that route towards the interior, and the Cherokees and Catawbas to the sea-board. The spot had been chosen for the new garrison and factory, some distance eastward of a direct route to the Cherokees, for the equal accommodation of the lower towns and Catawbas, as Savannah Town had been as far to the westward of it, for the convenience of the Over-hill Cherokees, and the more distant Creeks and Chickasaws.

It is quite probable that the Congaree and Chickasaw trails united, before reaching Charleston, at the present site of Dorchester; and that there was the residence of Peter St. Julien. From that point the former ran directly up the east bank of the Four Hole Creek, towards the nearest point of the Santee, thence across Amelia Township to the Congaree River, and up it to the fort at the falls. Beyond

* Forty years, rather.

† Bartram, p. 314.

these it followed the southern bank of the Saluda to the spot, where, in after-years, Ninety-six was built, and where it fell into a path that was, no doubt, even then known as the great Keowee trail leading from the lower towns to Charleston.

Fort Moore and the Congarees were the only garrisoned posts erected on the border by the government, at this early period, for the protection of the Indian trade. It must be reasonably supposed, therefore, that the first horse-paths from Charleston to the upper-country, touched at those points in their course. But, doubtless, before 1693, the year in which the Cherokees made their first formal visit to the English—perhaps in the earliest primitive times, an Indian foot trail ran by the most direct route from their towns to the main, at or near the mouth of the Ashley. This became gradually much frequented, as intercourse between the two people increased. In process of time the peltry traffic was inaugurated, and soon the Cherokees had grown so dependent upon the English for all the necessaries of life, that their greatly enlarged commerce required, if not a wider, a more direct thoroughfare than either the Chickasaw or Congaree path.

It was then that pack-horse trains began to frequent the Keowee Trail throughout its whole extent; and it became a great central high-way of communication between Charleston and the interior, and the mountain valleys of the Cherokee Nation. It formed a common track with the path last described, as far northward from Charleston as the present site of

Dorchester or its vicinity; thence after crossing Four Holes Creek, at the point, where, before the Revolution, the old Four Holes Bridge stood, it passed to the site of Orangeburg Court-house, and there crossing North Edisto, it pursued its course along the ridge between the main branches of that stream, to the head waters of the Little Saluda, the country on each hand abounding in rich pastures of cane. From Little Saluda, it ran to Gowdy's Fort and trading house at Old Ninety-six, where, having formed a juncture with the trail from the Congarees, it pursued its way, almost in a bee line, to the towns of the Lower Cherokees.

In the vicinity of Greenwood, it crossed Little Wilson's Creek at a ford long afterwards known, and used in the plantation formerly owned by the Rev. Joel Townsend, and ran thence through the lands of the late Capt. T. B. Byrd, and Capt. J. Johnson, having traversed, from Old Ninety-six, grounds now owned by Maj. R. A. Griffin and Nathaniel McCants. It passed a few paces eastward of the large granite rock, already described as standing immediately on the Barksdale Ferry Road, near the Rock Church.

A few miles north of the Pointing Rock, it crossed Rocky Creek, just above the site of Venning's Mill, and ran thence to the Corouaka, which it crossed at a spot famous as a camping ground with all the traders and Indians, who once frequented this celebrated trail. It lies on a plantation recently occupied by H. W. Leadbetter.

At that period, the creek, here, was shaded by a

notable grove of large white oaks, on which account it received from the Indians the name of *Quoo-ran-he-qua*—the place of very big white oaks. It was estimated, by the measurement of that time, to be fourteen miles from Ninety-six, and eighty-two from Keowee.

Adair mentions it as being a well-known camp-ground, and presents its name, to illustrate the manner in which the Cherokees frequently combined with their words a syllable or an initial letter of their sacred name for God, when they wished to express an idea in the superlative sense.*

From the Coronaka, it pursued its course towards the head branches of Mulberry Creek, passing a little to the west of the present site of Cokesbury. In the fork of the Mulberry, it turned suddenly, for a short distance, to the left, to take in its way the old trading post at Dewitt's Corner. Thence it ran across the head waters of Rocky River, and passed, in a similar manner, through the head streams of all the eastern tributaries of the Savannah, that flowed south of its point of destination, the town of Keowee on the ancient Isundiga.

Bartram, in his travels, thus speaks of the old Keowee Trail: "I chose to take this route up the Savannah River, in preference to the straight and shorter road from Charleston to the Cherokee country, by Fort Ninety-six, because, by keeping near this great river, I had frequent opportunities

* Adair's North American Indians, p. 70.

of visiting its steep banks, vast swamps, and low grounds. Had I pursued the *great trading path*, by Ninety-six, I should have been led over a high, dry, sandy ridge, and, a great part of the distance, an old settled or resorted part of the country, and, consequently, void of the varieties of original or novel productions of nature."*

The fort referred to here by the botanist, was not the star redoubt, whose remains are still conspicuous on the site of old Ninety-six; nor was it the temporary defence of palisades, thrown up on the opposite hill, a little south of the Child's House, by General Williamson and the Whigs of the Ninety-six District, in November of 1775. It will be seen, as our narrative progresses, that an older fort than either of those once stood at that famous spot.

There is scarcely a plantation, through which the Keowee Trail passed in the upper-country, that does not still bear the marks of its once well-worn track; and wherever the primitive forest, that shaded it in old times, has been left untouched, its deep, narrow bed is as plainly traceable as if English armies and pack-trains had gone over it—as of yore—but yesterday. Such traces of it are particularly noticeable in the vicinity of Cokesbury, and near its termination, as it goes down into the Valley of the Keowee.

This ancient highway is often confounded, at present, in Abbeville District, with the old Reed's

* Page 315.

and Pratt's Mill Road—a public work that had little, at any time, in common with it, and, in comparison, was but an affair of recent date. The Reed's Road was the result of an enactment by a Federal State Legislature; the Keowee Trail had its origin long previous, doubtless, to the period when any monarchy of the old world had obtained a foothold on American soil.

In the index to Dr. Cooper's Statutes of South Carolina, we find the following record: "An Act to make, and keep in repair, a road from Ninety-six Court-house, to the mill of George Reed, on Long-Cane Creek, and from thence to Pratt's Mill, on the north-west fork of Long-Cane.—Passed, March 5th, 1778."

It was not, however, until seven years after, that this enactment was carried into effect. Two years subsequent to the Revolution, a court—sitting at the Old Block House, or in the house of General Pickens, one of the presiding judges, (both of which stood under the south-eastern side of the hill on which the village of Abbeville has since been built,)—appointed, in accordance with the provisions of the Act, Captain John Irwin, Captain Hugh Wardlaw, and Colonel John Logan, to survey the designated route. This they soon accomplished, and the same year, (1785,) the Reed's Road was cut from Pratt's Mill, by Reed's, to Ninety-six.

The tradition goes, that one of the surveyors fixed the sights of his compass at Pratt's, and wagered the company a bottle of brandy that, at the end of his course, he would strike Ninety-six. The bet was taken, two to one, on the spot. The line ran out over the top of the hill, on which they were at that time preparing to build the old Cambridge College. The result was of considerable interest to the party; for they were men of no ordinary physical powers, and old Ninety-six never knew what it was to suffer from a dearth of brandy, of the best and purest bead.

Soon after leaving Pratt's, the Reed's Road fell into a part of the Keowee Trail, near Dewitt's Corner, on the plantation now owned by Captain J. R. Wilson; which, with its general direction, and lower terminus, well accounts for its being confounded with the Keowee path. Thence it ran by Reed's, (now Cochran's Mill,) through the parade-ground, at Lomax's, to the Deadfall, and the present site of Greenwood, where its track still deeply marks the lots occupied by R. M. White, and J. R. Tarrant. At a point between the latter and the Barksdale Ferry road, it ran into the old Ninety-six and Abbeville Road. Much of this old highway has been long out of use, and its former site well nigh forgotten.

The enterprise and progress of the present age have developed a fact in relation to the ancient Indian trading paths of Carolina, that is too remarkable to be omitted here; though we have never seen it noticed by any one. Nearly the entire railway system of the State has been constructed almost precisely on the routes of the old peltry trails of her infant commerce. The South Carolina Road passes between Charleston and Augusta, over the line of the great Chickasaw and Creek path; the Greenville and Columbia along that of the Cherokees; and the Carolina and Charlotte pursues, on the ridge between the Broad and Catawba Rivers, with no less fidelity, the old path that led from the Catawbas to the Congarees. But the correspondence does not cease here; one of the first railway enterprises in the State of Georgia was to construct, from Augusta, a continuation of the line completed in Carolina, over the Chickasaw and Creek trail; and but recently, Charleston has been rejoicing at her betrothal, by a tie of the iron rail, to the same prolific region, and in the main, over the same route, in the completion of the Memphis and Charleston Railroad, from which, a hundred and thirty years ago, she was accustomed to receive, on the backs of pack-horses, the bulk of her exports.

The great enterprise of the Blue Ridge Railroad, is only a continuation, by rail, of the ancient extension of the Keowee path from the site of Fort Prince George, across the mountains to the Over-hill settlements, and the teeming valleys of the Tennessee; and, when it shall have been accomplished, for which we have the obligations of a State that has never asked for more, as an incentive to noble action, than to know the path of her true interest and glory—and the long projected Savannah Valley Road, constructed over the route of the old Savannah, or Isandiga trail, which connected Augusta with the

Lower Cherokee towns—the correspondence will be general and complete, and the shrill echoes of the steam-car will be heard amid the same hills and valleys, in every part of the State, where, in the olden time, resounded the gentler notes of the pack-horseman's bells. "There is nothing new under the sun;" and, while we are wondering at these new combinations of science and art, an amazement no less great possesses us, on the discovery that, after all, they are only the more complete development of the ideas and practice of our less cultivated immigrant fathers.

The philosophy of this does not lie deeper than two simple facts: the one of history, and the other of political economy. The aborigines of America invariably displayed in their choice of lands, on which to form their settlements, a judgment as shrewd and business-like as that of the whites. Hence the same regions of country that were the productive hunting-grounds and maize fields of the Indians, are still the prolific sources of the valuable staples of modern traffic and exchange—and political economy teaches the fundamental principle that commerce is like the natural processes of crystalization—it best performs its work when left free and untrammeled. Here, therefore, we have, from her history, a powerful, but unobtrusive argument, for all that has been done or undertaken, in the development of the physical resources of our beloved commonwealth.

If the recent substitution of the railway for the old fashioned market thoroughfare has done away, in great part, with the suffering and exposure incident to the men and animals employed on the latter, the relief afforded the same objects, in an earlier age, by the widening of the narrow pack-horse trails into commodious wagon-roads. was no small approximation to the facilities and comforts of the present system. The abuse of horses, and the hardships of the drivers, on the trading paths, were sometimes dreadful, and never inconsiderable.

It may be truly said, that the bleaching bones of the former made white many a weary mile of the great trails leading from Charleston to the Cherokees, and towards the Mississippi; and not unfrequently mingled with them, were seen the ghastly skeletons of men and women. It is a curious fact, that the Cherokee Indians would leave their dead unburied on the path, rather than contract ceremonial uncleanness in the act of preparing them for interment, according to their custom, when at home, and in possession of their usual means of purification. In some instances, the bodies thus deserted, were covered up, out of reach of the wolves, by the traders belonging to the passing caravans. An instance of this kind occurred on the Keowee trail, just below Ninety-six, not long after the settlement of that place.

An Indian having died at that spot, in a party with which were Adair and several other traders, his body as usual, was about to be left by his savage comrades to the wild beasts, where it lay, when the white men, moved by feelings of humanity, buried it themselves. A more notable instance took place, about the same time, at or near the Congarees.

We described, in a previous chapter, the curious marriage of a young Indian woman, surnamed the Dark Lantern, to an Englishman of Charleston, and her initiation into the Establishment. Not long after that event, and her dismissal from the church, on account of her licentiousness, she fell sick, and died on the path near the Congarees, the scene of her marriage, and notwithstanding a twin-brother was one of the party, her body was left exposed in the woods.

In February, 1755, Gov. Glen invited a large number of the head-men of the Cherokee Nation to meet him in a talk, in Charleston, when he received in reply the following message from Old Hop, of Chote, the great head-chief of the Nation: "I have ordered my head-men to proceed no farther to meet you than the Congarees. From time to time, according to your Excellency's desire, I have sent down my best warriors to Charleston, who, by reason of fatal sickness contracted either there or on the trail, returned no more. Their *bones yet lie on the path, and are in many places to be seen.*"*

The abuse suffered, however, by the animals used in these pack-horse trains, was, in great part, owing to the savage treatment they received from the merciless drivers. They seldom decamped in the morning before the sun was already so high as to be hot

* Indian books in Columbia.

and disagreeable. Every driver carried a heavy whip, made of the toughest cow-skin. They started all at once, the horses ranging themselves in regular Indian file—the most experienced in the front, and the younger in the rear; then the chief driver, with the crack of his whip, and a whoop or a shriek, which rang through the forest and plains, spoke, often in the Indian tongue, commanding them to proceed, which order was repeated by all the company, and they set off at once in a brisk trot, which was incessantly urged, and continued as long as the miserable brutes were able to move forward. When they could go no farther, a camp was formed, frequently before the afternoon—the most favorable part of the day for travel—was more than half gone.

Bells were suspended from the necks of the horses, and these, though frequently stuffed with grass at starting in the morning, were soon loosened, by its jolting out, and they were not stopped again during the day; and, altogether, the incessant ring and clatter of the bells, the whoops, shouts and loud curses of the pack-horsemen, produced a noise and din on these primitive highways, scarcely less disagreeable and annoying, though not so loud and shrill, as the modern steam-whistle.*

---

* Bartram's Carolina.

CHAPTER XIII.

The Abuses already detailed, not the only source of Disorder and Disaffection in the Nation—France fiercely competes with England for the Sovereignty of the West—The advantageous position of the former firmly established in Canada and in the Mississippi Valley—Her magnificent Schemes, Finesse, and indomitable Energy—The English to be circumscribed, harassed, and, if possible, driven from the Continent—Upper Carolina exposed to French Emissaries, and menaced by encroaching French Settlements, &c.

The abuses arising in the Nation, from the indiscriminate granting of licenses, from the traffic in intoxicating liquors, and the pernicious influence of men, who falsely claimed to be missionaries of the Cross, though prevalent and lamentable enough, were not the only, nor the most exciting, sources of anarchy and disaffection. England had never been without formidable rivals in her efforts to possess the soil and dominion of North America.

The most powerful of these were the French, under the sagacious rule of Louis the Fourteenth; and never had France encountered her ancient rival on a more magnificent field, and never, in her history, had she displayed a more brilliant policy, or pushed her deep-laid schemes with greater energy. Firmly established in Canada and Louisiana, and rapidly connecting these extreme points by a chain of military posts, stretching through the entire length of the Mississippi Valley, and in close commercial alliance with several of the most powerful tribes of the Continent, her triumph was apparently beyond peradventure, and not far distant.

The design of the French was to secure the possession of the great Valley, and having circumscribed the English colonists within their narrow belt along the Atlantic, when everything was ready for the blow, to fall upon them with the hordes of their savage confederates, and exterminate or drive them from the soil.

In an old map constructed previous to 1741, by M. De L'Isle, geographer to the French King, a definite line is traced, marking the eastern limit of France's assumed domain on the American Continent.* It is set out from a point near the City of Charleston, ran north-eastward to Cooper River, which it crossed some sixty miles from the ocean—passed the Santee one hundred miles from its mouth, turned north-westward along the eastern bank of that stream till it reached the Catawba; pursued this tributary into the Alleghany Mountains, followed their course around the head waters of the Potomac to the Susquehanna, crossing it at a point some sixty-five miles from the head of the Chesapeak Bay—ran thence up its eastern bank to the North Branch, and along that stream to the Mohawk, which it crossed some fifty miles above its junction with the

* See Map accompanying Cox's Carolina.

Hudson—thence to a point near the lower extremity of Lake Champlain, and along the channel of that water to the mouth of the Sorrelle, by which it passed, finally, to the River St. Lawrence.

The sandy strip of country lying between this imaginary, defiant line of frontier and the ocean, was all that was allowed England for her portion of the continent. France claimed and ran off for herself the lion's share—the rich, inexhaustible domain of the Mississippi Valley, and an illimitable territory stretching back into the unexplored regions of the West. Had her diplomacy, skill and military energy, won for her the permanent possession of all that she had thus marked out, hers would have been the boast, that the sun never shone upon a more magnificent, territorial empire, than that she had acquired and planted in America.

As early as 1682, her enterprising voyagers had re-discovered the Mississippi, and explored it from its sources to the Gulf of Mexico.* The first expedition set out from Quebec, in Canada, three years after the English had formed their settlement on the coast of Carolina. It was led by a courageous Jesuit priest, named Marquette. His company was composed of Joliet, an experienced Canadian fur trader, five other Frenchmen, and several Indian guides. Their mission was to find the Mississippi River, of which they had heard many vague, though

* The Mississippi had been discovered by the unfortunate Spaniard, De Soto, one hundred and forty years before.

wonderful accounts from the Indians, and from Canadian traders, whose enterprise had led them as far south-westward as the region of the great lakes. Having ascended Fox River to the head of navigation, from Lake Michigan, with their birch-bark canoes on their shoulders, the voyagers crossed the country to the Wisconsin River, on which they again launched their frail boats and floated down to the Mississippi. Marquette, once on the bosom of the great stream he had come in search of, descended as far as the mouth of the Arkansas, charmed with the delightful climate, and the grand natural scenery that every day presented new features of beauty and sublimity to his astonished gaze. He here made the acquaintance of the Chickasaw Indians, who informing him that the banks of the river from their country to the sea, were inhabited by hostile nations, he decided to proceed no farther, and turning about his canoes, paddled northward on the Mississippi, till discovering the mouth of the Illinois, he ascended that stream to its source, and again bearing their canoes across the portage to the spot where Chicago now stands, they once more embarked on Lake Michigan, and, shortly after, Joliet reported their interesting adventures and discoveries to the authorities in Quebec.

A brave, enterprising young Frenchman, named La Salle, happened at that time to be in Quebec, and heard the glowing accounts brought back by those voyagers of the Mississippi and the South west. He had been educated a Jesuit, and had come to America in search of fame and adventure. Inspired by these discoveries, he conceived and resolved to execute the more daring exploit of exploring the Mississippi to its mouth. First, returning to France, in order to obtain a royal commission for his enterprise, with which he was also granted a monoply in the trade of buffalo skins, he sailed back to Canada, furnished with men and stores, and set out at once on this expedition by the way of the great lakes.*

Two years passed away, and La Salle was still on these waters purchasing furs and building forts. He had not, however, forgotten the main object of his voyage, and at length making his way to the Mississippi by the same route, doubtless, that had been pursued by Marquette, he there constructed a vessel better suited to the rough current of the Father of Waters, and was borne in safety to its mouth. Cox remarks, in his book on Carolina: "The River Meschacebe is so called by the inhabitants of the north; *cebe* meaning river, and *mescha*, great—the great river. The French, who learned it from them, pronounced the name corruptly, Mississippi. The correct name, "Meschacebe," it doth still retain among the savages during half its course. Afterwards, some call it Chucagua, others, Sassagoula and Malabanchia.

This history of the name, Mississippi, differs widely from that given us by the geographies in use.

Mooring his boat, and ascending a hillock in full view of the Gulf, he solemnly took possession of the

* Pickett's History of Alabama.

country in the name of his King Louis XIV., and in honor of him, called it Louisiana.

La Salle having thus accomplished the great object of his enterprise, returned to the country of the Illinois, there garrisoned Fort St. Louis, and hastened back to Canada and to France, to give an account of his discoveries.

On the fortunate results of these expeditions of Marquette and La Salle, France chiefly founded her claims to the Mississippi Valley, and the regions of the West; and began, without delay, to make ample provision for adding to her right of discovery—the better right of actual occupancy. Her first attempt to colonize the Mississippi proved abortive; but not discouraged, after a few years she renewed it with complete success, under the celebrated pioneer brothers, Iberville and Bienville.

This was in the spring of 1699, and, in three years more, these enterprising leaders had not only effected a settlement at Biloxi, in the territory of the present State of Mississippi, but had erected a fort and warehouses on Mobile Bay—had established a chain of military posts, as far up as the present City of Natchez, and were already in amity and commerce with various Indian tribes.

Louisiana, as defined by France, stretched northward from the Gulf, beyond the sources of the Alleghany and Monongahela.

It was about this period that the English of Carolina first began to harass the French, by sending emissaries to plot against them among the Muscogees and Alabamas.* These warlike tribes were induced to take up the bloody hatchet against the French; and they soon became so formidable as to threaten the existence of the colony. Those active emissaries from Carolina were no others, doubtless, than traders, whose interest in the Indian peltry traffic, just then beginning to be lucrative, as well as their inherent hatred and opposition to the French, moved them to adopt any, even the most unscrupulous measures to distress and ruin them. It does not appear that the public authorities of Carolina were yet fully aroused to a sense of the dangers which threatened them from the designs and encroachments of the French.

From a very early period after the settlement on the Cooper and Ashley, adventurous traders, both from Carolina and Virginia, had penetrated among the populous Indian nations, whose towns lay in the territory of the present States of Mississippi and Alabama. "These fearless British traffickers conveyed upon the backs of pack-horses such goods as suited the Indians, from distant Charleston to the remote Chickasaw Nation, over creeks without bridges, rivers without ferries, and woods pathless and pregnant with many dangers." † "Before the removal from Old Charlestowne, on the western bank of the Ashley, the proprietors forbade all trade with the Indians for seven years, that the settlers might become more numerous and better able to defend

* Pickett's History of Alabama. † Pickett, Vol. i., page 218.

themselves." "At the close of the Westoe war, in 1681, many individuals had added to their traffic the purchase of captives; and the proprietors endeavored to check abuses of this kind in the trade and intercourse with the natives, by taking under their nominal protection all the Indians within four hundred miles of Charleston. In 1691, it became expedient to limit, by a heavy penalty, the extent of trade and traveling to the vicinity of the settlement; but private enterprise must soon have rendered the enactment nugatory; for Archdale relates, not many years after, that the colonists had extended their inland trade to the distance of one thousand miles."*

The commerce, however, of Carolinians with the tribes on the Mississippi and Alabama, was as yet desultory and irregular—no trading posts had been established—it was sustained by private enterprise, and regulated wholly by private interest. It was not until 1717, that the Legislature deemed it proper to interfere in a traffic so distant and precarious. In the winter of that year, the House of Commons enjoined it upon the Commissioners of Indian Trade, to consult with Alex. Mackey and James Alford, in order to ascertain the most eligible spot on which to erect a factory for the uses of the trade with the Creeks and Chickasaws.† Several head-men of the latter nation were at that time in Charleston, and the

*Chalmers and Oldmixon Carr. Coll. Prof. W. J. Rivers's Topics of History.

† MS. Records in Secretary of State's Office.

question being referred to them, their reply was, that they had already intimated to the Governor their willingness to have a trading-house settled at the town of Coosa,* a place that could be easily furnished with goods by means of pack-horses from Savannah Town. It was decided at last, however, that the factory should be established at Talasse.† We have already remarked that, after the erection of this post, Colonel Hastings was withdrawn from the factory on Savannah, and made chief agent at the new house among the Creeks. It was at this time, that one Wm. McGilvery is mentioned as one of a party who had been employed to conduct twenty-three pack-horses from Charleston to the factory of the Creeks.

In the summer of 1718, Andrew Patterson, George Douglass, Wm. Parrot, Daniel Kennard, and an Indian, Sanhoe, were ordered by the Board to go up under Lieutenant Joseph Chambers in a periago to Savannah Town; after which they were to proceed, with their goods on horses, without Chambers, to the factory of the Creeks. Chambers was a lieutenant under Charlesworth Glover, at the Savannah Fort.

Three years before, the indefatigable Bienville had ascended the Alabama River from Mobile, and established at Tuskegee the famous old Fort Toulouse, in the very heart of the formidable Creek Nation. He had previously made frequent representations to

* Spelt in the old record, Coosatees.

† Indian Books in Secretary of State's Office, Columbia.

his government of the necessity of planting a fortress and trading post on the Alabama, in order to repel the aggressive Carolinians.* The bravery and address of Bienville had made him exceedingly popular with the Indians. Indeed, there was much in the French character that peculiarly fitted them for the business of intriguing among savages: their sprightly vivacity, their easy manners, and indomitable courage and energy, were qualities irresistibly fascinating to all the tribes with whom they came in contact in America. The erection of Fort Toulouse in a position that gave Bienville not only command of the Creek Confederacy, but the opportunity of tampering effectually with the Cherokees and Catawbas on the very borders of the English settlements, was observed by the latter with the most unaccountable apathy. It was not yet, by twenty years, that the fierce struggle began between Carolina and French Louisiana, not so much for the privileges and profits of the Indian trade as for the very existence of Carolina.

It appears from the recorded testimony in relation to these events, little of which has ever been published, that such, for that length of time, was the feebleness of her policy, and remissness of her public officers, compared with the persevering energy and admirable sagacity of the French, that she was chiefly indebted for her ultimate triumph and safety to her own extraordinary and unflinching chivalry,

* Pickett.

in the moment of trial, united with British valor in the field.

English writers, even of that day, did not hesitate to eulogize the skill and tact displayed by the French in America: "The French are a great, enterprising, polite nation, and fully sensible of the advantages of foreign colonies in reference to European trade; and use all manner of artifices to lull their neighbors asleep with fine speeches, and plausible pretenses, whilst they cunningly endeavor to compass their designs by degrees, even at the hazard of encroaching on their friends and allies, and depriving them of their territory in time of peace, and contrary to the most solemn treaties."*

Bienville was now well prepared to pay back to Carolina, with full interest, the intrigues and aggressions of 1703; and from this period, both French and Spanish emissaries, usually under the disguise of private inoffensive traders, began to frequent the Nation. Some of these, it has already been observed, were men of education and ability—a few of them Jesuits of rare learning and address—for Carolina was called upon in this exigency to contend not only against the power and skill of the French, but against secularized Popery and spiritual wickednesses from high places. The distinguished Jesuit *voyageurs*, whose exploits on the Mississippi have been described, were emissaries engaged in the prosecution of arduous enterprises, not for the aggrandizement of

---

* Cox's Carolina.

France only, but to win new and wider fields in which to disseminate the superstitions and mummery of Rome. Mr. Bancroft, when treating of the expedition of Father Marquette, closes an imposing period with this rhetorical flourish: "and France and Christianity stood in the Valley of the Mississippi;" when at that very moment, thousands of poor Huguenots, ruined and expatriated through the weakness and bigotry of Louis XIV., and the malice of intolerant priests, were crying to Heaven to avenge an *outraged* Christianity.

The same couriers who announced to Europe the successful exploration of the Mississippi, bore, after a short interval, the more astounding news that Louis had decreed the Edict of Revocation. The first centennial anniversary of the *Great Massacre* occurred while LaSalle was in the midst of his explorations; and though in the depths of the wilderness, and surrounded by savages, it is quite probable that the devout Jesuit did not fail to observe a day so sacred in the calendar of all true Papists with becoming ceremonies and respect.

"Facts are stubborn things," yet it is not seldom that, under beautiful figures of speech, they are found either perverted or wholly ignored. France and Romanism, very probably, stood in 1673, for the first time, in the Mississippi Valley; but it by no means follows with reason that the *genius* of Christianity accompanied them either in the person or inspirations of Father Marquette.

France, it appears, relied much upon Jesuit sagacity to carry out her plans for harassing and circumventing the English; but bold, learned and indefatigable as they were, the latter, when once in the field, were scarcely inferior to them, even in their own boasted art of moulding savages to their purpose. And it may be inferred too, from the following confession found in a letter written by one Father Vivier, that they were not always so busy with their traffic, so practical and plodding, as not to find time to hurl an occasional bomb into the theological magazine of the holy brotherhood. "The English, as well as the French, trade among the Alabama Indians. You can easily imagine what an obstacle this presents to the *progress of religion;* for the *English are always ready to excite controversy.*" Indeed, humble traders as they were, in the secret employment of neither church nor state; but trafficking among the Indians with the sole view of building up their private fortunes, they were not all of them unlearned or destitute even of the polished weapons of scholarship.

CHAPTER XIV.

James Adair, the Trader and Historian—His valuable History of the Southern Indians—Charleston Library—Colonel John Galphin—A narrative of adventures and hair-breadth escapes in the life of Adair.

James Adair, the author from whom we have so frequently quoted, and from whose valuable and now rare book the world has derived most that is known of the manners and customs of the Southern Indians, was for forty years, a trader among the Cherokees and Chickasaws. He was not only well versed in the dialects of those tribes, but was also learned in the Hebrew, the Oriental, and Latin languages; and displays in his writings much good sense, and rare powers of observation. His "History of the American Indians," was published in London, in 1775, the greater part of which appears to have been written in the midst of the arduous duties and turmoils of his adventurous occupation.

Its style is exceedingly figurative and characteristic—partakes much of the idiom of the Indian dialects to which the author was so long accustomed; and this imparts to it a quaintness, which, with the novelty of the subject, the remarkable life of the writer, the cogency of his reasoning, his ingenious philosophy, earnest truthfulness, and stalwart vigor, renders it one of the most interesting, as well as valuable works relating to American history.

The title of this book has a place in the catalogue of the South Carolina College Library, but it is no longer found in its alcove of American History—the copy having been unfortunately consumed with a private house that was burned down a few years ago in Columbia. The only remaining one that we know of in the State, belongs to the Charleston Library, whose shelves are peculiarly rich in collections of valuable, old and rare books. This copy has a history of its own worth relating. It was once the property of Col. George Galphin, the famous Indian trader and Whig of the Revolution, whose residence was at Silver Bluff. On one of its fly-leaves is inscribed George Galphin, and the year 1775, in that beautiful style of chirography peculiar to the business-men of his day. It afterwards fell into the hands of John Drayton, and was by him presented to the Charleston Library, in 1802. Galphin is frequently mentioned by the author in terms of flattering commendation.

It is to be regretted, however, that an observer so intelligent, and so admirably situated for obtaining the minutest information, in a field becoming every day more and more interesting, should have collected and used it mainly to illustrate the single idea which Adair appears to have fondly cherished, that the Indians of America were descended from the ancient Israelites. His arguments in proof of this are exceedingly plausible and well arranged; but the value of the history would have been greatly enhanced if he had presented his facts free from the bias and prejudices of any pre-conceived notion.

An interesting narrative of adventures and hair-breadth escapes in the personal history of Adair, could be gleaned from his work. He was a traveler, and valiant warrior, as well as trader and historian. The great Chickasaw path, and the Keowee trail, were the frequent scenes of his adventures. In the Cherokee war of 1760, he served as Captain, under a commission from South Carolina, whose interest and prosperity he appeared ever ready to promote. In the Indian country he was not unfrequently found on the war-path, leading bands of painted warriors against the French and their savage allies, whom he hated with all the hearty good will of which an Englishman of that period was capable. For the dangers and exigencies of war, as well as its toils, he seems to have been admirably fitted; for, besides the quick penetration of the Indian, he possessed audacity, cool self-possession, and great powers of endurance. These qualities did not fail to make him popular and a great favorite with the Indians.

One or two incidents, related in his own language, will be sufficient to illustrate his manner of life, and the peculiarities of his style as a writer. At the request of Governor Glen, in the fall of 1747, he visited Charleston on business connected with the trade, while residing among the Chickasaws; and, having been detained longer than he expected, winter overtook him on his return, before he had cleared the territory of Carolina: "I was detained so late in November that the snow fell upon me at Edisto, the first day, in company with Captain W——d, an old trader of the Okwhuske, who was going to Savannah. In the severity of winter, frost, snow, hail and heavy rains succeed one another in these climes, so that I partly rode and partly swam to the Chickasaw country; for, not expecting to stay long below, I took no leathern canoe. Many of the broad, deep creeks that were almost dry when I went down, had now far overflowed their banks, ran a rapid rate, and were impassable to any but desperate people. When I got within forty miles of the Chickasaw, the rivers and swamps were dreadful, by rafts of timber driving down the former, and the great fallen trees floating in the latter, for near a mile in length. Being forced to wade deep through cane-swamps or woody thickets, it proved very troublesome to keep my fire-arms dry, on which, as a second means, my life depended; for, by the high rewards of the French, some enemies were always rambling about in search of us. On the eastern side of one of the rivers, in taking a sweep early in a wet morning, in quest of my horses, I discovered smoke on a small piece of rising ground in a swamp, pretty near the edge; I moved nearer, from tree to tree, till I discovered them to be Choctaws* creeping over the fire. I withdrew without

* The Choctaws were the firm friends of the French.

being discovered, and apprehended no danger, as at the worst I could have immediately *inswamped*,† and secured a retreat with my trusty fire-arms and taken through the river and the broad swamp, which then resembled a mixed ocean of wood and water. I soon observed the tracks of my horses, found them and set off. At the distance of a hundred yards from the river there was a large and deep lagoon, in the form of a semi-circle. As soon as I swam this and got on the bank, I drank a good draught of rum; in the middle of the river I was forced to throw away one of my belt-pistols and a long French scalping-knife I had found where the Choctaws killed two of our traders. When I got on the opposite shore I renewed my draught, put my fire-arms in order, and set up the war-whoop. I had often the like scenes till I got to the Chickasaw country, which was also all afloat. The people had been saying a little before I got home, that, should I chance to be on the path, it would be near fifty days before I could pass the neighboring deep swamps. As I had the misfortune to lose my tomahawk, and wet all the punk in my shot-pouch, by swimming the waters, I could not strike fire for the space of three days, and it rained extremely hard during that time. By being thoroughly wet so long, in the cold month of December, and nipped with the frost, seven months elapsed before I had the proper use of the fingers of my right

† An expressive term to the woodsman of that period when the high forest lands were so open as to afford no concealment in the moment of danger.

hand. On that long and dangerous war-path, I was exposed to many dangers, and yet so extricated myself that it would appear like quixotism to enumerate them."

Two years afterwards, he passed over the same path, at the head of a party of Chickasaws; and though he was thus well guarded, and the trail free from the obstructions of floods and snow, his trials and adventures were numerous and interesting.

"I unluckily had the honor to receive from the Governor, another polite letter, dated September, 1749, citing me, under the great seal of the province, to come down with a party of Indians, as I had given His Excellency notice of their desire of paying a friendly visit to South Carolina. And having purchased and redeemed three French captives,* whom the Chickasaws had taken in war, under their leader, Pa-ya-matahah, I now bestowed them on him, to enable him to make a flourishing entrance into Charleston, after the manner of their American triumphs. He was very kind to them, though their manners were as savage as his own; excepting a few beads, they used to count, with a small silver cross fastened to the top of them, they had nothing to distinguish them, and were ignorant of every point of Christianity."

* From a very early period, in her conflicts with the French and Spaniards, South Carolina had humanely offered a constant reward to the Indians for every one of those people who chanced to fall into their hands. In this way many were redeemed, and saved from torture and horrible deaths.

We saw, among the records in Columbia, an instance of a Frenchman's being brought to Charleston, and delivered to the Governor, by a squaw, named Peggy; for which she received a yard or two of strouds cloth, and a piece of duffils. Also, another of a Conjurer of one of the Cherokee towns, who, about the same time—1716—delivered to the authorities a French-Canadian, for whom he was ordered by the Board to be presented with a coat and hat. Peggy appears to have been a character of some note in that day; she came to town with her son, accompanied by Col. Hastings, superintendent at Savannah Town, and put up with him, at Mrs. Elizabeth Gray's, at the public expense. A year later, we found another note of Peggy. Hatton, an agent, was removed from Keowee to Tugaloo, and among other orders, he was directed, before he left the latter place, to take charge of fifteen deerskins, two bags of bullets, and a remnant of strouds —public property—which had been deposited in Peggy's *corn-house.*

"I set off with about twenty warriors, and a few women, along with the aforesaid war-leader, for Charleston. As the French kept a watchful eye on my conduct, and the commanding officers of Tombeckbe garrison, in the Choctaws, and the Alabama, in the Muscogee country, kept a continual communication with one another, the former equipped a party of their Choctaws to re-take the French prisoners by force, if we did not previously deliver them to a French party of the Muscogees, who were sent by the latter, as in the name of the whole nation—though falsely—to terrify us into a compliance. We had to pass through the Muscogee country on our way to the British settlement; and though the French were at a great distance, yet they planned their schemes with consummate wisdom; for the two companies met at the time appointed, from two opposite courses, of about a hundred and fifty miles apart, on the most difficult pass from Charleston to the Mississippi, where the path ran through a swamp of ten miles, between high mountains, which were impassable in any other place for a great distance on either side. Here, the Muscogees left the Choctaws, and met us in half-a-day's march of their advantageous camping place. The foremost of our party had almost fired on the Muscogees who were ahead of the rest; but as soon as they saw their white emblems of peace, they forbore, and we joined company. The Muscogee leader was called, by the traders, the 'Lieutenant;' and he had been a steady friend of the English, till—by our usual mismanagement in Indian affairs—he became entirely devoted to the French." A long talk here ensued upon the path, which resulted in the Chickasaws holding fast to their prisoners. The Lieutenant, finding that his threats and entreaties, both, proved ineffectual, he was obliged to acquiesce. "Soon after, we set off. On that day's journey, a little before we entered the long swamp, all our Chickasaw friends staid behind, killing and cutting up buffalo. By this means, I was a considerable way before the pack-horses when we entered into that winding and difficult pass, which was a continued thicket. After riding about a mile I discovered the fresh tracks of three Indians. I went back, put the white people on their guard, gave my horse and sword to a corpulent member of the Sphinx Company,* and set off ahead, shunning the path in such places as the savages were most likely to post themselves. Now and then I put up the whoop on different sides of the path, both to secure myself and intimidate the opposite scout party; otherwise, I might have paid dearly for it, as I saw, from a rising point, the canes where they were passing to shake. I became more cautious, and they more fearful of being inclosed by our party. They ran off to their camp, and speedily from thence up the craggy rocks, as their tracks testified. Their lurking place was as artfully chosen as a wolf could have fixed on his den. When our friendly Indians came up, it was too late to give chase; they only viewed their tracks. At night, the Chickasaw war-leader give out a very enlivening war-speech, and each of us lay in the woodland form of a war-camp. As we were on our guard, the enemy did not think it consistent with their safety to attack us—ambuscading is their favorite plan of operations. The next day, the Indians—by agreement—led the van, and I brought up the rear with the French prisoners. A short way from our camp there were steep rocks, very difficult for loaded

* A mercantile corporation.

horses to rear and ascend. Most of them had the good fortune to get safe up, but some of which I escorted, tumbled backwards; this detained us so long that the van gained nearly three miles upon us. I posted myself upon the top of one of the rocks as a sentinel, to prevent our being surprised by the Choctaws, and discovered them crawling on the ground, behind trees, a considerable way off, on the side of a steep mountain, opposite to us. I immediately put up the war-whoop, and told a young man with me the occasion of it; but he being fatigued and vexed with his sharp exercise, on account of the horses, only cursed them, and said we were warriors, and would fight them if they durst come near enough. As I was cool, I helped and hastened him off; in the meanwhile, I cautioned the captives against attempting to fly to the enemy in case they attacked us, as their lives should certainly pay for it; and they promised they would not. We at last set off, and met with no interruption; the enemy having a sharp dread of our party ahead, who would have soon run back to our assistance had they attacked us. About an hour after our van we got to camp. The Choctaws, at night, came down from the mountains and crept after us. Our camp was too well pitched to be surprised; but they used an artful stratagem to draw some of us into their treacherous snares; for they stole one of the bell-horses, and led it away to a place near their den, which was about a mile below us, in a thicket of reeds, where the creek formed a semi-circle. This horse was a favorite with the gallant and active young man I had escorted the day before to camp.

"As he was of a cheerful and happy temper, the people were much surprised to find him at night peevish and querulous, contrary to every part of his past conduct; and though he delighted in arms, and carried them constantly when he went from camp, yet he went out without any this night, though I pressed him to take them. In less than an hour he returned safe, but dejected. When he sat down, he drooped his head on his hands, which were placed on his knees, and said the enemy were lurking, and that we should soon be attacked, and some of us killed. As I pitied the state of his mind, I only told him that yesterday he and I knew the French savages were watching to take an advantage of us; but, for his satisfaction, I would take a sweep on foot, while the Chickasaws painted themselves according to their war custom, when they expected to engage an enemy. I went out with my gun, pouch, and belt-pistols, and within two hundred yards of the camp discovered the enemy's tracks; they had passed over a boggy place of the creek, upon an old hurricane-tree. I proceeded with the utmost caution —posting myself now and then behind large trees, and looking out sharply, lest I should fall into an ambuscade, which the Choctaws are cunning artists in forming. In this manner I marched for three quarters of an hour, and then took to high ground, a little above the enemy's camp, in order to return for help to attack them. But the aforesaid brave youth, led on by his ill genius, at this time mounted a fiery horse, which soon ran into the ambuscade, where they shot him with a bullet in his breast, and another entered a little below the heart. The horse wheeled round in an instant, and sprung off; but in pitching over a large fallen tree, the unfortunate rider, by reason of his mortal wounds, fell off, a victim to the barbarians. One of them soon struck a tomahawk into his head, just between his eyes, and jerked off a piece of scalp about the bigness of a dollar; they took also his Indian breeches, and a handkerchief he had on his head, and immediately flew through a thicket of briars, to secure their retreat. When they fired their two guns, I immediately gave the shrill war-whoop, which was resounded by one of the Chickasaws, who had been out hunting from the camp. They instantly set off at full speed—naked, except their Indian breeches and moccasins. I put myself in the same flying trim, on the enemy's firing; we soon came to the tragical spot, but without stopping we took their tracks, gave chase, and continued it a great way; unluckily, as we were running down a steep hill, they discovered us from the top of another, and soon dispersed themselves, by which means, not being able to discover one track of those forces, on the hard, hilly ground, we were obliged to give over the chase, and return to camp. We buried our friend by fixing, in a regular manner, a large pile of great logs for the corpse, with big tough saplings laid over it and on each side, thrust deep into the ground, to secure it from the wild beasts. Though the whole camp at first imagined the enemy had killed me, and captured the other, yet the warriors did not show the least emotion of gladness, nor even my favorite friend, the war-leader, when they first saw me safe; but the women received me with tears of joy. I mention this to show the force of education and habit; those who are used to scenes of war and blood become obdurate, and are lost to all the tender feelings of nature; while they whose employment it is to mourn for their dead, are susceptible of the tender impressions they were originally endued with by Deity."

This adventure, it is very probable, occurred in North Alabama; the principal Chickasaw towns lay on the head waters of the Yazoo River, so that their great trail to Charleston would pass directly across the mountain-spurs of that State.

"Soon after this event, our Chickasaw friends were attacked by small-pox, which, becoming general in the camp, I was under the necessity of setting off by myself, between Flint River and the Ockmulgee. I came up with a large camp of Muscogee traders, returning from the English settlements. They told me that they had been lately assured at Augusta by the Cherokee traders, that above a hundred and twenty of the French Shawanese, might be daily expected near that place, to cut off the English traders, and plunder their camp; and cautioned me, with much earnestness at parting, to keep a watchful eye during that day's march. After having rode fifteen miles, about ten o'clock I discovered a head through the trees—an Indian ascending a steep hill; he perceived me at the same instant—for they are extremely watchful on such dangerous attempts. As the company followed their leader in a line, each at a distance of a few yards from the other, all soon appeared in view. As soon as I discovered the foremost one, I put up the shrill whoop of friendship, and continually seemed to look earnestly behind me till we approached near to each other, in order to draw their attention from me, and fix it in that way, as supposing me to be the foremost of a company still behind. Five or six soon ran at full speed, on each side of the path, and blocked up two valleys, which happened to be at the place of our meeting, to prevent my escape. They seemed as if their design was to attack me with their barbed arrows, lest they should alarm my supposed companions by the report of their guns. I observed, that instead of carrying their bows and quivers over their shoulder, as is the custom, they held the former in their left hand, bent, and some arrows. I approached and addressed them, and endeavored to appear quite indifferent at their hostile arrangement. While I held my gun ready in my right hand, about five yards distant from them, I struck my breast with the but-end of one of my pistols, which I had in my left hand, and told their war-leader, with that vehemence of speech which is always requisite on such an occasion, that I was an English Chickasaw, and informed him by expressive gestures that there were two tens of Chickasaw warriors, and more than half that number of women, besides children, a little behind just beyond the first hill. At this news they appeared to be much confused, as it was unexpected for such a number of warlike enemies to be so near at hand. This Shawanno party consisted only of twenty-three middle-sized, but strong-bodied men with large heads and broad, flat crowns, and four tall young persons, whom I conjectured to be of the Cherokee Nation. I spoke a little to a hair-lipped warrior among them, who told me he lived in Tukkaseche, a northern town of that country. The leader whispered something to his waiter, which, in like manner, was communicated to the rest, and then they all passed by me, with sullen looks and glancing eyes. I kept my guard till they were out of arrow-shot, when I went on at a seemingly indifferent pace; but as soon as out of sight of their view, I rode about seventy miles with great speed, to avoid the danger of a pursuit, as I imagined they would be highly enraged against me, for their double disappointment.

"About sunset of the same day, I discovered more Indians ahead; but, instead of sounding the usual whoop of defiance, I went on, slowly and silently, a little way, reasoning with myself about the safest method in so dangerous a situation. I had apprehensions of their being another party of the Shawanno company, separated in that manner to avoid a pursuit, which otherwise might be very easy, by the plainness of their tracks through the long grass and herbage. But at the critical time—when I had concluded to use no chivalry, but give them leg-bail instead of it, by leaving my baggage-horses, and making for a deep swamp—I discovered them to be a considerable body of the Muscogee head-men, returning home with presents from Charleston, which they carried chiefly on their backs. The wolf-king, as our traders called him—our old steady friend of the Amooklasah town, near the late Alabama—came foremost, harnessed like a jackass, with a saddle on his back, well girt over one shoulder, and across under the other.

"We seemed equally glad to meet each other; they to hear how affairs stood in their country, as well as on the trading path; and I to find, that instead of bitter-hearted foes, they were friends, and would secure my retreat from any pursuit that might happen. I told them the whole circumstances attending my meeting the Shawanno, with their being conducted by our deceitful Cherokee friends, who were desirous of spoiling the old beloved white path, by making it red; and earnestly persuaded them to be on their guard that night, as I imagined the enemy had pursued me, when they found I had eluded their bloody intention. I endeavored especially to arouse them against the Cherokee, well knowing that one pack of wolves was the best watch against another of the same kind. They thanked me for the friendly notice I gave them, and we parted company. The Shawanese whom I had eluded, after rambling about, and by viewing the smoke of fires from the tops of high hills and trees, and carefully listening to the report of guns, fell in with two Chickasaw hunters, who were adopted relations of the Muscogee, and killed and scalped them, and then ran off to the northern towns of the Cherokees. This was the true and sole cause of the last war between the Muscogees and Cherokees, whose direful effects are still feelingly known to great numbers of the suffering inhabitants. I insert this by way of caution to statesmen hereafter."

The remainder of his journey to Charleston, appears to have been made without the occurrence of any other incidents worth relating. "The next year," he resumes, (1750,) "I had occasion to go to the Cherokee country, and happened to have a brave, cheerful companion, Mr. H. F., of Ninety-six settlement. We took a hearty drink of punch about ten miles from Keowee town, opposite to which the late Fort Prince George stood, and were proceeding along, when we discovered the fresh tracks of Indians in the path, who were gone ahead. As we could not reasonably have the least suspicion of their being enemies, we rode quite carelessly; but they proved to be the above-mentioned Mononga-hela Indians. Their watchfulness, and our singing, with the noise of our horses' feet, made them hear us, before they could possibly see us; when they suddenly posted themselves off the path, behind some trees, just in the valley of Six-mile Creek, in order to revenge their loss by the Euchees, which they ascribed to the information given by the white man.* But their Cherokee guide prevented them

* This refers to an incident that will be related farther on.

from attempting it, by telling them that, as his country was not at war with us, his life must pay for it, if they chanced to kill either of us; and as we were fresh and well armed, they might be sure we would fight them so successfully, as at least one of us should escape and alarm the towns. With this caution, they forbore their hazardous attempt. They squatted and kept close, therefore, so that we did not see one of them, and suspected no danger. By the discontinuance of their tracks, we soon knew we had passed them. But just after we had hidden two kegs of rum, about two miles from the town, four of them appeared unarmed, stark naked, and torn by the thickets. When we discovered them, we concluded they had been below on mischief. If we had not been so nigh the town, my companion would have fired at them. We went into Keowee, and the traders there soon informed us of their cowardly design.

"We went as far as the mid-settlements, and found most of the towns much disaffected to us and in a fluctuating situation, through the artifice of the French. In a few days we returned, but found they had blocked up all the trading paths, to prevent our traders from making their escape. Just as we descended a small mountain, and were about to ascend a very steep one, a hundred yards before us, which was the first of the Apalache, a large company of the lower-town Indians, started out from the sloping rocks, on the north side of the path, a little behind us. As they were naked except their breech-cloth, painted red and black, and accoutred every way like enemies, I bid my companion leave the luggage-horses and follow me: but as he had left his arms at the lower-towns, and was not accustomed to such surprises, it shocked him till they ran down upon him. On this, I turned back, and stood on my arms, expecting they would have fired upon us. However, they proposed some questions, which I answered, as to where we had been, and were going, and that we were not any of their traders. Had it been otherwise the dispute would have been dangerous. We got over the mountain, and safe to Tomassee;* here we rested two nights, and found the people distracted for mischief, to which the many causes before mentioned prompted them."

After diligent research, we have been unable to discover with certainty, who H. F. of Ninety-six was. It is quite probable, however, that the initial F. stands for the name of Francis; for we met with a note in the Indian Books, which intimates that Adair was, about this time, living at Ninety-six, in the house of Capt. Francis. It may be that the publication of his initials, with several others from the same source, of prominent men, who, at this early period, figured at Old Ninety-six and the Congarees will lead to more than one pleasing recognition.

"The Governor,† in less than a month after this period, had the strongest confirmation of the ill intention of these savages and their allies, through an

* Adair writes this name Tymahse. † Governor Glen.

express I sent with the intelligence; but the news was pocketed, and my services traduced. The French, however, had a different opinion of them; they were so well acquainted with the great damages I had done to them, and feared others I might occasion, as to confine me a close prisoner for a fortnight when I went to the Alabama garrison,* in the Muscogee country. They were fully resolved to have sent me down to Mobile or New Orleans, as a capital criminal, to be hanged for having abetted the Muscogees, Chickasaws and Choctaws, to shed a torrent of their Christian blood; though I had only retaliated upon them, the long train of blood they had, years before, wantonly spilled. They wanted to have confronted me with the French prisoners I formerly mentioned, and with the long Lieutenant, whom we met two days before the Choctaws killed one of our people, below *Book Pharaah*, or the Long Swamp. I was well assured he was to have gone down to be baptized, and so become a good West-Florida French chieftain, in order to condemn me, the poor bloody heretic. I saw him, and they had by this time taught him to count beads; but I doubted not of being able to extricate myself some way or other. They appointed double centries over me, for some days before I was to be sent down in the French King's large boat. They were strictly charged against laying down their weapons, or suffering any hostile thing to be in the place, where I was kept, as they deemed

* Old Fort Toulouse, at the juncture of the Cosa and Tallapoosa.

me capable of any mischief. I was not indeed locked up only at night, lest it should give offence to our friendly Indians; but I was to have been put in irons, as soon as the boat passed the Indian towns, that lay two miles below the fort.

"About an hour before we were to set off by water I escaped from them by land; and though they had horses near at hand, and a corrupt town of savages settled within a hundred and fifty yards of the garrison, yet, under those disadvantages, besides heavy rains that loosened the ground the very night before, I took through the middle of the low land, covered with briers, at full speed. I heard the French clattering on horseback along the path, a great way to my left hand, and the howling savages pursuing my tracks with careful steps; but my usual good fortune enabled me to leave them far enough behind, on a needless pursuit. As they had made my arms prisoners, I allowed them, without the least regret, to carry down my horses, clothes, and other things, and punish them by proxy, in the manner they intended to have served the owner, for his faithful services to his country."

Once in the Choctaw Nation, while traveling the path alone towards Mobile, he was beset by enemies and dangers, to which, he affirms, he came nearer falling a bloody victim, than any he ever encountered in all his life besides.

Near the remote town of that tribe, called Yowanna, which appears on Adair's meager map, to have stood on Pearl River, somewhere between the present sites of Jackson and Monticello, in Mississippi, a party of strolling Muscogees, who were endeavoring to surprise its inhabitants, and failing in their purpose, savage-like, not to be disappointed in their thirst for blood, attacked a camp of two white traders, and killed and scalped both, after a desperate fight with one of them, who happened to be a man of courage, and muscular strength. The marauders then, having hung the bodies of their victims on a neighboring tree with the halters of their own horses, fled with the plunder of six horse-loads of dressed deer skins, towards the Mobile River. They were quickly pursued, however, by the Great Red Chieftain of Yowanne, who, fortunately coming up with them, killed and scalped two of the party, and recovered the horses and leather. With these, and the scalps of the enemy, he expected, on showing them to the English authorities, to procure for himself and warriors a fresh supply of presents and ammunition. But he was sadly disappointed, for so cold was his reception by the Deputy-superintendent of Indian Affairs, that he returned home deeply incensed against the English.

Adair continues: "I have reason to remember this too well, for a little while after those white men were murdered, business calling me to Mobile by myself, I chose to decline the eastern path, and the middle one that leads by the *Chakehooma* Old Fields, as they were much exposed to the incursions of the Muscogee, and rode through the chief towns of the Nation, along the horse-path that runs from the Chickasaws, nearest the Mississippi, to Mobile. About six miles below the seven towns that lie close together, and next to New Orleans, I met a considerable party of the leaders and head warriors, returning home from war. We shook hands together, and they seemed very glad to see me. They earnestly dissuaded me from proceeding any farther, advised me to return to their friendly towns, and rest a while among them, declaring that if my ears were mad, and would not hear their friendly speech, I should surely be killed, the enemy were ranging the woods so very thick. They were good judges of the danger, as they knew the treacherous plan they had concerted together at *Yowanne*. I thanked them, and said I wished business allowed me to act according to their advice, but it did not. However, if my limited days were not finished before, I would shortly have the pleasure to see them again. I then proceeded, and met several parties of the same main company, several miles distant from one another, carrying small pieces of a scalp, singing the triumphal song and sounding the shrill death whoop, as if they had killed hundreds.

"I encamped early and within two leagues of Yowanne, as it seemed to be a good place for killing wild game. I imagined, also, that here the people were awed by the Muscogee from ranging the woods, but it happened otherwise; for soon after the horse-bells began to ring, two sprightly young fellows came through the cane swamp, and, as enemies, they crawled up the steep bank of the creek near to me, before I discovered them. My fire-arms were close at hand, and I instantly stood on my guard. They looked earnestly around to see the rest of my company, as it is very unusual for any of the traders to take that journey alone. I asked them who they were, from whence they came, and what they were so earnestly searching for. They evaded answering my queries, and asked me if I did not come by myself? I told them, without hesitation, that some way behind, my companion rode out of the path to kill deer, as his gun was good, and he could use it extremely well. On this they spoke a little together with a low voice, and then told me that they belonged to *Yowanne*, and were part of a hunting camp, which was near at hand and in view of the path. I asked them to sit down, which they did, but their discourse was disagreeable, as my supposed fellow-traveller was the chief subject of it. They said they would go back to their camp and return to mine soon, to see whether the white man was come from hunting. They went and were as good as their word—for they did me the honor to pay me a second visit. As they were so very earnest in that which did not concern them, unless they had ill intentions, the sight of them would have instantly inflamed the heart of one not infected with stoicism, to wish for a proper place to make a due retribution. At this time the sun was near three hours from setting. The white hunter's absence was the first and chief subject of their discourse till evening. As on a level place all the savages sit cross-legged, so my visitors did, and held their guns on their knees, or kept them very near, with their otter-skin shot-pouch over one of their shoulders, as is usual in time of danger. I observed their mischievous eyes, instead of looking out eastwardly towards the Muscogee country, they were generally turned toward the north-west, the way I had come. As by chance I walked near to one of them, he suddenly snatched up his gun. No friendly Indians were ever known to do the like, especially so near home, and a considerable camp of their own people; innocence is not suspicious, but guilt is. He knew his own demerit, and, perhaps, imagined I knew it from concurring circumstances. To see whether his conduct proceeded from fear of danger or from accident, I repeated the trial, and he did the same, which confirmed me in my opinion of their base intentions.

"In this uneasy and restless manner we continued till sun-set, when one of them artfully got between me and my arms. Then they ordered me to stop the bells of my horses, which were grazing near the camp. I asked them the reason—they told me because the noise frightened away the deer. I took no notice at first of their haughty command, but they repeated it with spiteful vehemence, and I was forced to obey their mandate. They looked and listened earnestly along the edge of the swamp, but being disappointed of their expected additional prey, in about the space of ten minutes they ordered me to open the bells again. Of the manifold dangers I ever was in, I deemed this by far the greatest, for I stood quite defenceless. Their language and behaviour plainly declared their mischievous designs. I expected every minute to have been shot down; and though I endeavored to show a manly aspect, the cold sweat trickled down my face through uneasiness and a crowd of contrary passions. After sometime in this alarming situation, they told me the ugly white man staid long, and that they would go to their camp a little while and return again—they did as they said. To deceive them, I had made my bed as for two people, of softened bear and buffalo skins, with the long hair and wool on and blankets. My two watchmen came the third time, accompanied with one older than themselves; he spoke little, was artful and very designing. They seemed much concerned at the absence of my supposed companion, lest he should, by unlucky mischance, be bewildered or killed by the Muscogee. I gave them several reasons to show the futility of their kindly fears, and assured them he usually staid late to barbacue the meat, when he killed much, as he could not otherwise bring it to camp; but that he never failed, on such an occasion, to come some time in the night. The cunning fox, now and then, asked me a studied short question upon the main point they had in view, and my answers were so cool and uniform, that I almost persuaded them firmly to credit all I said. When he could no way trepan me—and there was silence for several minutes—he asked me if I was not afraid to be at camp alone. I told him I was an English warrior—my heart was honest—and as I spoiled nobody, why should I be afraid? Their longing eyes were by this time quite tired. The oldest of them very politely took his leave of me in French, and the others, through an earnest friendly desire of smoking and chatting with my absent companion, told me, at parting, to be sure to call them, by sounding the news whoop, as soon as he arrived at camp. I readily promised to comply for the sake of the favor of their company; and to prevent any suspicion of the truth of my tale, I added that if he failed in his usual good luck, they ought to supply us with a leg of venison, or we would give them as much if he succeeded.

"And now all was well, at least with me, for I took time by the forelock, and left them to echo the news-whoop. Yowanne lay nearly south-east from me, but to avoid my either being intercepted on the path, or heard by the quick-eared savages, I went a quarter of a mile up to the large cane swamp, and passed through it on a south-west course, but very slow, as it was a dark thicket of great canes and vines, over-topped with large spreading trees. I seldom had a glimpse of any star to direct my course, the moon being then far spent. About an hour before daylight, I heard from the top of a high hill my troublesome visitors fire off a gun at the camp, which was, I suppose, when they found me gone, and in order to decoy my supposed companion to answer them with the like report; conjecturing he would imagine it was I who fired for him, according to custom in similar cases. I kept nearly at the distance of three miles from the path, till I arrived at the out-houses of Yowanne."

CHAPTER XV.

French Policy and Intrigues continued—The Mountain Barriers of Upper Carolina the key to the Province—Cherokee's account of the first appearance among them of French Emissaries—Francis Nicholson—The English strangely indifferent to the dangerous encroachments of the French—The wonders and extent of the Great Valley, little apprehended by the settlers on the Atlantic—Gov. Nicholson meets the Cherokees in Council, &c.

The incidents of the last chapter, though interesting and truthful pictures of the times, and of their faithful chronicler, led us considerably in advance of the regular order of events.

The French, still bent on their grand scheme of uniting their possessions on the Gulph of Mexico, with those of Canada on the north, erected, in rapid succession, after the completion of Fort Toulouse, Fort Tombeckbe among the Choctaws, Fort Assumption on the Chickasaw Bluff, and Paducah at the mouth of the Cumberland River, besides numerous trading houses along the Tennessee, in close proximity to the Cherokees and Catawbas; the former occupying a position in the midst of their mountain barriers, on the immediate border of Carolina, which had long been regarded as the key to that province. The French knew this, quite as well as the public guardians of the people, who were most interested, and were now ready to take the last step—the seduction to their alliance and amity of the Cherokees, preliminary to the successful invasion and ultimate ruin of Carolina.

We found in the manuscript records the account given by the Cherokees themselves, of the first adventure made by the French among them in prosecution of these plans. They pushed a boat, loaded with goods and presents, as high up the Tennessee as they could approach in that manner the Over-hill settlements; and going boldly into one of the towns, proposed to hold a conference with the head-men. The Indians appeared to assent; the chiefs were assembled, and a scaffold erected, no doubt at the request of the French, in accordance with their notions of public dignity. On this the head-men and their new visitors took their seats with great solemnity, and entered upon the business that had brought the latter into the Nation.

All, in a short time, seemed greatly interested in the animated French talk, when suddenly the indignant warriors springing up, drew their tomahawks, and cut them all off with their friendly Indian interpreters; after which they threw their dead bodies from the scaffold and dragged them into the river. This account was preserved by a conjurer, who appears to have been an eye-witness of the scene. It is further related that this rebuff so discouraged the French, that for many years, they made no more attempts to entice the Cherokees from their alliance and commerce with the English.

In 1721, Francis Nicholson was appointed Governor of South Carolina. He was the first chief magistrate under the royal government ; and though all parties were now in the enjoyment of a delightful calm, after the fierce political struggle that had just freed the province from the hateful rule of the proprietors, it does not appear that either the new Governor or the Assembly had any adequate conception of the policy of the French, or of the dangers that threatened Carolina, from their splendid schemes of self aggrandizement.

Indeed, it is an interesting fact, that even at this period of American history, the whole of that vast region now known as the West, had made no definite impression upon the minds of the English inhabiting the Atlantic coast. To them it was an unknown world, shut alike to their view and their enterprise, by the impassable barrier of the Alleghany Range. It is true, that much earlier than this, a few bold spirits, allured by the profits of trade, or in search of new hunting-grounds and wild adventure, had found here and there a pathway which led to advanced points, from which they enjoyed magnificent views of the wonders of the Great Valley. But, like the ancient Northmen—whom we are told fortuitous winds wafted to the shores of the New World, long before its discovery by Columbus—the many strange stories they brought back of the scenes they had witnessed in their distant excursions, only served to fill the imaginations of the people with vague ideas of a mysterious region that lay far beyond the blue mountain summits that studded their western horizon.

"They little dreamed of the breadth, the length, and the resources of the Great Valley, whose verge they had approached; nor imagined that a region lay beyond them, wrapped in the silent splendor of unbroken forests, which, in extent and beauty, far exceeded the territories which had previously been subdued by our ancestors, at so great an expenditure of life and wealth. They were, perhaps, unaware, that the French were even then building forts and villages, planting the grape, and playing the violin, upon the borders of the Mississippi."*

We are not left, however, to mere conjecture on this point. An old chronicler of the times, thus quaintly writes: "We have very little or no correspondence with the mountainous parts of this province, and towards the country of the *Messiasippi*, all which we have strange accounts of, and some very large ones, with respect to the different and noble fruits, and several ornaments and blessings of nature, which Messiasippi possesses; more to be coveted than any of those we enjoy to the eastward of the mountains. Yet, when I come to discourse some of the idolizers of that country, I found it to be rather novelty than truth and reality, to induce those persons to allow it

* Judge James Hall.

such excellencies above others. It may be a brave and fertile country, as I believe it is; but I cannot be persuaded that it can be near so advantageous as ours, which is much better situated for trade, being faced all along with the ocean, as the English America is, when the other is only a direct river, in the midst of a wild, unknown land, greatest part of whose products must be fetched or brought a great way, before it can come to a market. Moreover, such great rivers commonly allow of more princes' territories than one, and thus nothing but war and contention accompanies the inhabitants thereof."*

The Colony, relieved from the agitations of its recent domestic troubles, and once more restored to quiet, under the mild sway of the royal government, had ample leisure to make provision for its commercial prosperity and security against the hostile encroachments of neighboring savages. With this end in view, Gov. Nicholson, soon after his arrival in the province, proposed to form with the warlike Cherokees a treaty of close friendship and amity.

He accordingly dispatched a messenger to the Nation, informing them of his desire to meet them in a general council, on the border, that he might distribute presents amongst them, and confer with their chiefs on the interests and claims of their growing commerce with the English. The Cherokees, pleased and flattered by a proposal so conciliatory and re-

* John Lawson's History of Carolina, published in London, at the Black-Boy, Paternoster Row, 1718.

spectful from their white neighbors, readily accepted the invitation; and the head-men of thirty-seven of their towns, came down with a great company of warriors, and women, and children, and met Gov. Nicholson. This council was held, it is quite probable, at the Congarees; just three years before this event, as has been related, the fort and trading-house had been built at that place; it was then the only advanced or fortified post on the Cherokee border. Ninety-six was not settled till about thirty years after, and Old Fort Prince George had not been dreamed of. The Cherokee Nation numbered in population, at this period, more than twenty thousand, and could send into the field more than six thousand bowmen.

It indeed behooved the colony of Carolina to cultivate the friendship of a people so truly formidable, and so well situated for harassing her, and, when directed by French emissaries, for effecting her total ruin. Well would it have been, if all her public agents and private citizens had constantly manifested towards these savage but generous warriors, the same respectful and kindly tone shown on this occasion by Gov. Nicholson. It would have been happier for the people on the sea-board, infinitely happier for the hardy pioneers and their defenceless families of the upper-country, whose blood, in after years, flowed in streams, to appease the wild spirit of revenge, which was at length aroused by the cruelty, oppression and neglect of English traders, and English government officials.

There is no chapter in our history which more strikingly illustrates the evil consequences that are sure to flow from the continued disregard of the great Scriptural truth—"With what measure ye mete, it shall be measured to you again"—than that which details the public and private dealings of Carolina with the Cherokee Indians, and the consequent retribution that in due time followed, when the frontiers were lit up with a flame of savage warfare, and the tomahawk and scalping-knife were doing their terrible work around the hearth-stones of the Scotch-Irish backwoodsmen.

The difference between the French and English, in their manner of treating the Indians, was just the measure of the specific difference in the social habits of the two people. The one was ever characterized by the mildness, suavity, and respectful consideration, so striking in the Frenchman, whether he is studied in Paris, or in his rude village on the Illinois; the other, by that selfish bluntness, and utter disregard for the feelings of others, not unfrequently pushed to the degree of brutality, equally inherent in the Englishman.

It may be replied by some that, after all, French suavity is only an exhibition of intense selfishness, under the form of a refined policy; but what is all the suavity and politeness of social life, but a refined policy, except that rare manifestation of it which springs from the heaven-born benevolence of true piety. It is pleasing to any man, be he Christian or savage, to be thought worthy of even that deference in the conduct of others, which yields only the semblance of true feeling. And that this much is an acceptable work, and does not fail of its earthly reward, is shown in the remarkable fact, that the French were enabled to penetrate into the very heart of the continent, and there form peaceful and flourishing settlements; when the English, with all their courage and dogged hardihood, had scarcely advanced a hundred miles towards the interior, from their first strong-holds on the Atlantic coast. During one hundred years, large communities of the French settled in the Mississippi Valley, planted their gardens, reared fruits, and embellished their cheerful homesteads—in the midst of vast savage hordes—with scarcely an instance of hostile interruption from those wild children of the wood, only confiding and gentle, when treated with kindness and respect.

Governor Nicholson, we are told, although recently from Europe, was not unacquainted with the character and habits of the Indians. Indeed, his conduct in this congress, with the Cherokees, and another, which he soon after held with the warlike Creeks—whose eastern boundary was the Savannah River—sufficiently indicated his estimation of their prowess, and their capacity for an alliance of friendship and amity with their civilized neighbors.

This first assemblage in council with the English, of the head-men and warriors of the Nation, was, without doubt, more striking and imposing than any that were afterwards held at Old Ninety-six, Nequossee, or at the same place—if the Congarees was really the spot—at which this was convened. There was scarcely a town or a village in all their settlements that was not represented; and the proud chiefs and warriors, and young females of the Cherokee Nation of that period, dressed in the wild, picturesque costume of their race, presented the finest specimens of the physical man and woman, to be found on the American Continent.

"The Cherokees," observes Bartram, "are yet taller and more robust than the Muscogees, and by far the largest race of men I have seen. Their countenance and actions exhibit an air of magnanimity, superiority and independence. The women are tall, slender, erect, and of a delicate frame; their features formed with perfect symmetry, and they move with a becoming grace and dignity. The complexion of some of them is so bright as to approximate quite closely to the bloom of European women."

The botanist saw the Cherokees at the period of the Revolution—when it was already the testimony of history that they differed as much in their moral and physical characteristics from what they had been in the time of Governor Nicholson, as the Greeks under Alexander differed from the Greeks who fought at Marathon and Salamis.

No minute record,* it appears, was ever made of

* It was not until Governor Glen's time, that any regular, and, at the same time, full records were kept of the public transactions with the Indians. It is to his intelligence, liberality and praiseworthy re-

the proceedings and incidents of this council, on the remote border; the name of but one, even, of the many head-men who took a part in it has been preserved; yet their speeches on the topics laid before them by the Governor, must have afforded examples of wild eloquence worthy of preservation and study.

The business in hand was soon dispatched, and the promised presents distributed; after which the Governor smoked, with the chiefs, the pipe of peace. He, on this occasion, regulated their weights and measures, and marked out the boundaries of their lands, that they might no more be intruded upon by English settlers. The Cherokees had made frequent complaints of encroachments upon their hunting-grounds. An agent was appointed to superintend their affairs; and, in order to have them united, as far as their notions of government would permit, under a common head, he selected and empowered, with their consent, Wrosetasato, to be the chief warrior, and commander of the Cherokees, endowing him, at the same time, with ample authority to punish the guilty and lawless, and to obtain redress for every act of oppression perpetrated by English settlers or traders, upon the Indians.* The Cherokees returned to their towns, from this congress, greatly pleased, both with their presents, and with

gard for system, that the State is indebted for those invaluable manuscript records in the Secretary of State's office, known as the Indian Books. They are contained in four volumes, and are themselves a deeply interesting and curious history.

* Hewit. Car. Col.

the excellent temper and good sense displayed by the Governor; and the tranquillity, as well as the rapid political developments of the twenty-two years immediately following, fully vindicated the wisdom that conciliated, on that occasion, the friendship and good-will of this formidable people.

The interval that elapsed between 1721 and 1743, were, without doubt, the most prosperous years of the peltry trade, and the most peaceful in the relations of Carolina and the Cherokee Nation; yet it is just that period in their mutual history, of which we have been furnished the fewest records. Some were lost in the subsequent turmoils and vicissitudes of the colony; some, perhaps, through neglect, were destroyed by the canker and damp; but much more, that would have been interesting and valuable, was either suffered to pass away unrecorded by any chronicler,* or lies locked up and useless in the British archives.

It was in 1716, as we have seen, that the first caravan or periago† of goods was sent up by the Board to the Cherokees; and, as late as 1731, there were collected from all quarters in Charleston, for exportation, as many as two hundred and twenty-five thousand deer-skins alone. And the annual rate of exportation was above two hundred thousand.‡

* Professor Rivers, in his Topics of Carolina History, gives a minute account of the sources of our history, and the condition of the manuscript records in the State archives.

† This is sometimes written pettiauger; periago is the word used in the journals.

‡ Professor Rivers's Topics of History.

It cannot, of course, be precisely ascertained how many of these peltries were contributed from the hunting-grounds of the Nation; but we found a single brief note in one of the Indian Books which enables us to venture something more than a mere conjecture as to the actual number. Nearly a quarter of a century later, 1755, it is stated, that Cornelius Dougherty anticipated, if the winter of that year was but tolerably favorable for hunting, collecting from his district alone in the Nation, fourteen thousand pounds of buck-skin leather. His trading-house stood in the town of Tugaloo. Three years before, the entire Nation had been mapped off into thirteen hunting-ranges or districts, and a trader appointed to every one, to superintend its traffic and business. If for one of these ranges only two-thirds of Dougherty's expected crop be taken as an average return, it would give for the entire Cherokee country an annual production of more than one hundred thousand pounds of buck-skin leather; no mention being made of the skins of the raccoon, the beaver and bear; all of which animals were still quite abundant in the upper-country and the mountains.

It was estimated in old times, and is still, that the average weight of deer-skins is four pounds to the skin; and there is little difference between its weight when dry and raw, and when taken from the vat, ready for transportation. In the winter of 1755, therefore, Dougherty expected the hunters of Tugaloo range to bring down with their rifles some thirty-five hundred deer; making for the whole Nation, according to our average, about twenty-five thousand annually.

This is, doubtless, far below the true number—four pounds being a large average per skin—larger, it would appear, from the following note taken from the same records, than that allowed in the practical estimates of 1716. The enacted price of deer-skins for this period were—for *white skins* of a pound weight and upwards, five shillings; *light*, two shillings and six-pence; raw buck-skins, of a pound and a half weight and upwards, five shillings; all raw, doe, and other light skins, two shillings and six-pence, or according to weight.

Tugaloo, early and late, was an important place in the peltry trade; it is frequently mentioned in the journals of the Board. June the 11th, 1717, it is recorded, that the Commissioners received from Tugaloo, nine hundred and one dressed deer-skins, fifty-six raw, thirty beaver-skins, and twenty-one slaves, purchased at that factory.

In 1755, one hundred deer-skins were worth, in Charleston, at the present value of the English pound in federal currency, two hundred and fifty dollars. A beaver-skin brought four shillings, three and one-half-pence. During the administration of Governor Glen, after the staple of rice, which had then grown to be of the first importance on the list of colonial exports, there was no commodity that surpassed in value the peltries yielded by the Indian hunting-grounds. An old chronicler quaintly informs us of the extent and value of the traffic in its earlier periods:

"They carry on a great trade with the Indians, from whom they get these great quantities of deer-skins, and those of other wild beasts, in exchange for which they give them only lead, powder, coarse cloth, red paint, iron-ware, and some other goods, by which they have a very considerable profit."

In 1747, there were exported from Charleston two hundred pounds weight of beaver-skins, and seven hundred and twenty hogsheads of deer-skins; worth, in Carolina currency, nearly four hundred thousand pounds. The latter commanded five hundred and fifty pounds per hogshead.

If such was the importance of the peltry trade in the last years of its existence, when wild animals had become comparatively scarce, and the degeneracy and indolence of the Indians a by-word and reproach, no reason is left for amazement at the assertion, that in the periods of its greatest prosperity it was the most lucrative business on the Continent. The wonder must be, how it was possible for the hapless animals, whose skins supplied this active commerce for the greater part of the eighteenth century, to continue to subsist so long in such incredible numbers.

It is a fact, not unworthy of notice in natural history, that long after most of the beasts of prey had become well-nigh extinct in the country, the gentle deer and inoffensive beaver were still numerous in their primitive haunts; though, during more than a century, they had been the constant objects of the toil and cunning of a nation of the best hunters in the

33

world, and had supplied, through their destruction, the greater part of that time, the most valuable portion of the colony's exports. Do not the meek, even among brute animals, inherit the earth?

It was once remarked by an old hunter, when speaking of the deer, "that the reason why they were not all cut off when young—as they breed but once a year, and were always surrounded by other animals which preyed upon them, as dogs, wolves, wild-cats and panthers—was, that no dog or other animal could smell the track of a doe or fawn while the latter was too young to take care of itself. He declared, that he had often seen it demonstrated; he had often taken his dogs over the ground where he had just before seen them pass, and they would take no notice of the track, and could not be induced to follow when led to the spot, while they would instantly discover the track of any deer not having young ones." This is but another proof from nature of the wisdom and goodness of God.

Great as were, however, the profits of the peltry trade, they began seriously to fall off so soon as the evil effects of the English policy, in its management, had time to develop themselves. The irregularities and abuses produced by the licentiousness and rapacity of a few bad men engaged in the traffic, no doubt, did it an injury—sometimes even endangering the peace of the province—but so far as they immediately affected the character of the Indians, they had a decided tendency to sharpen their wits, stimulate their energies, and increase their self-reliance, while just the opposite influence was brought to bear upon them by the government monopoly, through its fostering care and protection.

They were now taught to rely, in all their exigencies, upon the strong arm of the colony, instead of upon themselves, and their private traders, whom they had formerly met on terms of mutual freedom and independence. The whole affair had become a State concern, and neither trader nor Indian was any more free. The former, who, before only abused the Indians, now learned to cheat the government, and abated not one whit of his evil practices in the Nation.

But the blameworthy policy of the government did not stop at this; from a sad misconception of the Indian character—in which even Gov. Glen, with all his tact and ability, participated—they adopted the method of conciliating the savages by frequent large distributions of presents to their women and head warriors. No small portion of the revenue accruing from the Indian trade was thus expended.

A few years were sufficient to develop the evil tendencies and fruits of such a system. The Indian character degenerated with most alarming rapidity; its original manliness was soon greatly abated; the self-reliant energy, courage, and noble bearing, that, in primitive times, had distinguished the Cherokees as the most intelligent and formidable warriors in America, were exchanged for the indolence and empty, noisy parade of a nation of doomed, proud beggars.

A reliable eye-witness observes: "Before the Indian trade was ruined by our left-handed policy, and the natives corrupted by the liberality of our dim-sighted politicians, the Cherokees were frank, sincere and industrious. Their towns then abounded in hogs, poultry, and everything sufficient for the support of a reasonable life, which the traders purchased at an easy rate, to their mutual satisfaction; and as they kept them busily employed, and did not make themselves too cheap, the Indians bore them good will and respect—and such is the temper of all the red natives."*

In the early years of the traffic, as before remarked, the traders established their store-houses wherever they found a town or settlement favorably situated for their business. The commissioners decreed, however, about the year 1718, after forts and factories had been built, both at Savannah Town and the Congarees, that the Indians, for the future, should come down to those posts to obtain their goods and do their trading; "it being the resolution and sense of the whole country, not to have, any more, a settled store among the Indians, but, by degrees, cause them to come down to our forts, and purchase what they want."†

This arrangement would have been productive of a two-fold good effect: it would have withdrawn from the Nation the swarm of roving, unprincipled white leeches, who preyed upon both traders and Indians, and whose vicious example corrupted all

* Adair. † Commissioners' Journals.

who came within their reach; and have brought, as well, the Indians repeatedly, every year, under the influence of a better sort of men—whom it must have been the interest of the government to appoint as its agents at those factories.

An unaccountable whim, however, or a deep-seated prejudice of the Cherokees to coming to the forts for purposes of traffic, as well as the uncontrollable enterprise of the traders—great numbers of whom soon began to be licensed—effectually prevented this salutary measure.

The manuscripts add: "The Cherokees utterly dislike coming down to the garrisons to deal, and will not, on any account—except to procure *rum*—agree to that proposal." It is not at all improbable that the Indians were potently aided in contracting this prejudice to the trade at the forts, by the horde of white savages, who infested their towns; for the proposed arrangement was obviously fatal to their nefarious enterprises and licentious dalliance in the Nation.

The full blaze of day would have produced no greater commotion among as many skulking bats, than the removal of the scenes of their exploits to places where the eyes of upright men, and some portion of civilized influence, could reach them.

The fate of the Nation was now sealed. Long before the breaking out of the war of 1760, the Cherokees had become so thoroughly corrupt, as to be no longer able—as in the times of their primitive strength—to resist the insinuating address and tempting bribes of the French emissaries, who, well aware of their opportunity, had been, for years, hard at work, in their own dangerous way, in every part of the Nation. We are in advance, however, of some events too interesting and important to be omitted.

CHAPTER XVI.

The results of Gov. Nicholson's Treaty—They are soon rendered valueless by the successful Intrigues of the French—The English begin to be sensible of their danger—Active Emissaries once more at work among the Cherokees—Gov. Middleton dispatches Col. Chicken to the Nation, to counteract their influence—Adair's description of Herbert's Spring, near the Tugaloo—The Over-hill Towns encourage the French.

It was related in the last chapter how Gov. Nicholson had met the head-men of the Cherokees on the border, and formed with them a treaty of friendship and commercial union. The good effects of that alliance were long felt, both in the province and in the Nation; the frontier was free from violence, and the prosperity of the peltry trade greatly enhanced.

This era of peace and tranquillity was now rapidly drawing to a close; in less than ten years after Nicholson's treaty, the truth began to force itself, even upon English senses, that the French, of Louisiana, had in view the vast design of connecting, by military posts, their possessions on the Gulf with those of Canada—thus circumscribing, in menacing proximity, the whole north-western frontier of Carolina. They had once more taken courage, and having sent out into the Over-hill settlements several dangerous emissaries, were already exerting a most dangerous influence upon that portion of the Nation.

Arthur Middleton, who was now Governor, being informed of this movement of the French, dispatched Colonel George Chicken to the Cherokee towns, to counteract, by his influence, the designs of these skillful intriguers. And during the remainder of his administration, Chicken was enabled, by the exercise of all his address, to keep the Indians to the English interest.

Adair gives an amusing account of a spring, then famous as Herbert's Spring, situated only half a mile from the head of Tugaloo River, whose waters flow into the Mississippi, and were, therefore, called the French waters. It lay close to the trading path, and became a great resort for pack-horsemen, and other wayfarers. When a man drank of it, he was said to have partaken of French waters. It came, at length, to be regarded with a sort of superstitious awe, and the heads of many were completely turned by having tasted it but once. The belief grew current that it possessed the magical power of fastening a man for seven years in the Nation; a notion eagerly laid hold of by the dallying debauchees who sought a plausible excuse for their continued sojourn in the towns, when nothing detained them but the allurements of vicious pleasure. The river *French* Broad, is another notable memorial of the encroachments of the French, at this period, upon English territory.

The emissaries from the Valley now met with an encouraging reception among the Over-hills, and having distributed many presents in their villages, promised them a much more valuable contribution in the future, if they would only discard the English and look exclusively to French store-houses and traders for all their goods and supplies.* In order, however, to carry their measures, they did not trust alone to the influence of glittering gewgaws and trinkets; they maliciously proclaimed in all their *talks* with the Indians, that the English were a selfish and treacherous race—that their alliance with the Cherokees was solely for their own aggrandizement; their friendship was mere pretence, and as soon as it suited their purpose they would withhold from them goods and ammunition, and reduce them, with their wives and children, to the miserable necessity of using ashes instead of salt; and thus deprived of every resource and comfort, they would make war upon them and utterly destroy their Nation.

The British Government at length deemed it highly important that their alliance with the Cherokees should be of a tenure more reliable than a mere treaty of commerce and amity; but what steps to take to secure an object, now so desirable, was a practical question, the solution of which required no small amount of wisdom and a peculiar experience. The course at last decided upon, was not striking in its exhibitions of either.

---

* Indian Books.

They proposed to convert them suddenly into gentle and obedient subjects of King George—to exact of them the performance of duties, of whose nature they had no more conception than they had of the principles of the British Constitution.

A Commissioner must be sent directly to the Cherokee Nation, empowered by the king, to form, with its leading men and warriors, a treaty, whose provisions should bind them and their people forever to be the willing subjects of Great Britain, and their country an appendage of its crown.

Sir Alexander Cumming was selected as a suitable agent for this mission. He landed in Charleston early in 1730, and having collected a party of traders, with an interpreter, all of them well acquainted with the trail and the Nation, he set out for the mountains; and passing up by the site of Ninety-six, then an unbroken wilderness, reached Keowee, probably in the latter part of March.

The head-men of the lower towns hastened to meet him at that place, and, with many demonstrations of friendship, welcomed him to their country. From Keowee he sent an invitation to all the remaining chiefs of the Nation to meet him in a general congress, at Nequassee, a town on the Hiwassee. Accordingly in April, having crossed the mountains to the place appointed for the meeting, he had the satisfaction of finding himself surrounded by a gorgeous assembly of all the leading men of the Cherokees.

The pipe of peace was introduced, and Moytoy, the head warrior, having first smoked it with the usual solemnity, handed it to Sir Alexander, who smoked it in like manner, and passed it to the next in rank; and thus it went round, till the whole company had testified, by participating in this old national custom, their amicable feelings and intentions. Everything was now ready for Sir Alexander's business.

He arose, and doubtless, after a preface of some length, abounding in handsome compliments to the warriors present, and their magnificent country, made them a very plausible speech on the subject of King George's power, munificence, and the cheerful obedience of his happy people; and concluded by informing them that he had come a great way to their Nation to ask of Moytoy, and the other chiefs, an acknowledgment of the same obedience as faithful subjects of King George, in return for his love and protection of their country. This same plea was made by a later George to the rebellious colonists of America, in a similar exigency and with precisely the same amount of truth.

To all this handsome *talk*, delivered in a manner and style calculated to impress an Indian council, the chiefs, we are told, readily assented, with many demonstrations of *grateful humility*. Sir Alexander then proceeded, with the same easy acquiescence of the whole assembly, to name Moytoy as *Viceroy* and Commander-in-chief of the Cherokee Nation, and enjoined upon the subordinate head-men the obligation they had placed themselves under to obey and respect him as their *king*.*

The packs of merchandize which Sir Alexander had the foresight to bring up with him, and the display of which in the council had produced even a greater effect upon the supple necks and pregnant knees of the Indians than the eloquent speech of the Commissioner, were now opened and distributed; after which, the new-born loyalty of the warriors waxing enthusiastic, they presented to Sir Alexander the sacred tiara of eagles' feathers, usually worn by the great head chief of the Nation, and fine painted eagles' tails and four scalps of their enemies. These emblems of peace and friendship were to be laid at King George's feet on his arrival in England.

It was now proposed, however, as a happy suggestion by Sir Alexander, that Moytoy should delegate several of their chiefs to go with him to England, to offer in person, to the great king, their homage and emblems of friendship. This proposal was joyfully acceded to, and six of their most prominent headmen, were immediately selected for the mission across the great waters. These returned on the trail with the Commissioner to Charleston, where being joined by a seventh, who, it appears, had either been invited in that town, to join the embassy, or had

* The ideas conveyed by the words *king* and *monarchy* were not quite so clear to the Cherokees at this period as some of the principles of Newton's Principia; yet Hewit describes this whole scene with a gravity suited to the description of the event of signing the Declaration of American Independence.

been added to it after their departure from Nequassee, they all set sail in the English ship Fox, and landed the following June at Dover.

Their appearance on the road, in the passage from Dover to London, produced a sensation only akin to that awakened in Spain by a like cortege, which accompanied Columbus in his first return from the New World. On their arrival in the metropolis, plumed, dressed and painted, in the most elaborate style of American barbarism, bearing with them their bows and quivers, and the decorated emblems of their power and proffered friendship, they became, at once, objects, of intense curiosity to all classes of the people. Crowds of boys and idlers thronged them in the streets; they received many formal visits from the great, and were invited to the houses and tables of the nobility.

During their stay in England, they lived at the public expense, and no attentions were spared to impress them, in turn, with due admiration of English grandeur and munificence. Adair informs us, however, that the rooms assigned them in London were subterranean. We are not told by any records preserved in Carolina, what they said or how they acted on first beholding the architectural splendors of the great city, and the pageantry of its court; but the assertion may be ventured, that, however deeply they felt, not the least excitement or enthusiasm betrayed it in their outer movements. A Cherokee warrior, would have stood in view of London Bridge, and the dome of St. Paul's, with the same stoical indifference that he would go to the stake, and suffer the tortures inflicted by his enemies.

This apparent incapacity of the Indians to be charmed by the strange and wonderful sights they saw in Britain, must have disappointed, as well as surprised the English; but they were not themselves prepared to comprehend the depths of pride that locked up the bosom and lips of every one of those red warriors, nor the heroism and dignity of his native self-control.

Sir Alexander introduced them to the king; and the scene was, no doubt, such as to remind some who were present of the patriarch's interview with the ruler of Egypt. With the self-possession with which they would have conducted the business of the council-house in Keowee, they related to the English sovereign, how at Nequassee the chiefs of their Nation had met the British Commissioner, and formed with him a treaty by which they pledged themselves to be the loving friends and allies of Great Britain; in token of which, they had brought with them their national crown, the scalps of their enemies, and their painted emblems of peace, and now laid them at his Majesty's feet.

The king made them a suitable reply, and caused the treaty, thus confirmed, to be written out as faithfully, as could then be done in England, in the glowing, figurative style of the Cherokees. This English version of it mainly stipulated that the colonists of Carolina, should furnish the Indians with all manner of goods, and hasten to build houses, and plant corn towards their towns behind the great mountains. They, on their part, were to keep the path, where the English trod, clean and free from blood; to fight the enemies of Great Britain, and suffer the people of no other nation to build any forts or cabins, or plant corn upon the *lands belonging to the great king.*

Notwithstanding the long-threatened encroachments of the French, and the formidable position of the Cherokees on the north-western border of Carolina, this was the first treaty of any kind that was ever concluded between the Nation and the English Government; and this neglect or want of foresight, would have been sufficiently fatal to any promise of good in what was now done, if each provision of this high-sounding compact, had not itself been as empty as the wind.

The excitement and pleasure of a costless voyage across the Atlantic, to see a world new to them, and the gratification of displaying their fine things, and of acquiring more presents, were inducements enough for seven head-men of any Indian nation to go on a visit to a European sovereign. But King George exhibited, perhaps, a pardonable ignorance of Indian character, when he fell easily under the delusion that the Cherokees had, on this occasion, come over with their sacred eagles' tails, and painted scalps, from a profound sense of their duty as loyal, obedient subjects of Great Britain, to pay him their personal homage, having already voluntarily yielded him their magnificent country in exchange for a belt of wampum, a few flints and pots of red paint. England then began to fillibuster iń America.

The chronicler of these events thus piously comments on the article of the treaty, which relates to the fancied acquisition of the splendid domain of all Upper-Carolina, and much more besides: "The Cherokees, however barbarous, were a free and independent people; and this method of obtaining a share of their lands by the general consent, was fair and honorable in itself, and most agreeable to the general principles of equity, and the English Constitution. An agreement is made with them, in consequence of which, the king could not only give a just title to Indian lands, but, by the Indians becoming his voluntary subjects, the colonists obtained peaceable possession."*

But did they obtain peaceable possession. when they came to build their cabins and plant corn, towards the mountain villages of the Cherokees? Rather, did the warriors in London, and at Nequassee, intend to make any sort of title to King George, by which he could hold and grant their lands at pleasure? A curious incident occurred among the chiefs, while in England, that throws a flood of light upon this notable affair, revealing the shrewdness and consummate tact of those red statesmen of the American woods. It is preserved by Adair.

In the Cherokee language, the word *to-e-u-h-a-h* was regarded the most sacred form of affirmation.

---

* Hewit.

Its final syllable contained an essential part of Jehovah's name; and to once give it, and then deny its obligations, was deemed infamous blasphemy.

One night in September, in the dead hours, after they had returned to their subterranean lodging-place, they fell into a fierce debate, whether they should not kill, on the spot, one of the war-chieftains, and their interpreter, *Cheesto-Kaiehre*, the Old Rabbit; because, by the mouth of the latter, the chief had answered *to-e-u h-a-h* to the king's speech, in which he claimed not only their lands, but those of the neighboring nations, as his right and property. The difficulty was finally deferred till they should return home, to give an account of what they had done in their mission. They were carried back to America in the same vessel that bore Governor Robert Johnson—a second time appointed to the Chief Magistracy of Carolina—and, soon after reaching their towns, the two offending warriors were regularly tried before a great council of the Nation.

The charges preferred against them were, that they had betrayed the public faith, and sold their country for an acknowledged price, by a firm compact, as representatives of the Nation; the value received being a certain quantity of goods, and a decoying-belt of white wampum. The case was carefully discussed; but, on mature deliberation, it was decided to acquit them honorably, because it was judged that the interpreter was bound by an oath to explain their speeches; and that surprise, inadvertence, self-love, and the unusual glittering pageantry of the courtiers, had extorted the sacred assent, *to-e-u-h-a-h*, from the chieftain—both of them being, at the same time, greatly afraid lest they should say something amiss, owing to the difference in the idioms of the English and Cherokee languages.

The Cherokees were, at no time, loth to enjoy the profits and fine displays incident to the talks and formation of treaties with their liberal white neighbors; but they ever put a higher value on their lands than the consideration of any amount of the flints, belts, and other presents bestowed upon them by the English. Yet, shrewd as they were, and rich and valuable their domain, they, at last, received scarcely more for much of it than that miserable equivalent, save the sweet satisfaction of exacting a heavy interest of blood on the border. We shall have more to say on this interesting topic, when we come to treat more fully of the events of Governor Glen's administration.

Some six or seven years of comparative tranquillity followed Sir Alexander Cumming's treaty, so full of promise for the future; but not one advantage was obtained by it for Carolina, that had not already been secured by the more sensible negotiations of Governor Nicholson. Unfortunately for both the English and Cherokees, the magicians of France knew well how to do the same, and much more, with their enchantments.

We gave, in a former chapter, a brief sketch of the famous English trader and historian, James

Adair. At the same period that he lived among the Chickasaws and Cherokees, the French were represented among the latter, by a man whose genius and learning appear to have been of a very high order; but whose skill and untiring energy as an emissary, combined with an utter disregard of every moral principle and restraint, made him, perhaps, the most dangerous character that ever figured among our Southern Indians, or in any country.

His name was Christian Priber, a German Jesuit—"a gentleman of a curious and speculative temper." Having been deputed by the French as a special agent among the Cherokees, he came into the Nation in the year 1736, and, with admirable judgment, fixed his residence in one of the towns on the great Tellico River. His instructions were to ingratiate himself, by any means, with the Indians, and use all his influence to seduce them from the British to the French interest.

Though possessing, besides a highly cultivated mind, the refinements of manner that fitted him to adorn any position in civilized society, he adapted himself at once, with the utmost ease, to the life and habits of the savages. He began by exchanging his clothes—and every thing else he had brought with him into the Nation—with the warriors around him, and in this way greatly won upon their confidence. He now selected a handsome woman, and made her his wife; and ate, drank, slept, danced, and painted himself after the manner of the Cherokees. So completely had he succeeded in disguising himself, in a short time, by these arts, that his most intimate friends could scarcely have distinguished him from the natives with whom he lived. Endowed with a fine memory, and ready talent in the acquisition of language, he soon became perfect master of the Cherokee tongue; and now set to work in earnest to execute the immediate business of his dangerous mission.

His first object was to impress the Indians with sentiments of hatred and contempt for the English, which he effected by constantly representing them as a people both dishonest and rapacious; not omitting, at the same time, to flatter and inflame the pride of the savages, by reminding them of their valor, the great number of their warriors, and the formidable barriers of their mountainous country, against which no power of the English could ever prevail.

He was now prepared to put in practice a grand scheme, which appears to have been a conception of his own, and something additional to his main instructions as an emissary; and when viewed in relation to the late effort of the English Government to convert the Cherokees into loyal subjects of King George, it looks very like a plan of the skillful enchanter to foil them by a resort to their own arts, but with far superior abilities and opportunity to secure success.

Complete master of the minds of the Indians, he now proceeded to reörganize their Nation after the form of a European monarchy: their great beloved man was duly decorated for the occasion, and crowned the first sovereign of the new American empire; after which the cunning Jesuit, created for him a sort of court, composed of the several officers of state; for each of whom he invented a high-sounding title that the Indians might be the better pleased and conciliated. Himself he appointed to the responsible position of Chief Secretary of State, and actually corresponded as such, with the authorities of Carolina. Adair observes, that he received several letters from him himself, during the first year of his secretaryship. In these communications he insisted with consummate effrontery, upon having due respect and consideration shown his office.

South Carolina being thus informed of the threatening state of things in the Nation, dispatched Col. Fox over the hills, armed with full powers to arrest this bold Secretary of the new Cherokee empire. Fox came upon him while standing in the square before their council or state-house, and took him into custody; but before attempting to remove him, he deemed it prudent to explain, in quite a speech, his reasons and authority for acting in such a manner towards so popular and influential a functionary. He had scarcely got it all out, however, before a warrior interposed in a threatening manner, and ordered him to be silent, telling him that Priber was one of their own people, and had become a great beloved man among them; and to this the Secretary himself added, in his own defence, a most plausible apology for his presence and acts in the Nation.

Col. Fox, who was deemed to have more strength in the muscles of his arm than in his head, overwhelmed by these arguments, desisted from his purpose. It is more probable, however, that a man, whose courage and experience fitted him for so hazardous an enterprise, had the tact to see at a glance, in the threatening manner of the Indians, that it would be at his imminent peril to proceed farther in the matter.

They permitted him to go safely off, and Priber gave the finishing stroke to the insolence of his triumph, by granting him, with many assurances of regard, a party of armed warriors to escort him to the border.

Encouraged by his success thus far, the learned Jesuit now greatly enlarged his plan, and began to set up for himself. He proposed to constitute a vast territorial empire, by a union of the Cherokees, Creeks and Choctaws, with tribes beyond the Mississippi. It was his chief design, he afterwards asserted, in attempting to bring about this dangerous confederation of Southern and Western Indians, to inspire them with industry, to teach them the useful arts of life, and ultimately to unite them in a combined effort to crush every European colony in Southern America.

He selected a site for the capital of his proposed empire at a favorable spot in the Cherokee country of Georgia: into this, in imitation of the policy of the famous founder of Rome, were to be gathered the fugitives of all nations; the larger number of whom, it was expected, would be outlawed English, French and Germans; criminals escaped from justice, exiled felons and vagabond scoundrels of every hue. After the acquisition of these, and all the property they could bring with them into the new imperial city, it was particularly designed to be an asylum for the white slaves of Georgia, and runaway Africans from the plantations of the Carolinas and Virginia.

To this delectable crew, the Jesuit held out the alluring bait of unbridled licentiousness and full immunity for every crime, except murder and idleness. The marriage-tie was especially to be annulled, and a community of women to be established in its stead.

Such were the diabolical plans of this consummate schemer. Since the time of the Roman Cataline, history gives the details of no conspiracy vaster in its reaches, or more dangerous in its ends to the interest of mankind. Fortunately, Divine Providence cut them all short in a summary manner.

Some five years after his first arrival in the Nation, business having called him to Mobile, he set out for that place, attended by several of his Cherokee friends, and had proceeded on his journey by land as far as the head of navigation on the Tallapoosa, when the English traders in the neighboring Creek towns discovered his presence; and, being well-informed of his dangerous influence among the Cherokees, and suspecting the object of his present voyage, went in a body to his lodging-place in the town of Tookabatcha, and arrested him.

They found in his possession a large package of valuable manuscript papers, which they carried, with their prisoner, to the town of Frederica, on the Savannah. Oglethorpe was then Governor of Georgia; and in consideration of the Jesuit's having once occupied a position of rank in the French army, he committed him to a room of the prison separate from that of the common felons. Under these trying circumstances, he lost neither his courage nor his philosophy. An incident occurred soon after he entered the jail that put them both to a severe test. The magazine of the town, which stood close to the jail, took fire. The sentinels threw open the doors, and ordered him to run for his life, as they themselves hastened to do; but, instead of obeying, he threw himself flat upon his face on the spot where he stood, and, while in that position, the powder of the magazine, and thousands of shells exploded over and around him without the least injury to his person. On being afterwards rebuked for his rashness, he remarked, that experience had taught him it was the best means of escaping danger under such circumstances.*

Falling sick not long after this event, in his cell, death, happily for all, but himself, put an end alike to his life and ambitious hopes. During his imprison-

* Adair observes, that it was about the fifth year of his Indian empire that Priber was arrested. It would appear from this, taken in connection with a remark in McCall's Georgia, that his residence among the Cherokees extended to eight years. The latter thus speaks of the blowing up of the magazine at Frederica: "On the 22d of March, 1711, the bomb-magazine was blown up at Frederica.

ment he had won the notice and kindly sympathies of many of the citizens of Frederica by his uniform cheerfulness and the affability with which he received every one who approached him. Oglethorpe found leisure, before his death, to give him a thorough examination, and was astonished to discover, that though dressed in deer-skins and moccasins, he was a man of polished address and of singular learning and genius.

He was not only a perfect master of the English and Cherokee languages, but spoke fluently the Latin, French and Spanish. There are reasons to regret the loss of a large portion of his manuscripts; for, besides his private journal, there was found among them a complete dictionary of the Cherokee language. Adair remarks of him, in relation to these papers: "As he was learned and possessed of a very sagacious, penetrating judgment, and had every qualification that was requisite for his bold and difficult enterprise, it is not to be doubted, that as he wrote a Cherokee dictionary, designed to be published in Paris, he likewise set down a great deal that would have been exceedingly interesting to the curious, and serviceable to the historians of Carolina and Georgia; which may be readily found in Frede-

---

Very little damage was done, though it contained three thousand bombs. Whether fire was communicated by design or accident is not known; if the shells had not been well-bedded, the damage must have been very considerable. By some, it was attributed to an Irishman who arrived there a few days before, and disappeared immediately after the accident happened."

rica, if the manuscripts have had the good fortune to escape the dispoiling hands of military power."

His journal, with some other papers, appears to have been preserved. In the former, he gives the names of certain Indians and negroes who were to assist him in his conspiracy, and of a private treasurer in Charleston for managing the funds of the conspirators.

Another volume contains the elaborately digested rules and regulations for his proposed capital. "It was drawn up," remarks a writer* who had the privilege of examining it, "with much art, method and learning, and was designed to be privately printed and circulated."

It appears from certain confessions made a short time before his death, that in all his schemes and enterprises he was not seeking his own aggrandizement alone, or even acting under the direction of his own will. Some one who approached him had remarked, that his plans were necessarily attended with many difficulties and dangers, and that the establishment of his empire must require the labor and vigilance of many years. "Proceeding properly," he replied, "many of these evils may be avoided; and as to length of time, we have a succession of agents to take up the work as fast as others leave it. We never lose sight of a favorite point, nor are we bound by the *strict rules of morality* in the means, when the end we pursue is laudable. If we err, our

* Dr. Wm. B. Stevens, in his History of Georgia.

general is to blame; and we have a merciful God to pardon us. But believe me, before this century is passed, the Europeans will have a very small footing on the American Continent." *

This able Jesuit emissary was therefore acting, from first to last, in these nefarious schemes, chiefly under the direction of his order. Can the gloomy annals of any European court afford a more striking illustration of the desperate iniquity and moral abomination of the Mother of Harlots? Endowed with the great talents he certainly possessed, and having at his command so many of the physical elements of success, it would appear that nothing in the providence of God, but his timely death, saved Carolina and Georgia from destruction. It will be presently seen, however, that he lived long enough to inflict incalculable injury upon the former.

At that period, there were in the Cherokee Nation alone, six thousand warriors; a force amply sufficient, if firmly united and rightly directed, to crush in detail, at least, all the settlements of the infant colony. Had Priber confined his influence and ambitious projects to this warlike people, impressing them, as he began, with vengeful hatred of the English; marshalling, by his skillful tactics, all their military strength, and instructing them in the proper uses of the formidable advantages of their natural position, the chances would have been, if he had been suffered to live, wholly in favor of the complete success of his cherished design, to ruin Carolina.

* Dr. Stevens.

This special interference of Heaven in her behalf, did not, however, begin nor end with the death of Priber. Powerful causes had been operating for a series of years to reduce the strength of the Cherokees. Their lower settlements had suffered greatly from the hostile incursions of the Creeks; several important towns on the Tugaloo—among them Ishtatohe, Echia, and Tugaloo—were, about this time, totally forsaken or destroyed; while the Over-hills and valleys were no less harassed by the repeated attacks of the tribes on the Ohio and Mohawk.

In 1738—three years before Priber's fatal attempt to visit Mobile—a slaver from the coast of Africa arrived in Charleston, having on board the then deadly small-pox. It was communicated to the town, and thence a party of Indians or traders conveyed it to the Nation, where it acted like a spark upon the dry grass of the prairie.

Adair says, it was carried up by a pack-horse train, whose goods were infected with the disease. His description of its ravages is too graphic to be omitted:

"At first it made slow advances; and as it was a foreign, and to them a strange disease, they were so deficient in proper skill, that they alternately applied a regimen of hot and cold things to those who were infected. The old Magi and religious doctors who were consulted on so alarming a crisis, reported that the sickness had been sent among them on account of the adulterous intercourses of their young married people, who, the past year, had, in a most notorious manner, violated their ancient laws of marriage in every thicket. * * * To those flagitious crimes they ascribed the present disease, as a necessary effect of the divine anger. * * * However, it was thought needful, on this occasion, to endeavor to put a stop to the progress of such a dangerous disease; and as it was believed to be brought on by their unlawful * * * in the night-dews, when they formed their dancing-parties in the council-houses, it was thought most practicable to try to effect a cure under the same cool element. Immediately they ordered the reputed sinners to lie out of doors, day and night, with their breasts frequently open to the night-dews, to cool the fever. They were likewise afraid that the disease would pollute their houses, and by that means cause all their deaths. Instead of applying warm remedies, they at last, in every visit, poured cold water on their naked breasts, sung their religious, mystical song, "yo, yo," &c., with a doleful tune, and shook a calabash, with the bubbles, over the sick, using a great many frantic gestures, by way of incantation. * * * When they found their theological regimen had not the desired effect, but that the infection gained upon them, they held a second consultation, and deemed it the best method to sweat their patients, and plunge them into the river, which was accordingly done. Their rivers being very cold in summer, by reason of the numberless springs which pour from the hills and mountains, and the pores of their bodies being open to receive the cold—it rushing in through the whole frame—they immediately expired. Upon this, all the Magi and Conjurors broke their old consecrated physic pots, and threw away all the other pretended holy things which they had used as medicines, imagining they had lost their divine power by being polluted, and shared the common fate of their country. A great many killed themselves; for being naturally proud, they are always peeping into their looking-glasses, * * * by which means, seeing themselves disfigured, without hope of regaining their former beauty, some shot themselves, others cut their throats; some stabbed themselves with knives, and others with sharp-pointed canes. Many threw themselves, with sullen madness, into the fire, and there slowly expired, as if they had been utterly divested of the native power of feeling pain."*

The same author describes the particular case of a great head chief of the town of Tomassee, ten miles above the present site of old Fort Prince George, who, finding himself disfigured for life by the scourge, resolved to die rather than survive his imagined shame. And when his relatives, by dint of close watching, prevented him from destroying himself by the ordinary means, he darted his head with all his might against a wall; and this failing to effect his purpose, he finally succeeded by fixing a hoe-helve, nearly upright in the ground, upon which he threw himself in such a manner as to force the end of it down his throat, when he miserably perished.

* Adair's American Indians, p. 232.

In the course of a single year, this terrible disease swept off nearly one half of the Nation. This is asserted by the author just quoted; yet we are assured by another, that in 1740, the Cherokees numbered five thousand warriors, but lost one-fifth of that number the same year from small-pox.* It is very probable, therefore, that at the time of the establishment of Priber's Imperial Court, the military strength of the Nation was, at least, not less than that previously stated.

A more fearful agent of destruction, however, than either war or pestilence, had been, from the earliest period of their intercourse with the whites, silently but effectually preying upon the vitals of all the native tribes—it was the scourge of intemperance. There was something in the Indian's constitution or temperament that kindled, and kept burning in him an insatiable appetite for intoxicating liquors. His favorite beverage was rum; and this, despite all laws to the contrary, was supplied him without stint, as long as he was able to pay for it the required price. An interesting, as well as an instructive chapter could alone be written on the incidents of the rum traffic in the Nation. Thus, was Divine Providence bringing good out of evil; for these penal scourges, while they gradually humbled the pride and destroyed the power of the Cherokees, who, from their ancient purity and gentleness, had now become excessively insolent and corrupt, opened the way for

* Pickett's History of Alabama, page 157.

the permanent settlement of a nobler race upon the fertile hills and mountain valleys of the upper-country. It was not destined, however, that this should be consummated without long years of suffering, and a fearful expenditure of treasure and of blood. These were the penalties to be endured, in a measure, by the English, for crimes and violences which offended justice could not, in the presence of men, visit with a milder retribution.

These various evil influences before related, did effectually their work of corrupting the minds and habits of the Indians; and, from the time that Priber lived among them, there was no more peace in the Nation, till it was restored by the pioneer rifle and English musket.

CHAPTER XVII.

Traders from Virginia continued—A Deputation from the Over-hills, headed, it appears, by the famous Ataculiaculla, goes to Williamsburg—The Gov. of Virginia gives them an encouraging Answer—A hostile spirit towards Carolina manifest in the Nation—The Board cuts off their supplies of ammunition—The Over-hills in direct correspondence with the French, &c.

Notwithstanding the remonstrances of the Board, the intruders from Virginia continued, year after year, to disturb the Cherokee peltry traffic and lessen its profits. At length, in 1751, a deputation from the Over-hills, headed, it seems, by a chief who was greatly disaffected towards the English in Charleston, presented themselves before Gov. Lee, of Virginia, praying for a formal treaty of commerce between the Cherokees and the Old Dominion.

The Governor received them with great kindness, heard their *talk*, smoked with them the pipe of peace and friendship, and dismissed them with presents and assurances that a regular trade should be opened up between their people and the colony of Virginia. The Over-hills, disaffected towards Carolina, first through the intrigues of the French, had of late manifested so hostile a spirit, in their conversations with the traders, and by many overt acts of petty violences, that the Board ordered the latter to supply them with no more goods, till they should make reparation for what had been done, and give proper guarantees for their future good behavior. Their pressing necessities, therefore, at this time, as well as a spirit of opposition to Carolina, induced them to turn in any direction, whence they could hope to obtain sympathy and a good supply of goods and ammunition.

Soon after the death of Priber, seven of their towns hastened, in fear and dissimulation, to inform the traders that they had renounced the French and all their schemes, and were resolved to cling to their old friends, the English. Great Tellico, however, the chief scene of the Jesuits' operations and influence, declared itself still firm in the French cause. They corresponded with the French, says Adair, in the name of the other seven towns, which are the most warlike part of the Nation; and so strongly were they prepossessed with the notions their beloved secretary had infused into their heads, in the then weak State of Louisiana, that they had resolved to remove, and settle lower down the river, at a point where the French pettiangers could easily reach them; but the hot war they fell into with the northern Indians caused them to abandon this design.

The French had offered to build at that point a strong fort, to be well garrisoned, and supplied with every article of merchandize desired by the Indians. The valley and lower towns were yet steadfast to the English interest, but wavering and discontented. About the same period, a deputation similar to the one from the Over-hills, went up to the same authorities from the Catawbas. But nothing could have elicited this, except strong allurements held out by Virginia herself.

Gov. Glen was thoroughly aroused. No one better knew than he the political importance of the Cherokee and Catawba trade to Carolina, or better understood the Indian character. He immediately addressed a letter to Gov. Lee, couched in terms of strong remonstrance. The Governor replied in substance, that he had been deceived by the Indians who came to him from Chote. They passed themselves off as a king and eight nobles, sent with authority from their emperor to treat for the Nation.*

They complained of Carolina, that though she had promised them a constant supply of goods, they had received none, and were then in great want of many necessaries.† He adds, that he was moved by their pitiable condition, and asks of Glen, if he could have acted otherwise under the same circumstances; for, as the warrior of Israel was deceived by the cunning Gibeonites, they had presented themselves before him in a condition of apparent squallor and wretchedness.

---

* After the time of Priber, the terms emperor, king and noble, grew familiar in the Nation.

† "They had been receiving goods from Carolina," wrote Gov. Glen on this occasion, "during forty years." This would fix the commencement of the traffic with the Cherokees as early as 1711.—Indian Books.

That measure was difficult indeed, that an Indian could not carry by his cunning, if too great for the prowess of his arm.

In the Virginia Gazette of August, 1751, the following advertisement appears :

"As the Governor of South Carolina advises us that the Cherokees, who were recently in Williamsburg, under the character and denomination of ambassadors and nobles, were people of no eminence, or quality, or dignity, but obscure persons—that they had committed many cruelties and injuries upon the inhabitants of that province, and were to have been delivered up by their countrymen to be punished; that it is false that they ever made application to South Carolina for goods, and were refused—they having been supplied by that province abundantly with everything needed for near forty years. This intelligence is therefore inserted in the Gazette, that the inhabitants of this colony may be cautious in their commerce with them."

Nevertheless, the government of Virginia did not seriously design to check these encroachments of her traders; she rather claimed an equal right with Carolina to trade with all the southern Indians. These pretensions were soon after put in practical operation by Governor Dinwiddie, which drew from Governor Glen a very clear and able defence of the exclusive claims of his province to the commercial amity of those tribes.

"South Carolina," he wrote to the Governor of Virginia, "is a weak frontier colony, and in case of an invasion by the French, would be their first object of attack. We have not much to fear, however, while we retain the affection of the Indians around us; but should we forfeit that by any mismanagement on our part, or by the superior address of the French, we are in a miserable situation. The Cherokees alone, have several thousand gun-men, all well acquainted with every inch of this province—their country is the key of Carolina. We have been greatly alarmed by the behavior of the Virginians in regard to the Cherokees. Few or no Indians are in treaty with Virginia. By long experience, we have become thoroughly acquainted with their nature and inclinations, and have been so successful in managing them, as to keep them steady to the British interest, notwithstanding the vigorous and persevering efforts of France to seduce them from us. We can see no good end or wise policy in endeavoring to draw away these Indians from one of his Majesty's provinces to another. We have been enabled to fix the affections of the four great nations around us.* Let facts speak: they come when we send for them, and go when we bid them depart; they do whatever we desire of them. They now perfectly understand the injustice of punishing the innocent for the guilty, and the necessity of punishing the latter in conformity to the treaties between them and us. And when, under any circumstances, a white man is killed in their country, the offender is sure to die, though the greatest chief of the Nation.

* The Cherokees, Catawbas, Muscogees and Chickasaws.

"When a people, unacquainted with the nature of crimes and punishments, are brought to deal with offenders on principles that guide, under similar circumstances, the most enlightened nations, may we not safely boast of having progressed a great way in the education of savages? All this, we do aver to be truthful. What benefit, therefore, do you hope to gain for the common cause, by sending so many pressing invitations to those four nations, or the five of New York, to come to Virginia? I will answer for their good behavior with my life, if your province will let them alone. In my absence the council of this colony wrote, praying you not to intermeddle with our Indians. I have also requested the same thing in the strongest terms; yet you have sent messages lately to the Catawbas, and as many to the Cherokees and Chickasaws, inviting them to come and receive the presents sent over by the king."*

Little else than the mere variety of witnessing the extension of his influence and power over Indian hordes and vast territories could have instigated Dinwiddie in these abortive efforts to entice the four great southern tribes from their alliance with South Carolina, and their dependence upon her for the necessaries of life. They lay, in great part, far out of reach of her marts ; and, at that period, she was not so related, even in her most advanced settlements, to the boundaries of any one of these tribes, as to make it necessary for her safety to form with them treaties of commerce and reciprocity.

* Letter addressed to Dinwiddie, 1751. See Indian Books.

The tact and energy of Governor Glen arrested, at length, the danger from this source. It was an emergency that afforded him an opportunity of displaying, in no insignificant manner, his ability and prudence, as a guardian of the public weal.

One of the proximate causes of this threatened defection of the Cherokees, may have, indeed, been the temporary withholding of goods from them, by the order of the Board, until certain crimes and violations of the peace, committed in the Nation, had been investigated and atoned for. The records of this period abound in complaints and warnings sent down by the traders, and in details of agitations and terrors on the border from the hostile threats and violence of the Indians. The whole Nation was kept, for years, in a constant tumult of fear and alarm. The traders adandoned their stores, and fled for safety to the settlements; a man named Murphy was shot in cold blood at Oconee; one Barnard Hughes, had his store broken open, and rifled of its goods, himself escaping with difficulty; the frontier settlers hastily assembled, and fortified themselves, with their wives and children, at Ninety-six, the Congarees, and at other points most convenient for the pioneer communities.

In a conference, which Governor Glen held about this time, in Charleston, with several of the head-men of the Nation, in relation to these disturbances, Skiagunsta, a prominent chief, gave the following account of one of the most serious of these Indian outbreaks, in which the Cherokees were implicated:

"I am from Sugar Town, on the Keowee; last summer I and my people were hunting, near the Catawba Nation, and we were informed that several of the Creeks were with the Catawbas; they had come in search of some of their people, whom the Catawbas had retaken from the Northern Indians. We were also told that these Creeks designed to attack us as they returned home. News of this menace soon reached all our hunting-parties, then in the woods, and they hastily withdrew to their own country, except one little camp, in which were a man, a woman and child, who had heard nothing of the Creeks. The latter soon discovered and came upon them. The man was absent from the camp on a hunt, and they took the woman and the child, intending to make slaves of them. But they had not proceeded far before they were met by a party of Northern Indians, who killed nine of them on the spot, and retook the prisoners; the remaining five of the band made their escape. They were quickly, however, pursued by some thirty of my people, who, in a little while, came upon several horses they had taken from us, by which they knew that the enemy was lurking not far off.

"This was at sunset; and they remained still here until dark, and then sent out a scout to reconnoitre an old house that appeared in sight, and which they perceived to be occupied either by Indians or white people. He soon returned, and reported that he heard several talking in the Muscogee tongue, and one in Chickasaw, but heard no English; from which it was concluded there could be no whites among them. They determined to attack the party, and fired at once upon them, through the openings in the house. The fire was returned, and quickly the conflict became warm, several of my people being wounded with swan-shot. After the fight had continued for some time, we perceived that the reports of some of the enemy's guns were much louder than others; and we began to suspect and fear that, after all, there must be white men with them. Immediately after, a white man came out of the house; and one of us, who stood nearest him, running up, took him by the hand and led him aside out of danger. Soon after another came out, and was approached in like manner by one of the Cherokees; but who, instead of protecting him, knocked him on the head, notwithstanding all the rest of us called out to him to hold his hand, that he was striking a white man. The blow fell, and the Indian ran away. Your Excellency sent to have this man arrested and brought down to you; but it was long before the message reached me, and by that time the murderer had gone out to war—preferring to die by the hand of the enemy, rather than suffer death as a culprit, at home." He beautifully added: "I cannot write as do you and your beloved men. My tongue is my pen; my mouth, my paper. When I am looking upon the writing of the white man, I am as if I was blind and in darkness. We of our Nation have but one path, and that leads us to the English. It is now straight and clear;

on this hand and on that, there is nothing but darkness."*

The adroit cunning of the Indian is visible throughout this narrative, but we have from more reliable sources quite a full account of the sad state of things at this time in the Nation; and nothing more vividly illustrated the restless instability, not of the Cherokees only, but of any wild people, wholly dependent upon a neighboring government for subsistence, naturally subject to sudden and barbarous excitements, and with no employment but to roam from place to place in search of game. They were prepared to become the easy dupes of any well-directed influence, and the French were not so dull as to let the opportunity slip.

It must not be denied that Gov. Glen, with all his ability and apparent zeal for the best interest of the colony, rests here under the serious charge of being much more jealous from private motives, in the work of freeing the trade from the damaging intrusion of the Virginia traffickers, than in repelling the far more dangerous encroachments of the French. Says an old trader, who played, himself, an important part in these scenes—but was no friend to Glen: "The dormant conduct of the South Carolina chief, gave them an opportunity to effect that part of their design; though timely notice, even years before, had been given by the Cherokee traders, that the French priests were poisoning the minds of those Indians

* Indian Books.

against us, who live among the Apalache mountains, and were endeavoring to reconcile them to all the various nations of the Mississippi and Canada savages; and that there was the greatest probability they would accomplish their dangerous plan unless we soon took proper measures to prevent it. The informers had ill names and resentment for their news, and the Assembly was charged with mis-spending their time in taking notice of the wild, incoherent reports of illiterate, obscure persons.

But it afterwards appeared that the interest and security of South Carolina were in great danger. By the diligence of the French, their Indians entered into a treaty of friendship with the Cherokees, and their country became the rendezvous of the red pupils of the black Jesuits. Hence they ravaged South Carolina, beginning at the weak frontier settlements, and gradually advanced through the country, for the space of eight years, destroying the live stock, insulting, frightening, wounding and sometimes killing the inhabitants, burning their houses, carrying away their slaves, and committing every kind of devastation, till they proceeded so low as within thirty miles of Charleston.

The sufferers often exhibited their complaints in the most pathetic and public manner; and the whole country felt the ill effects of the late overbearing and negligent conduct. False coloring could serve no longer, and a few inconsiderable parties were sent out; but not finding any enemy, they were in a few months disbanded, and peaceable accounts were again sent home."*

We have already related how a party of these northern savages, now acting in open concert with the Cherokees, and all directed by French intrigue and energy, had made several captives from among the settlement Indians, near Charleston; and whose timely rescue by Hermon Geiger, cost that noble trader his life. We found in the manuscript records a minute account of more than one horrible butchery on the border, perpetrated at this time by the Notowegee or Savannah Indians, under the guidance and protection of the treacherous Cherokees. These have never been seen, except by the few whose curiosity, or a love of antiquarian research, prompted to look into the State archives.

On the 7th day of May, 1751, Mrs. Mary Gould came to the house of Martin Friday, severely wounded, and gave the following narrative to Capt. Daniel Sellider, of the Saxe-Gotha company: "Saturday, the fourth, two Indians came to my house, situated about half way between the Congarees and Savannah Town. They were Savannahs. It was nearly dark when they came in, and sat down quite civilly. My husband being able to speak their language, he conversed a great while with them. I gave them their supper, after which they asked my husband for pipes and tobacco, which he supplied them with, and we all sat up till midnight, and then went to sleep.

* Adair, p. 343.

The Indians also laid down, pulling off their moccasins and boots. One of them broke his pipe, and came to the bed to my husband, who handed him his out of his mouth, and he laid down again, when he dropped to sleep. When the cocks began to crow, they got up and came to the bed-side and shot my husband through the head; a young man sleeping on the floor was shot dead the same moment. The Indians, I suppose, thinking the bullet had gone through my husband's head, and mine too, struck me with a tomahawk under my right arm. Believing that they had killed me, one of them then went to the bed, where they were sleeping, and murdered, in cold blood, both of my children; after which they took the blankets from the beds, and having plundered the house of everything valuable, went off. In this condition I lay among my dead two days, when one of my horses providentially returning to the house, I was enabled to mount him and come to this place."* On another page it is recorded that this unfortunate woman died soon after, relating to Friday the above account of the ruin of her home.

A little later, but in the midst of the same agitations and dangers, a dreadful massacre took place on Buffalo Creek, somewhere in the present territory of York District. We have chosen to relate its history as we find it recorded in the Indian books:

"May it please your Excellency," writes Captain James Francis to Governor Glen, from the upper-

* Indian Books, Secretary of State Office.

country, October 7, 1754, "I should have written sooner concerning this cruel murder, perpetrated, as I suppose, by a camp of French Indians, if I had not heard that Mr. Wilcox of this neighborhood had already set off for town to inform you of the same.

"On a stream called Buffalo Creek, supposed by some to be in North Carolina, and by others, in the southern province, at the house of a Mr. Guttery, a sociable, hospitable man, and of good resolution, where several families, traveling from the north, had put up; at the same unfortunate time a family from the neighborhood had also come in to await the return of a young couple who had gone some forty or more miles to a Justice of the Peace to be married. In the mean time a party of sixty Indians came upon these unhappy people, twenty-one in all, and murdered sixteen of them on the spot. Their bodies were found scattered around in a circumference of some two or three hundred yards; the remaining five were either carried off or killed at a distance from the place where they were attacked. They have not yet been heard from; among them are a woman and three children—of the fifth one I could get no account.

"This, sir, is the exact story of this unhappy affair, as far as it relates to the murdered people. Immediately after dispatching these, the savages killed all the hogs, fowls, and cattle about the premises, and heaped their carcasses upon the dead bodies of the men and women. Twenty head of horses, some of them very valuable, that had belonged to the travelers, were driven off.

"But a single one of the butchered people fell by a gun-shot; the rest were all killed by means of arrows and tomahawks, many of which were found sticking in their bodies. The first who discovered this bloody deed were the newly-married couple, who returned soon after it was all over, and the Indians just gone. They were completely panic-stricken, but staid long enough to bury the dead, by throwing them hurriedly into a well, which was near the house.

"Buffalo Creek is about five miles from where the path crosses Broad River, that leads from the Cherokees to the Catawbas and Guttery's plantation, some twenty miles from that ford, which is one hundred from this Saluda settlement."

The Governor made praiseworthy efforts to recover these captive children, and restore them to their relatives. It is stated, that, the following October, he wrote specially to one of the traders in the Nation, to rescue, from a party of Savannahs, a little white child, which was supposed to be one of them. He directed it to be sent to him in Charleston.

A few days afterwards, he received a letter from John Elliott, at Chote, informing him that a party of Savannahs were at that place, having in their possession two white children, which they declared to the Cherokees they had obtained from the Indians who were engaged in the massacre on the Buffalo.

"I tried," adds the trader, "to get them from them, but could not succeed. I hope your Excellency will take some steps to rescue the captive children of our settlers from these savages."*

About the same period, a large party of the same troublesome savages came from the head of the Monongahela to the Cherokee Nation, where, having procured a willing guide, they set off down the Savannah, to make a bloody attack upon the inoffensive Euchees, who were regarded as *settlement* Indians, and therefore under the protection of the English. Like wolves, they came stealthily into a lurking place, near a small town of that tribe, situated two miles below Silver Bluff, and there waited an opportunity to do their murderous work, which was soon offered them, by the men all turning out to make a day's hunt; whereupon, springing from concealment, they butchered the women and children, and then darted off in different directions, to secure their retreat.

A striking instance was displayed, on this occasion, of the tender affection of the Indian women for their children; for every mother that escaped, bore her little ones safely off with her. The shrill war-whoop was soon ringing through the woods, the Euchee hunters flew to the assistance of their women and children, and, without stopping to contemplate the bloody scene that met their gaze, they dashed off up the river, in pursuit of the main party of the retreating foe.

The Cherokee guide, in order to avoid this, led

* Indian Books.

them a northern course, as far as the commencement of the open piny-woods country, where, turning to the north-east, they were stretching away—about ten miles north of the present site of Hamburg—for Ninety-six, which lay nearly in a direct line to the lower Cherokee towns, when luckily, they were discovered by an English hunter mounted on a fine white horse, which made him a fair mark for their guns; and they would have shot him, for their own security, if he had not spurred out of reach of them on their back tracks; for he wished to ascertain what the mischief was they had done, that their countenances and great haste plainly indicated.

He had not gone far before he met the enraged Euchees, pressing hard after them. He informed them, as they ran by, of the course the enemy had taken, and that they were twenty-six in company. Thus directed, they were enabled, in a run of twelve miles more, to come in sight of the marauders; and presently, running on each side of them, they fired upon and killed several of them. The rest, in order to make good their escape, were forced to throw away nine guns, a part of their plunder, and even to strip themselves of their clothes.

They were so terrified that they passed wide of the *then weak settlement of Ninety-six*, and continued to run—day and night—till they got in reach of the Cherokee towns. This occurred in May, 1750.*

These naked Canadians, as he called them, were

---

* Adair, p. 345.

the same savages who threatened the life of Adair, and his friend, H. Francis, (?) from Ninety-six, on the Keowee trail, near that town, as was related in a previous chapter.

The numerous communications sent down to Gov. Glen, by the traders and leaders of the companies of rangers which he had placed on the frontiers in the upper-country, at this troublous period, contain a faithful picture of the state of things on the border. In 1750, the following persons were acting as traders in the nation: "John McCord, Robert Gowdy, John Kelly, Bryan Salamon, Anthony Lantagne, Richard Smith, James May, Robert Emory, David McDonald, John Hatton, James Beamer, William Bates, and John Hook.

It was in the following year, that all the hunting grounds of the Cherokees were divided off into thirteen districts or ranges, and as many traders appointed to superintend them—one to every range—and two hundred Indian gun-men. There were, at that time, in the Nation, twenty-six hundred efficient warriors. It was found difficult to select from the number of traders thirteen men competent to be trusted with the superintendency of the hunting districts. They are generally described in the records as being without "substance, sense or character."

The following are named amongst those who were at last chosen: Robert Gowdy,* Antony Dean,†

* Gowdy was the first settler of Ninety-six.

† Dean has been before mentioned as a man of remarkable learning and skill

and Benn, for the Over-hills; Cornelius Dougherty and Grant, for the Valleys; James Mackey, and some others, for the middle settlements; Barnard Hughes, for the outer towns, with others not mentioned; and Beamer, Smith and Baldridge, for the lower towns. Several new rules for the guidance of the traders arose from this arrangement. Every one was to confine himself to his own range; no trader was to carry rum into the Nation, except *a few bottles for his own use;* a quantity of it was, however, to be lodged in the forts*—then preparing to be built—be distributed, twice a year, among the Indians of the districts—two kegs to a range: one to be given at the time of the green-corn dance, and the other on their return from the winter's hunt.

Several of the traders, about this time, repeatedly expressed the belief that a fort, properly built and garrisoned, among the lower towns, and another, equally efficient, over the hills, were all that was required to restore quiet and prosperity to the settlements and trade. The Indians, themselves, had, some time before, requested this as a special favor, in order to prevent the removal of the people of the lower towns to the settlements beyond the mountains, and the consequent ruin of this division of the Nation.

May 9th, 1751, Capt. Roger Gibson† wrote to Gov. Glen, from the Waterees: "I am informed, this day, by some of my company, just arrived from the Con-

* Prince George and Loudon. † Captain of Rangers.

garees, that the inhabitants of Ninety-six, Saluda, and the Upper Congarees, have fled to the fort at the latter place, to secure themselves from the Cherokees and northern Indians, who have killed several of the white people. As my company is the nearest to the enemy of all the Wateree inhabitants, we are in most danger, and are wholly unprovided with ammunition—there being no stores here to supply us—Charleston a great way off, and the people mostly new settlers, within the last two years.

"The increase of my company has been from thirty-five to eighty-three men; we, therefore, pray your Excellency will grant us a supply of ammunition, that we may defend ourselves and families against these heathens, who threaten our destruction."

A few days previous, Gov. Glen had written to order Capt. Gibson to raise a troop of rangers, consisting of fifteen men, besides officers, and five friendly Indians. He adds: "You and Capt. Francis, are to range, separately, with expedition, from the Congarees on Saluda, to Ninety-six, and between the Congarees and the Catawbas—but make no stay at the latter places; proceed, without loss of time, towards Ninety-six, where it is probable you will meet each other; and you are then to visit some of the settlements in those parts, and assure the people that nothing shall be omitted by this government that will promote their security.

"You are to endeavor to dispel their fears; encourage them to stand by one another, and keep possession of their homes and settlements; for to desert them only emboldens the Indians."

One Stephen Crell, of Saxe-Gotha, informed the Governor that a gang of Indians had been killing horses, *mares*, and cattle at the Congarees, and in the more northern settlements, after which they came to the house of John Geiger, and carried off his negro boy. Two women were the only members of the family at home at the time, and these dared to resist them, rather than give up the negro; but desisted, when the savages seemed resolved to murder them.

He advises the Governor, that the close settling of a number of people on the frontiers, is the best means of defending the country against the encroachments of the savages. The *lands lately purchased about Ninety-six*, and thence to Broad and Santee Rivers, and towards the Catawbas, being all very fertile and well adapted to close settlements, he did not doubt but that his Excellency would make all proper arrangements to have them settled under such regulations as would be most conducive to the safety of the country. There were several single young men at the Congarees, who were entitled to the bounty, and would settle higher up towards the border; but were deterred by the expenses and loss of time in going to Charleston, to prove their rights. They desired to be permitted to send down their oaths to the officers.

The tenth of the same month, Capt. John Fairchild, of Fairchildsboro', on the north side of the Congaree, wrote as follows to the Governor: "It is my duty to inform you, that several distressed families have been driven from their habitations and livings on the Little Saluda, and have, with great difficulty, retreated down to the Congarees, to escape the Indians. These savages have killed Isaac Cloud, with two of his children, and a young man living with him, as appears by Mrs. Cloud's affidavit.*

"This mischief, and the insolence of the several parties of Indians who are now in the settlements, plainly indicate their hostile intentions. They are ready for any violence, as opportunity offers, if not for a general war. This, I fear, must be the result; for those who have lost friends, or have been driven from their homes, will arouse themselves and seek revenge. At present, however, our corner of the country is not in a condition to defend itself. We have not the force nor the arms, and most of us are foreigners, and strangers to the methods and habits of the Indians; yet the men are full of spirit, and ready to engage the enemy in defence of their homes and country.

"We would, therefore, be most thankful to your Excellency for a supply of ammunition and warlike accoutrements; many among us are really poor and distressed—objects of compassion—and not able to purchase them for themselves. Having command of a company on this side of the river, for our better

* These are certainly identical with the Goulds, whose murder by the Savannah Indians has been related. The name is written differently in another place in the MSS.

defence, I have divided it into parties, some of whom I keep constantly scouting through the country; while the rest are employed in building a fort, into which our women and children may retreat. We would also petition your Excellency for a few swivels with which to mount the fort, when finished."

These were doubtless Scotch-Irish immigrants, who had come about this period into the present territory of Richland, and settled on the north-east bank of the Congaree. They are mentioned above as "strangers and foreigners," and they could not have been the Germans, who settled on Broad River, at the mouth of Kinsler's Creek. The following list of Capt. Fairchild's Company of Rangers, would seem to confirm the conjecture:

Capt. John Fairchild, Lieut. Philip Raiford, Cristis Colwell, Thomas Copeland, Ebenezer Howard, James Fletcher, William Low, John Evans, Richard Jones, James Myrick, Daniel Johnson, Solomon McGrow, David Jackson, Edward Bush, William Moore, Isaac Rhodes, Nathaniel Patridge, William Shetter, James Weston, William Hart, and William Raiford. These men were enlisted in May, 1751.

In the following August, Capt. Fairchild informed the Governor that he had ranged with his company as high up as Ninety-six, and built near that place a fort of puncheon-logs, for the protection of the people in that settlement.

CHAPTER XVIII.

The bank of John's Creek the probable site of Fairchild's Stockade Fort—The facts in the case—Description of the remains, discovered on the plantation, of P. D. Klugh, Esq.—Old John Youngblood and Wm. Buchanan—A search for hidden treasures; the excavation still visible on the ancient site of the fort—The old John's Creek settlement, &c.

After diligent search, we have had the satisfaction of discovering the probable site of the ancient fabric mentioned in the last chapter, which, though scarcely now perceptible, links the present with the earliest civilized period in the history of the old Ninety-six District. If our conjecture is correct, it was built—and as Fairchild wrote to the Governor—of puncheon logs, on the north bank of John's Creek, a rifle-shot from it, on the brow of a considerable hill, at present the property of P. D. Klugh, Esq.

The facts are these: On that spot, even previous to the Revolution, an old stockade fort was found standing in a ruinous condition. A slight embankment of earth had probably been thrown up, and on this the puncheons fixed in an upright position. The entire structure inclosed an acre or more of ground. On the west side of the hill, some sixty yards from the fort, ran a branch to which a covered ditch was cut, for the purpose of securing a supply of water for the occupants of the stockade, when surrounded or menaced by enemies. The remains of this ditch are still traceable.

Within the southern edge of the fort there yet stands a huge slippery-elm, which has been preserved by the proprietor of the plantation, in the midst of a cultivated field, partly for its medicinal virtues, but chiefly for the sake of its venerable associations.

Old John Youngblood—who removed about the close of the Revolution from the territory of Edgefield, and settled on the Jews'-land near this place—related, that when he first saw it, many of the tumbling palisades were still standing; particularly the heavier timbers about the gate, and on them were the marks of the augur and saw, proving it to have been the work of civilized men. Yet, Wm. Buchanan, an old settler, and a Revolutionary soldier, of the same neighborhood, stated, on being inquired of by Youngblood, concerning the origin of the fort, that he had often seen it, but knew nothing of the time or the occasion of its construction.

The truth is, the Buchanans and their neighbors had come into the country long subsequent to 1751—the period at which Fairchild built his puncheon fort—and the rapid changes incident to the population of every pioneer settlement had left not one of its previous settlers, who could have given the desired information.

A tradition having become prevalent at the beginning of the present century, to the effect, that rich treasures had been buried in troublous days of the olden time beneath the fort on John's Creek, a party, quite hopeful in their anticipations of success, sunk a pit near the foot of the ancient elm, which still remains, a monument of the cupidity of men, as the site of the old stockade inclosure is of the Indian hostilities and pioneer dangers and hardships of colonial periods.

To these circumstances, it may be further added, that the settlement on John's Creek corresponds well with Fairchild's statement, that he had built this fort near Ninety-six—it being only some fourteen miles north-west of the creek, a distance which was relatively much less in that age of widely-scattered communities than a modern estimate would regard it. And since, besides the fort built at the same period, by the Gowdies, at Ninety-six, and the block-house of Fort Boon, erected several years later by the Calhouns, Nobles and Houstons, on Cheves's Creek, there is no other known site of a similar structure in the present territory of Abbeville, we are almost driven to the conclusion, that it was at this spot, on John's Creek, Fairchild built the stockade fort of which he speaks in his letter to Governor Glen.

These facts shed a new and interesting light upon the history of the John's Creek settlement. They would prove incontestably, that on the fertile cane-bottoms of that stream a flourishing civilized community was founded; cotemporaneous with the first ever planted in any portion of the Ninety-six District. And there is much in the present aspect of this section of Abbeville, to corroborate this view derived from intimations already referred to in the records, and from others that have not been mentioned.

No part of the district, not even the Flatwoods or the lands around Old Cambridge, present a more worn or ancient appearance than that portion of the Long-Cane Valley lying between John's Creek and the Abbeville Branch of the Greenville and Columbia Railroad.

In May, Captain Francis, of Ninety-six, sent a letter to the Governor by Robert Gowdy, urging him to take into consideration the dangers to which the people there, and on the Saluda, were exposed from the incursions of the northern Indians, and the schemes of the French. The inhabitants had assembled, and forted themselves. James Maxwell rode an express from the Nation, and laid the following narrative before the Governor and Board:

"Having arrived at Keowee, a lower Cherokee town, I went to the house of Richard and Abraham Smith, traders there, and asked the news. They replied that the Indians had grown insolent and insulting; three nights before, they expected to be killed by them, several councils having been held to deliberate on their fate. A half-breed fellow came to the house, and, in an insolent manner, asked Abraham Smith what he thought? 'What should I think?' answered Smith. 'Why, I have killed a white man,' he replied, 'do you think your Governor will be cross? He may be cross if he will; I wish I could see an army of white men coming down yonder hill, I would be the first to strike my tomahawk in their heads.'

"A few days ago, when returning from a ball play, we heard the Indians laughing heartily at something that had been remarked in their conversation. We stopped to hear what they were talking about, and discovered that they were mocking the dying agonies and exclamations of the four white men they had murdered at the Oconees, such as, 'O! Lord, O! Lord have mercy upon us,' and the like, at which they laughed again most extravagantly.

"These Indians also declared that the traders should not leave the Nation till they had brought up the promised ammunition. The latter were in great fear of their lives. The same evening the good warrior of Tocquillo came to me—Maxwell further relates—and asked how his Excellency did, and the beloved men below? 'What does his Excellency say,' he added, 'of the murdered men at the Oconees?' 'I have not lately seen the Governor,' I answered. He asked again, what I thought of it, and if the Governor would resent the killing upon the whole Nation? I told him that such was not the way of the English, to punish the innocent for the guilty; the Nation would not be punished unless it was concerned in the deed. The Governor will, however, require satisfaction from the guilty. He answered that that would be very just.

"From Keowee I went to Cheowee and Tomassee,

and heard the same complaints from the traders at those towns. I now crossed the mountains to Hiwassee, and called on Dougherty, at his trading-house. He informed me that the Over-hills were well disposed—that the Raven of Hiwassee, and the chiefs of the Seven Towns, would not hear bad talks. I likewise met here Robert Gowdy and Samuel Bonn, who made the same report. From Hiwassee, I came to the town of Johree, on my return, where I had scarcely lighted from my horse, when I was told that a runner was in the house, sent from the lower towns to cut me off. I was struck with astonishment; and, calling the fellow out, demanded of him if what I had heard was true. He did not deny it. I then told him that such villainy should be severely punished.

"Next day, meeting three men who were walking very fast, I called out to one of them, James May, and asked what was the matter. He replied 'Bad news.' An Indian woman had come up from Sticoe, on the Tucosigia River, and reported that an Indian fellow had killed Daniel Murphy, a trader, and robbed the store of Barnard Hughes, who had taken refuge in Tucosigia. This was done by a man and a warrior. I now sent for the head-men of Johree and the neighboring town, and asked them if they had heard of the murder of Murphy, and the plundering of Hughes's store. Hoy answered that they had heard of it that morning. 'Why, then,' I asked again, 'did you not tell me of it?' 'We thought you knew it,' he replied. 'Do you believe it?' I asked. 'Yes; we have received messages that confirm it.' 'Do you approve of such acts?' 'No, we do not.' 'Will you protect me if they come to cut me off?' 'Yes, if it is in our power. They may be too strong for us. We will send for the Raven of the Valley, and be directed by him in the matter.' The white people now advised me to leave the Nation, and not to return by the way of Keowee or Ninety-six, as the Indians would certainly murder me; whereupon I procured arms for seventeen white men and two negroes, and, setting off at midnight, we made good our escape to this place, by the Augusta path."

The four men mentioned as having been killed at the Oconees, were Hugh Murphy, Bartholomew Hughes, Thomas Langley and Charles Grows.

In July, 1751, Captain James Frances wrote as follows, from Ninety-six, to Governor Glen: "We, therefore, beg leave, with all due submission, to declare to your Excellency, that to such lengths have matters now gone on the frontiers, that peace and quietness can no more be expected, unless a fort is built here on some commanding spot, and a company of rangers sent up, of sufficient force to drive these Northern or French Indians* from molesting and destroying our effects, which are our livelihood.

"When the Indians in other of his Majesty's provinces behaved formerly in the same manner, all

* These French Indians were the Natawegese, from the Ohio, a branch of the Shawannese, the devoted allies of the French.

efforts of the public authorities to keep them in submission were unavailing, until this method was proposed and carried out: a fort and body of rangers were put in force, which had quickly the desired effect; and those parts, though never so much encroached upon by the savages, soon began to be strong settlements, and made ample amends for the expenses the country was at to sustain them during their minority. And as the world can scarcely surpass this region in healthfulness of climate—in clear and wholesome streams running over a soil both fertile and beautiful—thousands would be induced to come and partake of it with us, when they understand that this government hath taken such methods that they need be under no concern or fear of danger from the Indians. It is certain that a fort in the Cherokee Nation will be of service on sundry accounts. It is absolutely necessary, however, to prevent the breaking up of the lower towns. But while the people believe it would secure the present settlements on the frontier, and all future settlements, it cannot, they think, be efficient without a company of rangers to scour the woods continually in those parts where the French Indians have taken possession.

"Captain Fairchild was very ill at the Congarees when I came by. His men, however, had gone on to Ninety-six, where they arrived three or four days before Captain Gibson reached the same point.

"Captain Minnick has also since met them there, who had previously acquainted those officers of the mischiefs committed, and of the necessity of concentrating the rangers at Ninety-six.* Capt. Gibson was so good as to come over to my house to inquire for the truth of the rumor of Indian depredations recently perpetrated; but as it was thought too late to pursue with success the retreating gang of northern savages, who had been killing the cows of the settlers, he returned to his company at Ninety-six. The neighborhood, however, humbly begs leave of your Excellency, that one, at least, of the ranging companies be appointed to range these woods back of the settlements, on the north side of the river; for it is only there that much damage can be done, there being no livers on Ninety-six to receive any."†

A few days after the reception of this letter by the Governor, Captain Roger Gibson sent down the following additional information. He wrote from the Coronaka: "According to the first instructions given by your Excellency, I visited with my troops the several places and inhabitants that had been designated, but without meeting with any Indians or accidents worth mentioning. I must, however, inform you of the miserable condition in which we found the upper settlers: they had been driven from their homes, their houses robbed, and their crops destroyed. I did all that I could to dispel their fear, by telling

* These officers were leaders of companies of rangers--a force that it had been the policy of the colony to maintain on the frontiers from an early period. None, however, had yet been posted higher up than Ninety-six.

† State Records vol. 5th.

them that your Excellency and council would do everything that could be done for their safety and protection.

"I have also, in compliance with the same instructions, ranged with my troops as far as Ninety-six. About one mile above that place we encamped, and, taking a small detachment of my men, I went up the river to Corouaka, to discover, if possible, the Indians who, we learned, had killed the cattle of the people there, cut down their corn, and committed other acts of violence.

"My Lieutenant and Captain Fairfield's company ranged likewise in another direction with the like object in view, but we saw none of the enemy. While we were gone, however, these Indians came to a house with long knives drawn in their hands, and having entered it, one of them fired off his gun, and immediately after re-loaded it. They told the people living in it, that they were Cherokees, and went off showing impudent airs, as if they despised and did not value us. So that from all we can learn, they meditate nothing but war; and it is the opinion of every one acquainted at all with Indian character, that as soon as they know your resolution by Mr. Bunyon, they will break out and fall upon us and the upper inhabitants, and cut us all off before your Excellency can come up with an armed force to our relief. I therefore advised Captain Minnick to join us, and delay his visit to the Catawbas; fifty or sixty men being too small a number to withstand three hundred Indians; for that number you may surely expect. It is the desire of these upper inhabitants that we go no farther up, but stay and build a fort near Ninety-six, to which they may resort when the danger comes. At that place we shall await further orders from your Excellency."*

Most deplorable was now the condition of the struggling settlers of the upper-country; never before, not even in the darkest hour of their partizan conflict in the Revolution, did they suffer more, or stand in greater need of assistance from a stronger arm than their own. Their territory over-run by roving bands of savages, more barbarous in some respects than the nest of restless hornets on their border; themselves murdered in cold blood at their fire-sides, or while wrapt in sleep, unconscious of an enemy's approach; their children carried into captivity, their houses burned, and their property destroyed or plundered—every settlement in a panic of fear, the frightened people hurrying at constantly recurring alarms to the friendly refuge of forts and block-houses, hastily constructed in some central spot.

And these dangers and agitations—this violence and invasion—were not endured for a week or a month; during many gloomy years they were more or less the constant portion of the early pioneers of the upper-country. From 1749, to the close of Col. Grant's campaign, in 1761, embracing a period of more than ten years, there was not a settlement in

* Indian Books.

this portion of the province that was not exposed to the inroads of hostile savages, and, at their hands, became the not unfrequent scene of bloody tragedies and domestic ruin.

Through the most critical and trying half of this period, the destinies of the colony were presided over by Gov. James Glen. The question forces its own consideration: Did he sustain his trust with fidelity? We have already intimated, that Adair, a sufficiently intelligent, though not altogether disinterested cotemporary, does not hesitate to charge him with the deliberate sacrifice of the public interest to the promotion of his own private aggrandizement;* and it must be confessed that an impartial review of all the facts in the case, drawn from various and the most reliable sources, does not restore his memory to the unqualified admiration of posterity.

He entered upon his office in the very midst of the energetic and open efforts of the French to seduce the Cherokees and Catawbas from their alliance with Carolina; Priber, the prince of the intriguers, was known to be among the former people, and busily preparing for the accomplishment of designs that must issue in the serious injury if not total ruin of the province; yet nothing is heard of a more efficient opposition to these encroachments than the occasion-

* The conduct of Governor Glen, in this respect, as estimated by many of his cotemporaries, was severely reprehended in a pamphlet published at the time, entitled, "A Modest Reply to J. G., Esq.," and which is, no doubt, still preserved among the other valuable collections of the South Carolina Historical Society.

al advice to the traders to keep a sharp eye upon the French and Spanish emissaries. A feeble effort had just been made to apprehend the scheming Jesuit* through the agency of Colonel Fox, which resulted in a complete failure, and the ejection of Fox from the Nation, under circumstances of mortification and disgrace; yet nothing more was done in the matter, till the accidental opportunity that was offered for his arrest by the Carolina traders, on the Tallapoosa.

A few years later, and the savage allies of the French, from the banks of the Ohio, were already over-running the settlements on the border, and even boldly depredating in the very vicinity of the capital. We have already related how, at this time, a band of them captured and tomahawked, in cold blood, Herman Geiger, a respectable and popular trader of the Congarees. But if any effort was made, even now, to vindicate the rights and secure the safety of the people of upper-country, or to receive Geiger during the considerable time that the savages were encamped with him in the Cherokee country, further than a simple message sent to the lower towns, and a petty reward offered for his re-capture, it does not appear in any record or chronicle of those times.

When, at length, after depredating, for years, with impunity, upon the property of the prisoners—for it has been shown that, in the absence of assistance from the government, the feeble settlements

* Priber was in the full tide of success with his plans, when Glen was appointed Governor, in 1743.

were utterly unable to protect themselves—the savages began the wholesale butchery of defenceless families, the minute details of which, with earnest prayers for deliverance, were constantly sent down to be laid before the Governor and his council; what shall be said of their continued indifference to these foul wrongs, or at best, their puerile efforts to remove and redress them through the instrumentality of a few patrol bands on the back of the settlements?

In the interval that elapsed between the murder of the Goulds, or Clouds, and the horrible massacre of the immigrants and wedding party on the Buffalo, Governor Glen was coolly sitting in Charleston, dictating, in a masterly manner, it is true, a correspondence with the Governor of Virginia, in relation to the interference of that colony with the business and profits of the Cherokee peltry trade. Like many, who had figured in responsible places of public trust before him, he seemed much better fitted to shine in the management of the etiquette and pageantry of a court or government, and in fostering its literature and arts, than in discharging the more arduous duties of the statesman and military leader.

Negociation was his strength. Negociation conducted with tact and vigor, must accomplish everything; and it must be confessed, that no Governor of Carolina ever presided in her councils or public conferences with a better dignity or more graceful address than James Glen. The Indians regarded him as a consummate orator; but were certainly never impressed with the least respect for his prowess as a warrior. An old chronicler thus briefly describes him: "He was a man of considerable knowledge, courteous and polite; exceedingly fond of military parade and ostentation, which commonly have great force on ordinary minds, and by these means he maintained his dignity and importance with the people."*

It was chiefly by diplomacy and management that he had hoped all along to quell the disturbances on the border. The manuscript abounds with mutual communications that passed, during these years, between him and the most prominent head-men of the Nation. The Cherokees with their usual shrewdness, soon discovered this bent of his genius, and showed themselves neither remiss nor unskillful in the art of amusing it. In the spring of 1751, the chiefs of the lower towns,† of Keowee, Tomassee, Cheowee, Ustustee, Estatoe, and Sugaw Town of Toxso, addressed him a letter, in which they express their sorrow for the outbreaks that had occurred to disturb the peace of the upper settlements; and promise that a better state of things shall be maintained in the Nation; concluding with the assurance, that it had all originated in the lies of those who went about to sow the seeds of discord.

* Hewit.

† The following names of chiefs were signed to this communication: Skiogusta, Little Conjurer, Howsuffe, of Keowee; Skiogusta and All Bones, of Cheowee; Chunroheke, of Ustustee; Tuckeoruftteke, of Tomassee; Oconaco, of Sugaw.

Similar communications, either written or in the form of a message, were frequently sent him by Old Hop of Chote, and the Raven of Hiwassee. We have seen that even the wary traders in the Nation were sometimes beguiled by these fair promises, and penitential regrets of the chiefs.

At length, in the summer of 1753, Governor Glen invited all the leading men of the Nation to meet him in a general conference in the town of Charleston. As many as were able to come at the appointed time promptly obeyed the summons, and as this was one of the most remarkable Indian *talks* that ever occurred in Charleston, developing important historical facts, as well as many interesting details illustrative of Indian character, we have ventured to quote its proceedings entire, as they are recorded in one of the volumes of the Indian Books.

Before introducing these, however, it may be well to recur to a few previous events. In 1751, tired out by the continued misrule and disorder on the border, it was seriously proposed in council to throw off altogether the commercial alliance of the Cherokees. This proposition met the wise and unqualified disapproval of Gov. Glen. His remarks on the occasion are, however, characteristic:

"It would be impolitic to resent, in the manner proposed, anything they have yet committed. To prove this, I would refer you to a few facts that must be fresh in your memories. Soon after the breaking out of the present war between France and England, the French were very busy with their agents and friendly Indians, endeavoring to obtain a foot-hold in the nations in alliance with the English. The Catawbas returned an answer to the overtures made to them, that they would have no connection with any other than the English of Carolina—they would stand or fall with them. These were overtures not of peace only, but to instigate the Catawbas to take up the hatchet against the English.* The same proposals were made to the Cherokees, and received a similar answer.

"These attempts of the French, however, very justly alarmed this government, the more especially as bad talks had been spread by them among the Creeks. These events gave great uneasiness to all our outer settlements and new townships, and they petitioned the council to have forts built on the border, which the council advised to be granted. I, at the same time, thought it important that I should have an interview with those nations, that these things might be looked into, and the Indians confirmed in the British interest. I accordingly went up and met them near their respective countries; I met the Catawbas at the Congarees, and the Cherokees at a place called Ninety-six. Head-men came to this place from almost every town in the Cherokee Nation; and in all their speeches they expressed so much attachment to the English interest, and

* Adair declares that the French, at this time, offered a standing reward to the Choctaws and other Southern tribes, for every scalp of an English inhabitant they should bring in.

spoke with so much sincerity, as not only to convince me, and the gentlemen who were with me, of their good intentions, but likewise all the *inferior sort of people*, to the number of two hundred, who had attended the meeting, and were very attentive to what passed, most of them being greatly interested in the consequences, as settlers in the new townships. And so fully were they persuaded of the friendship of the Cherokees, that they petitioned me that the money it had been proposed to expend in building forts, should be applied to the repairing of their highways.

"Soon after this, a French emissary came into the Nation; the Cherokees beat out the brains of an Indian, who had come with him, and he scarcely escaped with his life. Other instances of their friendship could be given. An Englishman happened to be killed some time ago in one of their towns—a pack-horseman of indifferent character. The town at first refused to avenge the murder; the warrior who committed the deed, they said, was a very great man, while the Englishman was a nothing. I insisted on satisfaction. A council of head-men was called, and they resolved to reduce the town to ashes, and massacre its people, if they did not yield up the murderer, or put him to death themselves. They consented to cut him off, and struck him in the town-house, but only wounded him; he ran and hid in a hollow tree; thence they dragged him, and cut him to pieces with a hatchet, having first chopped off his hands. His friends begged his body, that they might bury it: the chiefs refused, declaring that it should lie above ground, that the English might see how faithful they were to their engagements."* Such was Gov. Glen's confidence in the Cherokees, and such his plan for remedying the existing evils in the Nation and pioneer settlements.

A brief, but no less characteristic communication, was sent about the same time, by James Adair, the historian, to William Pinckney: "If the government designs to stand on the defensive, and will grant me, with sufficient credentials, that encouragement which, if possible, I might merit, as well in this as in the Choctaw and Chickasaw affairs, I shall induce the Chickasaws at Augusta, and many brave woodsmen, to join me in the service of Carolina; and, if I am not mistaken in myself, with such brave, wanton fellows in the field, I will accomplish something remarkable."†

A fierce war was now raging between the Creeks and Cherokees. It will be recollected that we related in another place, how that Adair, on one occasion, singularly escaped being murdered on the Chickasaw path, by a band of the prowling Savannahs. After he had got away from them, they fell in with a couple of Chickasaw hunters—adopted relations of the Creeks—whom they killed and scalped; and then, as they had been long doing in Carolina, ran and took refuge among the Cherokees. The exasperated

* Indian Books. † Ibid.

Creeks, having more respect for their national honor and private rights, and less confidence in Cherokee honesty, than the intelligent rulers in Charleston, made war at once upon that Nation.

Our credulity is now put to the test, though we are assured of the fact, that Gov. Glen summoned the Cherokee chiefs to meet him in the conference in Charleston, to which we have alluded, not for the purpose of giving them even the gentlest rebuke for the outrages they were obviously abetting, upon the defenceless settlements of the upper-country, nor to require them to make reparation for their recent insult to the Creeks; but solely to persuade them to bury the hatchet, and be at peace with the latter people.

The proceedings of the conference will tell their own story. A cotemporary* has discovered, however, an identical motive in this step of the Governor, with that which induced him to expostulate with Virginia, in relation to the Cherokee trade—the Creek war was greatly interfering with the *profits of the traffic.*

* Adair.

CHAPTER XIX.

Gov. Glen's Great Council with the Cherokee Chiefs, in Charleston—Attaculaculla makes the first speech—The Governor replies—Long Jack and other Chiefs follow—Certain Savannah Indians in the town-jail become the subject of an angry debate—The Chiefs depart for their Towns—Incident on the Path near Saluda Old Town, &c.

The Conference was opened in the Council-Chamber, July 4th, 1753, Gov. Glen presiding. Attaculaculla* appears to have made the first business speech. "I remember when I was in England, we were told by the great King George to defend ourselves against all our enemies, and that we should have ammunition to fight against the Muskogee and other southern Indians who might attack us. I want to know if you have any orders from the great King to make peace between us and the Creeks?

Governor.—You were very young at that time, and must have forgotten the talk. I have the great King's instructions on paper, in my keeping, and he

* This chief, when quite young, had gone with the famous Cherokee Embassy to England, and was better known to the whites by his surname of Little Carpenter. He was exceedingly small in his person, but eloquent, sagacious, and brave. His Indian name signifies the *most excellent wood-cutter*.

desires that all the Indians, who are friends to the English, should be at peace with one another.

Little Carpenter.—The great King desired us, when I was in England, to avenge the lives of his white people, whose bones lie white upon the ground of the Muskogee.

Governor.—What I say is the great King's talk; you are not to be guided by any one else.

Little Carpenter.—I shall be glad if you will let me go to England in the spring; I want to talk with great King George myself.

Governor.—It may be that in two or three years hence, after all things have been made easy, you can get leave to go; but your Nation is at present so engaged in war with the Creeks, that it would be injudicious to send so able a warrior as you are away from your country.

Little Carpenter.—There are other countries and places from which one could go to England besides this.

Governor.—The great King will see no one from this country but whom I send.

Little Carpenter.—I should be glad to hear your Excellency's talk about your white people and our trade; but as to making peace with the Muskogee, we have no directions about that; we can do nothing without the consent of Old Hop.*

Governor.—You knew for what purpose you were

* The King of Chotie and the great beloved wise-man of the Nation.

invited here before you came down; I am surprised that you did not bring full powers with you to conclude a peace, to which you had agreed above two months ago. (Then turning to the Little Carpenter, he continued:) I have been here now ten years, and never saw you before; many serious complaints have been brought down to me about your being a disturber of the peace; but as you are present to speak for yourself, I do not doubt but that you will clear yourself of these charges, and prove worthy of my good opinion.

Little Carpenter, (taking a lighted tobacco-pipe in his hand.)—This pipe was sent by Old Hop, of Chotie, who desired that it might be delivered to your Excellency and your beloved men, that all of you might smoke of it. (An Indian fellow, having a brass cross hanging from his ear, received the pipe, and hands it to the Governor, who, with the council and all the Indians present, smokes in the usual manner.)

Governor.—We have now smoked out of our pipe; this is a token of peace, and that we are all friends of your Nation. The last time I smoked the pipe of peace in this room, the Cherokees, Muskogees and Catawbas, all smoked it with me. I love such smoking, and should be glad to witness such a scene again, when they shall all once more be friends and united as brothers. The business you were sent upon was to conclude a peace with the Creeks.

Long Jack.—I came hither from my town, and from the place where Old Hop and our council meet.

I came to see the Governor at the edge of the great water. I have not seen your Excellency for a long time. There are many enemies on the path; I knew not that I should ever get here alive. But we have come safe, where we find all bright and clear, and we are thankful. I am with you; and I have seen the smoke of peace rising from your mouth on the air. I shall now return home, and if I get safely back, shall go directly out to war. Everything I have seen and heard here is clear and bright, but my people at home are dark. I shall go out to war only against my enemies; never against my friends. I shall go home as soon as I get down these stairs; this room looks to me like a great tree; but it is a tree that may fall and bury me under it, so that I shall hasten to get out of it. When we left my town, we brought our arms with us, and Old Hop desired us to hurry down with our people, and attend to what your Excellency should say about the white people and our trade; but to give no definite answer as to a peace with the Muskogee. Old Hop will settle that matter himself. He told us that he would be impatient of our return, and would keep his face turned towards Charleston, in the hope of seeing the smoke of friendship rise towards the clouds from the edge of the great water. (Pointing to the pipe.) This pipe is Old Hop's; he is as much a governor of his towns, as you are of your people here. We are only sent to your Excellency as messengers of peace, to smoke with you and your beloved men.

Governor.—If Old Hop was here, I should only

hear him speak; but if any others of the head-men have something to say, I shall hear them.

Several Indians.—We did not come down to give a talk; we were ordered by Old Hop to hear what your Excellency had to say.

Governor.—Your comparison of this government to a great tree was very just; but you are mistaken if you think it may fall; its roots are deep, and the branches strong and wide-spreading, and happy is that nation of Indians who shall find shelter under it.

Long Jack.—I did not mean that: your Excellency mistook my meaning in regard to the tree. I meant by it, that we are so much exposed to our enemies, particularly the French Indians, that we want a large tree to be planted in our Nation, to protect and shelter us from our enemies.*

Governor.—The English are very careful to provide for their friends; and you may depend upon all the assistance you need from this presence.

Long Jack.—We are in haste to be gone, and shall be thankful for a supply of arms and ammunition. The day here is bright, but not so on our path, which is full of enemies; they lurk in every bush and thicket to cut us off as we pass, and we know not that we shall live to see our homes again. When we came down we were safer than when we shall return, because the white men were with us.

Governor.—You shall have a supply of ammuni-

* Long Jack, no doubt, asks here, under a beautiful figure, for a fort.

tion, and I shall take care that it be carried a part of the way with you in a cart.

Long Jack.—We are greatly obliged to your Excellency. We also very much need pipes, hatchets, and pins with which to stretch our skins. We had these things from Virginia, and we wish to get them from you, so that we may show our people, that we can get as good things here as in Virginia.

Governor.—Yesterday you heard my talk, when I told you, the chief thing for which I sent for you was to make peace with the Creeks. There are other things, however, proper to be mentioned; but as you have not yet fully answered on that point, if you have anything more to say, I am ready to hear it. I have now in my hand a letter from Old Hop, attested by Beamer and Hatton, concerning a peace with the Creeks. "Before this," he says, "everything was cloudy; but since hearing from the Governor, all is clear and bright." I perceive that Ustinca and Tassite,* of Hiwassee, were present when it was written; I suppose they remember it, and as this is the last time we shall probably talk together before you leave, I desire that you will unburden your minds to me, and conceal nothing. I see (pointing to one of the Indians) you have in your hand the pipe sent me by Old Hop; I accept it as a token of friendship between us, and I and my people will smoke of it. (Orders a candle to be lighted.)

Indian.—Canachte, of Chotie, sent this pipe and

* The Raven.

these eagles' wings, as a token of friendship for the English, that when they see them they may remember Canachte.

Governor.—I do receive it as a token of peace and friendship (the Indian presenting it lighted, with the eagles' wings, and all present smoke; presently, the tobacco is exhausted, and the Governor continues): I perceive that the tobacco is all burnt out, and as sure as I now re-fill this pipe, I do publicly promise that the Cerokees shall be, hereafter, plentifully supplied with goods. It is the fault of the traders that there are frequent complaints on this head, who do not keep me informed of your necessities. When you are in want of anything, send a messenger to the Captain of the Fort at the Congarees.

Long Jack.—We thank your Excellency. While Robert Kelly and Stains traded in our towns, we were well supplied, and wanted nothing; but since they are no more, we are often necessitous. We are now in the great Council House, with your Excellency and beloved men, our brothers, and with our traders, also—several of whom, we know, have lost their lives in coming to our country, and for whose blood we shall yet have satisfaction of the French.* Last winter, when you sent up the talk desiring us not to go against the Muscogee, I did observe it, and begged our warriors not to go out on the war-path

* Long Jack here cunningly insinuates that it was Indians in the pay of the French, and not Cherokees, who had been guilty of the murders in the Nation.

against them any more. The last message that came up, was a request that we would meet you at the Congarees; but that failing, we have now come, at the request of Old Hop, to meet and talk with you here. We are not desirous to continue the war against the Creeks, for there are other enemies of our Nation to fight at present. But the making of peace with the Muscogee, is, in reality, making no peace at all; for a treaty of friendship and amity that they may make to-day, they will break to-morrow.

Governor.—I have given great attention to what you say. I am sensible that Kelly was a very good man, and supplied you well with goods; but as he is gone, we shall take care that you shall be as well supplied by others, as if Kelly were still alive. The name of Kelly brings to my remembrance the barbarity of the French in encouraging their Indians to kill our people, by giving them a reward for their scalps. They murdered Robert Kelly; but, in time to come, if any white man is killed on the path, or in the Nation, they may depend upon it, satisfaction will be required.

As Old Hop is head-man over the hills, and he appears desirous of a peace with the Creeks, I am hopeful that the latter people will be as ready to accede to it on their part. I am glad that you think the loss of one man is not a sufficient cause for war. If the murderer, himself, is punished, it will prevent further mischief. You, Cherokees, are much more beloved by us than the Savannahs; but should one of you come down and murder any of my people, we would insist upon having satisfaction, and yet, not make war upon your nation. This is our constant practice. There is an instance of it among the Muscogee; they came down and killed several of you, Cherokees, our friends, near this town. I sent up and demanded satisfaction. They complied without a murmur, and took away the life of one of their greatest men.

Little Carpenter.—When I was in England, two papers were given by the great King George, one for the Cherokees, and the other, I suppose, for the authorities of Carolina. I have not seen those papers since; doubtless, they are lost.

Governor.—The paper for Carolina, though it cannot at present be readily come at, being in a great heap of other papers, is not lost. I showed it to you the other day, printed in a book.

Little Carpenter.—This is the third time I have been here, and I remember the great king's talk. He promised that we should never want for goods; nevertheless, we have suffered much, because we could not procure them from the Carolina traders; we were forced to go for them to other countries. But now that your Excellency has given your promise that we shall lack these things no more, our hearts are straight, and we shall not look to any other people for supplies.

Governor.—I am glad that that was your only reason for going to Virginia.

Little Carpenter.—I heard that your Excellency

sent several times for me, and I was sorry that I was from home; for, perhaps, you may have thought that I had done something that made me afraid to come hither; but I was then in Virginia, where the Governor showed us his commission, and said it was the same as that of the Governor of Carolina. It was not from fear that I did not come; it was because the Over-hill people, being poor, and in great straits from want of goods, compelled me to go to Virginia, in search of a supply for them. There are now only two regular traders in our Nation, Mr. Beamer and Cornelius Dougherty; the others have no goods of their own, except what they get of other traders, with the view of speculating as they can. Now, it is to be hoped, however, that our traders will receive a supply sufficient for all the wants of the Nation. We need some small articles for our women. When I was in England, I heard what the great king said; and I remember that he directed in the paper he gave us, that the Governor of Carolina was to supply us with all kinds of goods, and if he failed to do it, we could get them from Virginia—that you were both one people, under the same great king.

Long Jack.—We are now almost ready to go home, and I would be glad to have an answer from your Excellency to Old Hop's letter, which mentions that he was not able to come down with us. We would rejoice if you would go up towards our country, as far even as the point at which Old Hop said he would meet you, if he had to be carried on the back of a slave.

Governor.—I will first reply to the Little Carpenter. I am very sorry that you were obliged to go through briars and thickets to obtain a supply of goods. For the future, they shall be sent to you in abundance. I am glad that you went into those parts; for, in your absence, your enemies gave it out you had gone over to the interest of the French; but now that you have returned, and given your own report of the matter, I shall no more give ear to what they say. It is very true what you remark about the goods. You have at present but two traders among you—Beamer and Dougherty; but, indeed, there is no encouragement for them; the price of goods is so very low, that the traders cannot live among you; notwithstanding, I recently sent you, by another trader, enough for your wants. I do not mention this in view of raising the price of goods; you shall have them always as usual; but you must pay for them. You cannot but be sensible of the fact, that they are much lower in price with you than with the Creeks. I shall mention one article only: The Creeks pay a pound of leather for but forty bullets, while the Cherokees get sixty for the same. I have read over the paper that you speak of, from the great King George, and find not a word in it about the government of Virginia, or of her supplying you with goods. It is true, that province belongs also to the great king; but if, at any time, I should send to its Governor, requesting him not to supply you with goods, on account of some misdemeanor committed by you, he would not dare do it.

Little Carpenter.—What I say about that is only talk. I do not assert that such is to be, or likely to be; but if it should so happen, that Carolina refuse to send us goods, there are many great waters and rivers to go down to, where they can be obtained. We hope, however, that we shall be laid under no such necessity; the first offence shall never be on our part.

Governor.—You would be at a great loss if you did desert Carolina; and ultimately as naked as the French themselves are. We shall always be good friends to the Cherokees.

Little Carpenter.—I have no desire to look elsewhere for goods; but Old Hop is a wise man, and can give your Excellency full satisfaction as to these things, were you to talk with him. We are only warriors, and have no great knowledge of many things, in which lies much good for our Nation; neither can we express ourselves, nor argue upon dark questions; we, therefore, refer you to the good and wise old man. Formerly, when we had more men than we now have, four traders trafficked in our towns. Mr. Elliott has brought us a great many goods; but, we fear, he will not be able to supply all our wants.

Governor.—Then, I will send more. You have pressed me very much to see Old Hop; but there are many affairs that require my presence here. If, at any time, however, I should go up as far as the Congarees, I will send for him to meet me there. (Pointing to Skiagunsta, he continued.)—I am glad to see you; you are always the messenger of peace and good news, and have come down at the proper time, to witness that all the reports against our government are false. You always give good talks to your people. We look upon you as our good friend, and hope always to do so. If Skiagunsta, the small-pox conjurer, has anything to say, let him speak.

Skiagunsta.—I am listening to hear if the upper towns have anything more to say, and kept silent because their two head-men did not appear to be done. When they are, I have something to say; for, it is not our custom, like the white people, to talk all at once; but when one is through, another begins. When they are all quiet, I shall begin to speak.

Governor.—It is a very good rule, and, indeed, we observe the same.

Skiagunsta.—We were talking about the trade. I believe your Excellency and we are imposed upon by some of the traders. When we tell them of it, they say they have the Governor's orders; and if we complain, we are ill-treated by them. The price of a white shirt is five pounds of leather; a broad hoe the same, and of a small shirt, three pounds; and when we complain of this the answer is, they have come a great way, and their horses break their bones carrying the goods over the hills and mountains. Some of them make us pay six pounds of leather for a fathom of calico.

Governor.—What the traders say is very true. They often sustain great losses in conveying their goods to your Nation. They are frequently spoiled in the carriage; and indeed the prices are so low that many of them cannot live. Sometimes they get no pay at all for their goods, and many other disadvantages there are which they labor under; so that you must not expect goods at too low a price. By the last treaty, you were to have them at the same prices as were usual before that treaty was made.

Long Jack.—Many of our Nation are often killed in war, while others fall by sickness on the path; and when we die thus, though we are in debt to the traders, they should not seize upon our horses. The little that is left is of service to the living.

Governor.—I am very sorry to hear that such things are done. If you will but mention the name of a trader who is guilty of it, he shall be punished. But you yourselves should keep an account of your traffic, that you may compare it with that of the traders. (He here reads the article in the last treaty relating to trade, and the names of all the head-men who signed it.)—"All goods shall stand at their usual prices, and if any trader imposes upon the Indians higher rates, he shall be punished." Let me know the man that does it.

Little Carpenter.—A flap was to cost one pound of leather, and six pounds were to be the measure of a match-coat.

Governor.—You shall take up with you an iron yard-stick, so that the traders cannot cheat you.

Skiagunsta.—When I and my people were here before, we were about to fix the price of a flap and a shirt at eight pounds of leather; but something intervened and put a stop to it.

Little Carpenter.—It was on account of the trade that we went to Virginia. When I was in England I was told to go and procure goods wherever I could get them cheapest. The price of shirts is dearer now than formerly.

Governor.—It was agreed that the prices should be as had been usual.

Little Carpenter.—The traders are very cross with us Indians. We dare not speak to them. If we do, they take our skins and dash them upon the ground, and deny us goods. We must give them whatever they demand, or go without goods.

Governor.—You have in your country right weights and measures; they cannot, therefore, cheat you. But as I before remarked, the prices are already so low, that the traders can scarcely pay for their goods and live. I desire you to show me one who ever made a farthing among you. One of the greatest traders who ever went to your Nation—from whom other traders procured their goods—being unable to get them elsewhere, has left you to go to another country, and there broken. Here is James Beamer, who went very young among you, and settled as a trader; he is now gray-headed, and yet in debt. Even among the Muscogee, the traders make but a shift to live. This is all they can do. Mr. Kelly, who was a long time in your Nation, left nothing. His wife and children are poor to-day. The day is now nearly spent; but if any of you have more to say, speak on.

Little Carpenter.—Do what we may, the white people will cheat us in our weights and measures—they will make them less. What is it a trader cannot do? They give us bad measure in our powder. Some of the white men borrowed my yard-stick, and cut it shorter, for which I was blamed.

Governor.—Let the yard-measure be kept by one of your beloved men, and then if any trader cuts it, send him to me.

Little Carpenter.—We are satisfied.

Skiagunsta.—I look towards the south-west, and it is bright. I am heartily glad of the peace. We are obliged to your Excellency. I am ready to confirm it. I like the talk of the Muscogee; but would like to have seen them here. We are but two towns, at present, in the Lower Cherokees; but we are men and warriors, as well as the others; we have a war-hatchet as well as they. But as soon as I heard the peace talk, we buried the bloody hatchet, and it shall appear no more. Since that time all has been quiet, and we have hunted without fear. A young man brought word that the upper towns were for peace, but the lower were not; then your agent came to the Nation and proposed peace; and you have obtained it, and I am glad. May it be lasting. I have always been obedient to the Governor's commands. I have followed him step by step. I have none other now to assist me. This is the last speech I shall make. Your Excellency must remember that you promised to build us a fort at Keowee. It has not been done. Should it not be built, my people must desert their towns, and remove beyond the blue hills.

Governor.—I have heard you; I hope the peace will be lasting, and there will be no occasion for a fort. I do remember that I promised it, and what I promise, I shall always perform; such is the custom of the English. But many things happened; some bad talks among the Cherokees prevailed; everything appears bright and clear now, however, and I shall endeavor to build you a fort at Keowee.

Skiagunsta.—I should be very glad to depart now; but I do not know when I shall get home, as I have lost my horse; perhaps some *rogue of a white man has taken him.*

Governor.—Diligent search shall be made for your horse, and if he cannot be found, I will present you with another to carry you home.

At the same time that these Cherokee chiefs arrived in town to hold their talk, it so happened that the identical Savannahs,* who were mentioned in a former chapter, as having been captured in the act of committing depredations near Charleston, and unwisely confined there, were brought in, and had undergone a slight examination in the presence of the Cherokees, before the conference began. When, to the surprise of the Governor, if not of other Englishmen present, they suddenly manifested a warm interest in their favor. The talk now turned upon the Savannah prisoners, and the speeches became shorter and somewhat spiced.

* Ohio Indians.

Long Jack.—I should like to know what is to be done with the Savannahs below; for the wise old man at home will be very anxious to know that; they have always acted like messengers of peace.

Governor.—They have not behaved well, and we have not yet decided what to do with them.

Long Jack.—They came to us with talks of peace.

Governor.—By their bringing talks of peace they may have had business at Chotie; but they had no business at all in our settlements.

Long Jack.—If they brought ropes, with which to tie prisoners, they did not design them for white, but red men. If they had had a mind to kill white people, they could have done it before they came here.

Governor.—It is for that very reason, the seizing of our friendly settlement Indians, that we punish them.

Long Jack.—If you will not take our talk about the Savannahs, we will not take yours about the peace with the Muskogee.

Governor.—You have no business with our affairs.

Little Carpenter.—We will not have a peace with the Creeks, while these prisoners are here.

Governor.—I am sorry to repeat my words again; it is the last time I shall do so. If any Cherokees had done the same, we should punish them and yet remain friends to the Nation. We never suffer Indians to meddle in our affairs. You say you came from Old Hop, and that you would declare nothing yourselves, till you should hear and tell him all that I say; therefore I do not regard what you speak concerning the Savannahs.

Little Carpenter.—I do not defend the Savannahs; it is for the safety of the white people, who come among us, that I contend. If these Indians are punished, the path will be made bloody, and no white man will be able to come to our country. You, (pointing to the Governor,) and those about you, are safe; but many a straggling white man will lose his life.*

Governor.—What Indian dare do it.

Little Carpenter.—Many of the five nations will join these people, and some of the Cherokees; we cannot prevent it.

Governor.—The Savannahs never go into the councils of the five nations; if they did, however, we would soon run them out.

Little Carpenter.—There are three towns of them.

Governor.—If there were thirty we are strong enough to destroy them all.

Little Carpenter.—I do not refer to numbers; we know you are able to cut them off, but in the mean time, they may do you much injury.

Governor.—We are not afraid of the French Indians; we are determined to defend our friendly red people. Old Hop says, he has sent me down his boys; I am sorry indeed to find them behaving like

* This was in good part verified by those savage vagabonds.

boys. If these Savannahs are guilty, we will punish them; if not, they may go free. It is not for our own sakes, we desire peace between you and the Muskogee; it is at your earnest desire. The upper, middle and lower settlements all urge its consummation. But if you covet war rather than peace, you may be gratified; I will write to the Creeks, and you shall have enough of it.

The next day the Governor resumed his speech:—I have read over this morning your treaty with the great King George in England. In that treaty you engage to keep the path free from blood, and to protect our traders in your Nation. You also promise that when his Majesty is at war with any nation of Indians, you are to go out against the same—his enemies are to be your enemies. When you return on the path I will send ten soldiers to protect you as far as the Congarees; and, hereafter, whenever this government shall have anything to say to your Nation, we will order some one to accompany you from the Congarees Fort to this town; the traders will come with you that far, from your country. I will send a letter by you on this occasion, to Old Hop, your emperor, and to the Raven of Hiwassee. I did not intend to say this much to you, after your behavior on yesterday. I have never met with like treatment before from any Indians; it was very different from what I expected.

Long Jack.—This is the last talk we shall have together, at this time. We have listened well to every word your Excellency had to say, and shall keep it in our hearts; the chain of friendship is bright between us and the English; it shall never rust, neither shall it ever be broken. We confess that our talk yesterday to your Excellency, about the prisoners, was very wrong; we beg you to forgive it. It was for the good of the white people. For our part we have forgotten it, in token whereof we present you with this piece of tobacco, (lays it before the Governor,) to smoke with Old Hop. Take it as a proof that we are very sorry for what we did. Old Hop knows that a peace has been agreed upon in general between us and the Muskogee; so that as soon as we return, the talk of your Excellency will be considered, and war heard of no more.

Usteneca here arose and delivered the Governor his commission.*

Governor.—Usteneca, your conduct has always been good, particularly since you have been in this place; I therefore return you your commission, and hope you will still continue good to the English.

Long Jack here hinted that a commission would not be displeasing to the Little Carpenter.

Little Carpenter.—What we had to say, we have already said; *but it is right to give these commissions.*

Governor.—It has been a long time since Attaculaculla† was here, I shall give him a new commission.

* In order to gain or conciliate the favor of the Cherokees, their head-men were frequently commissioned by the Governor as in his provincial militia.

† Little Carpenter

Little Carpenter.—When I was taken by the Northern Indians I lost my commission, and thought I should have lost my life. If I get another commission, we shall once more be alive together.

Governor.—Mr. Butler shall also go up with you. Do not forget that if you wish to have always a plenty of goods you must make good hunts, and induce no more traders to come among you. As old Hop is not able to travel, I am going to show him other countries in a glass, and he may show them to his people. (Here a mirror, with perspective prints, was laid on the table.)

Soon after the Indians took their leave and withdrew.

Skiagunsta was a head-man of the lower towns, Sugar Town, and Keowee; the Little Carpenter, Long Jack, and Ousteneca, were Chiefs of the Overhill settlements. Each one on leaving the council chamber, received a scarlet suit, a ruffled shirt, and laced hat, stockings, garters and buckles, and a set of ribbon buttons.

Near the close of this famous talk, Governor Glen made several interesting inquiries of the traders who were present, some of whom had acted as interpreters, concerning the state of things in the Nation. These traders were Beaver, Elliotte, and Butler. He learned from them that it was not probable the Cherokees were at that time in correspondence with the French; though several suspicious characters had recently come among them. There was one Lantiquae, with a Frenchman for his pack-horseman;

and Anthony Dean, a violent Catholic, and so learned as to arouse the suspicion that he was a Jesuit emissary. His pack-horseman was a Spaniard, who spoke also fluently in the French language. They mentioned another, though not by name, a very dangerous intruder—that the Indians were anxious for forts to be built in certain places in their country; these, they believed, would enable them to regulate everything in the Nation—to keep up the lower towns—repel enemies, and drive out dissolute, worthless white men, who only preyed upon the Indians. That some of the traders still continued to smuggle large quantities of rum into the Cherokee country. William Gawdy had recently carried up two hogsheads of it; it may have been intended, however, only for his store at Ninety-six. A trader, McDaniel, who had come down with the chiefs, refused to return with them on the path, because he was sure it would be certain death for any trader to do so while the Savannahs were held as prisoners. The Governor then declared that he would write to Old Hop and Cornelius Dougherty; he knew Dougherty to be a skillful and willing healer of differences.

The events, however, connected with this visit of the Cherokees to Charleston, were not confined solely to their business and display of eloquence before the Governor and council. We hear of them again before they reach their towns, and under circumstances, which, though trivial in themselves, afford with all the proceedings detailed above, interesting material for reflection to the student of our upper-country history, who would be informed of the manner in which the lives and property of his immigrant fathers were, at this trying period, watched over by the powers then existing in Charleston.

They returned by the path that led to the Congarees, and thence to Saluda Old Town. Near that place, on the Little Saluda, lived Stephen Holston; his house, it appears, stood not far from the trail. When the Indians reached that point, they had fallen short of provisions; Holston was absent from home; the ten soldiers sent to escort them had been left at the Congarees, and if any trader was with them, it was Butler alone. The party, forty in all, grew insolent and mischievous. They surrounded Holston's house and demanded of his wife a supply of provisions. Mrs. Holston readily granted it, and whatever else she could afford them; still they were not satisfied. At night two of them insisted on being permitted to sleep upon the floor of the house. After some hesitation, she yielded this also; and near midnight, when she and her servants were fast asleep, those on the outside again surrounded the house; the fellows, who had pretended to sleep on the floor, opened the doors—there being one on each side—and the whole party rushed in, after making a great uproar by whooping and firing off their guns. Mrs. Holston was greatly frightened, seizing her infant, that slept by her side, she sprang from the bed. At that instant one of them attempted to force the door of her room; she had sufficient presence of mind, however, to ask him what he wanted; but, before he could reply, she caught sight of the Indians, through the openings in the rude door, moving wildly about the house with their arms in their hands, upon which rushing to the window, she jumped through it to the ground, still clinging to her child, and did not cease to run till she had reached in safety the house of a neighbor, who lived several miles distant in the forest. The marauders did not pursue her—they may not have noticed her flight—they were content with the plunder of the house; for, on Mrs. Holston's return next day, she found they had robbed her of the best part of her pewter plates and dishes, of all her tea-cups and a kettle, besides thirty bushels of corn, and two valuable mares from the stables. Holston came home not long after, but too late to recover his property; he could only lay an account of his grievance before the Governor, and petition for an indemnity. Whether it was ever granted him does not appear; his letter to the Governor, on the subject, afforded us the data from which we have hus endeavored to commemorate an event long uppermost in the memory, at least, of his wife.*

* See Indian Books in Columbia.

CHAPTER XX.

The favorite object of Governor Glen accomplished—The Obligations of the public man and private citizen prompt—Vigorous Resistance to Wrong—Little Carpenter begins to rise in importance—His Character—Supplants Old Hop as Great Beloved Head-man of the Nation—The Responsibilities, and timid, temporizing policy of Governor Glen wonderfully suggestive of present political troubles and obligations—Many new and interesting revelations from the old MS. Records in Columbia, &c.

The Governor's favorite object was thus obtained with little pecuniary cost.* A firm peace was concluded between the Creeks and Cherokees at the very flood-tide of an opportunity that should have been seized by the authorities in Carolina to unite with the Creeks in punishing the insufferable insolence and treachery of the Cherokees. We shall presently see that when the crisis came, the former joined the latter, and carried fire and the scalping-knife into the infant settlements of Upper-Georgia and northwest Carolina.

It is very true that the admirable virtue of benevolence and good-will to men should ever be prominent in all our public and private acts; yet there are

---

* The chiefs of the Creeks met the Governor, in the same chamber, shortly after the departure of the Cherokees.

obligations that may rest upon the same individual, both as a public officer and private citizen, which should prompt vigorous resentment and the condign punishment of an offending party. Such a course, then, best subserves the ends of benevolence and a wholesome morality. The unscriptural doctrine of absolute *non-resistance* to encroachment and injury would be likely to find apologists and prevalency among fanatics,* but never among a people whose religion, and blood, and institutions, all approve a different standard. But Governor Glen was an Englishman, and making too much of an extraordinary opportunity to advance his own schemes of self-aggrandizement.

In the exigencies and obligations of this dark period of our colonial history, we are forcibly reminded of much that has transpired, and of much that constitutes the present crisis of our sectional struggle. Even the great council of *chiefs*—on nearly the identical spot where more than one hundred years ago Governor Glen met the assembled head-men of the Cherokee Nation—will not be wanting to complete the resemblance. And whatever may be the result of the approaching civilized *talk* in Charleston; whether, as suggested by an ex-Governor and sound politician, it end in simply ascertaining how much more insult, contempt and injury the South can possibly bear short of the ne-

* See the ethical deductions of free-soilism in the ethereal philosophy of one Daymond.

cessity of resistance; or in a political reconciliation among the discordant elements—the miserable odds and ends of a great temporizing, watch-and-wait party—the circumstances and pressing obligations of the two periods are wonderfully alike.

It is true that we are not now contending with savage hordes; but with fanatics, whom God appears to have demented. And they have invaded our country—have destroyed or forcibly seized our property; murdered, in cold blood, our peaceable citizens;—have applied the incendiary's torch to our cities and homes—have abused, villified and misrepresented us from the sacred desk and through a triumphant press; and, as the last act of the atrocious drama, are inciting our slaves to rise in arms against their masters, that the hellish work may be at once completed in the indiscriminate butchery of our people—of our women and innocents—in scenes of ruin and desolation, such as only savages can contemplate without remorse. The Little Carpenter, who figured so conspicuously in the recent *talk*, began, it appears, from that time to rise in importance both with his own people and the English. He had previously been, as he himself confessed, disaffected—had even rested under the suspicion of having entertained proposals of peace from French emissaries; and had once gone to Virginia to obtain from that province a regular supply of goods for the Over-hills. His love for the English was not, however, so strong as to restrain him from similar designs if he had possessed the power to carry them out. His fear of the great king, whom he had seen in England, had not wholly subsided, and the French were in no condition to supply all the wants of his people.

Deer skins were the chief staple of the Cherokees. For these the French traders found little sale in France, and her manufactures afforded few of the articles of prime necessity which the Indians required in exchange.

Eminently practical, sagacious and eloquent, he was also excessively vain and self-conceited; but much of this vanity was, no doubt, one of the results of the intense independence and love of liberty which characterized the Cherokees beyond any other native people. Partly by his own wisdom and address, and partly through the influence of the English, he attained, not long after the conference in Charleston, the chief seat of power in the Nation, in the room of Old Hop.

This change in his fortunes is thus mentioned by Adair: "Notwithstanding the Cherokees are now a nest of apostate hornets, pay little respect to gray hairs, and have been degenerating fast from their primitive religious principles for above thirty years past: yet, before the last war,* Old Hop, who was helpless and lame, presided over the whole Nation as *Archimagus*, and lived in Chotie, their only town of refuge. It was entirely owing to the wisdom of those who then presided in South Carolina that his

* War of 1760.

dangerous, pontifical, and regal-like power was impaired by their setting up Attaculaculla, and supporting him so well, as to prevent the then easy transition of an Indian high-priesthood into a French-American bloody chair, with a bunch of red and black beads, where the devil and they could as easily have instructed them in the infernal French catechism, as they did the Canada Indians—as who killed Christ? Answer, the bloody English.

Both Bartram and the author just quoted, describe him as the most diminutive Indian they ever saw; he was well nigh a dwarf, though belonging to a tribe whose men were more gigantic in stature, than any other American people.

The botanist, as late as June, 1776, while exploring among the Over-hills, accidentally met Attaculaculla, and thus describes the incident: "Soon after crossing a large branch of the Tennessee, I observed descending the heights, at some distance, a company of Indians, all well-mounted, on horseback. They came rapidly forward. On their near approach, I observed a chief at the head of the caravan, and apprehending him to be the Little Carpenter, Emperor or Grand Chief of the Cherokees, as they came up, I turned off from the path, to make way, in token of respect, which compliment was accepted, and magnanimously returned; for his highness, with a gracious and cheerful smile, came up to me, and clapping his hand on his breast, offered it to me, saying: 'I am Attaculaculla,' and heartily shook hands with me, and asked me if I knew it. I answered, that the Good Spirit, who goes before me, spoke to me, and said, 'That is the great Attaculaculla;' and added that the name of Attaculaculla was dear to his white brothers of Pennsylvania, whence I came.

"After this compliment, with which he seemed pleased, he inquired if I came lately from Charleston, and if John Stewart was well, saying that he was then going to see him. I gave him my compliments for the superintendent, and the emperor passed on towards Charleston."

This visit to John Stewart was, no doubt, closely connected with the Cherokee invasion of the first of July, that once more made the upper-country the scene of bloodshed and savage warfare.

We shall meet with him again, acting in more interesting scenes than any in which he has yet appeared; and the once flippant, testy Little Carpenter, will scarcely be recognized in the calm, dignified, politic Attaculaculla. It is proper to add, however, that in one of them he must be judged by the standard we are accustomed now to apply to many public men—not as Attaculaculla the great beloved man, and representative of the Cherokee Nation; but simply as an Indian most gloriously drunk.

We have seen how often and earnestly the traders, settlers, and even many of the Indians, petitioned the authorities for the establishment of well-garrisoned forts on the border, or in the Nation. As early as 1734, shortly after the return of the Cherokee Embassy from London, the importance of such a work had been apprehended in Charleston; but instead of promptly meeting the necessity with their own strength, and with the resolution with which, unassisted, they had achieved, in less propitious times, more difficult enterprises in their own defence, they laid it in a prayer, signed by the Governor, the President of the Council, and the Speaker of the Lower House of Assembly, before the British Government.

After detailing the numerous dangers that threatened the province from the French settlements and Indians, in the Mississippi Valley, and urging the necessity of planting forts in the country of the upper Creeks, the petition continues: "We find the Cherokee Nation has lately become very insolent to your Majesty's subjects trading among them, notwithstanding the many favors the chiefs of that Nation received from your Majesty in Great Britain, besides a considerable expense which this province has been at in making them presents, which inclines us to believe that the French, with their Indians, have been tampering with them. We, therefore, beg leave to inform your Majesty, that the building and mounting some forts likewise among the Cherokees, and making them presents, will be highly necessary to keep them steady in their duty to your Majesty, lest the French may prevail in seducing that Nation, which they may the more readily be inclined to do, from the prospect of getting considerable plunder in slaves and cattle. Several other forts will be indispensably necessary, to be a cover to your Majesty's subjects settled far back in this province, as those also of the colony of Georgia, both which, in length, are very extensive."

In conclusion, they observe: "This is the present state and condition of your Majesty's province of South Carolina; utterly incapable of finding funds sufficient for the defence of this wide frontier, and so destitute of white men, that even money itself cannot here raise a sufficient body of them."*

It is quite true, that the resources of the province were, at this period, not great. The united militia force of Carolina and Georgia, did not number more than thirty-five hundred efficient men;† but if their respective governments had been animated with a spirit of self-reliance, and had rightly used the strength they possessed, they would have found themselves fully equal to the task, not, indeed, of fortifying and defending their whole exposed frontier, but that portion of it on the north and north-west, where the most imminent dangers now menaced them, and whence the privations and helplessness of the suffering pioneers were calling loudly, not upon their patriotism and obligations as guardians of the public safety only, but upon their pity and humanity, as men.

A single fort and garrison among the lower Cherokees, aided by the companies of rangers already embodied, would have awed them into quiet submission, and, in a little while, repelled from the settlements the plundering bands of savages from the Ohio. At last, after years of criminal temporizing and delay, the province was forced to assume and perform this work at her own expense.

---

* Hewit in Carroll's His. Col. † Ibid.

The Council thus reasoned in regard to it: "Taking into consideration the several messages that have passed between the Assembly and the Governor, concerning the building of a fort among the lower Cherokees, the testimony of the traders, and the application of the Indians themselves; and the same having been frequently under the consideration of the Council, they deem it unnecessary to add further reasons; but are of the unanimous opinion, that it would be greatly for his Majesty's service and safety of the traders and settlements, that such a fort be built, and the Council, therefore, advise the Governor to give directions for its construction this fall,* provided it does not cost more than three thousand pounds; that the land on which it is built be purchased from the Indians, and the site selected as close as possible to the town of Keowee.†

Skiagunsta—a favorite chief with the English in Charleston—had thus closed one of his speeches before the late Council: "I live in the town of Keowee. I call it a town; but there are so few people in it now, that it scarcely deserves the name. I must, therefore, once more put your Excellency in mind of your promise to build us a fort, that our people and wives may come and go as safely as in your streets."‡

In obedience to the above directions of the Coun-

* 1753. † Indian Books. ‡ Ibid.

cil, Gov. Glen, in the fall of 1753,* visited the country of the lower Cherokees, and having purchased from them a quantity of land, erected the long-promised and earnestly desired fort, at Keowee.

In one of the first conferences held between Gov. Glen and the Indians, in relation to the fort at Keowee, the latter assured him that they would not only dispose of lands sufficient for its site, and the uses of its garrison, but would, themselves, assist in building it, they would supply provisions for the laborers employed in the work, and cut all the timbers that would be required.

"What assistance will you give us in building the fort?" asked the Governor, of the Raven of Hiwassee, in Charleston.

Raven.—"All that we are able to give; the lower towns will furnish provisions."

"What number of men will you lend to the work?" asked the Governor, again.

Raven.—"We will send ten men every day, from each town, alternately, till it is finished;† we can only cut and carry timbers, however."

The following is a faithful copy of the deed of conveyance by which the lands on which it stood were secured to South Carolina:

* Hewitt, and all after him, who have made mention of this event in our history, state that this visit of Gov. Glen was made in 1755. We know nothing of the authority on which the statement was first made; the records in Columbia are our sole guide.

† Indian Books.

"This paper witnesseth to all manner of persons, what has been transacted in the Cherokee Nation, between His Excellency, James Glen, Esq., Governor of South Carolina, and Corane, the Raven of Toxawa, in the presence, and by the approbation of many of the head-men, and most of the beloved men of the Nation. *Whereas*, the head-men of the said Cherokee Nation have, for many years, solicited the said Governor of the province aforesaid, to have a fort built in the Nation; and in order to induce him thereto, freely offered the land in any part of the said Nation he should choose to build upon.

"*And whereas*, some of the head-men are since dead, and the said Raven of Toxawa being now in their stead, and having consulted with many of the head-men of said Nation, and most of the beloved men of the lower towns, they do offer to make a free donation of all the lands on the north-east side of Keowee River, betwixt a creek, known by the name of Mile Creek, and the river aforesaid, for that purpose.

"But he, the said Governor, refusing to accept of the same by gift, and being desirous of purchasing it, *Therefore*, this present paper witnesseth, that for and in consideration of thirty stroud match-coats, a certain number of duffil blankets, striped flannels, shirts, guns, a certain quantity of powder and bullets, flints, knives and paint, the receipt whereof is hereby acknowledged; I, the said Raven of Toxawa, have, in the name of the Cherokee Nation, aforesaid, by the consent of many of the head-men, and most of the beloved men, granted, bargained, sold, alienated and confirmed unto the said James Glen, Esq., Governor of South Carolina, his heir in trust, nevertheless, for His Majesty, King George the Second, King of Great Britain, and his heirs and successors forever, for the use of his subjects of the province aforesaid, not only the spot of ground on which a fort is at present building, near Keowee, and all the lands betwixt that and a place called Long-Canes, of *the width of said fort;* but also, all the lands, as well corn-fields, as pasture-grounds, hills, woods and waters, all the right and title the Cherokee Nation can lay claim to in the said lands, forever.

"And I have put the said Governor in the possession thereof by giving him a handful of the earth, with what was growing thereon, and by delivering him a branch of a tree, with design that neither we nor our children, will ever lay any claim to the said premises, while the sun shines or the rivers run; and we shall, and will be, always ready to defend his said Majesty, King George the Second, his heirs' and successors' right thereto, against all manner of persons whatsoever.

"*In witness whereof*, we have subscribed these presents by putting our marks and seals to the same, in Fort Prince George, this 24th day of November, in the year of our Lord 1753.

Signed, sealed and delivered in the presence of Raymond Demere, James McKay, White Outerbridge, Thomas Glen, James Francis, Ludwick Grant, James Beamer and John Elliotte. Signed by

Corane, the Raven of Toxawa; Canacaugh, the great Conjurer of Keowee; Sinnawa, the Hawk's-Head warrior of Toxawa; Nellewagalehe, of Toxawa; Yahoma, of Keowee; Canasaita, of Keowee; Yorhalehe, of Toxawa; and Owasta, the head beloved man of Toxawa.'"*

Gov. Glen carried up with him to Keowee, on this occasion, the pipe Old Hop had sent him, and the eagles' wings, with a good supply of tobacco, intending to have a friendly smoke with the wise old man of Chotie; but he was so infirm as not to be able to meet him at Keowee. Hewit describes as follows, this meeting between Gov. Glen and the chiefs of the Nation: "After the usual ceremonies previous to such solemn treaties were over, the Governor sat down under a spreading tree, and Attaculaculla† being chosen speaker for the Cherokees, came and took his seat beside him. The other warriors, about five hundred in number, stood around them in solemn silence and deep attention. Then the Governor arose and made a speech in the name of his king, representing his great power, wealth and goodness, and his particular regard for his children, the Cherokees. He reminded them of the happiness they had long enjoyed under his protection; and added that he had many presents to make them, and expected they would surrender a share of their terri-

* Indian Books.

† Chulochculla, the name used by Hewit here, is evidently meant for Attaculaculla. No such name appears in all the records.

tories in return for them. He demanded lands to build two forts in their country to protect them against their enemies, and to be a retreat to their friends and allies, who furnished them with arms, ammunition, hatchets, clothes and everything they wanted.

"When the Governor had finished his speech, Attaculaculla arose, and holding his bow in one hand, his shaft of arrows, and other simbols used by them on such occasions, in the other, in answer spoke to the following effect: 'What I now speak, our father, the great king, should hear—we are brothers to the people of Carolina—one house covers us all.' Then taking a boy by the hand, he presented him to the Governor, saying: 'We, our wives and our children, are all children of the great King George; I have brought this child, that when he grows up he may remember our agreement on this day, and tell it to the next generation, that it may be known forever.' Then opening his bag of earth, and laying the same at the Governor's feet, he said: 'We freely surrender a part of our lands to the great king.' * * * Then showing his bow and arrows, he added: 'These are all the arms we can make for our defence; we hope the king will pity his children, the Cherokees, and send us guns and ammunition.' Then delivering the Governor a string of wampum, in confirmation of what he had said, he added: 'My speech is at an end; it is the voice of the Cherokee Nation; I hope the Governor will send it to the king that it may be kept forever.'"

We learn that at this Congress a territory of prodigious extent was acquired for the king, of no less than the valuable domain embraced in the present Districts of Abbeville, Edgefield, Laurens, Union, Spartanburg, Newberry, Chester, Fairfield, Richland and York. That, from this time it was claimed by the English, and their settlements began rapidly to extend towards the mountains, does not admit of a moment's doubt; but in view of the curious and exceedingly vague language used in the deed, as copied above, from the records, when defining the limits and boundaries of the lands disposed of by the Nation for the uses of the fort, may not the careful inquirer be pardoned for asking, if such was really the construction the Cherokees intended to be put upon it?

And, indeed, whether the Indians made a mental reservation of their rights or not, despite the tenor of the contract to which they appended their names, will any just interpretation of its present language admit of such a construction? It is impossible to ascertain from the deed itself, what were the precise extent and locality of the lands released on this occasion to the English; but that they did not embrace so large a territory as the one claimed, would seem to be clear.

Long previous to this event, the Cherokees, in order to obtain the benefits they hoped to receive from the establishment of a fort in their country, had proffered to give the English authorities land sufficient for its site, and for other purposes connected with a military post; and this, and nothing more, appears to have been the idea they sought to express, in the very cautious or very loose language of their deed.

It admits of but two constructions, neither of which yields to the King of Great Britain the shadow of a claim upon a foot of the upper-country, south of the north-branch of Long-Cane.* It may, possibly, mean just what it says, that besides the immediate site of the fort, and the surrounding woods, pastures and waters, quite necessary to a garrison, a strip of land was also released, the width of the fort, which extended thence as far southward as a place called the Long-Canes—a sort of thoroughfare or unalienable way of access to the future garrison.

Or again, by the phrase "width of the fort," they may have designed simply to convey the idea, that the ceded lands extended over the distance that intervened between the garrison and the Long-Canes—that is, so far south as the fort was wide of the latter place. This view is confirmed by a variety of cotemporaneous facts. A few months after Governor Glen's return from Keowee, the following dialogue took place in Charleston:

Governor, (to two Indians who had just brought him a message or letter from Prince George, the name that had been given to the new fort.)—This is

* Now Little River.

the paper (holding up the original deed) you gave me, when I bought the land; are not these the marks of the head-men of the Cherokee Nation?

Indians.—They are.

Governor.—Do you know the Raven of Toxawa?

One of the Indians.—He is my grandfather.

Governor.—Are those who made these marks beloved men of the lower towns?

Indian.—Yes, they are all beloved head-men.

Governor.—By this paper you gave me all the *land between the River Keowee and a place called the Long-Canes;* together with all the trees, corn-fields, pasture-grounds, hills, woods and waters. Of these you put me in possession; but a letter from Thomas Harrison, commandant of the fort, informs me, that your people—which very much surprises me—refuse to let the English plant their corn on these lands.

Indians.—We heard nothing of that before we came away; there is land enough for us all. We design to plant our corn at Ustenate.

Governor.—Very well; I think it is better for you to plant your corn near your own river; there will then be no dispute. If, however, you have already planted on our lands, you shall be welcome to it this year. One of the head-men was out hunting when the land was sold me; what is that warrior's name?

Indians.—His name is Washatchee.

Governor.—As he was not at Keowee when the paper was signed, I shall send it up that he may put his name to it; and I will also send him the pistols and saddle he asks for.*

In February, 1756, James Beamer informed Gov. Glen, that the Cherokees were extending their hunting excursions into the advancing settlements; and were complaining bitterly of these encroachments upon their lands. He adds: "There are several families who have this fall settled too high up. They say they have fixed their settlement above the *dividend path* on a stream called Rocky River, which is about three miles within the dividend path on Tugaloo road.†

What is meant here by the Tugaloo road is not apparent, unless it was the old trail that passed up from Augusta along the east bank of the Savannah, already described; but in regard to Rocky River, there can be no uncertainty; it still bears its primitive English name, and lies almost wholly in the District of Abbeville, a few miles north of the larger branch of the ancient Long-Canes.

The term "dividend‡ path" is still more inexplicable than "Tugaloo road," if it does not relate to the narrow strip of land which the deed of conveyance seems to describe as extending from the base of the fort to the Long-Canes.

An old chronicler,§ of a neighboring province, detailing events connected with the Cherokee Indians,

* Indian Books.

† Ibid.

‡ The word dividon is used here in the manuscript records.

§ McCall's History of Georgia, p. 305, Vol. i.

nine years later, observes: "This tribe had also shown some discontents, arising from encroachments on land claimed by them as hunting grounds to the north-west of Little River, afterwards Wilks County; and similar complaints were made against encroachments in Carolina upon a creek called Long Cane."

We have seen no complaints of encroachments upon their lands, sent down at this period by the Cherokees to the Governor of Carolina, that did not relate to those about Long-Cane Creek; yet, at this very time, the rapidly advancing settlement had already progressed considerably northward of a line running from the Long-Canes directly across to the Catawba, through territory now included in the Districts of Laurens, Newberry and Fairfield. In the latter district, eight crops of corn had been gathered from the rich bottoms of Broad River by the hardy pioneers of the Scotch-Irishry, and Newberry was settled at least a year before the establishment of Fort Prince George.

The truth is, the only satisfactory explanation that can be given of these conflicting facts is, that the Indians—true to their old habit of dealing deceitfully with the whites in all contracts and treaties, no matter how deliberately and solemnly formed, which related to the disposal of their lands—never once designed by the deed of conveyance, signed and delivered at Keowee, to yield the English any real possession of an acre of their soil.

But they knew, that, ever on the alert to seize and appropriate new lands, their pioneers would hasten to build cabins and plant corn on the territory which they now regarded as their own—the lands that had been designated as lying between Keowee River and Long-Cane. Hence these were to be guarded with peculiar care; though few, if any, complaints had ever been made of the encroachments on their hunting grounds farther south—on the present territory of Richland, Newberry and Fairfield, where settlements had been gradually progressing for years—one of them having been founded as early as 1740.

The first attempt made by the garrison of Fort Prince George to plant corn on the surrounding lands, it has been seen, was promptly resisted by the Indians; the same resistance was offered when the advancing pioneers began to overleap the waters of the Long-Cane; and so determined were the Cherokees to debar the English from these lands, that the latter were forced to yield, and rest satisfied, as well they might, with the magnificent domain they had already peaceably acquired, and were holding by no better title than that of simple possession.

It has, all along, been supposed, that Gov. Glen purchased, from the Cherokees, in the famous treaty at Keowee, the whole upper-country with the present Districts of Richland and Fairfield, as far north as the ancient boundary line which separated this territory from that of Old Pendleton; and that the latter was only fairly obtained by the treaty of 1777, at Dewitt's Corner; whereas, Governor Glen himself being judge, if any reliance can be placed in a large and interesting portion of our State records, certain lands, afterwards embraced in the Districts of Greenville, Anderson, Pickens, and a portion of Abbeville, were the first and only part of their soil ever acquired by a formal purchase or treaty from the heads of the Cherokee Nation, previous to the Revolution.

The people of the upper-country, who live between the Keowee and the northern boundary of Abbeville, hold lands by purchase, or inheritance from their fathers, for which there may be found in the archives, sound original titles, preserved in as many as two distinct State documents, each of which are associated with most interesting events in the history of Carolina.

The treaty at Dewitt's Corner removed the Indians above the old boundary line, which ran from near the mouth of the Chatuga, across towards the Estatoe Mountain. This was obliterated in 1817, when the Cherokees gave up the last foot of their ancient territory in the present limits of Carolina.

Fort Prince George was erected in gun-shot distance of the town of Keowee, and designed to be a much more formidable structure than the ordinary stockade inclosures which the agitations and dangers of late years, on the border, had made familiar in every community of pioneers.

It was built in the form of a square, with a rampart or wall of earth some six feet in height, on which stockades were fixed; a ditch, and natural glasis strengthened two sides of it, and strong bastions the angles upon which were mounted sixteen small cannon—four on each bastion. Its barracks were sufficiently spacious for a hundred men.

Twenty-three years after the completion of this fortress, the spot was visited by Bartram; in that brief period it had become hallowed by many thrilling events of deep historical interest. A war, disastrous to the frontier, and well nigh ruinous to the Cherokees, had swept, as with a besom, this whole lovely region; its natural beauties were, however, indestructible, and these rendered doubly interesting by the surrounding vestiges of the former handiwork and hostile collisions of savage and civilized men, did not escape the observant eye of the botanist.

"Keowee is a most charming situation, and the adjacent heights are naturally so formed, and disposed, as, with little expense of military architecture, to be made almost impregnable. It lies in a fertile vale at this season enameled with fragrant strawberries and blooming plants, through which the beautiful river meanders, environed at various distances by high hills and mountains, some rising boldly almost upright upon the verge of the expansive lawn, so as to overlook and shadow it, whilst others more lofty, superb, misty and blue, majestically mount far above.

"The vale of Keowee is seven or eight miles in extent, that is from the little town of Kulsage,* about a mile above, thence down the river six or seven miles, where a high ridge of hills on each

* Sugaw town.

side of the river almost terminates the vale, but opens again below the narrow ridge and continues ten or twelve miles down to Seneca, and in width one and two miles. This fertile valley, within the remembrance of some old traders with whom I conversed, was one continued settlement; the sides of the adjacent hills were then covered with habitations, and the rich level grounds beneath lying on the river were cultivated and planted, which now exhibit a very different spectacle—humiliating indeed to the present generation, the posterity and feeble remains of the once potent and renowned Cherokees. The vestiges of the ancient Indian dwellings, are yet visible at the foot of the hills bordering and fronting on the vale, such as posts or pillars of their habitations, and the scattered fragments of their hearths and utensils.

"There are several Indian mounds or tumuli, and terraces—monuments of the ancients, at the old site of Keowee, near Fort Prince George—but no Indian habitations, at present; and here are several dwellings belonging to white people concerned in the Indian trade; Mr. D. Homes is the principal trader at this time. The old fort bears no marks of a fortress, but serves for a trading house."

These observations were made in the spring of 1776—one month later began the last Cherokee war—of that we will speak in its proper place.

The founding of Fort Prince George, purchased but a brief peace for the Nation, and a short-lived confidence on the border. The very next year, occurred the massacre on Buffalo Creek, already described; and soon the fickle savages, were as restless and annoying as before. Gov. Glen sent up and invited the head-men to meet him, in another talk in Charleston. It was on this occasion that Old Hop replied that he could not expose his warriors to the fatal sickness which they often contracted in town, and on the Keowee trail; this message, or one of the same import, was brought down by Attaculaculla, accompanied by an escort of nineteen warriors;* upon which the Governor consented to meet their head-men in council, at some point mid-way between the Nation and Charleston. The meeting was accordingly held at Saluda Old Town.

All that is known of its proceedings must be gleaned from a communication addressed the following year, (January, 1756,) to the Governor by one Moses Thompson, in which the writer presents a valuable synopsis of the Governor's official career, and takes occasion to speak of its acts in terms sufficiently flattering to his pride, if not to the judgment of most of his cotemporaries.

"I cannot forget my impressions of your paternal care of South Carolina since you came among us. First, your journey to Ninety-six, to settle a peace with the Cherokees; and thence to Savannah, to make peace with the Creeks. Second, your long journey to the Cherokee Nation to build a fort.

* Letter to Glen, from Harrison, commandant of Fort P. George. —Ind. Books.

Third, your journey to Saluda, in the heat of summer, to settle a second peace with the Cherokees in troublous times;* which act crowns all the rest; for, I verily believe, there was never such a firm peace made with any Indians before, and all resulting in the advancement of the indigo manufacture. And likewise your great care of our back-settlers; for, when I was major under your Excellency, I cannot forget your care, by your instructions to me on several occasions; besides, your private letters to me to inform your Excellency of any event, that proper steps might be taken for our safety. I think your successor will have nothing to do but to walk in your footsteps: for you have paved the plainest road that can be taken, which, I think, will keep your memory in the minds of the people when you are dead and gone."†

His successor, Governor William Henry Lyttleton, soon had an opportunity to test the virtue of this famous gubernatorial highway. He was shortly after superceded; and one of the first official acts of the new Governor was to send a formal message‡ to Old Hop, informing him of his appointment and arrival; and what was more pleasing to the aged chieftain, that the men were already on their way up, with implements to build, for the Over-hills, the fort on the Tennessee, which Governor Glen had so long before promised them.

---

* Summer of 1755.

† Indian Book.

‡ This occurred June 3d, 1756.—Indian Books.

This step had now become absolutely necessary in order to preserve the peace of the Nation and safety of the border, the agitations and hostile threats of the Indians having grown fiercer than ever before. They were beginning even to talk openly of killing all the whites in their reach. These discontents were greatly aggravated by the prevalence, at this time, of famine, especially among the Over-hills, where they were reduced to a state of nakedness, having disposed of all their clothing for food; and some had actually died of starvation. Added to this, a party of Creeks, who had paid their towns a visit, seeing their restless, discontented state, maliciously sought to increase it, by insinuating that the policy of the English was at the bottom of it all, and that their design was to rob them of their lands, and reduce them to slavery.*

The energy of the French, it may be well conjectured, did not slumber over such an opportunity as this presented to advance their schemes. Indeed, as has been shown, the potency of their dangerous influence had not once ceased to work in the Nation, since the days of Priber.

A great council of the head-men was now held at Keowee, and all but five in the upper and lower towns, were urgent to fall at once upon the traders and settlements. It required all the influence of Old Hop and the Little Carpenter, to arrest the outbreak.†

* Letter from Commandant Harrison to the Governor, June 2d, 1756.—Indian Books.

† Letter from Harrison.

"Yet," remarks Adair, "his Excellency, our Governor, neglected the proper measures to reconcile the wavering savages, till the gentleman who was appointed to succeed him had just reached the American coast. Then, indeed, he set off, with a considerable number of gentlemen in flourishing parade, and went as far as Ninety-six settlement; whence, as most probably he expected, he was fortunately recalled, and joyfully superceded. I saw him on his way up, and plainly observed he was unprovided for the journey. It must have proved abortive before he could have proceeded as far as the Over-hill settlements. He neither sent before, nor carried with him any presents wherewith to soothe the natives; and his kind promises and smooth speeches would have weighed exceedingly light in the Indian scale."

The condition of Fort Prince George at this juncture was little calculated to inspire confidence on the border; it had fallen, through neglect, into an almost ruinous state; the palisades had tumbled from the ramparts, the ditches were partially filled up, and gaping breaches had been washed or wantonly cut in the walls. An officer, who inspected it, reported it in a worse condition than the old stockade at the Congarees, the defenceless condition of which was then well known in Charleston. "For my part," he adds, "I would rather be in an open field than in such an apology for a fort; the Indians may, at any time, pass over both the ditches and walls." When the fort was first built, the ditches had been dug five feet wide at top, two at bottom, and five deep, with a parapet, or breast-work, also five feet in height, and a *banquet?* or foot-bank on the outside.

Under the superintendence of Capt. John Crayton, it was now speedily repaired, by widening the ditches to seven feet, bridging them, and mounting a swivel upon each bastion.* This was in July, 1756.†

The speedy erection of Fort Loudon—for that was the strong-hold it was now proposed to build on the Tennessee—would, it was fondly hoped, not only put an effectual barrier against the French in that accessible quarter, but so gratify the Indians as to quell all their discontents. Gov. Lyttleton, though patriotic and indefatigable, was profoundly and unfortunately ignorant of the savages with whom he had to deal.

The previous year Governor Glen had promised the Little Carpenter to build a fort for the Over-hills on the Tennessee, provided he and his people would surrender themselves to be the subjects of the King of Great Britain, and their lands his possession forever;‡ and from this, no doubt, or from the treaty formed at Little Saluda, has originated the reiterated statement that Governor Glen, in 1755, purchased from the Cherokees the greater portion of the present territory of Upper Carolina.

Three months later he again informed the same chieftain that the regard he entertained for his Nation had moved him to make the promise to build

* What had become of the twelve others originally placed upon its walls?

† Letter to Gov. Lyttleton from Capt. Raymond Demere.

‡ In a letter dated October 1755.—Indian Books.

for them, that spring, a fort on the Tennessee; and that the bearer of this communication had been sent up for the express purpose of selecting for it a suitable site. His instructions were that it should be fixed on the above-mentioned stream; but convenient to the towns, and chosen in view of the health of its garrison—in reach of good water—out of gun-shot of any neighboring eminence, and in the midst of good pasture and corn-lands.* It was ultimately built one mile above Chotie, and five from the spot selected for it first, according to the above instructions, by Pearson.†

The Carolinians were assisted in building Fort Loudon by one hundred men, sent for that purpose, from Virginia, under Major Lewis and Captain Overton, by the Earl of Loudon—in honor of whom it was named—who had been appointed commander-in-chief of the king's forces in America, and Governor of the Old Dominion.

At the same time that Governor Glen hurried off the party destined to be employed in erecting the fort, he had ordered, it appears, several companies, with those of the provincial troops, to concentrate at Ninety-six, in case an out-break in the Nation should require their services: among them were two that hastened to that point from Fort Moore. In the mean time, he was superseded by Governor Lyttleton, but not, as we have seen from Adair, before he

---

* Letter to Little Carpenter, dated February 1755.

† Dr. Ramsay of Tennessee fixes its ruins five miles from the site of Chotie. We have followed the records.

himself had set out for the Cherokee towns with several wagons, laden with provisions for the workmen. The provisions were taken in at the Congarees, and presents for another *talk* had, no doubt, been procured in Charleston, which Adair was not permitted to see.

The new Governor, having learned, soon after his arrival, the result of the council of chiefs at Keowee, and informed, from other sources, that the Indians did not then meditate hostilities, dispatched a messenger to overtake the ex-governor, and deliver to him, with other important information, an order for Captain Raymond Demere, of the provincials, to the effect, that those troops should be disbanded.

The wagon train arrived safely at Ninety-six, the provincials were disbanded, the two companies from Fort Moore returned to that post, and Demere, with the ex-governor and young Ensign Coytmore, proceeded to Fort Prince George, at the head of the party going to the site of Fort Loudon. Before setting out, however, he prepared a communication for Governor Lyttleton, from which we have gleaned these facts.* It concludes as follows: "I find myself alone here, with a young officer, Ensign Coytmore, who, although quite capable, is yet too young

* Dr. Ramsay, of Tennessee, states, that Captain Demere had been sent, with a corps of two hundred men, by the Earl of Loudon, to garrison the new fort; yet in these letters to the Governor of Carolina, which we find in the Indian Books, Demere declares himself in command of Carolina troops, and subject to the orders of her Governor.

for such a command, unassisted, at this time. I shall, therefore, march with the whole party myself as far as Keowee, and there await further orders from your Excellency." *

While resting his men at Fort Prince George, several incidents occurred worth relating. A few days after his arrival, he was honored with a visit from the Little Carpenter, who staid and took breakfast with him, appearing in excellent humor; warming up, however, with the conversation that ensued between them, he suddenly announced to Demere that he regarded both him and the ex-Governor as arrant liars: the latter, he said, had promised him two kegs of rum from town, but had deceived him, and Demere's promises were no more to be relied upon.

The captain expostulated, and demanded why he addressed him in so abusive a manner? "I have said what I have said," replied the defiant chief. Demere at length conceiving it to be all assumed, in a style well becoming the address and cunning of the Little Carpenter, for the express purpose of extorting the objects he coveted, ordered a keg of rum to be given him; and soon after, in his presence, dispatched eighteen men forward towards the upper-Cherokees. This restored his good humor; he seemed greatly pleased, and made Demere many apologies for his rudeness, declaring, among other things, that he was vexed at the moment.

He soon left the fort; but returned in the evening

---

* Indian Books.

with the King of Chotie,* and begged of Demere, as one of the greatest favors he could bestow upon him, one more keg of rum, to drink with his friends; promising that no one should get drunk or cross the river that night to the fort. The rum was granted him; and taking the keg upon his shoulder he recrossed to Keowee, and there, in the presence of the Chotie King and the assembled town, proclaimed Demere the Commandant of Keowee, of the inhabitants thereof, and all the whites of the Nation.

"Nothing more was heard of him till about eight o'clock next morning, when he came into the fort reeling drunk, supported by two young fellows of the worst class; for no decent man would venture with him in that condition, especially, as he was well known to be exceedingly troublesome, when under the influence of rum. He happened to get a sight of me as he entered the gate, and I was obliged then to ask him to a seat, and sit with him.

"He soon became so annoying that I got up to leave him; he made a motion as if he would strike me with a bottle which he held in his hand; I instantly ordered several Indians, who had come in, in the meantime, to seize and carry him to Keowee, which they did, and once more relieved me of his presence.

"Early next morning he was back again; but this time perfectly sober and respectful. He quickly began with all the apologies he could muster for his bad conduct the previous day—declared that it

* Old Hop—Oconostota.

was not he who was guilty of the offense, but the rum that was in him, and hoped it would all be forgotten. I said to him that, notwithstanding my civilities to him, he had twice used me ill, and that the English had never treated him in such a manner; that if he had struck me, the consequences might have been very serious.

"He continued to apologize, and to assure me that there were three persons engaged in the difficulty, and not two only;—that I was the *first*, himself the second, and Rum the third.* He moreover informed me, that the people of Keowee had that morning stripped and dry-scratched him with snakes' teeth to remind him of his bad conduct, and make his blood good. Upon this I promised to forgive him."

The Captain adds: "It is true the Little Carpenter has great power and influence in the Nation; but it renders him excessively insolent and saucy. I have a bad opinion of him for his brutish disposition, and regard him as very deceitful when sober, and an impertinent fellow at all times."

Demere, soon after his arrival at Fort Prince George, summoned the head-men of the five lower towns to meet him in Keowee, on which occasion he made them a suitable speech. Among other things, he said to them that it was to be hoped they were now convinced that the English were in ear-

* This was, no doubt, the first temperance lecture ever delivered in that region.

nest to fulfill all their promises, in view of the great number of wagons, big guns, presents, cattle and provisions they had just brought with them to the Nation; and that besides these, they also had with them all the tools necessary for building the fort on the Tennessee;—that this work would have been performed long ago, but for the neglect of those to whom it had been entrusted. He concluded by giving them a general invitation to dine, the next day, with him at the fort. These remarks, and especially the closing sentence of the speech, pleased them prodigiously; they immediately sent off runners to the five towns, and called together that night, at Keowee, a great council of the lower Nation.

They sat in the council-house all night, and next morning sent a messenger to Demere with word that they would wait upon him with their compliments, in mass, at ten o'clock. The Captain relates: "I immediately gave orders to the men to be in readiness to receive them. In a little time they appeared in regular procession, a numerous train, dressed in their most gaudy apparel, their faces being painted over every part. Large belts of wampum and plates of silver hung from their necks on their breasts, with bracelets of the same around their arms.

"In front of the procession appeared a body of young men, moving in a slow, solemn pace, at the same time singing, and displaying, above their heads, eagles' tails and rattle-boxes. On each flank marched a young man, playing on a flute of their own manufacture. In the midst was borne a large bough of a sycamore tree, and, in another place, a white flag, tied to the end of a stick. Just as they entered the fort, I ordered the men to fire a salute from the swivels.

"They took their seats in one of the houses, inside the walls, and there delivered their talk, which consisted in expressions of joy and delight at our present friendly demonstrations. Ever since I arrived here I have had nothing but mirth and rejoicings. A runner came to me yesterday, with the compliments of the *ladies* of the towns, and also informed me that they would give me a dance the next day.

"This also came off in due time, and was handsomely performed, by a large number of them; after which, in return for our presents, they made offerings of cakes and bread, baked by themselves, and green peas and squashes; every woman bringing her own present in a basket, and setting it down before me. At this time, like the Over-hills, they were nearly naked, and in a starving condition."*

These timely supplies, particularly of cattle and provisions, with the erection of Fort Loudon, gave a short respite of tranquillity, and a hope to the infant settlements along the Cherokee line. But no human instrumentality could have availed to reform a people so hopelessly degenerate as the Cherokees had now become. While the flesh was yet in their

* Letter to Gov. Lyttleton's Indian Books.

mouths which the English had brought, at great expense, to relieve their starving condition, the murmurs and discontents broke out afresh.

Major Lewis informed the Governor of North Carolina that on his arrival at Chotie, he had received the kindest attentions from Old Hop and the Little Carpenter, and that the Indians in general, expressed their readiness to comply with all their treaties and promises; but this disposition was manifested only while the fort was building. As soon as it was finished, and they were urged to fulfill the obligation they had assumed to send their warriors with the English against the French, they began to equivocate. He also observed, that the French, with their Indian allies, the Savannahs, maintained a regular correspondence with the Cherokees, especially with the head-men of Great Tellico. It was evident that some measure was on foot for the distress of the back-settlers in the Carolinas and Virginia, and that the Indians were greatly disposed to join the French.*

This, indeed, was the fast-hastening consummation of the long years of abuse, neglect and mismanagement, whose various details we have, from the beginning, endeavored to portray. The special topics, however, which last engaged our attention, carried us some distance in advance of the main events of this troublous and memorable period.

France, with the ripened schemes and experience

*Dr. Ramsay's History of Tennessee, p. 52.

of nearly half a century, was now preparing to put every nerve to the stretch, in a final struggle with Great Britain, for the dominion of North America. Before the site of Fort London had been marked out, the old French and Indian War—or, as the people of the upper-country better knew it—Braddock's War, had begun.

The famous battle of 1755 had been fought at the ford of the Monongahela, where that presumptuous, though unfortunate general won nothing more honorable for himself than a soldier's grave. War had been formally declared by England;* and now, at the conclusion of three campaigns, all terminating in the success and exultation of France, William Pitt assumed the direction of affairs.

The fourth campaign—that of 1758—opens; Admiral Boscawen invests Louisburg; Abecrombie marches upon Ticonderoga; Forbes is sent to retrieve, by the capture of Fort Du Quesne, the terrible disaster at the Monongahela. And now the train of events begins rapidly to transpire, which were to prove the proximate cause of inflicting upon Upper Carolina the horrors of another Indian war. This was the Cherokee war of 1760; but its story of carnage, and thrilling scenes of savage vengeance on the border, must be reserved for another volume.

---

* 17th of May 1756.

END OF VOLUME FIRST.

Made in United States
Orlando, FL
26 March 2023

31409050R00321